HISTORY OF MODERN EUROPE

Kings and Philosophers
1689-1789

HISTORY OF MODERN EUROPE

General Editor: Felix Gilbert,
Institute for Advanced Study, Princeton

Kings and Philosophers
1689-1789

LEONARD KRIEGER

Columbia University

Weidenfeld and Nicolson
5 Winsley Street   London W1

ISBN   0   297   00493   X   (cased)

ISBN   0   297   00494   8   (paper)

PRINTED IN THE UNITED STATES OF AMERICA

Contents

v

PART III   The Philosopher Kings

Illustrations

Maps and Charts

Introduction

On February 13, 1689, some two weeks after it had declared the throne vacant because King James II "endeavored to subvert the constitution of the kingdom" and "abdicated the government," the Convention Parliament invited William and Mary to accept the crown along with the parliamentary version of the constitution enshrined in the Declaration of Right, and thereby consummated England's Glorious Revolution. On June 17, 1789, some six weeks after it had demanded common convocation with the noble and clerical orders, the Third Estate unilaterally transformed itself into the National Assembly, and three days later it formally voted its intention of writing a constitution, thereby initiating the French Revolution. In terms of gross results, the intervening one hundred years would seem a long time for constitutional government to have taken to cross the twenty miles of channel between Britain and the Continent. And since, in these terms, the result only marked a stage in the process of homogenizing Europe politically—a process that began before and would continue after—the eighteenth century would appear not only laggard but unremarkable in its political development.

And yet it was a most remarkable age politically. Even if we look more carefully only at its gross political results we must grant that the growth of the movement for constitutional government from an insular to a general and exportable system was no mere quantitative extension but a crucial stage in the development of modern politics. We shall find, moreover, that the manner of this growth during the eighteenth century will help us to define its political effects, for the way it happened perpetuated more of the achievements of political absolutism than one would suspect from a mere registration of results. And if we look beyond the slow evolution of states in their political orbits, we see an eighteenth-century European society in full movement, spawning the economic connections, the social attitudes, and above all the ideas that met, dissolved, and recombined in associations and conflicts dramatic in themselves, contributory to political change, and prodigal with the seeds of modernity. It is, indeed, the engagement of the stable institutional structure, fixed especially in the political order, with the unsettling dynamism of the society, crystallized especially in its intellectual activity, that gives the authentic flavor of the age. From the running interaction between the political institutions that channeled the social movement and the "enlightened" ideas that challenged the institutions comes the essential outline of eighteenth-century culture. From the activities of rulers and writers come the characteristic strands of the history that filled it.

There are many valid ways of approaching the general history of an age. Historians who use a comprehensive chronological approach divide the age into periods and compose as full a picture as they can of men's assorted activities in each period. Historians who use a comprehensive functional approach analyze successively all the institutions or fields of human activity that make up the structure of the age, admitting chronological events only to show the effects or the internal development of these institutions and fields. The approach in this book will not utilize either of these familiar formats, for our purpose is not to compose a comprehensive portrait or to make a comprehensive analysis, but rather to follow the shifting course of the different institutions and fields of activity that men at different stages of the age found most important, and thus to trace the central process that both reflected and molded the character of the age. Since this process consisted in the production of a political stability that then nurtured a social and intellectual movement, we shall first focus on the formation of the state system that was in fact the cynosure of early eighteenth-century activity and then shift, along with our historical subjects, to the social and intellectual activities that were the main outlets of cultural energy during the second half of the century. We shall conclude, as the century did, with the series of confrontations, first between kings and philosophers and then between kings and societies, that ended the long status-bound epoch of European history.

Part I

THE KINGS, 1689–1748

CHAPTER 1

The Nature of Kingship

IT WAS AN age of kings. Never before had so much effective power accompanied the prestige of kingship and never again would this power prevail with so little resistance as in the half century that spanned the last years of the seventeenth century and the first part of the eighteenth century. For Louis XIV, that paragon of monarchs, to be a king was a "delightful" profession, and the Continent was to be crowded with colleagues who obviously enjoyed it almost as much as he. The unbridled gusto of their reigns has made Peter the Great and Charles XII the individual heroes of Russian and Swedish history. The Electors Frederick August of Saxony and Frederick III of Brandenburg were sufficiently envious of the royal title to intrigue earnestly for the acquisition of one, the Saxon ruler by converting to Catholicism and getting himself elected to the vacant Polish throne (1697) and the Hohenzollern by arranging for the recognition of his self-announced elevation from duke to king in Prussia (1701). Less spectacular but more far-reaching in their effects were the achievements of the kings Charles XI, Frederick William I, and Charles VI, in establishing bases of unified authority in Sweden, Prussia, and the Habsburg dominions respectively. And if the Glorious Revolution of 1688 had frustrated what seemed like the Stuart attempt to institute a continental type of monarchy in England, still at the start of our period William of Orange, as the English King William III, did take with him, from the covert military dictatorship which he had exercised in the Netherlands as their general *stadholder* since 1672, the jealous care for royal prerogative that helped to moderate the constitutional results of the revolution.

The vogue of kingship meant something very definite in the history of Europe. In its most general meaning, to be sure, it was simply part of that respect for order that had dominated European political life since the early

1

Middle Ages and that persuaded men to accept a network of undisputed authorities by the end of the seventeenth century. If we think of monarchy in its broadest sense as government by a single ruler, whatever his title, then we may well say that, with a few minor exceptions of which the Swiss cantons were the most important, Europe as a whole was organized into monarchies by 1700. But if this fact testifies to the prevalence of political authority in general, the particular emergence of kings out of the welter of monarchs testifies to the precise kind of political authority that was becoming prevalent. The practical conditions of government and the attitudes of men now converged to establish an actual hierarchy among the monarchs, and the rise of the kings to the top of the pyramid illuminated the conditions and the attitudes that were at work.

Grand dukes, dukes, counts, and Electors could exercise the same kind of supreme or even absolute dominion over their subjects as the kings over theirs, but the days were long gone since a Duke Henry of Rohan (1579–1638) could wage a regular war against and conclude a peace with a king of France, or when a duke of Bavaria (Maximilian I, 1573–1651) could be a preeminent power in Germany, or when an Albrecht von Wallenstein (1583–1634) would get himself invested as duke of Friedland, the better to play an independent role in a war between the great powers. Even more impressive in underlining the distinctive role of kingship was the relatively sad plight of emperors in this age of kings. The once-powerful Ottoman Empire entered now into the long period of decline which later led to its personification as the Sick Man of Europe: the treaties of Karlowitz (1699) and Passarowitz (1718) affirmed the military defeats that marked the definitive end of the centuries-old Turkish threat to Europe, and the sultans responsible for them were ultimately deposed. The Holy Roman Empire, which Voltaire was tellingly to characterize as neither holy nor Roman nor an empire, remained the nominal political organization of the 360-odd principalities that comprised the German nation. It was, indeed, by now more usually referred to simply as the German Empire (as it will henceforward be called here), but it added little beyond the title to the Habsburgs who were usually elected its Emperors. It was precisely during our period, indeed, during the reign of Charles VI, that the Habsburgs began deliberately to choose southeastern expansion on the basis of their real ducal and royal powers in Austria, Bohemia, and Hungary over central European hegemony on the basis of their imperial function in Germany.

Only Russia, where Peter confirmed the imperial implications of the traditional title, Tsar ("Caesar"), when he proclaimed himself Imperator (1721), seemed to escape the derogation of empires. But even here, after Peter's death in 1725, the strain of imperial expansion developed flaws in the structure of state and society that made the position of tsar (or tsarina) unstable in a way that European kingship no longer was.

The advantage which the conditions of the time gave to kings over both dukes and emperors was more than a matter of preferred nomenclature. In the theoretical terms of traditional public law, kings ranked above dukes and below the emperor. It was precisely this intermediate position, paradoxically enough, which established the preeminence of kings in the first half of the eighteenth century, for it was the intermediate region, larger than a city, city-state, county, province, or duchy, smaller than the multinationed span of an empire, and usually identified with the "realm" of a king, that now proved itself to be the most effective unit for the exercise of political power abroad and the organization of social energies at home.

Internationally, the hallmark of the period was the ascendance of a plural system of great powers which would dominate the destiny of Europe until the Second World War of the twentieth century. This system was a practical response to a series of real challenges. It evolved as the fittest means of repelling the claims or aggressions of *de jure* empires like the German and the Ottoman and of aspirants to *de facto* empires like sixteenth-century Spain and seventeenth-century France. Just as a system of independent realms became superior to a hegemonical empire, so the powers which composed this system began now clearly to dominate the several city-states and smaller principalities whose competitive position until recently had rivaled their own. England, France, Austria, Prussia, and Russia—this was the pentarchy whose relations were to determine the issue of war and peace in Europe for two centuries, and it was in the age of kings that it appeared as an authoritative institution on the international scene. The countries whose political decline it signified included, to be sure, kingdoms like Spain, Sweden, and Poland as well as the republican Netherlands and the Electorate of Bavaria, but whatever the titles of the excluded sovereigns the essential fact was that inclusion within the circle of great powers henceforward required the possession of physical and human resources great enough, and the government over them unified enough, to be fit for a king.

Domestically, the hallmark of the period was the development of the king's realm from a set of legal claims to an actual district of administration and of the king's government from a superior magistracy to a supreme authority. At different times in different countries over the previous two centuries, kings, like sovereigns by any other name, had already succeeded in abridging the autonomy of such constituted authorities and corporations as governors, syndics, bailiffs, assemblies, churches, aristocracies, and municipalities, and in asserting, by fair means and foul, a lawful dominion over them. The individual constituted authorities—"subordinate magistrates" in customary legal parlance—were either successors of earlier royal agents who had settled down into local autonomy or the heads of self-administering corporations who exercised public functions. The corporations themselves remained, at the end of the seventeenth century, closer to what they had been in the Middle Ages than to what we now recognize by the term. Each corporation was still a combined social and political association which reflected in its organization the order of rank of a hierarchical society and in its function the interpenetration of private and public services. Each still was sanctioned by a legal charter which authorized it to exercise a monopoly of its assigned function in the community of its assigned region and which guaranteed both its right of governing its own members and its privilege of policing the community in the administration of its function. The most characteristic of the seventeenth-century corporations were the "estates," which referred to both the organized ranks of the society at large and the political organization of representative bodies ("parliaments" or "diets") by social rank; but villages, guilds, churches, and nobility (except in Russia and England, where for different historical reasons nobility as a social corps had no legal standing) equally exemplified the combination of internal hierarchy, self-governing association, and public-service administration which defined the pre-nineteenth-century corporation. At the turn of the eighteenth century most Europeans were still members of such corporations, high and low, but the tendencies were already at work which were limiting both their social monopoly and their administrative rights. As their hierarchical structure hardened into oligarchic exclusiveness the excluded men turned to individual enterprise, and whether as capitalists or day laborers increased the numbers of the unincorporated. As the political and economic demands upon public administration increased, the more mobile and open-minded response of the royal bureaucracies led to the community's acceptance of the king's sovereignty both over the members and over the functions of the corporations.

But the actual administration of this legal power had traditionally been left in the hands of the intermediate authorities and corporations except for those particular matters such as war, diplomacy, high justice, and finance, in which the sovereign had an urgent and continuous interest. As long as the public domain was shared out in this fashion, the difference between kings and other authorities was, in fact if not in law, a difference of degree rather than of kind. Toward the end of the seventeenth century, however, this system of indirect rule was increasingly overlaid by agencies of direct government responsive to the will of the sovereign. The realm of the sovereign became the effective unit for the exercise of political power, claiming jurisdiction over public business of all kinds and administering a growing share of it. The sovereign now became an authority different in kind from all others, and since this development pointed unmistakably to a single center of overall responsibility, it redounded to the advantage of kingship over the plurality of intermediate aristocracies and corporations. The key fields for the transition from particular regalian to general sovereign powers were justice and economics, for these were the activities in which the royal bureaucracies now established direct contact with the mass of the subjects and through which the state became a real force. The traditional authorities in these fields either became themselves instruments of the king's government or witnessed the appearance of new supervisory provincial and local organs that were such instruments.

Although the establishment of governmental agencies and policies that looked to the realm as a whole, and the parallel reorganization of myriad local and provincial communities into larger polities of citizens who looked to the regional state as the primary source of benefits and obligations, were the novel elements in the exaltation of kingship around the turn of the eighteenth century, they were not the only domestic factors in the veneration of kings. Historical changes rarely come in wholesale lots, and in this situation too men clung to accustomed practices and attitudes not simply out of nostalgia or inertia but because there was still a vital need for them. The bureaucratic service state that was coming into its own did not, after all, require a king at its head. That kings, with the regional scope of their legal authority and the practical convenience of their mediating position above competing social groups, should have been more appropriate to this function than more circumscribed nobles and oligarchs is clear, but other, more traditional functions explain why the new needs did not bypass kings as well. These functions were rooted in the psychology of early-eighteenth-century Europeans, in the structure of their society, and in necessary conditions of administration.

However real the activities of its organs, the state as such was an abstraction of which most Europeans were barely aware. Of the three elements that constitute a state—territory, people, and government—territories shifted with the fortunes of wars and dynasties, the people usually had no visible organs of direct participation in the state, and the government was made up of a congeries of authorities undertaking a variety of activities which added up to no visible system. For a minority of intellectuals, trained by philosophy to see abstractions as real things and by legal studies to see a rational order behind the apparent confusion of current practices, the state was the tissue of relationships that actually existed. Another small group, composed of politicians and administrators in the central governments, recognized the reality of the state as a whole because they had increasingly to deal with it in practice. The great majority of men, however, accustomed to recognize reality only in what was visible, tangible, or

incarnate, dimly sensed the effects of this new institution which was providing security and services from afar, but could identify it only through its incorporation in the royal person who led and symbolized it. Thus the divine right of kings, which had been replaced among the vanguard of intellectuals by a secularized natural-law theory of sovereignty, remained well into the eighteenth century at the root of the popular attitude toward monarchs. The idea of divine right, in its application to *kingship*, went

EUROPE IN 1689

——— Boundary of the German Empire

Spanish Habsburg territory

Austrian Habsburg territory

DEN

SEA

PRUSSIA

RUSSIA

Volga R.

•Warsaw

POLAND

•Kiev

Vistula R.

Dnieper R.

PODOLIA

Dniester R.

TRANSYLVANIA

MOLDAVIA

GARY

•Zenta

Karlowitz

WALLACHIA

BLACK   SEA

Belgrade

OTTOMAN

0   500 miles

EMPIRE

MOREA

VENICE

back to the Middle Ages; in this sense it signified the sacred origination of
the royal office, or the king's "body politic." The divine right of *kings*,
however, was a more modern product, developing during the sixteenth and
seventeenth centuries to extend the sanctity of the king's "body politic" into
his "natural body." This extension was a response both to the psychological need for a visible symbol of the ever more palpable activities of the
invisible state ("body politic") and to the political need for a distinctive

blessing upon kings vis-à-vis the more indiscriminate anointment of any officeholder in the hierarchy of public authorities. Through the dynasty, personal heredity became the natural counterpart of the permanence of the state and the person of the king the embodiment of the state itself.

There were good social as well as psychological reasons for the particular exaltation of kings in the early eighteenth century. The growth of the state, with its exercise of power from one central agency or set of agencies upon all subjects alike, inevitably extended the fields where traditional social distinctions were irrelevant. Economically, this meant the official encouragement of the commerce and industry run by commoners at least as much as of the agriculture dominated by aristocrats. Legally, it implied a community of subjects equal in their common subjection to the laws of the state. Administratively, it entailed the construction of a bureaucratic apparatus which required a technical training and a standard of practical efficiency transcending class origins. In all these ways the seventeenth century had witnessed an improvement in the fortunes of the middling sectors of society in contrast with the nobility. But, not for the first time in history and not for the last, what appeared to be the linear course of an apparently simple progressive development came a cropper during the early eighteenth century. Not that the bourgeoisie either declined or diminished. Powered by the dramatic expansion of overseas trade and by the first stage of the modern population explosion that continues to this day, the European economic growth of the eighteenth century infused wealth, leisure, and culture into an ever-widening circle of enterprising burghers. Nor was the centralizing process of state making reversed. The claims and effective force of bureaucracies continued to increase, and with them the opportunities for trained and talented commoners on the way up.

What was reversed was the precipitous descent of the aristocracy, a descent that had accompanied, and that had seemed a necessary counterpart to the rise of the bourgeoisie and the emergence of national sovereigns during the sixteenth and seventeenth centuries. In the eighteenth century, surprisingly, aristocracies—or at least important parts of them—were resurgent. Appreciating the principle of what would later become a proverbial prescription for men to join what they could not beat, nobles in the several countries of Europe picked themselves up and began to appropriate commanding positions in the governmental structures of the new states and even in the network of commercial relations. The Whig oligarchy that ruled Britain without serious challenge between the accession of the Hanoverian dynasty in 1714 and George III's assertion of royal influence after 1760 represented a landowning aristocracy that was sponsoring a capitalized and scientific agriculture in response to demands of the market and that had economic ties with merchants and bankers of the

City. The French peers, refueled by Louis XIV's calculated infusion of subsidies, made a serious bid to refashion the monarchy in their own image after the death of the Sun King in 1715, and when this attempt failed, a more economically progressive and modern-minded judicial and administrative aristocracy (*noblesse de robe* and *noblesse d'office*) rose to continue the counteroffensive on behalf of the privileged. In Russia various sections of the military and landed nobility dictated the succession to the throne—in general they preferred tsarinas in the expectation that they would behave consistently as members of the "weaker sex"— and dominated the social policy of the government from the death of Peter the Great in 1725 through the accession of Catherine the Great in 1762. The long period from 1718 to 1772 that the Swedes euphemistically called their "era of liberty" was actually an age of aristocratic sovereignty, exercised constitutionally in a nominal monarchy through the nobles' oligarchic control over both the *Riksdag*, or parliament, and the bureaucracy. The Dutch gave the same high-flown label to the period from 1702 to 1747, when the small but influential class of Regents, an oligarchy comprised of urban patricians, resumed its sway after the death of William III and kept the office of *stadholder* vacant. The seven provinces that made up the Dutch "Republic" were, in this respect, expanded versions of the independent city-states in Europe. Concentrated mainly in Switzerland and Germany, they too were stabilized during the first half of the eighteenth century under the rule of exclusive patrician oligarchies.

Only in Spain—an early achiever of state building—and in Austria and Prussia—two relative latecomers to the field—did the aristocracy register no visible resurgence, but the reason was the lack of need or occasion rather than of will or capacity. With Philip V (ruled 1700–1746), the first of the Bourbon line, the attempt was indeed made to rejuvenate the Spanish monarchy through bureaucratic centralization on the French model, but Philip's own political lethargy and the persistence of the Spanish predilection for government by committee throughout the administrative system enabled the nobility to carve their niches of influence in and around the reformed bureaucracy. Austria's Charles VI did obtain the legal recognition of the variegated Habsburg dominions as a single monarchy, but the Pragmatic Sanction of 1720, which secured an indivisible succession, was finally enacted only with the approval of the sundry aristocratically dominated estates of his realms, and their power sufficed to prevent the establishment of any real institutional unity on the basis of it during his reign. When, under the pressure of military defeat, his daughter, Queen Maria Theresa (ruled 1740–1780), did create unified institutions extending throughout Austria, she had to operate through an ambiguous policy of "gentle violence" which spared both the organizations and the feelings of the different kinds of aristocrats in the various Habsburg territories. The Prussian aristocracy, finally, could offer only passive resistance to the implacable mopping-up operation conducted by Frederick William I against the remnants of their political autonomy, but despite the hostility and grim satisfaction he expressed in his statement: "I am destroying the authority of the *Junkers*," Frederick William never even attempted to divest the *Junkers* or any other section of the Prussian aristocracy either of their social privileges in the army and on their estates or of their monopoly in the exercise of the state's administrative and judicial power over the local countryside. Thence they could be returned by Frederick the Great after 1740 to their wonted posts in the upper echelons of the government.

The aristocracies' new lease on life for the eighteenth century was thus predicated upon the modernization of their premises, and they thereby shifted the arena of social conflict from outside to inside the structure of the state. Where they had formerly defended their privileged rights to land-ownership, manorial lordship, judicial immunities, and tax exemptions by denying the jurisdiction of the central governments, they now defended these privileges by occupying and controlling the governmental agencies which exercised the jurisdiction. This aristocratic penetration of the state ran counter to the standards of general law, equal citizenship, and uniform administration which had served and continued to serve bureaucrats as guides in extending the scope of central government. But the hierarchical tendency was no mere atavism. Despite the obvious and reciprocal hostility between it and the leveling tendency with which it shared the state, the coexistence of the two tendencies, however mismatched in logic, was a faithful response to a fundamental social demand of the age. European society required, for the military security of its inhabitants, for the direction and subsidization of its economy, and for the prevention of religious turbulence and popular disorder, the imposition of unified control over a larger area and more people than the contemporary instruments of government could manage. Hence the employment of the traditional social and corporate hierarchies by the government as extensions of the governing arm into the mass of inhabitants. All people were subject, but some were more subject than others.

The necessity both for a social caste and for a bureaucracy which undermined the social caste redounded to the advantage of the kings. For effective political operation an authority was required which was recognized by bureaucrats and aristocrats alike as their representative in the adjudication of rival claims and in the allotment of appropriate powers. This authority could only be the king, for only the king combined in himself a social position as the highest-ranking noble with a political position as the supreme magistrate of the community. For centuries the notion of kingship had joined the idea of a natural man who was preeminent among aristocrats with that of a political man who symbolized the unity of the entire civil society, and the development of the aristocracy as well as the growth of bureaucracy in the late seventeenth century made this two-headed monarch indispensable.

And if the king was necessary to this anomalous mixture of hierarchy and equality in early-eighteenth-century society, he had an interest in perpetuating the anomaly, for it was equally necessary to him. The king's development of organs and policies to perform services needed for the security and welfare of the whole community was an obvious means of combating the dispersion of public power among the traditional corporations, but just as essential albeit not so obvious was the interest of the king in maintaining and even sustaining the privileged corporations—not simply for his administrative convenience but in their own social right. He needed the support of a hierarchy against the dangers of leveling as much as he needed the support of middle-class officials against the ambitions of the notables. The continuous threat and frequent outbreak of popular disorders through the seventeenth and eighteenth centuries were a constant reminder of how unreliable a basis of loyalty the appreciation of governmental services could be. The existence of a hierarchy which made the inequality of rights and functions an ultimate and unquestionable necessity of social organization accustomed men to accept the relationship of inferiors to superiors as a primary fact imbedded in the very nature of things. For kings, their position at the apex of the divinely constructed social ladder called for obedience even when the benefits of their government were not in evidence, and they never dreamed of destroying a support which linked their own preeminence with the general constitution of human society.

Thus peoples were related to their kings in two different ways, one primarily political and uniform, the other primarily social and pyramidal; and each of these relations in its own way supported the king and was in turn supported by him. But such a general characterization should not mislead. The development of kingship into this form may be clear to us, but it was not so clear to the men who developed it and lived under it. For this shape of the institution was being defined as a result of piecemeal practical necessities rather than of a deliberate program. It was no accident, then, that in the period from 1690 to 1748, between Locke's *Second Treatise on Civil Government* and Montesquieu's *Spirit of the Laws*, no important political theory emerged that commanded consensus: the mixture of institutions and principles that were going into the monarchical state was too new, too loose, and too attached to the particular circumstances of its origin for contemporaries to conceive it as a system. There were standard political theories for each of the ingredients, but their basic ideas stemmed from earlier periods.

We have already noted the divergence between the natural-law doctrine to which many of the intellectuals adhered and the divine-right ideas cherished by the populace. None of the great names associated with either theory belong to the period—not Grotius, Hobbes, or Locke for the former, nor James I, Filmer, or Bossuet for the latter—and they had no successors of like stature.

Contemporary political writers attempted to combine natural law with divine right or natural law with historical institutions, but emerged with works that were too special and occasional to command influence. Of the best-known thinkers which the period produced, neither Leibniz, nor Berkeley, nor Hume, nor Voltaire succeeded in concocting a coherent political philosophy. Those who did succeed in communicating some political ideas, on the other hand, had a limited effect in their time and fell into obscurity thereafter. Samples of this genre were Henry St. John, Viscount Bolingbroke (1678–1751), who covered his confusions of nature and history under the slogan of an English "patriotism"; Archbishop Fénelon (1651–1715), who recommended a mélange of royal absolutism, popular reforms, and the restoration of the French aristocratic constitution; Jean Jacques Burlamaqui (1694–1748), who put a bewildering amalgam of individual rights, sovereign authority, and corporate privilege into the deceptive format of a legal system; and Christian Thomasius (1655–1728), who tried to bring rationalism and German Pietism together in an unstable alliance of natural law and divine right.

The inchoate quality of political thinking during the first half of the eighteenth century not only reveals the primacy of practice over theory but hints at the primacy of circumstances over policies even within the area of practice. The historical pattern of the age confirms this. From 1688 until 1713 in western Europe and until 1721 in central and northern Europe, what was important—that is, of lasting effect—in public life was crystallized into a succession of dramatic events. Thereafter, until almost midcentury, what was important in public life was the creation of new institutions, i.e. new agencies for and ways of doing things, that set up changed conditions for later events. Events occurred too in this second quarter of the eighteenth century, to be sure, but they were relatively insignificant alongside the reorganization of public life which provided new routines for men's daily lives. The subdivision of the period 1688–1748 into this sequence of stirring events and stabilizing institutions indicates a significant characteristic of the period: from the circumstantial events of the first phase monarchs and ministers learned the lessons that they embodied in the institutions of the second; and from this sequence came the pattern and preeminence of kingship in Europe.

To see how this development worked as a process, we shall follow each stage in turn.

CHAPTER 2

The Kings at War, 1688-1721

DURING THE generation that separated Louis XIV's invasion of the Rhine Palatinate in 1688 from the Treaty of Nystad in 1721, the states that were evolving into the great powers of recent memory enjoyed but one brief year of peace (1699-1700). In the manner of the age, the number of belligerents was never constant, the motives even of allies were frequently obscure and local if not divergent, and the actual fighting was intermittent; but when the war aims and the battles are strained through the sieve of history, they separate out into two great conflicts which had fundamental effects upon the development of European society. There was a western war and an eastern war, and the future of Europe was determined by the unity within each and the connection between the two.

The war in the west was diffused through two stages—the War of the League of Augsburg from 1688 to 1697 and the War of the Spanish Succession from 1701 to 1713. Its continuity was further disturbed by the shift of focus from Germany to Spain, the shift of some states from one side to the other, and the mutual suspicions and incessant squabbling among ostensible allies. But it was nonetheless essentially one war, pitting the Grand Alliance against Louis XIV for the domination of western and central Europe.

To the east, similarly, the renewed nameless struggle of Habsburg against Turk in the southeast from 1683 until 1699; its succession by the duel between Sweden and Russia from 1700 until 1721, celebrated under the grandiose name of the Great Northern War; the sporadic pattern of hostilities in both stages; and the complications of Venetian, papal, Polish, Saxon, and Danish participation: these ill-assorted pieces obscure the historical meaning of one long conflict. Essentially, it was the counterpart of the western war: it decided the balance of power in eastern Europe.

Considered separately, then, these wars determined which of the myriad states and principalities would be most influential in shaping European destinies for the next two and a half centuries. But the western and eastern wars can also be considered together. They were connected with each other by belligerents and motives common to both, and their political effects converged into the formation of a single European political system composed of similarly organized states.

THE WAR IN THE WEST: FIRST STAGE, 1688–1697

The war in the west broke out over the issue of Germany, was resumed over the issue of Spain, and was actually fought for purposes which transcended both. Ostensibly the War of the League of Augsburg, or the War of the Grand Alliance, as the phase of it that terminated in the peace of Ryswick of 1697 has been alternatively called, was fought to determine the possession of the German Rhineland and had its origins in the usual escalation of reciprocal suspicions about the intentions of the main powers in the area. The struggle opened in September, 1688, when Louis XIV decided to take advantage of the Austrian involvement with the Turks and to forestall the unfavorable consequences of the imminent Austrian triumph for French influence in the German Empire. He embarked upon a preventive military invasion of the Rhine Palatinate, one of the politically sensitive German Electorates (*i.e.* the eight principalities whose rulers elected the German emperor and constituted the First Estate of the Imperial Diet, or Reichstag)—ostensibly to anticipate an attack on France by the Emperor's League of Augsburg, but actually to prevent the accession of an anti-French Elector in the Palatinate. Leopold I, Habsburg ruler of the Austrian dominions and German Emperor, countered this gambit with a formal declaration of war. Not only the occasion but the underlying cause of the war seemed to be the assertion of hegemony over western Germany. For Louis, addicted like so many aggressors to the policy that may be characterized as "creeping defense," the purpose was to force, through conquests on the right bank of the Rhine, the legal recognition of the irregular holdings in Alsace and Lorraine which the French had acquired at Westphalia in 1648 and in the "reunions" of 1680 and 1681—holdings which the Emperor had refused to recognize as legal in the Truce of Regensburg (1684) and which, indeed, in Louis' eyes, were threatened by the recent addition of Hungary to the Habsburg power (1687) and by the Emperor's previous sponsorship of the League of Augsburg in 1686. Constituted by the Bavarian, Saxon, and Palatine Electors and by the Kings of Sweden and of Spain in their capacities as princes of the German Empire—plus the Emperor—the League was indeed an alliance against the presumed aggressive program of Louis XIV for Germany.

But beyond these appearances more profound causes were at work. The German situation brought into focus fundamental factors that had previously been diffuse but would henceforth play important roles in the war and its aftereffects. These factors had broken the surface of European politics only in the repeated but aborted attempts by William of Orange to organize an offensive coalition against Louis XIV. Now, with the League of Augsburg as a core, William's effort bore fruit. His Protestant, commercial initiative and the Emperor's Catholic, traditional, landed defensiveness converged into a single definite military alliance against France, thus forging the political integration of economic, religious, and dynastic interests that had been incapable, by themselves, of producing a common issue around which Europe could be organized. But now the German problem was broadened into precisely such an issue.

This first of the European "grand" alliances was effected, under William's prodding, by the formal Treaty of Vienna (May, 1689) between Austria (on behalf of the German Empire), England and the Netherlands, bringing these maritime powers into the war against France, and by the subsequent inclusion of Spain, Sweden, and Savoy in the coalition (although the Swedes would be belligerents in name only and the Savoyards would change sides in 1696). The German issue formed the initial basis for the alliance, but it obviously was not, for many of the participating powers, a sufficiently vital interest to bring about their adherence. In the Netherlands and England, for example, Louis' German demarche triggered a long-standing resentment born of the commercial war which Louis' minister Colbert had waged for so many years against them, and nurtured on French territorial aggression in the Spanish Netherlands—an area strategically vital to both maritime powers—during the Dutch war of 1672–1678. The Bourbon threat to the lifelines of their respective economies readied influential business interests in both countries for an accounting with France. The Dutch move into the German conflict was actually preceded by a new tariff war against the French in November, 1688.

It is easy to overestimate the impact of the religious animosities which followed hard upon Louis XIV's revocation of the Edict of Nantes in 1685; actually the sound and fury of the Huguenot émigrés and the wild talk of their English, Dutch, and German Calvinist coreligionists about a crusade against France hardly explain the alliance of Catholic and Protestant powers that came into play against Louis. And yet it seems clear that even if this recrudescence of sectarian rivalry was not a general cause of the war it certainly contributed sufficiently to the belligerency of some states to be a cause of the war becoming general. Thus William of Orange, whose implacable hostility to Bourbon France far antedated Louis' Huguenot persecution and far transcended religion, could exploit outraged Protestant emotions to bring such erstwhile rival bargainers for Louis' favors as Sweden and Brandenburg-Prussia into a defensive accord against France (1686), and as William III of England he could develop the English revolution against the Catholic James II into participation in the war against France (May, 1689). The religious sensibilities of Frederick William, the Great Elector of Brandenburg-Prussia (ruled 1640–1688), combined with his political disappointment in the results of his French alliance to put him into a general anti-French posture after 1685. His son, Elector Frederick III (ruled 1688–1713), could use the historic fear which associated Catholic and political aggression to found the Magdeburg Concert of north German Protestant princes (October, 1688) for the war against France, despite the absence of a direct threat to their immediate interests.

In addition to the economic and religious factors, there were also dynastic considerations that were activated by the German crisis but went far beyond it. The most potent of these was undoubtedly the Habsburg claim to the Spanish succession. This issue, which was to appear in the open and dominate the second phase of the western war after the death of the Spanish king, Charles II, in 1700, was already covertly at work a decade before. It helped to remind the Habsburg Emperor, Leopold I, of his German patriotism and to take the incursion into the Palatinate by his rival Bourbon claimant to the Spanish crown as the occasion for the declaration of war (October, 1688). Indeed, he insisted upon a secret article recognizing his own right to the Spanish succession, as a condition of his adherence to the alliance against Louis which was formalized in the Treaty of Vienna.

Nor were Leopold's the only dynastic interests at stake or the only family ties involved. Louis XIV himself was continuously concerned with asserting Bourbon rights against the Habsburgs, and the Bourbon claim to the Spanish succession. In this instance he was representing the claims of his sister-in-law, the duchess of Orléans, to holdings in the Palatinate that would have given the Bourbon family a seat in the German Reichstag. The Great Elector's turnabout against France was connected with his hope of satisfying Hohenzollern claims to western Pomerania and parts of Silesia which he had failed to obtain through his policy of French alliance. Moreover, his kinship with William of Orange, his nephew and the chief architect of the anti-French coalition, eased his change of fronts. William, in turn, acquired the possibility of directing English foreign policy toward war with France through his marriage to Mary, eldest daughter of King James II, and through his own more distant claim, as the King's nephew, to a vacated throne. His plans for intervention in England were predicated on these dynastic ties, and in fact, the cautious alliance of Tories and Whigs which made the revolution would hardly have accepted him as the new king without them. A prime motive for Sweden's accession to the coalition went back to the French appropriation, during the "reunions" of 1680 and 1681, of the Zweibrücken principality whose succession had been promised to the Vasa dynasty. Even the Spanish Habsburg, Charles II, long a plaything rather than player in the game of European power politics, bestirred himself into joining the alliance in conformity with the change in his family relations following the death of his French wife in 1689 and his remarriage to an Austrian later in the same year. Even the occasion of the war took a dynastic form, for it was set off by the election of Joseph Clement, a prince of the Bavarian Wittelsbach line that had long controlled the See, to the archbishopric of Cologne, over the candidate from the pro-French Fürstenberg family.

Thus economic, religious, and dynastic factors, activated by Louis XIV's German invasion, all entered into the opening of the war in the west. Obviously, there was nothing new or remarkable either in the martial incidence of any of these factors or in the role of Germany as the battleground of Europe. What was remarkable was the new interrelationship among these factors which could make them all operative on the same occasion. In foreign as in domestic affairs, it signified the growth of a collective interest above the special interests which fed into it. For the government of Louis XIV, the move against the Palatinate fell into line with the commercial, religious, and dynastic aggression that had preceded it, and became a piece in a general policy of expanding a unified France. It was rightly taken in the rest of Europe as a part of such a policy. Among the rest of the European powers, the French action in Germany brought various partial interests together in the general agreement that Europe should be restored to the settlement created by the treaties of Westphalia (1648) and the Pyrenees (1659), with France deprived of its several intervening acquisitions. This was the core of the consensus embodied in the Treaty of Vienna. It indicated that Europe had caught up to the French in assessing transient business, confessional, and familial concerns by the standard of long-range, political aims. However varied the spur for the different powers, the effect was common: fear and resentment at the obstruction posed by French ambitions.

The perception of an overriding political interest, different in kind from other human interests and arbitrating among them, was not so much a rational conclusion from a political ideal as a lesson of practical experience. It is true, certainly, that systematic theories along this line had become ever more influential since Jean Bodin (1530–1596) in the sixteenth century, until by the late seventeenth century, they were represented in every major country by publicists and academicians who installed them as part of the mental equipment carried about by educated administrators. But men were accustomed, in Europe, to a wide span between theory and practice, and these ideas were not applied until conditions called for their application. And even then, they were applied not systematically but piecemeal, to meet particular situations. For the decisive authorities in the late seventeenth century were not the intellectuals or the administrators, but the kings—violent, poorly educated, distracted, or pious, diligent, pettifogging, but in any case attending to particular decisions rather than to general policies.

Yet it was in this period that the kings emerged who responded to their experience by permitting larger points of view to inform these decisions. History is always the result of the meeting between a situation and a personality (whether collective or individual), and in this case the personalities relevant to history were the royal figures who, in one way or another, were sufficiently attuned to their environment to meet its challenge and exploit its possibilities.

Louis XIV

Still holding the center of the stage was the Sun King, Louis of France (ruled 1643–1715), the scourge and the envy of Europe. In many ways he seemed the same as ever, only more so. The manliness and the presence that made him "every inch a king," the unquestioning self-righteousness, the untiring conversion of his private life into the public business, the unblushing identification of the public community with his private person, the active foreign policy of creeping defense: all these marks of his regime since 1661 were indelible until his death in 1715. But however persistent these fundamentals may have proved, a subtle change in their operation took place during the decade of the 1680's that set off the subsequent years as a new era. In part, the change was external to Louis, initiated by the converging decisions of other European monarchies to meet his challenge by acting up to the standards of power and policy which he had so successfully established. But in part, too, the change was internal to Louis and his regime, a dislocation of the parts which made up the pattern of his government.

The inconsistencies in Louis' absolutism have been noted often enough, but in his office as in his policies it was precisely the fine balance between opposites that constituted the chief strength of his regime during the first twenty years of his personal rule. There were contrasts between his private pleasures and his public dedication, between his vaulting ambitions and his bureaucratic pettifoggery, between his preference for commoners to do his work and his concern for the nobility that got his pensions, between the centralized administration which he imposed and the local institutions which he preserved, between maritime and continental policies, and between the arts of peace and the arts of war. But by holding these factors in equilibrium he had managed to draw strength from each of them in an age when neither the techniques of government nor the modest tempo of change permitted radical solutions.

From the 1680's the texture of his life and his policies coarsened, the delicate balance was disturbed, and the interest of state, which, as balance wheel, had enjoyed the joint support of the countervailing parts, began now to tilt. In this historical case as in so many others, the data hardly suffice to substantiate a psychoanalytic explanation of politics, but we must at least note the coincidence that the start of Louis' political excesses was accompanied by a rupture in the intimate habits that had contributed to his emotional stability. It was said of Louis that "he could not do without women," and from adolescence to middle age his amorous disposition had

Louis XIV praying. *Sculpture by Antoine Coysevox. The aging monarch in a characteristic pose. Notre Dame, Paris.*

found ample outlet in a continuous succession of affairs with partners of high and low estate. But when, in 1684, he married the last of his mistresses, the pious and frigid Madame de Maintenon (1635–1719), he broke with the habit of extramarital dalliance that had balanced the intensity of his application to the profession of kingship. It is at least ironical, if not revealing, that Louis should have reached simultaneously the states of conjugal fidelity and political concupiscence.

Not only in his morality but in his religiosity as well did Louis alter the previous pattern of his life. Louis' piety was an unquestioning, external commitment. He subscribed to the whole panoply of Catholic formulas and rituals, which he accepted, as he accepted all established institutions, insofar as they manifested the divinely ordained order and recognized the Most Christian Majesty—*i.e.* Louis himself—as its supreme caretaker. He had always abominated Huguenots and Jansenists, both because they fomented disorder in religion and the church, respectively, and because they appealed to principles of faith above the instituted authorities of which he counted himself the chief. Both groups did indeed share the same general doctrinal tendency to stress the role of divine grace over human free will in the awakening of faith, the role of faith over good works in the attainment of salvation, and the rigorous role of good works over accommodations to human frailty in the living of the good Christian life. Both groups shared too the same general ecclesiastical tendency to resist Catholic authorities who espoused contrary doctrines. To this extent Louis' opposition to both groups as rebellious heretics of similar stripe had a basis in general fact, but the specific differences between the two groups also reflect two different dimensions in the policy of suppression which the later Louis would visit upon them. The Huguenots were French Calvinists with their own separate churches whose autonomous corporate rights were recognized by law. Jansenism was originally a theological and ethical movement *within* the Catholic Church, claiming to represent a purified version of traditional Catholic dogma and morals and to oppose only the particular Jesuit influence whose emphasis upon free will, good works, and adaptability supposedly was corrupting the tradition. Stressing religious inwardness and personal ethics, seventeenth-century Jansenists tended rather toward reform of theology and clerical morals within the French Catholic Church, and when threatened, toward quietism, mysticism, and passive resistance, than toward ecclesiastical separatism or political action. Their organization as a church party and political movement during the eighteenth century would be more a result than a cause of the Papacy's alignment with the Jesuits and of Louis' with the Papacy at the start of the century.

During the earlier part of his reign Louis' antipathies to religious heterodoxy had been held in check by his suspicions of the Ultramontanists—advocates of papal authority in the French Catholic Church and activists against Huguenots and Jansenists alike—on the other side of the clerical spectrum. Then he had chosen to promote political Gallicanism, a middle-of-the-road position which sponsored the claims of religious orthodoxy against the deviants, of the French Church against the Papacy, and of the monarchy as the protector of French orthodoxy. In this activity as in others, the fundamental features of Louis' policy remained constant, but from the mid-1680's their internal relations shifted. Whatever the particular occasion that inspired Louis to end the toleration of the Reformed (Calvinist, or Huguenot) Church in France by revoking the Edict of Nantes in 1685—the anxiety of a literal-minded, middle-aged believer over the eternal consequences of a misspent youth, the growing influence of an entourage led by Madame de Maintenon and the royal confessor, Père La Chaise (1624–1709), the momentum of the ever-expanding list of disabilities imposed upon the Huguenots since the time of Cardinal Richelieu (1585–1642), or Louis' belief in the reported mass conversions to Catholicism of the Huguenots, whose few lagging brethren would need only the encouragement of law to bring about a religious unanimity—the importance of the act for our purposes lies rather in the general change of attitude which it betokened and initiated. For it was followed by Louis' rapprochement with the Papacy in the 1690's and climaxed by the enthusiastic cooperation of king and pope (Clement XI) in the persecution of Jansenists. The high points of their joint campaign came in 1709, when the community at Port-Royal, long a Jansenist haven, was evicted by royal troops, and in 1713, when, with Louis' approval, Clement issued the bull *Unigenitus*, which condemned one hundred and one propositions of France's leading Jansenist, Father Pasquier Quesnel (1634–1719). By 1715 the bitter conflict over his acceptance of the bull awakened even Louis, in a last flash of insight before his death, to a belated futile recognition of the political perils entailed by the unbalanced sectarian course of his latter years.

The meaning of Louis' religious shift at mid-reign, then, was not the simple growth of his authoritarianism, for his passion for unbrooked power was as strong before as after, and indeed was more surely attained in the earlier than in the later form. Its meaning lay rather in its revelation of his growing preference, in part deliberate and in part compulsive, for uniformity over balance as the better means of enhancing his authority.

The same pattern is observable in the final change that was to mark off the second half of Louis' personal government as a new era in the history of France and Europe: the replacement of Colbert by Louvois as the king's leading political counselor. Until the 1680's Louis had balanced adroitly between his two great ministers—ennobled scions, both, of bourgeois families, but exemplifying very different qualities of their class. Jean Baptiste Colbert (1619–1683), merchant's son, was the very model of the successful burgher. Icy by temperament (he was nicknamed "the North"), unbending, parsimonious, diligent, he dedicated himself to the same kind of calculation, rationality, and orderliness in the administration of the state as he would have in the management of an established business, and even the flaws in this granite character were those of his type—the nepotic provision for the expanded family and the uncritical reverence for his king. Controller general of Finance, Minister of Commerce, of Colonies, and of the Navy, Colbert had assumed direction of economic control and development. Through these functions, he directed the general internal administration as well as an appropriate part of foreign policy. To these functions he brought, and from them he drew, an equilibrated view of French interests. In domestic affairs he held a middle line between innovation and tradition, commercial liberty and regulation, bureaucratic leveling and aristocratic hierarchy. In foreign affairs he alternated between recognition of the economic need for peace and the mercantilist advocacy of limited war, and he approached these alternatives in terms of an oceanic rather than a continental orientation.

François Michel Le Tellier, Marquis of Louvois (1641-1691), represented another branch of the ascendant bourgeoisie. Middle member of a bureaucratic dynasty—he was to pass his office on to his son just as his father had bequeathed it, extralegally, to him—Louvois ran the Ministry of War like a hard-driving entrepreneur. Tireless, obsessed, brutal, he rode roughshod over traditional restraints and fed the king's authority through the restless expansion of his means of control. He had remade the army into a reliable royal instrument by leveling aristocratic privilege and rationalizing the conditions of promotion, training and administration. He agitated incessantly against foreign neighbors and French Huguenots alike, prescribing disciplined force and unbridled terror as equally permissible means for smashing all resistance, whether actual or potential, to the royal will. He had contested the direction of French foreign policy with Colbert, seeking for it a continental orientation that would increase the contiguous territories under French dominion.

Louvois' rise to power in the government of France was an important influence in changing the tenor of Louis' reign. Colbert's death in 1683 was a fortuitous removal of a rival influence, but the role of chance was not as crucial as this circumstance might seem to indicate. Colbert's star was already on the wane at the time of his demise. Louis' acquiescence in Louvois' policy of "reunions" as early as 1680–1681 showed that the subsequent triumph of the war minister was part of a general shift in Louis' approach to politics. If the French aggression which triggered the War of the League of Augsburg was a Louvoisian act, it was of a piece with the preceding developments of the 1680's which marked Louis' turn to the drastic over the balanced, the coarse over the fine, in his politics. Louvois was himself to die in 1691, and the unofficial place of policy maker for the king which Colbert and he had occupied was henceforth to remain vacant. Relying now upon his own devices, Louis held his course for the remainder of his reign, as if through a kind of inertia, in the direction that Louvois had impelled him. Whatever moral or even political judgment may be levied upon the constant warfare and increasing oppressiveness of Louis' later years, they paradoxically manifested the growing preponderance of the institutional over the private factors in kingship. For Louis' monopolization of decision making, his adoption of unitarian and expansionist policies in the style of Louvois, and his readiness to use repression and war in pursuit of them were accompanied by his growing tendency to think of kingship rather as a responsible public charge which acted through law for the general welfare than as the office of a divinely ordained person. This anomalous combination of increased despotism in the act and increased limitation in the concept is explicable only by Louis' developing conviction that he was trustee for a body politic that required uniformity at home and absolute removal of all risks from abroad.

William III

Louis' great rival was William, coincidentally "the Third" both as prince of Orange and as king of England, where he ruled between 1689 and 1702. On the surface the conflict between the two seems like one of those spectacular personal duels which have, independently of time and place, pitted individuals of titanic mold against each other recurrently throughout the recorded history of man. The confrontation has been generalized even further by the added attribution of an epical moral dimension: Louis is the archetype of the villain, William the model of the hero. But however dramatically satisfying, the tableau is flawed. The house of Orange has had a good historical press as dynasties go, and there is reason to suspect that some of the luster indelibly associated with his great-

William III, *stadholder* of the Netherlands and King of England.

grandfather, William the Silent, protagonist in the previous century's resistance to Philip II of Spain, has rubbed off on the descendant. Despite the common traits of persistence, determination, and courage in the face of adversity, the common position of *stadholder* over the Netherlands, and the common championship of national independence and Protestantism, William III evinced, in addition, unsympathetic qualities that were wanting in his forebear. Rigid, cold, calculating, as authoritarian in his politics as he was dogmatic in his Calvinism, William was a bully in his private life and a dictator to the nominally free and formerly tolerant republic of the Netherlands.

William's ultimate political purpose, moreover, in terms of which his severity has been extenuated, was and remains doubtful. Certainly he was consumed, all through his career, by his antagonism against Louis, and certainly too he saw in Louis a threat to the very existence of the Netherlands and of Protestantism, to both of which he was equally and sincerely devoted, as he was to the traditional constitutions of the European system and its several states. But it is also clear that personal ambition played an undue role in his antipathy to the French king. The restoration in the Netherlands of the *stadholder*ship, which had been suspended between 1650 and 1672, had stemmed directly from the needs of the war against France, and the preservation of the hereditary quasi-monarchy into which William converted it depended upon continued hostility. Again, William had English expectations of his own which were rooted in his Stuart blood, encouraged by his marriage to an English royal princess, and ultimately confirmed by his insistence upon an equal share of the English crown in 1689. Hence it was perhaps as much because Louis supported the Catholic

King James and whatever Catholic male heir he might sire—including the belated son he did sire in June 1688—and thus threatened to block William's access to the most exalted of honors, as because he cherished the patriotic project of using the English crown as an additional weapon in the Dutch fight against France that the *stadholder* persisted in his hostility to the French king. It should be added, as a final touch in the disparagement of William's heroic role, that he was but an indifferent general; his triumphs were generally attributable to his mastery of the valuable but unglamorous art of diplomacy.

The meaning of William's role lay neither in the principles, whether political or religious, nor in the personal or Dutch interests that he represented. It lay rather in his will and capacity to convert a variety of principles and interests into a system of countervailing power. Against the new organization of social force from a single political center pioneered by the government of Louis XIV, he educated the sovereigns of Europe in equally novel means of associating their various centers of social force against it, thereby introducing the concert as the alternative to hegemony in the mobilization of political power.

The sphere in which William thus modernized European politics was the sphere of international relations. He had, to be sure, proved himself adept at building an effective political machine out of the motley Dutch constitution, and he drew from it more force than any single authority had ever succeeded in amassing before. But he changed no institutions here any more than he was to change any in England when he assumed royal authority there. His domestic policy in both his realms varied with the needs of his wars and his diplomacy, and it was in foreign policy alone that he was truly constructive. In this arena he broke through to the perception of *political* interests as the general currency of diplomacy into which special dynastic, religious, or economic interests must be converted if the relations among states were to be negotiable and controllable. Because William himself perceived and brought his fellow monarchs to perceive the primacy of security from aggression as the political value on which all other public values hinged, he was able to convert the heterogeneous fears of and animosities against Louis XIV into the awareness of a unified European political interest against the military extension of the French political system. Piecemeal, through the indoctrination of one prince after another through the decade of the 1680's, he built informal understandings, agreements, and partial coalitions into the great alliance that fought the war.

The Lesser Monarchs: Charles XI, Leopold I, Frederick I

Measured alongside Louis and William, the two pioneers of modern statecraft, other European rulers of the period seem puny. And yet, despite the traditional, partial, and myopic cast of their political personalities, the King of Sweden, the German Emperor, and the Elector of Brandenburg manifested, each in his own way, an admixture of political consciousness that made them at least responsive to the challenge posed by Louis and the lead offered by William.

Among the participants in the western war, it was Charles XI of Sweden (ruled 1660–1697) who was closest in political stature to the great ones and who approximated, along with them, the type of royal state builder characteristic of the period. From one point of view, Charles's personal government was simply an oscillation in the customary cycle of nobiliar and monarchical preponderance that characterized Swedish history throughout the early modern period. Personally shy, ill-educated, and opportunistic as he was, the King was certainly driven by no doctrine or plan of political reorganization, and to this extent he belongs to the traditional rather than the modern pattern of government. And yet, from the way in which he reacted to his opportunities and from the unintended integration of his piecemeal policies, a new element emerged, important enough to earn for Charles the historical credit of having established the bases of the modern Swedish state.

Only Sweden's imminent decline from great-power status, a decline already visible in the Swedes' diminishing influence upon the destinies of western Europe in the latter seventeenth century, has cast Charles into the rank of secondary political rulers. Like Louis he grew up in the disorder of a noble-ridden regency, and like William he rose to power by assuming the role of national savior which he associated with his position of military commander at a time when the ruling oligarchy was militarily impotent. The autocratic political power which was consequently vested in him after 1680 was at once analogous to Louis' and William's and something new in Swedish history. The Swedish parliament, the *Riksdag*, like the Dutch estates, continued formally in being with its wonted constitutional powers, but it now expressly recognized in Charles its "absolute sovereign King, responsible to no one on earth." Utilizing every occasion to establish his independence and increase his authority at the expense of the compliant assembly for the purpose of expanding Sweden's military resources, Charles's particular policies—hardly unfamiliar in themselves—of recovering crown lands, destroying the political and bureaucratic predominance of the old nobility, and creating a new service aristocracy alongside the old on the land, and above it in the government, took a permanent institutional form: there emerged a rational budget, a reorganized regular army, and a centralized administration staffed by officials loyal to the king as head of state.

This work of internal consolidation absorbed the bulk of the king's attention and energies after the Treaty of Nijmegen (1678–1679), in which Louis XIV's studied neglect of his Swedish ally seemed to confirm the near disaster of Sweden's military fortunes during the precedent war,

Habsburg Emperor Leopold I in his later years.

but if Charles's foreign policy was muted its influence was nonetheless pervasive. It was, indeed, in the light of Sweden's diplomatic position that the domestic reforms were undertaken, and Charles's approach to international relations was analogous to the pattern of his internal politics. For internationally too, a series of particular policies added up to a general policy which, however unconscious, testified to the reality of a state interest transcending traditional motives. Charles's resentment of French "tutelage" at Nijmegen, his reaction to Louis' violation of the dynastic rights he claimed in the Palatinate, and his opposition to the Huguenot persecution all had an effect upon his policy, but they did not dominate it. They fed into a larger attitude that did dominate it. Under their influence Charles entered into the various anti-French combinations of the 1680's to redress the balance upon which the restoration of Sweden's independent role depended, and he climaxed this phase by participating in the formation of the Grand Alliance of 1689 against Louis. But once the alliance was formed Charles deliberately repressed his own anti-French motives, since they no longer served the Swedish interest. This depended, in his view, upon a balance of the powers that now existed without him. Sweden remained militarily neutral through the War of the League of Augsburg, for Charles and his advisers now saw Swedish interests best served by a mediator's role. As a matter of fact, the calculation was, for the short run at least, quite correct. Sweden was instrumental in bringing about the peace conference at Ryswick and did draw a commission for its services as honest broker—the recognition (only until 1718, as it turned out) of its king's dynastic claim to the German Rhenish duchy of Zweibrücken. The real payoff for the performance of Charles XI was to come shortly there-

Pleasure-yacht of the uncharacteristically fun-loving Hohenzollern, Frederick I of Prussia.

after in the early successes of Charles XII, for the father supplied the son not only with the institutions but with the mentality appropriate to the age of power politics.

Leopold I (ruled 1658–1705), Holy Roman Emperor, *de jure* ruler of the Austrian archduchies and King of Bohemia, *de facto* ruler of Hungary (he had the royal title transferred to his son Joseph in 1687), was a monarch in the traditional Habsburg mold. Full of family pride and the sense of his own prerogatives, Leopold was yet pacific by temperament, aesthetic by taste, and sectarian by religious conviction. He was therefore, for much of his reign, the very model of the passive autocrat in which the Habsburg line has been so prolific. Interested rather in music, the theater, and Catholic piety than in royal politics, his had been rather a responsive than a provocative role on the European scene, with the characteristic exception of his energetic repression of Hungarian Protestantism.

But under the pressure of experience he developed a new political concern, which he introduced as a permanent trait into the Habsburg dynastic character. From the defections among the German principalities during the Dutch war he discovered at first hand the futility of Austria's Imperial position and from the conjunction of Hungarian revolt, Turkish invasion, and French aggression he discovered the vital military importance of the Habsburg non-German dominions, the priority of the political over the religious aspects of the confessional conflict, and the unity of Austrian interests amid the apparent multiplicity of issues. There was, then, a new political awareness in Leopold's perception of the common danger from east and west, in his decision to turn the war against the Turks into a two-front war against the French as well, and in his participation in a coalition with the Protestant powers of Europe.

Frederick III, Elector of Brandenburg (ruled 1688–1713), was undoubtedly something of a sport in the Hohenzollern line of strong rulers. Such has been the common historical judgment upon him, and it is sustained by his propensities toward extravagance, luxury, display, indecisiveness, dependence, and pessimism—traits obviously uncharacteristic of the dynasty. Dwarfed by the state-building activists who preceded and suc- ceeded him, Frederick's reign is usually considered a hiatus, notable only for his acquisiton of the royal title of King in Prussia (as Frederick I), during 1701—and this too has been criticized as an empty form of pomp too dearly bought.

But still, even aside from the cultural innovations which were included among Frederick's diversions—the Academy of Sciences and the Univer- sity of Halle were the most important of these foundations—Frederick made a positive contribution to the age. He did have a feeling, articulated both in the quest for kingship and in the emulation of the Sun King's manners and tastes, for the standards appropriate to the new appreciation of the state and its representatives, and the presence of such a feeling in such an unpolitical personality was a mark of how far the appreciation had come. It was Frederick who, immediately upon his accession in 1688, set aside his father's testament and saved the unity of the Hohenzollern domi- nions, which the Great Elector had willed to be divided. It was Frederick too who, just as immediately, led the northern princes into the war against France and was thereby instrumental in creating the solid front against Louis out of which the multipower international system of modern times was to come.

WESTERN LINKS WITH THE EASTERN WAR:
FIRST STAGE, 1688–1699

The War of the League of Augsburg was itself as deceptive as the poli- cies and personalities that produced it, for its events, when viewed individ- ually, gave one impression, but when taken together, had quite a different meaning. Once the French had been driven back across the Rhine by the German Imperial victories at Mainz and Bonn in 1689 and into a defen- sive naval posture by the Anglo-Dutch defeat of the French fleet at La Hogue in 1692, the war seemed to drag on interminably and without direction, with the gods bestowing local victories on either side apparently at random. The campaigns were far-flung—the Rhineland, the Spanish Netherlands, Spain itself, northern Italy, Ireland, North America, the Car- ibbean, and India were all theaters of war—but everywhere equally with- out decisive issue. The conflict soon took on the familiar aspect of a stale- mate, with separate peace feelers and negotiations starting as early as 1693 and gradually leading to separate agreements until the Habsburg Emperor Leopold, left isolated, was forced to acquiesce in the general peace at Ryswick in 1697.

The settlement at Ryswick confirmed the fruitless and unfocused course of the war, for not only was it articulated into several bilateral treaties between Louis XIV of France and each of his opponents but it restored, with a few apparently inessential changes, the territorial arrangements in force before the war. The only noteworthy provisions of the settlement were the French agreement to return German territories seized since the Treaty of Nijmegen with the notable exception of Strasbourg and Alsace; the French agreement to end its tariff war against England and the Netherlands; the French recognition of William III as legitimate king of England; and for the French concession, as a symbol of Dutch security, the right of the Dutch to garrison the "barrier" fortresses in the Spanish Netherlands to the south—"barrier," of course, to French invasion.

And yet, beneath the surface of these apparently aimless and fruitless maneuverings the events formed certain significant clusters. First, the war and the treaties that concluded it adumbrated the outlines of a multi-power international system. French claims to hegemony were repulsed on the Continent, on the sea, and in the colonies, but in each of these arenas the French status as a great power among others was confirmed along with the recognized rise of England and Austria to a similar status. Second, beneath the apparent military and diplomatic dispersion of allied forces there remained elements of cohesion within the Grand Alliance—notably, the force of English subsidies and the influence of William III, who in fact although not in form negotiated with Louis on behalf of the whole alliance. Finally, for the first time the colonies of the European powers around the globe were drawn into a conflict initiated on the mother continent. The synchronization of these colonial conflicts attested to the power of the invisible bonds which the states were drawing around their agents and their citizens, however distant their situation and however limited their stake.

Contributing to the important long-range effects of the apparently sterile western war were its connections with the first stage of the eastern war which ran a course parallel to it. Once more we must look beneath the surface for relationships that were not obvious in the actual events. In appearance the eastern war of the 1690's was simply a continuation of the conflict which opened with the Turkish invasion of Hungary and Austria in 1683 and with the ensuing formation of the Holy League, in which Venice, and later Russia, joined the German Empire and Poland under the aegis of the Papacy in a military alliance against the Turk. In its origins this eastern war was independent of the growing tensions in western Europe: not only was the Turkish attack free of French complicity but the Christian crusade against the infidel and the territorial ambitions in eastern Europe which spurred the counteroffensive of the Holy League were equally separate from the turmoil in the west. The struggle in the east persisted without formal break through the entire War of the League of Augsburg until it was terminated by the Peace of Karlowitz in 1699, and its insulation was attested to by the refusal of the maritime powers (England and the Netherlands) to expand their alliance with the German Emperor against France into an alliance against the Turks as well.

But the two wars were related nonetheless. Their main link was the Habsburg monarchy, both through its own dominions and, to a lesser extent, through the states of the German Empire, whose foreign policies were actually—albeit not legally—controlled in this period by the Habsburg monarch in his capacity as German Emperor. The sequence of successful military campaigns in the Turkish War of the 1680's brought additional territories under Habsburg rule—particularly through the conquest of Hungary—so that Leopold was encouraged to resist Louis XIV in the west; on the other side, it was Louis' invasion of the German Empire that spurred the Turks to continue the war against the Habsburgs and the Empire despite the telling losses of Budapest in 1686 and of Belgrade in 1688. Moreover, the eastern war did take a new turn in the 1690's because of the diversion of Imperial troops to the west. The Turks took the offensive, and although stopped at the Danube in the Battle of Slankamen, reconquered during the 1690's the bulk of the Balkan territory lost during the 1680's.

Another link between the two wars developed in the successful candidature of the Austrian protégé, the Saxon elector Augustus the Strong (1670–1733), for the Polish crown (1697) against Louis' candidate, François Louis, Prince of Conti (1664–1709). As a result of this strand reaching across the continent, Poland was held in the anti-Turkish camp, Saxony in the anti-French, and the eastern Imperial army, which had been inefficiently led by Augustus before his convenient elevation to the Polish kingship, received a brilliant new commander in Eugene of Savoy (1663–1736), who crushed the Turks at the Battle of Zenta in 1697 and prepared them for the acceptance of peace.

The eastern peace itself, embodied in the Treaty of Karlowitz (1699), was conditioned by the situation in the west, for the mediation by the Dutch and the English and Leopold's acceptance of the terms of the treaty despite his commanding military position were undertaken in the light of the incipient resumption of the western war on the issue of the Spanish succession. The terms of the peace treaty indicated the inconclusiveness of this eastern settlement that was made under western influence: not only were the declining powers of Poland and Venice conceded territorial acquisitions—Podolia and the Morea respectively—that would soon have to be disgorged again, but Russia, the new power in the European constellation, refused to participate in the treaty and instead signed its own reluctant truce with the Turks at Constantinople in 1700, leaving still unsatisfied the Russian claims to free navigation of the Black Sea. The one definitive provision of Karlowitz related, significantly enough, to Austria, the swing power between east and west: by recognizing Habsburg sover-

eignty over Hungary and Transylvania it established the Habsburg monarchy as a power in eastern Europe and made it the pivot of the continental system of states that was aborning.

THE WAR IN THE WEST: SECOND STAGE, 1700–1713

The second stage of the western and eastern wars, running a convergent
course, brought the continental system into existence. Each of the wars,
formally separate from the other and from its own first stage, now took on
a new name. The western conflict became the War of the Spanish Succession, the eastern, the Great Northern War—a label which obscured Russia's new orientation toward all of eastern Europe. Along with the names
the character of the conflicts changed. Not only were campaigns now punc-
tuated by decisive battles but warfare and the domestic political considerations stemming from the demands of warfare temporarily replaced diplomacy as the main fields in which fundamental decisions were taken.

The character of the new historical personages who entered upon the
scene at the start and during the course of the renewed conflicts typifies
the new focus of events. In the west Louis the Sun King, old and somewhat tarnished, continued in power throughout the war and provided the
main thread of continuity with the past. But he outlived his opponents,
whose replacements created a new atmosphere and a new historical situation. His old archrival, William III, died in 1702, shortly after he had
brought his diplomatic career to a fitting climax by re-forming the Grand
Alliance against Louis. Based once more on the triple entente of the two
maritime powers (England and the Netherlands) and the Habsburg
Emperor, the alliance was once again extended to include the bulk of the
German principalities. But it had now to do without Spain (under its new
Bourbon king, Philip V), Bavaria, Cologne, and Savoy (which would once
again switch sides, in 1704): all these powers, for sundry hopes of dynastic
and territorial gain, went over to Louis XIV.

The leadership which William had supplied was now assumed by the
English commander, John Churchill, Duke of Marlborough (1650–1722),
and the militant grand pensionary of Holland (the chief legal counselor of
the province and the most influential civil official in the whole Netherlands), Antonius Heinsius (1641–1720). The Emperor Leopold, whose
decision to resist Louis XIV once again, as in 1688, precipitated war, lived
on until 1705, but once again too this singular show of determination was
followed by the resumption of his chronic indecisiveness, and he turned
over the active direction of Habsburg policy to the most energetic and
effective of his generals, Prince Eugene of Savoy. Eugene retained his
influence with Leopold's successor, the fun-loving Emperor Joseph I
(ruled 1705-1711), and when it waned with the accession of Emperor
Charles VI (ruled 1711–1740), it was replaced by the personal government

of a monarch equally addicted to a forward course. In its unprecedented concern with the cohesion of the Habsburg dominions, Charles's reign marked a new era in the history of central Europe. Toward the end of the western war, finally, the grim Frederick William I replaced the flighty Frederick I at the helm of the Prussian state (1713), and therewith the Prussian oscillation between western and eastern orientations of foreign policy gave way to the determined construction of a highly centralized bureaucratic monarchy.

In the eastern theater, similarly, the cast changed. Augustus the Strong, unscrupulous and ineffective as ever, remained on the scene but paled into insignificance beside the two new titans whose duel was to assume epic proportions for European history: Charles XII of Sweden and Peter I of Russia. Both monarchs risked the destinies of their countries on the decision of the battlefield. Both achieved the national glory of the military hero, and through them Russia and Sweden became strong monarchies forged in war and justified by war.

The new protagonists, then, were either generals like Eugene and Marlborough, who played the role of kings, or kings like Charles and Peter, who played the role of generals. Common to this quartet was the set of beliefs which, in league with their undoubted talents at the court and on the battlefield, channeled their actions into epochal achievements: the faith in their states as the supreme agencies of earthly values, the conviction that decisive military victory was the primary condition for the effective existence and functioning of these states, and the focus upon the individual sovereign as the bearer of the state's destiny. But if these were common tenets, each of these history-making individuals held them in his own way and reflected, in his particular personality, a different feature of the age.

Eugene of Savoy

Eugene, dedicated, ascetic, self-disciplined, manifested the kind of secular conversion that was making war and politics the cynosure of men's attention toward the end of the seventeenth century. Eugene's origins reflected the variety and the insecurity of the age, and his development reflected the direction in which it sought order. Son of a Savoyard prince in the service of France and an Italian-born niece of Cardinal Mazarin, Eugene was French by birth and rearing albeit not by descent. He grew up, moreover, with an attachment to his dissolute mother and to a licentious juvenile coterie at the free-living French court of the youthful Louis XIV that comported ill with his destination for the clergy. Physically weak and unprepossessing, known sardonically as "the little Abbé," Eugene responded, at some undetermined stage in his adolescence, by transforming himself into a proud, self-driven, puritanical Spartan, wholly committed to the profession of arms. Stung by the successive humiliations of his mother's banishment and Louis' personal rejection of his application for a commission, Eugene resentfully turned his back on France and in 1683 entered the service of the Habsburgs. However much the fortuitous circumstances of momentary pique and fraternal example—his older brother entered and abandoned French service before him—contributed to Eugene's decision, it was the fundamental character of the Habsburg dynasty—its polyglot staff, multinational base, and pan-European outlook—that harnessed the lifelong loyalty of this uprooted aristocrat.

His loyalty to the Habsburgs became the constant and certain center in his life toward which Eugene of Savoy could unleash restless energies and around which he could organize them. He broke through the military conventions of his time, which were oriented around the strategies of position and of siege warfare, to act single-mindedly for the mobility of his own armies and the destruction of the enemy. At Zenta, in 1697, where he first proved himself as a commanding general, he drove his army forward in a forced march, surprised the Turks crossing a river toward the end of the day, attacked their main body in a pincers movement, and destroyed it. He exhibited the same restlessness, the same concentration on the main goal, in the realm of politics. His categorical judgments, acerbic impatience, and fanatic obsession with the conditions of military victory made him alternately indispensable and *non grata* at the easygoing court of Vienna, according to the greater or lesser degree of crisis. Although his actual influence vacillated, he was, for most of his career, president of the Imperial War Council and chairman of the Privy Conference of Ministers, posts that expanded his attention from purely military concerns to the more general problems of wartime administration and the diplomacy of war and peace. In government as in command Eugene was rigidly committed to efficiency. He worked to clarify the lines of authority; he was indifferent to inherited rank, and judged performance by results; and he concentrated, without pomp or sentiment, on the effective operation of existing institutions.

But the public life to which he was so devoted could not, in an age and a country still so reverent of tradition, absorb all the force of this dynamic and versatile personality, and the forces of inertia ruling at the court first limited and then ended his exercise of political power. But the cultural life of the era was infinitely more dynamic, and Eugene's application of the same traits in this arena was more continuously successful. He became one of the largest collectors and most appreciative patrons of the arts in history: his library, his gallery, his places, his friendships (*e.g.* with Leibniz) all manifest an intensity, a tenacity, an impatience to conquer the realm of beauty that are reminiscent of Eugene's martial disposition. It was characteristic of the late seventeenth century—and this is a trait that sets it off from the century to follow—that his two passions, government and the arts, should remain as separated as they were in Eugene. Still, the religious-style fervor that he brought to each represented something new. Earlier in the century, another Austrian general, Johan Tilly (1559–1632), like Eugene foreign-born and like Eugene single-mindedly and puristically devoted to the Habsburg cause, had been known as the "monk in armor" because of the open Catholic fervor behind his military efficiency. Eugene reflected the change of the times: the monk had become a lay brother.

Marlborough

The other guiding genius of the allied cause in the War of the Spanish Succession was John Churchill, Duke of Marlborough, a soldier-statesman whose military and political domination of the English war effort after the death of William in 1702 paralleled Eugene's position at the Habsburg court. An intriguing puzzle surrounds the relations of the two leaders, for they were collaborators in policy, partners on the battlefield, friends off as well as on it—and yet not only was each a military virtuoso, solitary in his own genius, but Marlborough's indulgent character and reputation were a far cry from those of the austere Eugene.

Born into the obscure country gentry and launched upon his career by the patronage of the duke of York, Churchill worked his way up toward wealth and power, using appointments in the military arm of the English state as his stepping-stones, and he became what the parlous political conditions of seventeenth-century England might be expected to make of a man naturally endowed with uncommon ambition and prudence. He became expert, that is, in the management of his armies and his wealth, in the enchantment and manipulation of men, in the facile assumption and discard of loyalties, depending on his estimate of the main chance.

For his manifold military and diplomatic services to the Stuarts, James II had granted to him and he had accepted an English peerage, the rank of lieutenant general, and command of the royal army against William of Orange. But Churchill had been in contact with William, and in November, 1688, on what seemed the eve of battle, deserted to him, receiving in exchange a place on the Privy Council and the earldom of Marlborough. He had indeed protested against James's Catholicizing policies, but although James's religious policies were a factor in his shift to William's side, Marlborough characteristically resumed communication with the exiled James after the revolution—a connection which was the basis for the unproved charges of treason levied against him in 1692 and again in 1696. By the turn of the century he had once more insinuated himself into William's favor, and in 1702, with the accession of the last of the Stuarts, Queen Anne (ruled 1702–1714), to whom his wife and he had long and foresightedly paid court, he became, along with his lifelong friend and political ally Sidney Godolphin (1645–1712), the effective ruler of England. His one abiding concern thereafter became the prosecution of the war against France, and he shifted nimbly from Tory to Whig collaboration in his search for support. Godolphin and the Whigs were dismissed in 1710 but Marlborough hung on for another two years, and when he was then removed, his fall was characteristically accompanied by a formal charge of peculation and the informal charge of betraying the national interest—*i.e.* prolonging a futile war for pecuniary gain.

And yet, through all these manipulations, unquestioning friendship and cooperation between the overshrewd English tactician and the direct Eugene never faltered. Behind the visible contrast between the two personalities and behind even the political bond arising out of their common implacable hostility to Bourbon France lay a fundamental sympathy of disposition. In their military as in their personal careers, both were mobile, both were aggressive, and both believed in decisive and thorough action as the only means of public survival in their age.

That men of this stripe should dominate the second stage of the western war—the War of the Spanish Succession—was an indication of the quality of the epoch that was being ushered in with the new century. Whereas Louis' triumphs had manifested French primacy in consolidating stability, order, and authority as the means of power, the repeated successes now of Marlborough and Prince Eugene in outflanking, outmaneuvering, and outracing these same French symbolized the new possibilities that would make movement, energy, and the rapid concentration of force the new means of superior power.

The War and the Peace

The origins of the war, to be sure, continued a familiar pattern. The readiness of the English and Dutch to make concessions—short of endorsing the hegemony of one continental power—where their commercial interests were not involved had produced two successive partition agreements with Louis XIV, providing for disposition of the Spanish possessions upon the death of the ailing and childless Charles II. Even when the latter issued a deathbed will bequeathing the whole of the Spanish empire to Louis' grandson, the Duke of Anjou, the maritime powers had recognized the arrangement on Louis' assurance that the crowns of France and Spain would never be united.

Representing the rival Habsburg claim to the Spanish succession, Emperor Leopold, stubborn as usual where the Habsburgs and Bourbons were concerned, had refused to accept either the treaties of partition or the Spanish will. Louis, also as usual, played into his hands by using the formalities of the law to commit actual aggressions. With the death of Charles II in November, 1700, the Duke of Anjou acceded to the Spanish throne as Philip V, and in the nominal role of agent of the new king, Louis immediately moved French troops into Italy and occupied the Spanish Netherlands, including the barrier forts. In his own name as King of France, moreover, he now recognized the rights of his grandson—who also

The Battle of Turin, 1706. *Imperial troops under Eugene of Savoy smashed the French siege of the Piedmontese city and ended the French military presence in Italy until Napoleon.*

happened to be King of Spain—to the French succession. As signatory of an agreement with the sovereign state of Spain, finally, he secured for a French trading company a temporary concession of the coveted *asiento*— the right to import Negro slaves into Spanish America—and thereby offended the mercantile susceptibilities of the maritime powers. William III's renewal of the Grand Alliance in September, 1701, was a response also in the traditional mold, for it stipulated as war aims, provisions designed to divide the opposing powers: the eternal separation of Bourbon France and Bourbon Spain, the Austrian acquisition of the Spanish Netherlands and Spanish Italy, and English and Dutch monopolization of the Spanish colonial trade. When the Elector of Bavaria remembered the old hostility of the Wittelsbachs against the Habsburgs and attached himself, like many of his ancestors before him, to the French, and when his brother, the Archbishop of Cologne, followed suit, the juncture with tradition seemed complete.

But from this point Marlborough and Eugene took over and infused a new spirit into European affairs. The premium that was now placed upon energy and initiative found expression in the new domination which England exercised both within the Grand Alliance and over the course of the war as a whole, thereby opening the era of British preponderance over Europe and the world that was to last for two centuries. Marlborough was commander in chief officially of the combined English and Dutch armies and unofficially of the whole Grand Alliance. Similarly, Eugene's solo triumphs over the French in Italy and his active participation in the most notable of the allied victories in Germany and the Low Countries reflected

Louis XIV's ratification of the separate armistice between Great Britain and France in 1712. *Detail from a stylized announcement welcoming a "happy augury of the peace" which was concluded in 1713 and 1714.*

the adroit adaptation which the Habsburg monarchy was making to a dynamic multiple-power system that was coming to life. At the same time, the timorous, defensive, and obstructionist tactics of the Dutch were a true index of the general decline in vitality that would cause the Netherlands to fall from the ranks of the first-line powers in the eighteenth-century system of states.

Thus English participation was the common element in all the decisive actions of the war, and when the English lost their verve for the war the decisiveness went out of it. Fleets under English command took Gibraltar (1704) and Minorca (1708). On land, after Imperial losses inflicted in Germany by the French and in Hungary by a rebellion under the resourceful Francis Rákóczi (1676–1735) during 1703, Marlborough and Eugene converged rapidly upon the French on August 13, 1704, to combine forces and commands in the epic victory of Blenheim on the Bavarian Danube, one of the decisive battles of history because it destroyed the aura of French military superiority and initiated the long era of British hegemony over a balanced continent. Two years later Marlborough and Eugene, at Ramillies and Turin respectively, blunted the French push north and expelled them from Italy for almost a century. In July, 1708, it was once more as a smoothly functioning team that the two generals swooped down upon the French at Audenarde on the Scheldt and destroyed Louis' hopes for the conquest of the Spanish Netherlands.

But despite these spectacular exploits an actual balance of power, which was henceforth to dominate international relations, now showed itself as an inescapable military fact. Audenarde proved to be the last decisive battle of the war. When Marlborough and Eugene pressed southward a little over a year later the French met them at Malplaquet, and although the allies were left in possession of the war's bloodiest battlefield, the Pyrrhic quality of their achievement was such that the French Marshal Claude Villars (1653–1734) could with justice remark that "the enemy would have been annihilated by another such victory." Malplaquet fed the growing war-weariness in England that edged the Tories into power as the peace party and led to the covertly negotiated Preliminary Articles of October, 1711, between the English and the French. In May 1712, the English withdrew their subsidies and armies from combat. Without the English, the Dutch and imperial armies quickly lost the initiative to the resurgent French. A series of defeats in the Low Countries and on the Rhine convinced the reluctant Dutch to join the English in making peace with the French at Utrecht (1713) and the even more reluctant Austrians to conclude the separate Treaty of Rastatt (1714).

This complex of bilateral treaties, commonly subsumed under the general title of the Peace of Utrecht, takes its place, along with Westphalia (1648) which preceded it and with Vienna (1815) and Versailles (1919) which followed it, as one of the fundamental settlements in the history of international relations. To settle the chronic international conflict stemming from the role of competing world-religions in politics the signatories at Westphalia had legislated the sovereignty of the several territorial rulers into international law. After this principle bred its own continuing international conflict stemming from the indefinite extensibility of the rulers' claims, the signatories at Utrecht broadened the principle to make the plurality of realms—that is, of settled territories and peoples—as well as of rulers subjects of international law and co-beneficiaries of its guarantees of sovereignty. In this form of an international order made up of the several sovereign states, formally equal in their rights and necessarily represented by their rulers, Utrecht's contribution would be preserved at Vienna against unsettlement in the name of world revolution and at Versailles by the merger of nationality with the traditional sovereignty of the territorial state. At Utrecht, moreover, the signatories not only registered the sovereignty of the several states but explicitly introduced the principle which would henceforward be inseparable from it: the balance of power was formally prescribed as the standard to which the mutual relations of the several sovereign states should conform.

Just as the course of the war had established the military conditions for the open recognition of balance of power as a goal of foreign policy, the preliminary negotiations leading to the peace had laid down its diplomatic base. The favorable reception which the English accorded French peace feelers ripened into agreement when the death of Emperor Joseph I in

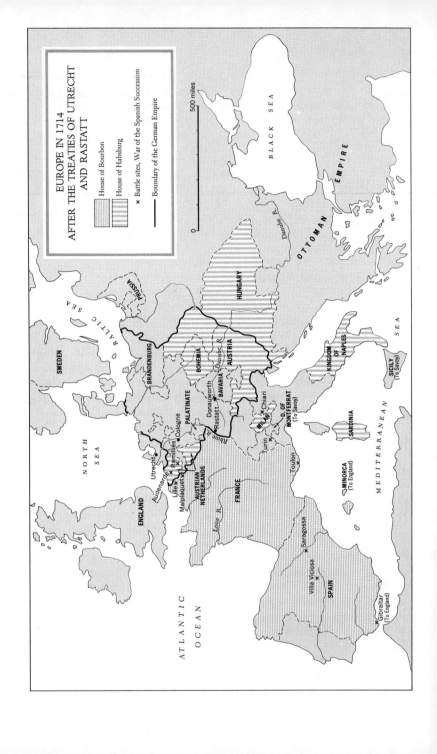

EUROPE IN 1714
AFTER THE TREATIES OF UTRECHT
AND RASTATT

House of Bourbon
House of Habsburg
× Battle sites, War of the Spanish Succession
— Boundary of the German Empire

0   500 miles

BALTIC SEA

SWEDEN

PRUSSIA

BRANDENBURG

NORTH SEA

BOHEMIA

Danube R.

HUNGARY

AUSTRIA

OTTOMAN

BLACK SEA

EMPIRE

PALATINATE

Cologne

ENGLAND

Utrecht

Audenarde

Lille × Ramillies

Malplaquet

AUSTRIAN NETHERLANDS

Donauworth

Rastatt

Rhine R.

Danube R.

BAVARIA

Chiari

MILAN × D. OF MONTFERRAT (To Savoy)

Turin

Toulon

KINGDOM OF NAPLES

SICILY (To Savoy)

SEA

SARDINIA

MEDITERRANEAN SEA

MINORCA (To England)

ATLANTIC OCEAN

FRANCE

Loire R.

× Villa Viciosa

× Saragossa

SPAIN

Gibraltar (To England)

1711 made the Archduke Charles, designate of the Grand Alliance for the throne of Spain, head of the house of Habsburg and all its dominions, for the English were no more disposed to Austrian than to French hegemony over Europe. Hence in the Peace of Utrecht they recognized the Bourbon Philip V as legitimate monarch of Spain in exchange for the formal renunciations of the French succession by Philip and of the Spanish succession by Louis' French heirs, stipulated the removal of the sensitive Netherlandish and Italian territories from Spanish to Austrian control, and accepted Louis' recognition of the Protestant succession in England as established by the parliamentary Act of Settlement in 1701. This agreement revealed that in the association of dynastic with state interest the latter had become the dominant factor. The force that could be exerted by the separate sovereigns of the several European states became a more important consideration, in international law as well as practice, than the larger family connections within and between dynasties.

In addition to its factual and formal exposition of the balance of power, Utrecht also initiated the paradoxical but persistent pattern that joined this balance to English hegemony. Not only were the English the chief architects of the peace but the provisions upon which they insisted reveal the political logic in the apparent paradox of hegemony through balance. For one thing, the provisions sponsored by England to achieve a general equilibrium among the great powers obviously prevented the mobilization of continental resources against the island kingdom, but the English went further to assert a positive influence upon continental affairs by initiating local balance-of-power arrangements in the coastal areas sensitive to English naval power. At Utrecht they utilized several kinds of arrangements to check the domination of such areas by the large states. They now took from Bourbon Spain the one European possession they permitted themselves—Gibraltar—to supplement their patronage of Portugal. In the former Spanish and now Austrian Netherlands, moreover, the new Habsburg overlord submitted to English pressure and concluded a self-denying treaty with the Dutch Republic: Emperor Charles VI granted the right of garrisoning barrier forts within Austrian territory to the Dutch, whose marked decline in naval and military strength was reducing them to the status of English clients. In Italy, finally, the English made analogous arrangements for their naval security; they enlarged the role of the landlubberly Austrians whose dominion replaced that of Spain in the principalities of Milan, Sardinia, and Naples. But at the same time, the English limited any possible Habsburg pretensions to maritime power by endorsing the acquisition by Savoy (the core of the future united Italy) of the Duchy of Montferrat in the north and of Sicily in the south (later—in 1721—bartered, under English pressure, with the Habsburgs for Sardinia, after the Savoyards had shown their incapacity to defend Sicily against Britain's more pressing Mediterranean foe, Bourbon Spain). England secured, moreover, the formal declaration of "the neutrality of Italy," under general guarantee.

The free hand which this policy of interior and peripheral balance on the Continent secured to the English they chose to exercise for the acquisition of colonies and trading rights. Aside from Gibraltar and the island of Minorca, England's immediate gains at Utrecht, however modest by later eighteenth-century standards, were all of this kind, and they served as the foundation for subsequent conquests: France ceded Newfoundland, the Hudson Bay area, and Nova Scotia; the Spanish yielded the right of *asiento* and associated rights of naval protection, and gave the English an opening wedge into the Spanish colonial carrying trade. A European balance of power was indeed tailor-made for the extra-European expansion of the English.

What made possible these local agreements for British advantage was the stalemate into which the Bourbons of France and the Habsburgs of Austria had finally settled after their struggle of more than two centuries for predominance in Europe. The general lines of the settlement laid down at Utrecht were to endure for almost a century: the Rhine was formally recognized to be "the frontier between France and Germany"; German particularism was perpetuated undiminished with the restoration, at French insistence, of the anti-Imperial princes (the Electors of Bavaria and of Cologne) to their offices and possessions; Austria was compensated by a preeminent place in Italy, from which France was henceforward excluded.

At Utrecht the new mobility of the western powers, reflected in the dynamic strategies of the war, came to a temporary halt. That the halt would be only temporary was ensured by the persistence well beyond Utrecht of the eastern war and by its drift into the western orbit of international politics. For it was at this point that the European states arranged themselves into a single system of international politics in which the issues of the entire continent were mutually related. Here was the origin of that fateful pattern through which the instability of eastern Europe has time and again in the past two and a half centuries upset the more stable arrangements of the west.

THE WAR IN THE EAST: SECOND STAGE, 1700–1721

As in the west, the war in the east took a unique form from the two personages who supplied its political and military direction. Like Eugene and Marlborough, Charles XII of Sweden and Peter the Great of Russia represented that fusion of military and political considerations under whose aegis the states of Europe were beginning to assume their characteristic modern form; to all four, this fusion exalted an undogmatic and thoroughly pragmatic passion for organization and efficiency; for all four, mobility and aggressiveness in favorable circumstances, mobility and resilience in the face of disaster, kept organizations in being and were the marks of efficient performance.

Charles XII

Charles XII (ruled 1697–1718), the soldier-king of Sweden, presided over the definitive descent of his country into the ranks of the secondary powers, but so splendid was his defeat, so strong his grasp of what it took to be a great power, that he has remained a national hero, a symbol of what Sweden had been and of what it might have become were population and resources not the equivalent of will and intelligence in the ranking of modern states. Charles exploited and expended what his able father, Charles XI, had carefully constructed and husbanded. In particular, the wars which the elder Vasa had both prepared for and avoided the son fought unremittingly, at first by necessity, then from deliberate policy, and finally through obsession.

Effectively nurtured in the arts of government, Charles followed the spirit rather than the letter of his father's legacy in 1697 when, at the tender age of fifteen, and mere months after his father's death, he took advantage of a conflict between regents and nobility to reestablish the *de facto* autocracy of Charles XI. There is no telling what direction his government might have taken had he been left undisturbed, for his domestic administration of the next two years was fairly nondescript, compounded equally of a sovereign diligence reminiscent of Charles XI and a fresh tone of gaiety customary in the court of a teen-age monarch. The unique cast of his career, like that of so many other kings in this epoch, received its initial mold from outside, in the kiln of international politics. In 1699, the rulers of Denmark, Saxony, and Russia, foreshadowing the parallel re-formation of the Grand Alliance against French domination of the west, entered into a coalition with the aim of partitioning the Swedish empire and terminating the Swedes' hegemony over the Baltic. The following spring the allies launched a three-pronged attack against Schleswig-Holstein (a Swedish protectorate), Livonia and Ingria (Swedish possessions), thereby confronting Charles with the situation that revealed his calling and crystallized his character.

It was as a soldier that Charles XII found himself, as a soldier that he lived the rest of his life, and as a soldier that he has gone down into history. Charles's stern moral code would probably not have allowed him to start the war; but once he was convinced of the moral evil in those who had started it, this same moral code supported his professional desire not to let it end. And in truth, for the next eighteen years of this Great Northern War, Charles literally abjured capital, court, administration, marriage, civil and polite society, for the saddle and the sword—a chivalric preference that made him the last of the kings to retain personal leadership of his men in battle as the most continuous, the most characteristic, and the

Charles XII at the disastrous battle of Poltava (1709). *Characteristic representation of the wounded Swedish monarch.*

most exalted duty of a King. His atavism made his life a national epic. Like Eugene of Savoy, he was celibate, ascetic, single-minded, reserved, and blunt. Like Eugene, he focused his energies and passions upon the waging of war, and he waged it with a determination and a momentum that brought him victories beyond his resources.

But Charles was unlike Eugene in his lack of the iron self-restraint and of the cultural tastes that made the Prince of Savoy a success both as a commander and as a man. There was in Charles the passion for the infinite, the inability to rest content with any given achievement or limit, that have driven conquerors from Alexander to Hitler and that led him to ignore prudence and despise diplomacy in an age when the distribution of power was making a political necessity of both. This passion of the conqueror was joined in him, moreover, with a moral purism that ennobled it as it has rarely been ennobled in human history but that contributed nonetheless to its fateful political influence. When Charles hounded Augustus the Strong until he forced the deposition of that weaselly Saxon Elector from the throne of Poland, he undoubtedly performed an ethically satisfying act, but he also enmired himself in the bog of Polish politics and granted precious convalescent time (almost four years) to his mortal enemies, the Russians.

Just as he had rejected all peace offers from Augustus he declined them equally from Peter, and for essentially the same reason—that they came from an unworthy source. When he set off after Peter he was drawn, as by a magnet, into the boundless reaches of the Russian interior, passing up the much more reasonable and possible option of recovering the Baltic provinces. Even after he had been sucked deep into the Ukraine, had been grievously weakened by the remarkable Russian defensive combination of scorched earth and "General Winter," had been smashed by Peter at the battle of Poltava (1709), and had been reduced, as a solitary fugitive in Turkey, to an intriguer for war between Russia and the Ottoman Empire, Charles refused all offers of compromise, of mediation, or neutralization. We can guess why the Turks called him "ironhead."

The result of intransigence and weakness in combination was what might be expected—the ultimate expansion of the anti-Swedish coalition, by the time of his return to Sweden in 1714, to include all powers whose interests touched the Swedes in any way: Russia, Saxony, Denmark, Prussia, and Great Britain (in support of King George I, who as Hanoverian Elector, had covetous interest in Sweden's north German possessions). Aided by divisions among the allies, Charles performed heroically in the defense of Sweden, and he paid unprecedented lip service to the necessity of diplomatic negotiations for peace. But war had become an obsession with him, and even in these straitened circumstances he was ready to support militarily the Scottish invasion of the Stuart pretender and to embark himself upon an invasion of Danish-owned Norway. It was in the midst of this enterprise that he met his death (1718).

In many ways Charles XII was an atavism, and in these respects he reflected the anachronism of Sweden as a great power. Like his country he tended toward isolationism in diplomacy and monomania in war. Perhaps even more important, he reflected his nation's past in the ambiguous mixture of religion and morality with politics and war. In the earlier seventeenth century, under Gustavus Adolphus (ruled 1611–1632), the combination had worked to Sweden's advantage, and much of what seems inexplicable in Charles's personality and policy is attributable to his persistence in attitudes which were no longer appropriate. "Have princes the right to commit actions which in commoners are dishonorable?" he asked. "I should be incapable of it, though ten royal crowns were at stake; and could I win a hundred cities I would not do so in the manner of the King of Prussia. . . ." But the present belonged to the king of Prussia and his ilk, who recognized that politics had its own demands, its own morality, and its own limits. Charles's moral intransigence, however honorable the repute it brought him, now appeared extreme and fanatic, alienating him from reality and justifying unlimited war.

And yet there was also a modern facet in this last king of Sweden's great age. His taste and capacity for mathematics, itself in the latest mode, went into the strategy of mobility which he shared with the most advanced army commanders of the period. More fundamentally, his association of morality with the absolute inviolability of the state and its frontiers, however old-fashioned in his rigid application, did reflect the ethical and even sacred character that was passing over into the modern state.

Peter the Great

In Peter of Russia (ruled 1682–1725), Charles's great antagonist, we find the same boundless energy, the same vaulting ambition, the same dedication to the martial side of statecraft. Yet the historical destinies of the two monarchs were diametrically opposed, since the one presided over the demise of his state as a great power while the other ushered his dominion into that status. This divergence of political destiny was paralleled by the widely different traits which accompanied the common qualities of the two leaders. Where Charles was xenophobic, Peter sought out the foreigner. Where Charles was ascetic and abstemious, Peter was coarse and self-indulgent. Where Charles viewed politics from the apex of military command, Peter viewed it from the closer angle of military organization and supply. Where Charles subscribed wholeheartedly to an integral code of honor, Peter constructed his guidelines piece by piece, according to what did and what did not bring success. In short, where Charles looked to the past, Peter looked to the future, and both were right, since the greatness of their countries lay in those respective dimensions.

Like Louis XIV, Peter acceded to the throne during his minority (in 1682, on the eve of his tenth birthday) and grew up under a regency which left him in chronic want and sporadic danger. Like Louis', his youthful experience bred a lifelong mistrust of the old court and aristocracy, but under Russian conditions this mistrust found a different expression. Because the danger came from the *streltsy*, or palace guard, Peter's attention was early riveted on things military; because the regent exiled him from the Kremlin, he grew up outside the Muscovite tradition dispensed in the court; because Russian techniques were backward, he turned to foreigners within Russia.

From the age of eleven Peter absorbed himself in playing at war, but as he organized his attendants into increasingly elaborate and professional formations, staffing them with foreign officers and directing his education to mathematics, engineering, and military studies, the pastime grew into a profession and helped to frame the Tsar's career. So involved was he that even after he attained his majority in 1689, his concern was with his regiments and their "military ballets," as their exercises were called, rather than with politics and government. It is in this context, indeed, that his famous visit of 1697 to western Europe in the guise of a carpenter is to be understood. The guise was more truthful than the reality, for the artisan-tsar went more as an artisan than as a tsar. He went to learn at first hand the industrial, the military, and particularly the naval technology to which the foreign colony in Russia had alerted him and Russian naval deficiencies in the Turkish war attracted him. This addiction to the instrument,

A Russian woodcut caricaturing Peter the Great's campaign of westernization through depilation.

the means, the procedure, rather than the system, the theory, or the process was to characterize his whole regime.

He returned to Russia in 1698 and immediately proceeded to demonstrate both his impulsiveness and the enthusiasm for western things that directed his impulsiveness by energetically striking out on such varied activities as exterminating the old Muscovite *streltsy*, proscribing the traditional Russian beards and dress, and building a fleet on the Sea of Azov. He made free use of torture and execution in the elimination of the *streltsy*, and he himself wielded the razor on beards of his reluctant courtiers, thereby initiating the simple and brutal resort to direct means for the attainment of an immediate result that would become the hallmark of his regime.

The Great Northern War, which followed almost immediately, had the effect of magnifying rather than submerging these tendencies. The stress of this struggle, coming hard upon the military predilections of his youth, fixed once and for all in his mind the priority of war for the state and the derivative status of all other concerns. Earthy, coarse, incontinent on the one hand and curious, sensitive, shrewd, cognizant of his official duties on the other, Peter learned through doing. Around the incessant warfare in which his own predilection and his conception of imperial responsibility coincided, he introduced, step by step, the total reorganization of the Russian state as experience revealed its necessity to military security. At first indifferent to ideas, principles, and theories, but ever more aware of western political and technical superiority, Peter applied with violence the progressive reforms which he paradoxically designed to increase the voluntary contribution of the society to the state.

Peter's participation in the Great Northern War, from which his personal rule stemmed, was itself a response to a situation rather than a deliberate change of system. He had, during the 1690's, accepted the Turkish war which he had inherited and he had directed his naval plans toward the Black Sea. The shift toward the Baltic and the north which was forced upon Peter by the Austrian defection from the anti-Turkish coalition in the Peace of Karlowitz (1699) resumed an alternate line of seventeenth-century Russian foreign policy. With no alliance against the Turks, but with an anti-Swedish alliance in the making to which he had merely to accede, the reorientation toward the north was scarcely a revolutionary act. But if Peter was not the architect of this policy, still the western orientation which was his passion before his entry into diplomacy led him to accept wholeheartedly the proposed change of fronts from the south center (on the Azov frontier, gateway to the Caucasus) to the northwest of his dominions. Although he would offer Sweden many concessions during the twenty-one continuous years of warfare upon which he now embarked, he always excepted the frontier post, near the mouth of the Neva River in the captured province of Ingria, which he began in 1703 to develop into the unofficial capital city of St. Petersburg. However fortuitous in origin, the Great Northern War provided him with the stimulus for the military, political, and social reorganization of his state because it embodied for him the fundamental decision to enter into the competitive system of the European powers.

Peter proceeded not by prearranged plan, but from measure to measure as the circumstances seemed to dictate, and these circumstances, as he intelligently perceived them, called for an ever-widening scope of governmental reorganization. Between the disaster at Narva in 1700 and the epochal triumph at Poltava in 1709, Peter devoted himself entirely to the recruitment, training, and support of a reliable and efficient army through a desperate succession of *ad hoc* decrees. The standard set by such a highly organized military power as Sweden drove him, by 1705, from the irregular induction of raw volunteers and conscripts into regular general levies, incumbent upon all classes of the population, and providing a continuing supply of trained reserves.

The civil counterpart of such an armed force, required to feed it a steady stream of loyal soldiers, uniforms, up-to-date muskets, artillery, and the tax monies to pay for it all, received in these years before Poltava the sporadic measures which military emergency obviously called for, such as the sponsorship of armaments industry and the imposition of retroactive taxation. But after Poltava, Peter by his own admission extended his purview to "the administration of civil affairs." He expanded military political reorganization into domestic affairs just as he now learned to surround military policy with a diplomatic context in foreign affairs. He utilized the temporary alleviation of the martial crisis after 1709 to rebuild the northern alliance, add Prussia to it, and embroil himself in central European affairs. To the persistent war, there was thus added a permanent entangle- ment in competitive international politics, and it was this new, long- range pressure that turned Peter to the enactment of basic legislation and the establishment of fundamental institutions in the effort to harness, western-style, the energies of the society to the power of the state.

What Peter said of the Senate, the organ which he created in 1711 on the Swedish model to unify and centralize the whole of internal govern- ment, held for his entire work of reform: its purpose was "to collect money, as much as possible, for money is the artery of war." Around this core he subsequently built a whole network of new or reformed agencies: the "colleges"—*i.e.* boards—into which, again on the Swedish model, the older languishing departments were reorganized to serve as the various branches of central administration; the office of procurator-general, a kind of prime minister to supervise and control the colleges; a system of provin- cial government newly specialized to exclude judicial and military func- tions (now under separate agencies) and include a host of educational and welfare activities; and a system of municipal government reorganized to promote urban self-administration by guilds under central governmental control. Accompanying these efforts to equip government for the mobili- zation of the society's resources was Peter's direct approach to the society itself, to galvanize its energies and direct them into governmental channels. His chief target here was, characteristically, the aristocracy—the military class par excellence—for whom he made, through punishment, education, and blandishment, the old nominal and sporadic obligation to state service a compulsory and permanent reality. The enforcement of military regis- tration upon threat of attainder was supplemented by the imperial spon- sorship of secular education for the aristocracy, at first abroad and after 1714 at home, in practical subjects that would increase its usefulness to the state. The formerly revertible and divisible service-fiefs of the aristoc- racy were converted into entailed hereditary estates—a measure designed to stabilize the economic basis of one part of the service nobility and to send its unpropertied siblings wholly into state service. The climax of Peter's social legislation was the enactment in 1722 of the famous Table of Ranks, which made both the nobility and the newly created distinctions of status within the nobility dependent upon service to the state—that is, upon the grade attained in military or civil office. Revelatory of the ulti- mate motive of this far-reaching social reform were Peter's prescription that two thirds of the nobility fill military functions and his grant of precedence to the military over the civil branch of the same rank. The reform was capped by the legislation in 1724 of the poll tax, a household levy which fell primarily upon the peasantry. This act confirmed the official function of the aristocrat as governmental administrator as well as private landlord of his serfs.

As Peter was thus led insensibly from the makeshift military measures of his early years to the fundamental political and social reforms that they entailed for him, his consciousness of the connection kept pace with the reality. The peremptory tone of the early decrees gave way to the rational explanatory prefaces of the later laws as he became increasingly aware that military security required both political unity and social cohesion. As he matured in his understanding of the network of relationships that bound governor and governed together in the modern state, his receptivity to western culture broadened from his appropriation of its techniques to the employment of the ideas which westerners used to direct their techniques. The rationales which he came to append to his laws showed more and more the influence of the western political ideas that had developed during the seventeenth century to account for and spur on the growth of the modern state. Secular and utilitarian like himself, these ideas conformed to Peter's own. They were imported, together with German and Swedish legists, to articulate the Tsar's convictions of the preeminence of "interests of state," the equal subjection of all citizens to the sovereign, the toleration of dissident—if politically loyal—religious sects, and the subordination of church to state.

And as Peter grew in political self-consciousness with the aid of western notions, his attitude toward the Russian Orthodox Church, with its traditionally ambiguous relationship to the tsar, developed apace. Where he had initially expropriated Church property and income for military purposes, he proceeded by 1721 to a fundamental reorganization of the Church which abolished the patriarchate, feared by Peter as "a second sovereign" in the eyes of his subjects, and established in its stead a Holy Synod, appointed by Peter and organized analogously to the executive colleges which ran his secular departments of state. This reform, sweeping and permanent as it proved to be, was not intended by Peter to be revolutionary, either in a religious or even an ecclesiastical sense. He was himself a believer who accepted without question, so far as we know, not only the divine governance of the world but the Orthodox doctrinal and liturgical formulations of worship. What he intended was not the principled assertion of tsarist supremacy over the spiritual organization of Russian life, but rather the tsarist authority over those aspects of clerical activity which his own experience and his western models had demonstrated to be relevant to the interests of the state—above all, over the role of the Orthodox Church in civil obedience, education, and public morals.

The institutional changes which Peter sponsored proved so fundamental that they mark the decisive turning point in Russian history down to the revolution of 1917. Obviously they could not have taken root if the soil had not been prepared for them, and as a matter of fact much of what Peter wrought had been begun before him. To this extent his statesmanship consisted in his selection, from the several possibilities available to

A picture worth a thousand words. *Depicted by an unknown artist and purporting to show the interrogation of Prince Alexis by his father, Peter the Great, because of the son's involvement in the conservative and clerical opposition to Peter's reforms. The facial expressions anticipate Alexis's fate: he was tortured and thrown into jail, where he died under mysterious circumstances in 1718.*

him, of the long-range policies that would materially strengthen the competitive western position of the Russian state, and in his ruthless execution of them.

And yet the future was to bear the marks not only of the long-range but also of the circumstantial factors that went into the policies of this age of kings. For Peter's growing realization of his state's needs betokened a broadening of his interests rather than a radical change in him. Both the violence and the despotism that were native to him continued to accompany his rule, even in its more enlightened phases. He outlived the Great Northern War, but war was as much a law of life to him as to his great rival, Charles XII of Sweden, and the year after the victorious Treaty of Nystad with Sweden (1721) he was again in the field, carrying on the struggle which he had fomented for the conquest of Persia's Caspian provinces.

His achievements at home pacified Peter no more than those abroad. He passed his last years, indeed, in a state of deepening depression, interrupted by the recurrent coarse revelries and dissipations that testified to the persistence of the unrestrained autocrat in the aging ruler. His bouts of melancholy stemmed from the conjunction of his growing conviction that only he was the reliable agent of Russia's welfare with his growing recognition of the massive scope of activities that the state, as the arena of that welfare, demanded. He imprisoned, tortured, and perhaps murdered his son Alexis, the heir apparent (the precise circumstances of Alexis' death in the prison into which Peter had cast him are unknown), and he was unable, to the day of his own death, to settle upon his successor. He despaired of the Russian will either to obey or to execute the law. During the last years he intensified the prosecution and execution of officials for malpractice, and at the time of his death he was planning a massive campaign against the bureaucracy.

When Peter died, in January, 1725, his country was as relieved as the France of 1715 and the Sweden of 1718 had been at the passing of the kings whom they too had nonetheless accounted great. All three countries were paying the price, as Stuart England had before them and Hohenzollern Prussia would after them, for the concession of their entire collective concerns to the care of a fallible individual. The incorporation of a whole society in one man in each case gave to that society a specious unity it could not otherwise have attained, but by the same token the confusion of the body politic with the royal person infused the still pliant structure of the new service states with a lasting tincture of arbitrary and violent compulsion.

CONVERGENCE OF THE WARS: FORMATION OF
THE EUROPEAN POLITICAL SYSTEM, 1709–1721

The general course and results of the Great Northern War follow obviously from the careers of the two titanic antagonists who dominated it. Charles's early successes had driven Russia's allies from the field and turned the war into a duel for hegemony in the Baltic which Peter's decisive triumphs of 1708 and 1709 secured for Russia. Thanks in good measure to Charles's stubborn rejection of any compromise or mediation, Peter's victory held through a decade of intermittent warfare and was registered in 1721 in the Treaty of Nystad through the Swedes' cession to Russia of their eastern Baltic provinces—Livonia, Estonia, Ingria and southern Karelia, on the southeastern border of Finland. With this transfer of coastal territories Russia replaced Sweden as mistress of the Baltic Sea and as one of the European great powers as well.

These gross facts are clear enough, but a few of the more obscure details which attended the latter phases of the war give an indication of their implicit meaning.

First, the further decline of the Ottoman Empire underlined the new ascendency of the Russians. True enough, the Turks took advantage of their temporarily favorable military position when Sweden's Charles XII instigated them to attack the Russians in 1710, and in the Treaty of Pruth

(1711) Turkish power not only checked the Russian surge to the Black Sea but forced Peter to disgorge Azov (the Russians would regain it permanently in 1739) as the price for the Turks' desertion of Charles. But this fleeting triumph was overbalanced by the subsequent defeats of the Turks at the hands of the Austrians. In 1714, immediately after the conclusion of peace with France, Emperor Charles VI turned east once more against the Ottoman Empire to resume the struggle that his father had suspended in 1699. The doughty Eugene, reaching the pinnacle of his illustrious military career, led the Austrians to smashing victories at Peterwardein (1716) and Belgrade (1717). The importance of this flareup in the age-old Habsburg-Ottoman conflict was not its overt result, for however impressive the Austrian gains from the following Peace of Passarowitz (1718) may have been—and indeed, the cession of northern Serbia, parts of Bosnia and Walachia, and the Hungarian Banat seemed to open the way to the Black Sea—the bulk of them had to be surrendered again in 1739. The settlement of 1718 served indeed only to mark out the lines of future Habsburg policy. The real importance of the Austrian triumph was rather that it neutralized the prior Russian setback and allowed Peter to assert Russia's position as the eastern and not simply a Baltic power. By the spring of 1717, with the Turkish armies in retreat, Sweden's Charles XII limited to the Scandinavian peninsula, and Poland reduced to a Russian satellite, Peter could offer France an alliance against its traditional Habsburg rival in which Russia would replace all three of the eastern states with which France had traditionally cooperated. In its effects, then, the Great Northern War became an eastern war, and as such it radically simplified the international power structure of Europe.

A second set of details attendant upon the concluding phase of the Great Northern War revealed still another facet of the European system that was coming into being: the convergence of its eastern and western spheres. As might be expected from the geography of the Continent, the crucial function in this connection belonged to the central European states of the German Empire. When the western war drew toward its close at Utrecht the north German principalities of Hanover and Prussia turned their attention to the coveted possessions of stricken Sweden on the German shores of the North and Baltic seas and were drawn, on their account, into the Great Northern War as allies of Russia. Indeed, the first of the Russian-Prussian treaties that were to prove so fateful for the future history of Europe was signed in 1714 on the grave of the Swedish empire and on the basis of their common interest in the conquest of Swedish provinces. But the same favorable tide that then (between 1714 and 1720) brought Bremen and Verden to Hanover, and Stettin and western Pomerania to Prussia, also brought Peter and his army into the north German states of Mecklenburg and Holstein, which became virtual Russian protectorates.

By 1716 the shock of the Russian presence in central Europe had been transmitted through Germany into western Europe. The frightened hostility of Russia's Baltic neighbors and Germany's Habsburg Emperor to the new eastern power communicated itself to the Atlantic maritime powers. Peter's German occupation and naval preponderance, which threatened to convert the Baltic into a Russian lake, brought the western naval powers, Britain and the Netherlands, unofficially into the war as naval supporters of the Swedish cause. In response, Peter sought an alliance with France, and the first of the Franco-Russian agreements which have spanned the politics of the European continent was signed in 1717. It was not the military pact for which Peter had hoped, but it was a treaty of friendship which recognized the connection between the late western and the ongoing eastern wars, and as a matter of fact it provided for the French mediation that helped to bring about the Treaty of Nystad and thus to complete the pacification of Europe.

And so was concluded, hardly more than a century after the outbreak of the first, Europe's second thirty years' war. Together, they determined that Europe would neither be dominated by any one power nor be split up into myriad local combinations of states and issues. What emerged was a limited group of superior powers whose interests spanned the whole continent in a connected set of relations. This was the system that was to produce the decisive wars and diplomacy over the globe for more than two centuries. This was the system too that was to set the standards of national security and thus to determine the limits of what could lawfully be done by and for citizens at home.

CHAPTER 3

The Kings at Home:
The Old Powers, 1689-1748

FOR A WHOLE generation the attention of the European monarchs and their governments had been fixed upon the battlefield and the conference table. Domestic policies had tended to assume convulsive and haphazard forms, since they were immediate responses to the necessities of war. And yet the effects of these domestic policies were enduring. They faithfully reflected longer-range tendencies of the respective states, and in the post-war period of the early eighteenth century many of these policies were translated into fundamental peacetime legislation which incorporated the military function into the very structure of government. The wartime generation of 1689–1721 was succeeded by the peacetime generation that focused its attention upon domestic institutions until the 1740's.

Foreign relations remained, of course, objects of continuing concern to the statesmen of the period, but they were no longer either explicit or primary for the formulation of governmental policy. The international rivalries that did break into hostilities, such as the War of the Polish Succession (1733–1735) and the Russo-Turkish war of 1736–1739, were limited in their participants, in their commitments, and in their effects. Even when, toward the end of the period, European energies were again caught up in a more general war—the intermittent and overlapping armed conflicts that have been misleadingly lumped together as *the* War of the Austrian Succession (1740–1748)—the obscurity of the war aims and the indecisiveness of the results show the struggle to have been in many ways the consequence of the domestic preoccupations which had made for peace and prepared for war. The bellicosity of the "war parties" was in part a psychic reflex from the boredom of well-solved domestic issues, in part an external explosion of internally well-ordered economic and social energies, and in part a rational determination to make use abroad of the political instruments that had been developed at home. And so, by the end of the period the European states had created the pattern of reciprocal influence between their international and internal policies which was to form so prominent a threat in their subsequent history.

There were four different kinds of domestic response to the challenge of the competitive European state system which was crystallizing out of the eastern and western wars spanning the Continent around the turn of the century. On a scale ranging from passive to active accommodation to the new international situation, we may identify: first, the states like Sweden, the Netherlands, Poland, and the Ottoman Empire, which found the strain too great and gave up on the task of forming an appropriate internal political organization; second, states like the Spanish and Habsburg empires, which adjusted only enough to maintain a stubborn but precarious defense against the dangers of partition and dissolution; third, the singular case of France, which now reached the crisis of the autocratic state as precociously, vis-à-vis the rest of Europe, as it had earlier found the key to its organization; and finally, the aggressive states of Great Britain (the official title of the island kingdom after the union of England and Wales with Scotland in 1707), Prussia, and Russia, whose rulers saw in the emergent system of international relations not simply new necessities but also new opportunities for expansion, and consequently went furthest in modernizing the constitutions of their respective states.

The differential development, in this period, of the basic institutions concerned with the security of states produced the European political system which would dominate the next two centuries. It broadened the gap between "small"—i.e. weak—states and the great powers, and it accounted for the remarkable geographical pattern which the system would assume. Henceforward the two states on Europe's periphery, Russia and Great Britain, held a balance within the continent and prosecuted aggressive designs outside it; a new central power, Prussia, would function as the organizing core for reordering the centuries-long chaos of the mid-continent; the two southern empires, Habsburg and Ottoman, would continue amid repeated convulsions to brake the forces of change; and France, that crossroads of Atlantic and continental influences, would absorb all the possible alternatives of the new state—absolutist, aristocratic, and popular—and would become the first victim of its tensions.

Success or failure in three main fields accounted for the rise or decline in power of the various European states in the eighteenth century. First, their administrations were more or less successful in mobilizing available resources. Second variations in resources, in population, and in the degree of opportunity for participating in the international seagoing trade—now a driving force in economic development—were clearly crucial factors in the rise and decline of states. But over and above these facts of political and economic geography was a variable social factor: running through the whole tendency toward the centralization of political and administrative power in the early eighteenth century was the contrapuntal resurgence of the European aristocracies. The resurgence affected ascending and declining powers alike, but the different ways in which the aristocracies met the challenge of political reorganization furnish the key to the emerging differences in the pattern of states.

THE DECLINING POWERS

The particular path of descent taken by the declining powers varied with the local conditions, but their terminus was remarkably uniform: a long era glorified as "liberty" but actually signifying a return to government by a traditional oligarchy which stifled and limited the central authority of the state in favor of aristocratic privileges and exemptions.

In the East: Poles and Turks

For Poland and the Ottoman Empire, where this oligarchic condition persisted throughout our entire period and the heights from which descent could be made lay far in the past, the decline was of a relative kind, referring to the growing gap separating these stagnant states from the active governments that were making domestic readjustments rather than to any important changes within the disorganized polities themselves. In Poland, the chronic foreign intervention and a federal constitution which conferred blessings upon aristocratic anarchy had relegated the state—if such that sanctum of nobiliar immunities may be called—to a secondary rank long before the start of our period. In the absence of any unifying institutions (the posts of what was only nominally the king's government were held by the same class of independent nobles that rendered the Diet incapable of common action) or any loyal body of citizens (the aristocracy was faction-ridden, the peasantry was enserfed, and the little there was of a middle class was composed of aliens), neither the Great Northern War of 1700–1721 nor the War of the Polish Succession of 1733–1735 could stimulate any domestic reorganization. Poland remained more a battleground than a protagonist, and only the vain dreaming of a viable Polish monarchy by its ineffectual Saxon king, Augustus, mislabeled "the Strong," affords a measure of what might have been.

For the Ottoman Turks, it was neither the constitution nor foreign intervention but military weakness stemming from the long process of *de facto* limitation of absolutism since the mid-sixteenth century that now caused the empire to drop from the ranks of the great powers. The brief surge of effective government in the third quarter of the seventeenth century, stemming from the massive enlistment of Phanariot Greeks into the Turkish administration, faded as the Greeks followed the pattern of Ottoman officialdom and built their offices into centers of independent aristocratic power. By the eighteenth century the sultan and his central government were at the mercy of the unruly corps of janissaries in the capital and of fractious warlords—Greek in the Rumanian principalities of Moldavia and Walachia, Turkish elsewhere—in the provinces. Instability at the heart of the empire manifested itself not only in the chronic insecurity of the position of the grand vizier (the sultan's chief minister) but in the violent deposition of the sultan himself—Mustafa II in 1703, and Ahmed III in 1730.

The weakness was one not so much of persons as of institutions. Even if the pacific bent and the cultural patronage of the sultans Ahmed III (ruled 1703–1730) and Mahmud I (ruled 1730–1754) be accounted political liabilities, certainly Mahmud's grand viziers, Yegen-Mohammed and Mohammed-Pascha, measured up to the current standards of statecraft. As a result of the military reorganization over which they presided, the Turks gained the surprising victories over the Austrians and the Russians in the war of 1736–1739 which brought to them the return of the Austrian Balkan conquests of 1718 (including Belgrade and excluding only the Hungarian Banat). But these successes scarcely outlasted the two grand viziers, because the Turks still had no permanent institutions that could make habitual the loyalty of the provincial paschas and hospodars, the secular collaboration of Moslems and Christians, or the impersonal devotion of the bureaucracy. Only French diplomatic and technical aid checked the descent of Turkish power during the first half of the century, but even this aid could not prevent the resumption of Turkish decline after the disastrous Russo-Turkish war of 1768–1774. Thenceforth, the Russians' presence on the shores of the Black Sea, and the acknowledgment of their claim to be protectors of the Christian population in the Ottoman Empire, effectively circumscribed Turkish freedom of action in Europe.

In the North: Dutch and Swedes

In the Netherlands, which had reached the apogee of its power only during the previous century, the decline was more perceptible, albeit hardly dramatic. The dictatorial authority which William III of Orange had wielded over the United Provinces as their *stadholder* had been rooted in his personal prestige and indispensability and administered by a personal party. It had effected no permanent institutional or constitutional change and did not survive his death in 1702. The Regents, as the urban patricians who had dominated the governments of the Dutch provinces through most of the century were appropriately called, resumed their sway, purged the Orangist partisans from the provincial and local administrations, and were able, since the succeeding Prince of Orange was still a minor, to prevent the appointment of another national *stadholder*. Behind their spokesman, Antonius Heinsius, grand pensionary (chief magistrate) of Holland, the Regents did unite in support of the alliance with the English against France in the War of the Spanish Succession, but even the Dutch share in the ultimate victory of the alliance could not long maintain the illusion that their state was still a great power, eroded as it was by the conservative administration of resources and the effects of a constitution that had fallen out of line with the requirements of the competitive system of international trade and politics. The obstructions placed by the Dutch deputies at Marlborough's headquarters in the way of that commander's dynamic strategy were symptomatic of the narrowing defensive mentality with which the Dutch ruling group was now facing its problems. Saddled with its Protestant, privileged, and particularist traditions, it made no serious effort either to expand its limited territorial base by appealing for national reunion to its former Netherlandish confederates in the Catholic but detachable Spanish (after 1714 Austrian) Netherlands to the south or to make the extraordinary levies of men and taxes demanded by the protracted warfare against Louis XIV. The result was the growing dependence upon British military subsidies and the growing proportion of British, as against Dutch, components in the nominally combined fleet. The remarkable attempt of the seven united provinces that had attained a federated independence from Spain to assert both a continental and an oceanic position of the first rank thus ended with the loss of both to Great Britain.

But it was the violent break in Swedish history at the end of the Great Northern War that made the domestic retreat of the declining states most perceptible. The Swedes had built their military power, at once awesome and exemplary to the rest of Europe, upon strict regimentation of men and resources and upon the fierce loyalty of the entire citizenry. The conversion of these relationships into the institution of absolute monarchy by Charles XI toward the end of the seventeenth century was apparently capped by Charles XII, who followed the standard practice of absolute kings when he set up his own centralized executive agencies—the Defense Commission and the Purchasing Deputation—on top of the traditional administration to carry through the conscription, special taxation, and forced loans that he required for his Great Northern War.

And yet, at Charles's death in 1718, not only the executive agencies of his own creation but the whole structure of absolute monarchy in Sweden collapsed. Aided by the fortuitous extinction of the Vasa dynasty and the advantages inherent in electing a new monarch, the *Riksdag* formally assumed supreme power and established a system of government in which the actual exercise of sovereignty lay with the aristocratized bureaucracy. Still deliberating and voting in separate houses and with the requirement of three majorities for the passage of legislation, as of yore, the four estates—nobles, clergy, burghers, and peasants—checked one another too thoroughly for the diet to function as an effective sovereign authority. Government redounded in fact to the ennobled officials who ran the Council of the Realm and who were careful to disturb neither the nobles' monopoly of high office, nor their privilege of tax exemption, nor their hostility to the further expansion of the noble class, nor the right of Crown peasants to purchase freeholds. Under the prudent leadership of the Counselor Arvid Horn (1664–1742), a Swedish oligarchy of aristocratic officials, supported by burghers and peasants, managed until Horn's fall in 1738 to endow the "era of liberty" with a pacific policy abroad and at home. Reconciled to the loss of empire and careful to respect the traditional privileges and immunities of all corporate groups, the oligarchy remained in office by avoiding the impositions and tensions of great-power status.

THE PERSISTENT EMPIRES

While the aristocracies of the declining states thus used their recovered strength to roll back the concentration of power in the sovereign authority, the aristocracies of the persistent empires struck a bargain with their monarchs. The notables of these states acceded to the extension of imperial power on condition that their own privileges and immunities would not be infringed thereby.

Spain

The fall of Spain had seemed virtually complete by the end of the seventeenth century under the combined weight of the nobiliar oligarchy whose councils frustrated the central government, the local nobility who secured the autonomy of their provinces through their domination of the influential regional cortes (diets) of Aragon, Catalonia, and the Basque Provinces, the urban oligarchies who jealously guarded the medieval immunities of their communes, and a degenerate dynasty of Spanish Habsburgs who reached their moral as well as physical conclusion under the feebleminded Charles II (ruled 1665–1700).

When the War of the Spanish Succession assumed the shape of a civil war within Spain, with Aragon and Catalonia espousing the cause of the Austrian Habsburg Charles against the Bourbon Philip, the state seemed on the verge of dissolution. But once recognized as the legitimate monarch by the powers of Utrecht the Bourbon Philip V checked the decomposition of the central authority by imposing an overlay of a French-style administrative system upon the traditional governing organs. Setting a series of ministries over the councils on the central level and placing intendants and military commandants over the cortes on the regional level, Philip reestablished royal authority over the basic functions of military security, finance, colonial relations, and general administration. He forcibly repressed the rebellious provinces and the Aragonese Cortes, but he otherwise asserted absolute power without violent alteration of the wonted constitution. The other provincial diets and the executive councils, with their corporate organization and aristocratic personnel, remained in being,

Charles II, last of the Spanish Habsburgs. *Childless and feeble, his death in 1700 triggered the War of the Spanish Succession.*

and the Councils of Castile and of the Indies even retained a considerable administrative importance.

Although the continued existence of the political preserves of the privileged classes marked the limits of change in Spain, the administrative reorganization did enable a bureaucratized monarchy to wield effective authority in the colonial and naval fields—the activities most relevant to the reassertion of Spanish power.

The Spanish empire was strengthened economically by King Philip's mercantilist policy of industrial protection, by the centralization of the financial administration, and by the encouragement of private participation, through new trading companies, in the exploitation of the colonies. Under the direction of such able ministers as Giulio Alberoni (1664–1752) and José Patino (c. 1666-1736), the revived central government restored its navy to a third-ranking place, behind those of Great Britain and France. The result was a surprising reassertion of Spanish power, giving the state a respectable, if not preeminent, position in the shifting alignments of eighteenth-century international politics. Spain indeed was in the thick of the minor wars that kept breaking out during the generation that followed Utrecht, and emerged not only with its empire intact but with its sphere of influence modestly expanded. The primary issue of contention was Italy, the one area whose disposition had been left unresolved by the Utrecht settlement. Spurred on by Philip's domineering Italian-born queen, Elizabeth Farnese (1692–1766), Spain was an aggressive claimant to the southern and central territories of the disorganized peninsula.

The Spanish ambitions in the Mediterranean brought open conflict with the Austrians in 1717, 1733–1735, and 1741–1748, and with the British in 1718–1719, in 1727, and, abetted by Anglo-Spanish colonial rivalry in America, most seriously in 1739–1748. As long as the Spaniards had to contend with a common Anglo-French front—an unusual combination for these rival Atlantic powers, explicable by their mutual interest in preventing any change that might threaten the Utrecht settlement—their tactical victories over the Austrians in Italy were to little avail. But then, in the 1730's, the revival of the traditional French anti-Habsburg policy and the increasing colonial frictions with the British shifted the orientation of Bourbon France toward the family compact with Spain that was to persist as a stable factor in European diplomacy until the French Revolution. The Spaniards then managed to stalemate the British in America and to roll the Habsburgs back from southern Italy. In 1738, the Treaty of Vienna, which formally concluded the War of the Polish Succession, recognized a Spanish Bourbon dynasty in an independent Kingdom of Naples (including the island of Sicily). Although formal union with Spain was barred by the provision that the succession in Naples was to be through the dynasty's second sons ("secundogeniture"), southern Italy would remain within the orbit of Spanish ambition until its conquest by Napoleon, and dynastically related to Spain until the unification of Italy in 1860.

Habsburg Dominions

The other realm which was characterized by astonishing powers of survival was the empire of the Habsburgs. From the heady days of Prince Eugene's victories against the French and the Turks in the early years of the eighteenth century—victories crowned by the territorial gains registered in the treaties of Rastatt (1714) and Passarowitz (1718)—Austrian fortunes went into a rapid decline until the state seemed destined for partition in the War of the Austrian Succession, which began in 1740. For this war was not a sudden catastrophe: the groundwork for it had been laid by a whole series of losses in the international arena and by the neglect of needs at home. Between 1725 and 1728, the Habsburgs had briefly seemed to be reaping the fruit of their earlier triumphs by becoming the core of a continental bloc, which included Russia, Prussia, and Spain. But the bloc soon disintegrated, and Austria, isolated except for some inadequate support from post-Petrine Russia, lost during the disastrous decade of the 1730's the bulk of the territory acquired during the glorious decade of the teens. Through the War of the Polish Succession, Naples and Sicily were lost to the Spanish Bourbons and the satellite Duchy of Lorraine to France. As a result of the Turkish war of 1736–1739 the Serbian, Walachian, and Bosnian acquisitions of 1718 were returned to the Turks. The Habsburgs did receive Parma, Piacenza, and through an indirect dynastic arrangement, Tuscany, in partial compensation for the Italian cessions; and they did retain the Hungarian Banat. But at the time these territories seemed to be outposts in a general retreat rather than the bases for the expansion of Austrian influence that they would in fact become.

The post-Passarowitz military failures were related directly to diplomatic ineptitude and indirectly to the government's passivity in domestic affairs. On the diplomatic side, Austria's isolation in western Europe led to the defeats in the War of the Polish Succession and to a dependence upon Russia that pulled the Habsburgs into their pointless and disastrous participation in the Turkish war. On the domestic side, the *de facto* political absolutism—that is, the hereditary succession of Habsburg monarchs and the acceptance of their legislative sovereignty by all their dominions—which had been erected at the time of the Thirty Years' War on the basis of Catholic uniformity remained static while other governments were energetically extending their effective authority over their peoples. Provincial diets and county estates retained far-reaching rights of self-administration and economic privileges under royal governments in Vienna (for Austria and Bohemia) and in Pressburg (for Hungary) which were not organized actually to make the policy they had the acknowledged authority to make. In the Viennese central administration itself, only the Court Chamber for the supervision of finances and a Court War Council had general jurisdiction. Otherwise, government in Vienna was conducted by separate agencies for the various lands of the Austrian archduchy and the Bohemian monarchy. The aristocracies of the sundry dominions that made up the Habsburg realm were loyal to the dynasty, but only within the limits of a mutual respect for the traditional way of doing things. When the sovereign's ministers did make tentative efforts to effect a more intensive mobilization of the dominion's resources, the notables withheld their cooperation —a posture which their crucial role in provincial and local administration made tantamount to a successful campaign of passive resistance. Aristocratic self-government and privilege in regard to land taxes stymied financial reform; provincial and local obstructions to trade and traffic stymied economic development. Thus the growing expenses of the new political demands met a static supply of resources, and the result was a chronic financial crisis that undermined the state's capacity for decisive action.

But if the predominance of the aristocracy in the provinces and at the court helped to prevent the *extension* of the central power, this same aristocracy did acquiesce in the monarch's *retention* of the basic functions which made it possible for him to exploit his various dominions as a single state for purposes of international relations. However diverted in the execution, the central administration retained supreme control over the command and organization of the army and over federal tax assessments, and its agents levied and collected these assessments on towns, royal domains, and commodities. However divided and impotent in practice, a Privy Conference did exist as a supreme advisory council. It included the highest officials from the various branches of the government, and their deliberations were intended to form the basis for a unified policy.

The political connections among the Habsburg territories were close enough, moreover, to make Austria the original home of "cameralism," the version of mercantilism that was to become characteristic of eighteenth-century German economic policy. It was to the Habsburg monarchy of Leopold I that the typical programs of this school had been first addressed, in the last quarter of the seventeenth century, and it was in the Habsburg monarchy of Charles VI that a tentative application of them was made during the first third of the eighteenth century. What was distinctive in cameralism, vis-à-vis the more familiar versions of mercantilism which furnished the guidelines of policy in the western European countries, stemmed from the conditions of Habsburg rule, and Habsburg cameralism became the model for other German states where conditions were similar. Definitive of these distinctive conditions were an economy that was laggard in comparison with those of competing countries, a society with few traditions of cohesion, and a government in which the distinction between the definite rights of the ruler over his own domain and his indefinite rights over the rest of the state was still a real one. The cameralists, taking their name from *Kammer* ("chamber"), the territorial lord's own exchequer, responded to these conditions not only by working out a set of policies, as the mercantilists did, but by elaborating a theory, as the mercantilists did not. There were three distinctive attributes of Austrian and German cameralism. First, cameralism was not simply, like mercantilism, a set of economic policies for an operating administration, but rather an entire administrative "science" to modernize the operation of government in general, including economic policy as one of its essential parts. Economics, in this context, was central to the extension of the sovereign's control from his private domains to the very different conditions of his subjects' domains, of which he was ruler but not lord. Second, greater emphasis was put, in economic policies, on the positive role of public agencies in both stimulating and operating new economic enterprise than on their role in controlling existing private economic activities. Finally, the financial purpose and interest of the sovereign in cameralist controls were far more explicit than the covert fiscal motives lurking behind the more general political, economic, or social mercantilist goals of the more advanced societies. The adoption of cameralist standards by prominent officials in Charles VI's regime testified at least to their belief in the possibility of imposing from the top the institutions and policies that would galvanize and coalesce the separate classes and regions of the Austrian society. But until the catastrophic War of the Austrian Succession

Charles VI. A *stylized portrait of the ineffectual Habsburg emperor and life-long salesman of the Pragmatic Sanction.*

(1740–1748), the notables would not accept these institutional consequences of the monarchy they did accept, and the measures initiated
against internal trade barriers under Charles VI, for example, were frustrated by provincial opposition.

The balance in Austria between the general recognition of monarchical
sovereignty and the limits within which the valid exercise of that sovereignty was recognized explains the history of the famous Pragmatic Sanction, the central issue in the reign of Charles VI. The Pragmatic Sanction,
declared by Charles VI to his closest advisers in ₁713 and submitted
officially to his territorial estates for ratification from 1720, was a royal
ordinance with the status of fundamental law. It made Leopold I's family
compact of 1703 a constitutional amendment. This compact had provided
for female succession to the Habsburg throne, and thus to the rulership
over all Habsburg possessions, in default of male heirs. But the Pragmatic
Sanction reversed the compact's specific order of the succession, transfer-
ring priority from the daughters of the older brother, Joseph (died 1711),
to the daughters of Charles VI. The domestic importance of the Pragmatic Sanction lay in the potential conflict between the principle of the
indivisibility of the Habsburg territories asserted in it and the still valid
fundamental laws of those Habsburg territories which excluded female succession. Charles's protracted but successful negotiations with the estates of
his territories for their consent to this amendment of their fundamental
laws faithfully expressed the relations between the Habsburgs and their
aristocracies: by 1732 all the estates had agreed to the Pragmatic Sanction

and its principle of an indivisible empire but had underscored the voluntary basis of their assent by making the reaffirmation of their consitutional rights an essential part of their compact with the ruler. Certainly the Pragmatic Sanction represented a net gain for the unity of the Habsburg dominions, for it placed the integrity of the state beyond the accidents of succession. But the necessity of securing the consent of the aristocracy and of confirming its traditional privileges and immunities left Charles VI with little disposition or energy to struggle against this group, and without such a struggle he could not extend the authority of his central government.

The international history of the Pragmatic Sanction was similarly marked by protracted and successful negotiations for endorsement, but in this arena the result, in the final balance, was a net loss. In his diplomacy, as in his bargaining with his estates, Charles purchased the formal recognition of the territorial integrity of Habsburg lands for his heiress, Maria Theresa, by nominally conceding the long-asserted claims of his rivals. But in foreign affairs, unlike domestic, the stagnation of the monarchy invited not loyalty but attack. Prussian impatience at the Austrian failure to deliver the succession rights to the Duchy of Berg, promised in 1728 as the price for the Prussian guarantee of the Sanction, formed a grievance which, together with the conviction that Austria was impotent, impelled the young Frederick II of Prussia to attack and acquire Austrian Silesia in 1740. Similarly, the Habsburg concession of the Duchy of Lorraine to the French protégé Stanislas Leszczynski (1677–1766), in 1735—a concession that helped to buy France's recognition of the Sanction—encouraged the rise of the French war party which soon resumed expansionist policies against the apparently vulnerable Habsburgs along the Rhine and in the Austrian Netherlands. The same party urged the Franco-Prussian military alliance which was actually concluded in 1741 against Austria.

Thus the efforts to secure international agreement to the Pragmatic Sanction aroused the resentments and stimulated the greed that led to the War of the Austrian Succession. Ironically, the concessions promised by the Habsburgs to ensure the undivided succession of their dominions brought on a war that threatened to divest them of dominions to succeed to. Prussia, Spain, and Saxony sought to slice off peripheral Habsburg territories, and the French had plans to set up a Bavarian Emperor of Germany and to partition the Austrian and Czech heartlands of the Habsburg dominions.

Obviously, the Habsburg policy of bargaining was a diplomatic failure, but the entrenchment of the dynasty effected by the domestic counterpart of this policy, abetted by a military alliance with Great Britain, limited Austrian losses to Silesia and to trivial cessions in Italy. Moreover, the combination of the domestic success of the Pragmatic Sanction with the military losses which it failed to prevent nurtured the seed of Habsburg revival which was to flower in the second half of the century.

FRANCE: CROSSROADS OF EUROPE

The domestic history of France between Louis XIV's last great war and the middle of the eighteenth century uncovered the tensions which were subsequently to isolate this nation as the one revolutionary power in Europe. The gap which favorable geography, available resources, and superior political organization had opened between France and the rest of Europe during the seventeenth century began to tell against the leader. The comparative superiority of the French, which had enabled them to make martial expansion a national tradition, now imposed a serious strain upon the state. Not only did French governments fail to recognize the mounting costs of maintaining such a tradition in the face of effective foreign competition both from Great Britain on the ocean seas and from modernizing land powers on the Continent but the French position on the crossroads of the Atlantic economies and the mainland societies opened the internal organization of France fully to the paralyzing countercurrents of economic growth and social resistance.

The most convulsive symptom of this strain was the financial crisis that darkened the latter years of Louis XIV's reign and deepened during the course of the eighteenth century. The financial crisis was not simply a symptom of too much war and too much royal extravagance. It also testified to the arrival of an advanced stage of state making in which the central authority was faced with the necessity of invading areas of economic and social privilege hitherto inessential to it. The paradox whereby the most centralized state in Europe experienced, during the eighteenth century, the most effective aristocratic resurgence is explicable by the new economic and social level which the confrontation of state and aristocracy now reached in France. This conflict remained a stalemate, and the chronic financial crisis was the most prominent reflection of it. The very success of the nation in meeting the challenge of the international exchange economy made large sections of the aristocracy dependent on support by the state to meet their rising costs and their growing indebtedness. But the state in turn looked to the contributions of all classes for the support of its own officials and their activities. The financial crisis became the battlefield wherein aristocracy and bureaucracy fought for control of the state they both needed. While other states, with their socially detached bureaucracies and their relatively undeveloped economies, were still reaping the benefits of a political unity that by common consent only the central government could provide, the French were progressing to the critical stage of social politics wherein the bureaucracy and the corporations represented mature, aggressive, and opposing groups which aimed at turning political unity to their own social advantage.

France under Louis XIV: Last Phase (1689–1715)

Under the pressure of the incessant warfare that filled the last twenty-five years of his reign, Louis XIV had extended the instrumentalities of royal absolutism ever more obtrusively into the internals of French social life. In part the extension stemmed from the expansion and specialization of the royal agencies. It was a matter rather of administrative practice than institutional change, for the system of government through central councils and functional departments of state, unified by the supreme will and common direction of the king, persisted actually to the end of Louis XIV's regime and nominally until the revolution. But wherever government affected people rather than policy, the balance between corporate and bureaucratic institutions which had made the increase in monarchial power not only acceptable but even welcome to the society of seventeenth-century France was now, in the latter stage of Louis' long reign, upset by an excess of bureaucratic pressure. The *intendants*, general regional agents of the king, extended their control over provinces and towns; the inspectorates, agencies of the central administrative departments, were multiplied for the most varied kinds of products and activities; the office and powers of the police lieutenancies, both in Paris and in the provinces, grew inexorably.

But in part, too, the increasing regimentation of the French society was an indirect product of fiscal need: the ever more frequent resort to the creation and sale of offices generated a plethora of officials whose competition for control and for fees multiplied the points of contact between government and people. The growing pressure of the state upon the society was concentrated particularly in the fields of economics and religion, and the character of this pressure set the stage for the profound divisions that tore the nation throughout the eighteenth century and beyond.

The mounting financial requirements of the state at war furnished the spur for the extension of mercantilism into an ever more rigid and inclusive system of controls. The institutions that had been designed by Colbert to trigger economic growth were now developed into a fiscal machine to siphon off all surpluses from working capital and current income. Import tariffs were raised to prohibitive proportions. Exports of food and raw materials from France and even from one region of France to another were prohibited. Internal tolls were raised as a matter of tax policy. Available resources were diverted to the industries which armed and clothed the military forces of the king. Hordes of inspectors supervised every stage in the process of production, setting standards and collecting taxes for their stamps of approval. Capital was in effect confiscated, both by the enforced circulation of paper currency and by compulsory loans to the treasury. The result of the wars and of the economic policy geared to wars was a severe depression of the French economy—affecting all its branches save the armaments industries—and the literal bankruptcy of the government, complete with the virtual repudiation of a large proportion of its debt to those citizens who by choice or under duress had invested their capital in it.

The tax needs of the state grew increasingly more critical as the tax base shrank. Louis XIV's government, consequently, sought to expand this base by canceling the age-old exemption of the aristocracy from direct taxation, and by imposing new levies upon all citizens, with capacity to pay the only principle of discrimination. A royal decree of 1695 enacted a head tax *(capitation)*, dividing all French subjects into twenty-two classes according to assumed income, and proportioning the tax according to the class. Since these revenues proved inadequate, the king announced still another presumably egalitarian direct tax in 1710: the royal tithe *(dixième)*, a 10 per cent income tax modeled on the church tithe. Although both taxes were limited to the duration of the war (the head tax was indeed suspended during the truce of 1697–1701), they clearly signified the intention of the monarchy, under the pressure of necessity, to breach the financial privileges of the aristocracy and the clergy, privileges whose retention had formed a crucial part of the tacit agreement which had reconciled these corporations to political obedience.

The royal policy that sought to abridge the tax immunities of the privileged classes coincided with royal infringements upon the ecclesiastical rights of clerical bodies in their own religious capacity. We have already seen what Louis' later brand of religiosity meant for him (see pp. 20–21), but in the event, it proved to be more than a personal matter, since the long-run residue of the change in Louis' religious policy was a thorn that festered in French public life as a source of conflict throughout the eighteenth century. For the country as a whole, Louis' shift away from the mixture of Gallicanism and qualified toleration that had aided the rise of both Bourbon and French power since the age of Henry IV (ruled 1589–1610) implied as fundamental a rift in the network of corporate privilege as his simultaneous financial enactments. If the spectacular suppression, by agencies of the state, of the Reformed (Calvinist, or Huguenot) Church and the Jansenist movement within the Catholic Church may be seen as the elimination of recalcitrant minorities with the aid of the official church, certainly the accompaniment of these measures by Louis' quiet revocation of the charter of Gallican liberties which had guaranteed the rights of the French Catholic Church as a national institution threw new light upon the policy. Whatever the motivation, the effect of the policy was to put the power of the state into areas that had been under the competence of corporate bodies.

The impact of the financial and religious measures of Louis' later reign was twofold: the customary privileges of traditional corporations were violated, and individuals were thus confronted directly with the state in areas of social activity which had formerly been the terrain of corporate mediation between state and individual. The immediate response of the society to the innovations was correspondingly twofold: on the one hand, the privileged orders sought to resist the royal incursions and recover their specific exemptions; on the other hand, representatives of those orders sought to redefine those exemptions, changing them to general rights which would bring the will of the whole society to bear against the overextension of state power.

The most characteristic response of the first type was the aristocracy's forceful opposition to and effective frustration of the new equalizing taxes of Louis' wartime administration. The aristocracy evaded the intended incidence of the taxation through a combination of bargains with the government for reduced rates, redistribution of the levies within the provinces on the model of the traditional and unequal *taille*, and simple noncompliance. Nor was the aristocracy the only corporation in the France of the aging Louis XIV to oppose his growing intervention in fields of vested interests. The merchants, still grouped by the myriad of privileges and obligations stemming from the palmy days of the commercial guilds, grew restive under the increasing burden of indirect taxation and direct regulation imposed by the agents of the central authorities. Their spokesmen in the royal Council of Commerce (the official advisory body of bureaucrats and elected merchant representatives which had been formed in 1699) began to complain aloud of the obstructions to and decline of trade, while in the towns they themselves initiated the practices of evasion which, during the course of the eighteenth century, undermined in fact the mercantilist policies that grew ever more stringent in the lawbooks. Presaged now, too, was the social lineup which, whatever the class frictions in other contexts, permitted aristocratic initiative against autocracy to represent other organized groups in French society until the very eve of the revolution.

Characteristic of this traditional and corporate type of response too was the reaction to Louis' religious aggressions. Against his arrangements with the Pope and his sympathy with Ultramontane Jesuits, the Gallicans rallied to the defense of the national church, and the Jansenist cause was adopted by the royal courts (*parlements*). Louis' extraordinary measures adumbrated ordinary royal policy throughout the eighteenth century, and the opposition to them adumbrated the corporate resistance to this policy. Not surprisingly, tax privileges and religion remained the two primary issues of conflict between king and notables until the revolution.

Equally prophetic of the internal struggles to come was the progressive form taken by the articulate response from the threatened groups. This kind of response was pioneered, during Louis' own lifetime, by aristocratic and religious writers who transmuted the traditional claims of corporations into general programs of political reform. In the process they rationalized and modernized their defense of privilege by reconciling it with the political sovereignty of the monarch and by connecting it with the claims of the whole community upon the monarch.

Among the spokesmen for the aristocracy, that inveterate gossip, Louis de Rouvroy, Duke of Saint-Simon (1675–1755) with his nostalgic and

The Duke of Saint-Simon. *Unreconstructed aristocrat, nostalgic grumbler, and gossipy memorialist of the court of Louis XIV.*

impotent grumbling for the good old days of noble and royal partnership in the government of France, may have been close to what his peers were thinking; and certainly the French histories of his contemporary, Henri de Boulainvilliers, Count of Saint-Saire (1658–1722), were unashamed exaltations of those days with the purpose of bringing about their restoration; but the up-to-date thinking of Archbishop François Fénelon (1651–1715), Sébastien de Vauban (1633–1707), and Pierre de Boisguillebert (1646–1714) announced the main line that the aristocracy was to take in the coming century.

Noble-born, royal tutor (of Louis XIV's grandson, the Duke of Burgundy), maverick Archbishop of Cambrai (inclining toward heterodox Quietism), Fénelon combined elements of tradition and innovation in his writing as in his life. In his banned utopian novel, *Telemachus* (1699), as well as in his essays on the responsibilities of kings, Fénelon stressed, in good traditional fashion, both the inherent obligation of the king to govern for the good of his subjects in accordance with the law of the land and the necessity of an edifying moral education to inculcate him with fitting self-restraint. Neither such pious discourse nor Fénelon's fulminations against the evils of despotism were particularly new. What was new was his project for the constitutional reform of France, in which he sought to renovate the political function of the aristocracy by making it the pivotal factor in maintaining a balance between the sovereign monarch and popular rights. He would check the king not by pleading for special class immunities, but by placing general constitutional limitations upon the sphere of recognized sovereign power which the king exercised. The guarantor of the royal limits, accordingly, was not simply the noble caste, but a whole hierarchy of assemblies, stretching from the local to the national levels, which would represent the entire people and would be led by its aristocratic section in its primary function of confining the royal authority within proper bounds. Fénelon did not shrink from giving his proposals immediate point by blaming Louis XIV's excesses of power for miseries of all classes of the population, and he thereby initiated the role of spokesman for the nation which the French aristocracy was to assume during the eighteenth century.

In Vauban and Boisguillebert, the other facet of the aristocracy's representative function during the eighteenth century was adumbrated. Where Fénelon initiated the modernization of the nobility's constitutional claims upon the state, Vauban and Boisguillebert opened the way to new versions of its administrative prerogatives within the government. Both were aristocrats by birth and bureaucrats by profession, Vauban as a military engineer and Boisguillebert as a jurist. Both were convinced monarchists who were led by their specific criticisms of Louis XIV's monarchical policies into seminal proposals for the reorientation—albeit not the reformation—of royal absolutism. Both developed their proposals in the context of avocations adjacent to their administrative careers—Vauban as a writer on military science, Boisguillebert as a political economist—and the import of both recommendations was the simultaneous limitation and strengthening of monarchy through the elimination of what was capricious and arbitrary in its policies.

The beginning of Vauban's disaffection can be traced to his precise estimate, in 1689, of France's loss—and its enemies' corresponding gain—in soldiers, cash, and industrial resources as a result of the Huguenot emigration after the revocation of the Edict of Nantes. In a crucial position to observe the destructive effects which Louis' subsequent exactions had on the military fortunes of the French state as well as on the welfare of its inhabitants, Vauban ultimately worked up his disapproval into his *Plan for a Royal Tithe* (written in 1698 and published in 1707), wherein he demanded equality of taxation and postulated as its corollary a monarchical state governed in accordance with general laws. During the same period Boisguillebert, an avowed supporter of Vauban, was making the same points in a broader economic argument. First in his *Economy of France* (1695) and again in his *Memorandum on France* (1707), Boisguillebert expanded his criticisms of the inequities of the French tax system into a general attack upon the bullionist and restrictive policies of governmental mercantilism and made a general defense of agriculture as the main source of the national wealth. What these writers resented was civil rather than social privilege. They found special rights and exemptions incompatible with the requirements of the state, and they insisted upon the contribution of all classes to the support of the state for the purpose of making the social hierarchy compatible with a state predicated upon the equal obligations of its citizens.

Not only the aristocracy but confessional Christianity too responded to Louis XIV's subversion of traditional corporate institutions by developing new intellectual bases of their rights. Among the Christian churches, it was dispersion of the Huguenots, the most persecuted of Louis' ecclesiastical corporations, which produced the most progressive theory of the free spirit. Pierre Jurieu (1637–1713), the exiled Huguenot pastor who fulminated against his former sovereign from his refuge in the Netherlands, was the transitional figure in this intellectual development, and through the ambiguities of his writings we can see how it worked. In his *Pastoral Letters* (1688-1689) and his *Sighs of Enslaved France* (1689–1690) he asserted nominal doctrines of religious liberty, natural rights, popular sovereignty, and contractual government side by side with commitments to Calvinism as the one true faith, to the sanctity of historical tradition as the basis of valid constitutions, to the hierarchy of corporate estates as the political spokesmen of the people, and to the exclusive right of this corporately organized people as a whole to defend both individual and collective liberties against violation. Thus he gave a modern libertarian cast to the old sixteenth-century monarchomachic doctrine of ecclesiastical resistance to religious oppression, but he added rather than combined the newer and the older ideas.

It was left to Jurieu's fellow Calvinist and exile, Pierre Bayle (1647–1706), to use the same kind of bitterness as a goad to the clear enunciation of a new liberal principle. Author of the *Historical and Critical Dictionary* (1697), which was to become the source book of the French Enlightenment, Bayle deepened his criticisms of Bourbon France, arriving at a general principle of doubt that was directed against all propositions, beliefs, and institutions not founded on sound reason or a solid empirical base. He broadened the special claim for toleration of the Reformed Church into a general principle of liberty of conscience, applicable by right to every religious belief and grounded in the priority of universal moral reason over particular religious dogma. Bayle's intellectual advance, so far beyond the stymied religious corporation from which he started, was an early harbinger of the philosophical breakthrough which would lead men from the defense of corporations to the assertion of individualism later in the eighteenth century.

The Regency (1715–1723)

The death of the Sun King, in September, 1715, followed hard upon the last of the conventions composing the Utrecht settlement. Both events announced the start of a new era: within France there was a visceral reaction against all that the grasping, failing Louis had stood for; outside of

France one-power hegemony was ended, and a multipower balance began to emerge. The immediate consequence of Louis' death was the swing of the pendulum in domestic political and economic affairs, for some five years, to the opposite extreme. Where autocratic wartime control had been the rule, the pursuit of peace, pleasure, and profit became general.

The shrewd but licentious Duke of Orléans (1674–1723), who had brought into focus the growing discontent under his uncle Louis XIV and now became regent for the five-year-old Louis XV, set the tone. The court moved to Paris and became the model for the relaxation of manners and morals from the recent constraints of Versailles' somber piety. The Duke himself embarked upon notable experiments in government, finance, and foreign policy quite different in tendency from the former system.

In government, he attempted to restore the political influence of the high nobility by instituting a set of central councils—from feudal times the most appropriate kind of institution for the aristocracy's participation in the business of monarchy—as the supreme executive organs of the state. But this *Polysynodie*, as the conciliar system was called, was no mere throwback to the unprofessional conciliar governments of the Middle Ages. Composed of bureaucrats as well as nobles and organized by function (war, navy, foreign affairs, interior, finance, and religion), it represented an effort to work the old-line aristocracy into the actual administration of a modern bureaucratic state. There was no inherent necessity for the experiment to fail, as the contemporaneous experience of Prussia was to show, but in France fail it did. It was dismantled as early as 1718, because, as one of its most strenuous proponents, the Duke of Saint-Simon ruefully admitted, the nobility that manned it evinced neither the taste nor the competence for the job.

The Regency thereupon accomplished the restoration of the balance between aristocracy and bureaucracy, which had been displaced in favor of the latter under Louis XIV, by deliberately returning a traditional right to an aristocratic party and inadvertently removing the crucial lever of control from the bureaucracy. On the first count, Orléans returned the right of remonstrance—*i.e.* of protest against the king's edicts—to the royal *parlements*, and he thereby conferred upon the judicial nobility that composed them the political weapon that would make them the aggressive leaders of the aristocratic resurgence. On the second count, the Regency initiated the diffraction of central authority that would prevent any unitary resolution of its internal tensions. No person or agency could replace the king as synchronizer of councils and ministries in the French system, and the failure of the *Polysynodie* brought not only the dismantling of the new councils but the gradual atrophy of the established ones. The actual work of government settled firmly in the hands of the chancellor (the chief legal officer) and the ministers (the four secretaries of state and the controller general), with their specialized departments. The Regency did revive the post of prime minister, dormant since the tenures of Richelieu

Mass anger and bitterness in Paris in 1720 after the collapse of John Law's Mississippi project.

and Mazarin in the previous century, to coordinate activities of the ministers, separately appointed and responsible as they were. For a few months before his death in 1723 Orléans took the post himself in fact and in title, but it was not revived after Louis XV (ruled 1715–1774) assumed his majority in 1723. From 1726 until 1743 Cardinal Fleury effectively occupied it in fact albeit not in title. But the post proved to be only a way station on the central government's road to confusion: not only was it discontinued both in name and in function after Fleury, but even during its revival it served more as an adjunct of the foreign office than as a source of general policy and unified control.

From the Regency on, the government operated through agents who recognized that the source of their powers lay in royal authority but who claimed that the right to exercise these same powers inhered in their offices and was inviolable by the royal authority which was its source. Here was the institutional basis of the political issue that seems so anomalous to modern minds but was to dominate the constitutional debates of eighteenth-century France: the issue of the limits that, according to fundamental law, could be imposed upon the sovereign power in the state by its own derivative agents.

Orléans' financial experiment was perhaps bolder and certainly more modern. Envious of the stability which had enabled Great Britain and the Netherlands to weather the long wars without suffering the quasi-bankruptcy that was the French memento, Orléans was persuaded by the Scottish adventurer and sometime banker John Law (1671–1729) that a two-pronged program of credit expansion and tax reform would finally resolve France's long-standing financial crisis. The Regent entrusted Law with both parts of the program. By 1720 Law had, with official approval, founded a trading company and a state bank, and united both into a single institution. He was, moreover, issuing both paper money and stock certificates on the joint basis of the trading monopoly (in North America) and of state credit. In 1720, too, Law was appointed Controller-general by Orléans, and in this capacity he sketched a progressive scheme of reform reminiscent of Vauban's in its provision for an equal tax and a uniform system of tax collection by state agencies. But the influences favoring a boom were too strong: the upward turn of the economic cycle following upon the long wartime depression, the beginnings of the spectacular growth in overseas trade that was to mark the century, the heady atmosphere of postwar abandon, and the unfamiliarity with the new credit instruments all generated the speculative fever which found expression in the scheme, which was subsequently known as the "Mississippi bubble." When it burst, in October, 1720, the downfall of Law and his projects confirmed an opposition to central banking and tax reform that was successfully to frustrate both until the end of the *ancien régime* (the shorthand term for the political and social structure of France between the fifteenth century and the revolution of 1789; in its anglicized form of "Old Regime" it can be applied to all Europe in the same era).

The financial experiments of the Regency signalized a basic problem of eighteenth-century France. Just as the administration became the arena of social conflict in absolutist France, so did the administration's tax question become the social issue appropriate to this arena. The recurrent fiscal crisis certainly had its own financial roots: the inefficient and corrupt habits of the government's semi-independent agencies; the continued shortsighted sale of public offices—and the multiplication of public offices to sell—with the effect of draining long-term revenues into private fees; the state's pensionary support of an idle and restive nobility; and its repeated foreign overcommitments on the land and on the sea. But the financial crisis was also widely believed to stem from an inadequate tax base caused by exemption of the privileged. The persistence with which the proposal for a tax upon all classes of people was raised and obstructed throughout the century indicates its status as the one issue in which the government confronted the question of social privilege.

In foreign affairs, finally, Orléans pursued a policy diametrically opposed to that of his bellicose uncle: he sought the friendship of Great Britain and in 1717 concluded a formal alliance with both of Louis' most persistent enemies—Britain and the Netherlands—to preserve the Utrecht settlement that sealed Louis' lost war. Orléans' interest was a personal one. He was interested in the continued exclusion of the Bourbon Philip V of Spain, his rival to the status of Louis XV's heir apparent, from the French succession. Coming as it did in the midst of the long period from 1689 to 1815 which, by reason of the profundity and persistence of Anglo-French hostility, has been dubbed by historians—with their customary casual arithmetic—"the second hundred years' war," the alliance with Great Britain has seemed like just another example of eccentric and unnatural dynastic diplomacy. But the entente—and the French policy that pushed it—

actually made more sense under the circumstances than its dynastic occasion indicates, for it was predicated on the coincidence of French with British interests in trade with the Spanish empire and in the Mediterranean, and of British with French interests in preventing a restoration of Austro-Spanish hegemony on the Continent. The first set of those interests was threatened by the remarkable Spanish resurgence of colonial exclusiveness and Mediterranean offensives after 1717; the second was threatened by the even more remarkable Austro-Spanish alliance of 1725, which opened the prospect of its joint domination of Italy, of Austrian participation in Spanish overseas trade (through the new Habsburg "Ostend Company"), and of dynastic union. But the results of the Anglo-French cooperation were not lasting enough to include the arrangement among the diplomatic revolutions for which the century was to become notorious. Once Spanish and Austrian designs in Italy had been checked, Austrian trading privileges canceled, and the Austro-Spanish alliance split in 1731, France resumed the independent policy that gradually fretted away the understanding with Great Britain until the resumption of actual hostilities in 1744.

Thus the Regent tried but failed to find a permanent solution for the international problem whose irresolution throughout the century was to intensify domestic social and financial problems and to strain the faulty administrative instrument to distraction. The problem was the choice between an oceanic and a continental orientation. The definite option for one would permit, on at least the other of these fronts, the preservation of the peace that France urgently required for the repair of the domestic establishment. Orléans' attempt was optimal from the point of view of prudence if not of glory: the British alignment kept the peace both at sea and—aside from an occasional skirmish—on the Continent. But the unpopularity of this policy signalized the problem that would weigh upon France as upon no other nation in the eighteenth century: the vital commitment to both colonial and European ambitions. Because the French could not choose between the options, they blundered into every conflict on either of the two fronts and had to fight in every major war on both.

France under Louis XV: First Phase (1723–1748)
After the Regency, only an undemanding foreign policy could postpone the day of reckoning. The leader primarily responsible for the persistence of this salubrious international orientation and its concomitant happy domestic inertia was André Hercule de Fleury (1653–1743), third and last of the great cardinal-statesmen who did so much to consolidate and prolong the Bourbon monarchy. Deceptively amiable and supple in demeanor, always dependent for his power on the shaky ground of Louis XV's personal, quasi-filial, reminiscent regard for his original role as the indulgent royal tutor, Fleury exhibited unexpected force, determination, and even arrogance in keeping the French state within the consistent lines of peace

Cardinal Fleury. *France's leading minister and architect of peace and prosperity in the early phase of Louis XV's reign.*

and retrenchment that he deemed necessary to the country's rehabilitation after the ruinous wars of the previous regime. Between 1726, when he succeeded to the *de facto* prime-ministership, and 1740, when his grasp began to slip, he collaborated with his like-minded British contemporary, Robert Walpole, in keeping the general peace. When dynastic ties and the growing strength of a war party at the French court embroiled France in the War of the Polish Succession, Fleury succeeded in limiting and focusing the French commitment to an extent that kept Great Britain neutral and acquired Lorraine definitively for France.

Similarly, Fleury influenced the appointment of ministers—particularly Henri d'Aguesseau (1668–1751), the law-codifying Chancellor, and Philibert Orry (1689–1747), the tightfisted Controller-general—who cooperated with him to give France the conservative and restrained domestic administration appropriate to the sobriety of the foreign policy. In internal affairs, as in foreign, when violence did break out it was quickly limited in its scope and effect as it dissipated in the placid atmosphere of an expanding economy and a government that watched benevolently over it. The social and religious conflicts that, in tandem, were to provoke corporate opposition to the royal government later in the century did not merge under Fleury. The only outbreak was occasioned during the 1730's by what has been called the "new Jansenism." Developing as an institutional and political movement in the stead of the pious, fideistic, and moralistic coterie that had been smashed by Louis XIV and the Bull *Unigenitus* (1713), the new Jansenism became the rallying point of the lower clergy, which used it against the ritualistic and Ultramontane hierarchy, and of the *parlements*, which associated it with their own Gallican claims to jurisdiction over the national church as nominal agents of the king. Between 1730 and 1732 the Archbishop of Paris, supported by Louis XV (who was already exhibiting the anti-Jansenism that, along with his passion for autocracy, represented the whole of his philosophy of government), sought to force acceptance of *Unigenitus* upon a recalcitrant lower clergy, and the subsequent disorder in the Church was paralleled in the state when the *parlements*, both in Paris and the provinces, supported the clerics who refused to accept it. But the agitation subsided in 1732, as a result of Fleury's alternation of firmness and amnesty, the notables' revulsion at the mass hysteria triggered by "miracles" around a Jansenist grave, and the absence of other grievances upon which to feed.

A decade later, the war and disorder that Fleury had kept limited and insulated began to join in the pattern of chronic crisis ultimately fateful to the monarchy. The break came, as it did so often during this century, in the field of foreign policy. In 1741 a war party led by Marshal Charles Louis de Belle-Isle (1684–1761) and constituted by court nobility of the sword gained the confidence of the king, and, taking the direction of foreign affairs away from the failing Fleury (he was a ripe ninety when he died in office during 1743), renewed the militant anti-Habsburg and anti-British policies which had for so long occupied the French warrior class. Resuming Louis XIV's lineup of a Spanish alliance and a south German clientele, the French involved themselves in the War of the Austrian Succession with an attack on Austria in 1741, extended the war to the Austrian Netherlands, and by 1744 found themselves confronted by a coalition of powers led by Great Britain and reminiscent of the Grand Alliance. The war lasted until the Peace of Aix-la-Chapelle in 1748—for the French a mere truce in the armed conflict that would drain their strength until the end of the century and beyond—and in its crucible the political chain of persistent crisis was forged.

The first link, on which all else hung, was the emergence, from behind Fleury, of the king whose character would set the conditions of government for the next thirty years. Louis XV, it turned out, was a monarch who would neither rule nor let anyone else rule. This stultifying indecision became a permanent feature of French public life, for it was the political expression of a cleft that ran deep in the king's character. Heir apparent since the age of two and king from the age of five, Louis grew up as the public ritual figure that his great-grandfather had meant the French monarch to be. But the heir reacted schizophrenically to the legacy: he clung to the plenitude of royal power and prerogatives as his by unquestionable right, and he hated all the business associated with the kingship. After Fleury's death, consequently, he would have no more chief minister, nor would he direct or coordinate the government himself. Bored with all affairs of state, he simply permitted each department to run itself, its insulation broken only by sporadic and fortuitous interference from a changing panel of favorites.

Probably the most constant and possibly the most beneficial of these

Louis XV. *The French Bourbon's alternation of political indifference with sporadic meddling in affairs of state dissipated the popular good will which good looks, native intelligence, and the peaceful prosperity of his early regime had secured for him and his dynasty.*

extra-political interlopers who entered into the political vacuum left and filled by the King's fancy was the notorious Madame de Pompadour (1721–1764), royal mistress from 1745—for five years in fact, and fourteen more in name. More intelligent than generally reputed, she balanced her well-publicized extravagance by her encouragement of literature and the arts and by her patronage of liberal intellectuals. Yet she had persons rather than policies as channels of her public influence. She practiced, indeed, a kind of royal favoritism in the second degree. Even within this personal orbit she was only moderately successful in eliciting desired actions from the King. Orry, the Controller-general whom she resented, she could get fired, but not the Count d' Argenson (1696–1754), the war minister whom she hated—at least not for twelve years. Nor was she able to get action brought against the Jesuits, whose influence at court she passionately opposed. Their expulsion in 1762 was welcome to her, but it was not a consequence of her hostility. Again, she could not protect her favorite Controller-general, Machault, when his reform policy—which she backed—was at stake, although she did succeed in getting him dismissed as naval minister later when he seemed to intrigue against her personally. Certainly it is true that her positive political power has been overestimated, but it can hardly be denied that in more senses than one she contributed to the distraction of the government.

Louis himself had but two interests that could bestir him to sporadic political activity—his hostility to Jansenism and his concern for the independence of Poland—and these stemmed more from family prejudice than

Madame de Pompadour. *Revised estimates make the mistress of Louis XV less sensual and less influential than was formerly thought and they show more appreciation for her intellectual tastes and for the real protection she afforded* philosophes.

from national policy (the first from the legacy of Louis XIV and the second from the Polish heritage of Louis XV's queen, Maria Leszczyńska, 1703–1768). To the sins of omission which were the continuing results of imperious boredom were added parallel sins of commission. On the few items of public business with which he did concern himself he tended to be devious rather than direct, a tendency which led to the proliferation rather than the coordination of agents purportedly executing the king's sovereign will. When he dabbled in foreign affairs he used a personal and covert organization of secret agents that confused and at times even opposed the regular organs and policies of French diplomacy. When domestic opposition to the policies of his own government became so strident as to disturb his indifference and sour his pleasures, he tended to remove the source of the annoyance simply by giving in to it, thereby endowing the opposition with a *de facto* veto upon the administration and preventing any consistent policy in government.

After Fleury, then, there was no force in the French state to prevent the issues of social crisis that had been suppressed by Louis XIV and assuaged thereafter from festering and erupting into sporadic political disorder. The war against Austria and Great Britain that Fleury had not wanted ended in 1748, but only to initiate the effects that Fleury had feared from it. In 1749, the Controller-general, Jean Baptiste de Machault d'Arnouville (1701–1794), member of the judicial aristocracy by birth but of the royal bureaucracy by career (he had been an *intendant*—royal district agent— before becoming controller-general), instituted a new direct tax of 5 per cent, called the *vingtième* ("twentieth"), on all incomes, from landed and mobile property alike, to succeed the wartime *dixième* ("tithe") and help pay for the late war. No doctrinaire but rather a rigid, logical, and practical administrator, Machault came to his edict from the simple observation that the deficit, once more becoming chronic with the resumption of French belligerence, could be made up only with the permanent submission of the formerly exempt classes to regular taxation. Unlike the *capitation* and the *dixième* that had preceded it, the *vingtième* was a peacetime tax and was accompanied by a newly trained corps of royal tax inspectors to provide for its equal administration. Supported in general by the merchants, Machault retained the support of the King long enough to fend off the protests from the judicial aristocracy in the *parlements* and the landed aristocracy in the provincial estates, but when the assembly of the French clergy, dominated by its hierarchy, added its remonstrance, the will of the King broke. In December, 1751, he formally exempted the clergy from the *vingtième*, and with the principle of equality thus fundamentally violated, the other privileged corporations quickly acquired their customary share of immunities, simply passing the *vingtième* along with the *taille* on to the peasantry for payment.

The resumption of the struggle over taxation, and the frustration of its reform, signalized both the growth of the financial problem into a continuing drain upon the monarchy and the united front of the privileged orders against any attempt of the bureaucracy to resolve it by equalizing the burden. But the active participation of both the entire nobility and the clergy and the overt primacy of the latter in the corporate resistance to the reform obscured a second significant development implicit in the conflict: the rise of the judicial nobility to preeminence among the privileged orders. This shift of influence within the aristocracy implied a shift of the aristocracy as such from a traditional to a popular defense of privilege, for it was precisely with its formulation now of a progressive and popular appeal that the judicial branch became spokesman for the whole aristocracy. Arguing from its distinctive constitutional position as direct organ of the sovereign power for the declaration of law, and from its distinctive social position as the most functional and most recently elevated service aristocracy out of the commonalty, the judicial nobility claimed to be the modern heirs of the ancient Estates-General and thus to represent the entire nation as the guarantor of its fundamental laws.

Having ascribed to themselves a unique position among the defenders of privilege in the tax conflict, the *parlements* assumed the same role in the renewed Jansenist conflict. Erupting in 1751, simultaneously with the climax of the tax struggle, the renewed ecclesiastical struggle pitted against each other the lay and clerical aristocracies whose collaboration was about to gain the day for their common financial exemptions. Once more, just as they had twenty years before, the Ultramontane hierarchy opened the fight by attempting to coerce the clergymen who still refused to accept the bull *Unigenitus,* and once more the *parlements* took up their defense. But here the historical resemblance stopped. The form of coercion now chosen by the clerical hierarchy—the requirement from the laity, under penalty of excommunication, of "tickets of confession" issued by priests who accepted *Unigenitus*—obviously broadened the conflict beyond the clergy and strengthened the claim of the *parlements* to a rightful jurisdiction. The *parlementaires* did not this time fall back before either the displeasure of the King or the popular disorders fomented by their resistance to King and Church. The conflict was in fact never resolved. It was prosecuted in full bitterness for some six years. Priests refused sacraments to Jansenists and were prosecuted by the *parlements*; the King threatened the *parlementaires* and issued decrees evoking all such cases to more submissive tribunals; the *parlements* refused to register such decrees, were dispersed by the King's order, and—as the court dockets overflowed, the pamphleteering war sharpened, and the urban disorders rose—were recalled by the King's order. Not until the outbreak of war in 1756 and an assassination attempt on Louis XV in January, 1757, did Madame de Pompadour's efforts at mediation bring a truce. But it was a truce that resolved none of the issues in the conflict. The internecine struggle between the Church and the courts, the two main institutions of privilege, was to continue through the expulsion of the Jesuits in 1762 until the end of the autocratic and aristocratic regime which was necessary to both but which they both thus helped to end.

By mid-century the pattern of the eighteenth-century French monarchy lay exposed. It was riven by a division between the divergent requirements of the national community and the corporate aristocracy that were its dual supports. It was riven further by a division between the different corporations of this aristocracy, and each of these corporations in turn itself issued contradictory claims both to exercise the powers of the sovereign and to enjoy immunity from control by the crown. These successive divisions not only affected the relations of the state and the society but were themselves reflected within the state itself with the result that no organ of the state was itself unified enough to reverse the process. In a France where only the accident of a strong king could compel unity, and only a policy of peace abroad could perpetuate the delicate balances of social and political division—in such a France, a Louis XV reigned over a government whose only consistent policy was commitment to war.

CHAPTER 4

The Kings at Home:
The Ascending Powers, 1714-1748

THAT STATES with internal political systems as different as Great Britain's on the one hand and Prussia's and Russia's on the other should have risen to great-power status in the first half of the eighteenth century testifies both to the stubborn variety of all historical experience and to the abstract character of what was common in the sundry examples of state building. The obvious political facts, certainly, were such as to warrant the usual classification of the constitutional island-monarchy and the two continental autocracies as opposite extremes of the European political spectrum. According to this overt scheme, the implications of the Glorious Revolution, confirmed by the circumstances of the Hanoverian succession a generation later (1714), made Great Britain into the very model of a limited monarchy at the very same time as Prussia and Russia, untroubled either by the tradition of fundamental laws or by the autonomy of the subordinate authorities nestling under them, were replacing France as the archetypes of absolute monarchy. Corresponding to these differences in political systems, moreover, were the differences in social conditions to which these political systems were the respective appropriate responses. Thus the British blend of monarchy and representative government can be seen as the most potent form of state for a commercially integrated society which specialized in the production of ships and services and which required a government authoritarian enough to defend and further trading interests abroad and respectful enough of property rights to command the confidence of the mercantile community at home. The administrative autocracies of Prussia and Russia, on the other hand, were the most efficient possible instruments of collective power for territories whose historic divisions, artificial connections, and economically localized communities offered few points of social cohesion.

The importance of the differences in conditions and institutions between the constitutional and the absolutist states can hardly be overestimated, not only for what they obviously meant in the subsequent history of east and west but less obviously for their schizophrenic effect upon the typical eighteenth-century man, who was attracted simultaneously to constitutionalism and to authoritarian monarchy. And yet, although this dual attraction complicated eighteenth-century political attitudes, the commitment of the same men to constitutionalism and absolutism at the same time pointed to a political reality common to both. This reality was the unity of the governing organs, which, regardless of the differences in their number and names in the different countries, collaborated effectively and intentionally in the common achievement of diplomatic and military power.

The distinctive organs and forms of government exhibited by each of these new great powers reflected the historic differences of location, circumstances, and cultural values that were forming each of these states into a separate nation. But the parallel coordination of these organs and forms of government also reflected an important historical process—the impact of competition among states, actualized by war or the continuous threat of war, as a general force for rationalizing and modernizing the political relations among institutions within the separate nations. The homogenizing role of international politics in the molding of the new great powers that arose during this period is easily visible in the cases of the Russian and Prussian administrative monarchies, where the new needs were literally translated into new institutions. It is discernible too in the more difficult and obscure British case, where intangible conventions and relations long prevalent among older institutions were now revised under the pressure of European war and overseas rivalries.

RUSSIA

Peter the Great had revolutionized the old Russian state and society in a series of reflex responses to international military and diplomatic competition. But his creation was so much a product of his personal force and the force of the extraordinary circumstances in which he had embroiled Russia that the form and the relations of the institutions which would make the revolution permanent remained a question for the future. Between the death of Peter in 1725 and the accession of Catherine II ("the Great") in 1762 these institutions took the basic shape which they would retain for almost two centuries. The six monarchs who ascended the throne in this interval reigned but did not rule, and thus the relations of government and society could find their own level. Of the three emperors—who reigned for a scant four years out of the thirty-seven—Peter II (ruled 1727–1730) was an adolescent dupe, Ivan VI (ruled 1740–1741) an infant, and Peter III (ruled 1762) an infantile "monster," as his aunt the Tsarina Elizabeth called him.

It was, then, an age of empresses in Russia, or more precisely—since they had personal commitments but no political interests—of favorites and factions. However varied their characters and attachments, the reigns of the ignorant and ailing Catherine I (ruled 1725–1717), the bitter and cruel Anna (ruled 1730–1740), and the charming but capricious Elizabeth (ruled 1741–1762), alternating with those of their short-lived male kin, resulted in the relaxation of actual royal authority and in the resurgence of aristocratic influence. But in Russia as in the rest of the European states which retained or acquired great-power status in the eighteenth century, the revitalization of the nobility was deceptive. In Russia no less than in France the revival took peculiar forms that made it something quite different from the regression toward the feudal decentralization with which the aristocracy had been traditionally associated.

Certainly the leading events of the period testified to the expanded public role that was being assumed by the Russian nobility. In the absence of a fixed rule of succession, the accession of emperors and empresses alike usually depended on the toleration or revolution of the palace guard—the worst kind of elective monarchy, as one contemporary characterized it. Again, not only did the older noble families strive—successfully in institutions like the exclusive cadet schools established in 1731—to reassert their precedence over the new service aristocracy, but the post-Petrine regimes progressively alleviated the service aristocracy's own compulsory obligations. Thus state service was limited to twenty-five years and leaves and exemptions to care for family estates were provided, and finally nobiliary compulsory service as such was abolished in 1762. Other edicts consolidated and extended the rights of noble lords over their serfs: the ownership of peopled estates became the exclusive privilege of the aristocracy, and a land-credit bank was set up to finance the cultivation of such estates; Peter the Great's provision for individual peasant emancipation through army enlistment was revoked; to the recruiting and taxing powers which Peter had conferred upon the lords was now added the authorization for the lords to enserf peasantry through inscription on their tax lists at their own pleasure, to supervise the conduct of their serfs, and to decree punishments for them—including deportation.

But closer inspection reveals that all these aristocratic gains were victories not at the expense of the state but in behalf of the state. They were, indeed, the results of a *de facto* agreement by monarchy and the combined nobility that the nobility would be the prime agents of the absolute state. Thus the weight of the palace guard invariably came down on the side of autocracy, crystallizing at the very center of the state the alliance between the Crown and a combination of the newer and the lower aristocracies. The decisive affirmation of this alliance came as early as 1730, when the group of old great nobles which had controlled Peter II and dominated the Supreme Privy Council tried, at Peter's death, to make Anna's accession conditional upon her subscription to the "Articles" drawn up by Prince Dimitri Golitsyn (1654–1738) and prescribing joint sovereignty of the Crown and a cooptative, oligarchic supreme council of the high nobility. In spite of Golitsyn's attempt to sweeten this plan for a nobiliar *coup d'état* by presenting it as a constitutional reform based on revived assemblies of estates, it furnished the occasion for the actual cooperation of the service and the lesser landed aristocracy with the monarchy. The palace guard and the country nobility, fortuitously in Moscow for a royal wedding that had been called off and left them with nothing to do, combined to reject the "Articles" of the old families and to install Anna as an absolute monarch. The counterpart of this commitment to absolutism, as the spoilers' projects and proposals on the occasion made clear, was their affirmation of their role as servants-in-chief of the autocracy.

The coup and countercoup of 1730 furnish the key to the meaning of the aristocratic resurgence in Russia during the era which ended in 1762 with the abolition of compulsory service and the accession of Catherine II (ruled 1762–1796). The weakness of the monarchs during this period did not signify the dissipation of sovereign authority in favor of aristocratic immunities, but the depersonalization of that authority in favor of the collective institutions of the state. Not only did the bureaucratic structure of administration by boards—the set of nine functional colleges under a Senate—instituted by Peter the Great persist and, at least in terms of quantity of business, expand during the first half of the eighteenth century, but the ambitions of favorites and factions tended to be embodied in a superinstitution which, under varying titles, was an instrument for the direction of the bureaucratic machine. Known under Catherine I and Peter II as the Supreme Privy Council, under Anna as the Cabinet of Ministers, and under Elizabeth as the Conference, it associated nobles and high bureaucrats in the formulation of unified policy.

In the country at large, similarly, the increased powers and privileges of the nobles over serfs and estates were not concessions to their corporate rights or their traditional jurisdictions—for it was the distinctive quality of the Russian aristocracy that it was invested with neither—but rather assignments of authority to them as local agents of the state. Russian serfdom has been characterized as an institution not of private law, as in the rest of Europe, but of public law, since it was a legal relationship imposed by the state to fix and to reach the floating population of a vast domain. Certainly the shift in emphasis, which accompanied the extension of Russian serfdom during the eighteenth century, from the real—*i.e.* propertied —to the personal bondage of peasant to lord confirms this interpretation, since it shows servile status to come with the development of peasant-lord relations from private obligation to civil obedience. From this point of view, the progressive alleviations of the compulsory service obligations which were granted the aristocracy after the death of Peter the Great, like the repeal of his legislation on entailed estates and the reversion to subdivision of estates, may be seen not as private or corporate exemptions extorted by a recalcitrant nobility, but rather as a shift of governmental policy changing from feudal to social the kind of service required from the aristocracy.

Several developments favored the new partnership of autocracy and aristocracy. The nobility grew into the habit of state service and made it an accepted custom in the aristocratic way of life. At the same time, the westernized education to which preparation for state service exposed the nobility began to produce an aristocratic cultural elite. Encouraged by these movements, the government tended increasingly to shift the chief weight of the aristocracy's role from compulsory service in the regular offices of the administration, where it was decreasingly needed, to the more diffuse control by the state of the society at large, where it was increasingly needed. The period between the great Peter and the great Catherine thus becomes the period in which the Russian nobility was weaned from its administrative swaddling clothes, inculcated with broader concepts of state service, and thus prepared for its subsequent role as the social complement of political autocracy.

PRUSSIA

The rise of Prussia to great-power status in the first half of the eighteenth century paralleled in many ways that of Russia. Both were "northern" monarchies—that is, benefactors of the Swedish decline and newcomers to the competitive world of European politics. Both were expansive states—externally oriented, and molded by the conditions of international competition. Both found their chief internal problem to lie in the organization of the variety of territories added piecemeal to the original centers of Brandenburg and Muscovy, respectively. Both, finally, responded to these external and domestic pressures by creating bureaucratic autocracies which were originally imposed by the imperious wills of forceful monarchs and subsequently maintained by a network of royal administrative agencies that absorbed every power of the state.

But despite the similarity of general type, there was enough variation in the situations, the social structures, and the action-sequences of the two states for them to represent different species within the same type of administrative absolutism. As old member of the Holy Roman Empire as well as new rising power on the Baltic, Brandenburg-Prussia was involved by the simple facts of past history and present geography more intimately and continuously than its eastern neighbor in the culture, society, and politics of western Europe. From this involvement stemmed the distinctiveness of the political forms which its rulers adopted—forms which were to leave a permanent impress upon the Prussian and ultimately upon the

German state. The individuality of these political forms had to do first with the special timing of the Prussian Hohenzollern dynasty's creation of centralized institutions, in comparison to the sequence of actions typical of the rest of Europe; and second, with the special relationship of the Prussian state to the Prussian society which this historical timing produced.

The actual pattern of events which marked the Prussian kings' consolidation of their power minimized the habit of empirical response to immediate competitive conditions that characterized the politics of so many European states and maximized the habit of rational planning for potential competition that was ultimately to become so prominent a feature of the German reputation. The great wars which ended the seventeenth century and created the conditions for the basic political institutions of the eighteenth in most of the European states had no such direct effect upon Prussia. Obversely, the postwar period after 1721, which in most of Europe was a time of aristocratic resurgence, with no expansion of governmental powers, fomented a drastic extension of royal controls in Prussia. This Prussian counterpoint stemmed partly from the accidents of royal succession and personality. After the shrewd and forceful Great Elector, Frederick William, had initiated Brandenburg into the European pattern of absolutism in direct response to the Thirty Years' War, the successive reigns of the ineffectual Brandenburg Elector Frederick III during the Wars of the League of Augsburg and of the Spanish Succession, and of the imperious King Frederick William I for the most part in a period of peace for Prussia, reversed the usual sequence of royal strength and weakness which other successful European states found appropriate to the sequence of war and peace. In King Frederick William's political personality, indeed, the contrast between the energetic authoritarianism of his domestic rule and the timid pacifism of his foreign policy demonstrated the Hohenzollern pattern of centralizing the government in preparation for rather than in response to war.

But factors more fundamental than accidents of personality were involved in the distinctive timing of the Prussian development. Both the state's Janus-faced involvement in the relations of eastern and western Europe and the geographic discontinuity of the Hohenzollern territories turned the Prussian rulers from the external to the internal extension of their authority and thereby reversed the usual pattern of state building.

Prussia fought in the War of the League of Augsburg, the War of the Spanish Succession, and—briefly—in the Great Northern War. The failure of this participation to produce in Prussia the kind of immediate and far-reaching political reorganization it produced elsewhere was accountable as much to the position and tradition of the state as to the frivolity or timidity of its kings. Prussian territorial ambitions at the time were directed primarily toward Swedish Pomerania in the north and Austrian-held Silesia in the east, but the exposed position of the isolated Hohenzollern possessions

Frederick William I. *Organizer of Prussian absolutism.*

along the Rhine and Brandenburg's membership in the threatened Holy Roman Empire combined to push the Brandenburg Elector Frederick III (from 1701 Frederick I, King in Prussia) into the anti-French and pro-Austrian policy of belligerency in the two western wars. It was as much because the Prussian interest in these wars was marginal and the participation of Prussians reluctant as because King Frederick's tastes were lavish and his political habits slothful that the Prussian government risked military dependence by financing the war through foreign subsidies rather than risk the domestic consequences of increased taxation and the institutional reorganization it usually required.

The entry of Frederick William I (ruled 1713–1740) into the Great Northern War during 1714 was, indeed, more conformable to the contemporary assessment of Prussian vital interests; but the Prussian participation was limited to the brief siege of Stralsund, and the Prussian acquisition of Stettin and Western Pomerania was more the gift of Peter the Great than the firm war aim of the Prussian king. Hence the immediate effect of this war too upon the state was minimal. Since, moreover, Frederick William's subsequent peace policy was centered on the now traditional Austrian entente and since his ambitions were limited to the lawful realization of equally traditional dynastic claims upon Jülich and Berg along the Rhine, the new style of power politics can scarcely be said to have infected this old-fashioned German prince.

And yet this Frederick William I was the very king who, in these same years, established the most modern administration in Europe, trained the bureaucracy to run it, and thereby fathered the Prussian state—all this, moreover, with a deliberate focus upon the growth and financial independence of a standing army for which his foreign policy envisaged no use. This riddle of a war machine created for a pacific policy, of internal innovation in the service of international tradition, was in part, of course, an expression of the ultimate riddle that was the political personality of Frederick William I. A tyrant to his family, a despot to his people, a fussbudget to his Emperor, an obedient servant to his God, and a driving executive to his officials, Frederick William merged the traits of ancestral patriarch, divine-right ruler, and rational administrator in a blend that reflects the mixed qualities of the age. He has been described as a violent, passionate, and limited man who, fundamentally unsure of himself, held all the more stubbornly and unqualifiedly to the few simple truths and precepts which the Lutheran pietism he preferred (formal Calvinist though he was) and the royal absolutism he preached and practiced afforded him. But the riddle remains: hating and fearing whatever smacked of reason and innovation, from theology to all things French, this throwback to sixteenth-century princely paternalism could yet find himself completely at home with the general policies that made a rational system of the Prussian administration. Thus he interposed between his aristocracy and himself a categorical barrier that was in everything but name the modern principle of exclusive sovereignty.

But if the surprising internal reorganization of the Prussian state in peacetime owed much to the personal accident of a weak war king and a strong postwar king, it owed even more to the basic needs and opportunities afforded by the Prussian population. The people were too poor, scattered, and caste-ridden either to supply immediate resources for piecemeal wartime levies or to resist the systematic peacetime organization and exploitation of their resources for long-range military needs.

Thus the reign of King Frederick William I established the characteristic pattern of Prussia's permanent institutions: it was military in principle even when it was pacific in fact, and it made military considerations not merely a seasonal or external, but a continuous and habitual feature of the Prussian state and society. The most spectacular tangible results of Frederick William I's reign were all connected with the army, and they were accomplished only by his making it the end and model of his government. Between the beginning and the end of his reign he doubled the size of the Prussian army from forty to eighty thousand men, guaranteed its independence from foreign subsidies by carving a secure financial base for it out of normal revenue, and even accumulated a considerable war chest for its support in the event of hostilities. To mobilize such human resources from a state of some two million people inhabiting an area poor in natural resources required a political concentration of social energies that was remarkable for the age.

Not only did the King assign an unparalleled 80 per cent of the state's revenues to the army but he exerted the entire force of his political and social position toward its conversion from a hired service into an absolutely loyal instrument of the crown. He created the Prussian officer corps and made it into the aristocratic pillar of the state it was thenceforward to be, by abolishing both recruiting contracts and the feudal type of military obligation, reserving officers' posts exclusively for the nobility, forbidding them foreign service, granting to the military a definite precedence over civil officials, and adopting the officers' uniform as his own daily habit. With the *Junkers* of the sword thus converted from feudal vassals into military bureaucrats, Frederick William acquired reliable agents for the recruitment of a native militia through the enactment of the canton system in 1733. Far from the universal conscription for which it was later to serve as a precedent, the canton system exempted the privileged classes, propertied citizens of the towns, and workers in loosely defined essential industries, but the peasant boys and journeymen who were regularly enrolled on the recruitment list of the neighborhood—*i.e.* canton—regiment and conscripted according to need anchored the state deep in the ·Prussian society. The incessant drill, in which this king with the proverbial sergeant's temperament delighted, worked officers and men alike into an efficient political as well as tactical machine.

The Prussian army exercised two kinds of formative influence upon the state. First, military standards entered into the civil administration, and this for the simplest of all reasons—because at the top and the bottom of the two hierarchies there was a personal identity between the military and civil officials. This was clearly the case at the apex, for the same king who created the characteristic Prussian institution of the officer corps also created, at the same time and in its image, the equally characteristic institution of the Prussian bureaucracy. Through appointment by examination, through a strict system of accountability enforced by the king's own regulations, his inspectors (the "fiscals"), and his punitive displeasure, Frederick William created an instrument of civil government that paralleled the military in its blend of personal and public loyalty to him and in its disciplined power over the rest of the society.

Nor did his system of "cabinet government" differ essentially from a chain of military command, since it consisted of the King's governing directly through the department heads whom he called individually to his *Kabinett* ("chamber") for the purpose of eliciting reports and giving orders. At the lowest end of the hierarchy, where the bureaucracy met the public, the military style had a similar personal base. The posts of the lower officialdom were habitually filled from the ranks of former noncommissioned army officers, and it is hardly surprising that the virtues of corporate devotion and honesty were balanced by the tendency to petty tyranny so often ingrained in the breed.

The second kind of military influence upon the Prussian state went through the institutions of civil government which were required by the needs of the army. Prussia, indeed, demonstrates more transparently than any other state the logical sequence that led from military requirements to the general centralization of government. Frederick William's primary concern, during the first decade of his reign, was the provision of an adequate tax base for the expanded army that he planned. For the efficient collection of what taxes there were he embarked on a throughgoing reorganization of the central and provincial financial agencies, aimed at establishing greater rationality and uniformity. But because tax yields in a poor state like Prussia were depressingly low in comparison with the scope of the military project, these financial agencies were commissioned with powers of economic development—*e.g.* the right to grant licenses, exemptions, subsidies—and control for the purpose of increasing the taxable resources. In order, finally, to secure the civic conditions required for an economy directed and in part operated by the government, the economic jurisdiction of these royal organs was broadened into a general competence over internal affairs.

This unbroken chain of cause and effect that led from the Prussian army into the very heart of the governmental system took explicit form both in the treatment of the Prussian aristocracy and in the structure of the royal administration itself. The same legislation that abolished the anachronistic feudal military obligations of the aristocracy also abolished the conjoined conditional tenure of their estates and replaced the military condition with a tax upon the same estates, which were now recognized as absolute private property. This special tax was obviously deemed the modern counterpart of the old knights' service, and was the only tax to which the aristocracy was subject.

Analogously, the development of the royal administration under Frederick William was essentially the story of the growth of military agencies into standard civilian bodies, exercising financial and economic functions which can be considered as war waged by other means. Frederick William's great administrative achievement was to merge into one uniform authority, on both the central and provincial levels, the two separate financial hierarchies which he found in existence and in competition upon his accession. The hierarchies administered, respectively, the traditional dues from the king's own domain and the public taxation which had originated in and retained the character of military levies; they were, accordingly, called "domain chambers" and "war commissariats." In establishing the supremacy of a central joint organ—the "General Directory," to abbreviate its mouthfilling German title, *General-Ober-Finanz-Kriegs-und-Domänen-Direktorium*—Frederick William assured that the standards of the war commissariats would prevail in the merger. Not only were the provincial domain chambers, which had enjoyed far-reaching autonomy, now definitely subordinated to the new central body, but the officials who were henceforward to dominate the state's administration on the local level came from the war-commissarial branch.

Even before the accession of King Frederick William the local war commissioners in town and countryside separated, as they became permanent officials. They became *Steuerräte* ("tax counselors") in the towns and *Landräte* ("county counselors") in the countryside. These officials were thus specialized because of the age-old economic differentiation and social distinction between the burgher caste which dominated the Prussian towns and the aristocratic caste which ran the Prussian countryside, and because of the difference in the kind of taxes to which each area was consequently liable. The urban tax counselors were simply royal officials whose primary job was to collect centrally imposed excise taxes. The rural county counselors combined in their persons the offices of royal appointee and local representative—in practice, of the local aristocracy—for the assessment of the "contribution," as this permanent land tax upon the county's peasantry was still misleadingly called in memory of its equally misnamed sixteenth-century origins in the occasional "contribution" voted, upon the ruler's special request, by the local assemblies of the exempt aristocracy on behalf of the peasantry who had actually to pay it. Under Frederick William I it was the urban tax counselor who made royal sovereignty a fact over the nominal rights of the decadent urban oligarchies, and it was under the same king that the royal capacity of the rural county counselor, despite all local attachments, was confirmed.

Much in these reforms recalls the political reorganization of France under Louis XIV and of Russia under Peter the Great. Like the work of these illustrious forebears, Frederick William's achievement was military in its purpose, centralizing in its means, aristocratic in its preferences for the army, bourgeois in its preferences for the civil service, and practical in its style. But there were shadings in both the purpose and the structure of the Prussian reform that set it off from precedents and contemporary parallels. Frederick William built his state around a powerful army not to fight with it, but as he said, to be able to negotiate diplomatically and make himself heard. In part this caution was a response to the temporal circumstance that saw Prussia already surrounded by powerful states even while he was only building its army, but even more it was a response to the internal conditions that were reflected in the distinctively comprehensive quality of monarchical sovereignty in Prussia. Where the conflict of bureaucratic and corporate elements within the French state obstructed any rational system of government and where the triumph of the bureaucratic service state in Russia absorbed traditional social groups wholly into the state and frustrated any direct connection between the state and the rest of the society, the Prussian system was unified in itself and, particularly through its officer corps and rural officialdom, continuous with the traditional aristocratic organization of society.

The reasons are not far to seek. Where France was rich in people and goods and Russia rich in people and land, Prussia was blessed in none of the three. Where France and Russia governed contiguous territories from the natural center that had expanded through them, Prussia was spread discontiguously across northern Germany in a congeries of distinct territories whose only center was the personal identity of a ruler who chanced to reside in Berlin. In Prussia, therefore, government had to supply, through the artifice of reason, all the connections that nature, history, or social intercourse had helped to provide elsewhere. There were, to be sure, in the municipal and aristocratic corporations autonomous social connections that Russia did not have. But in Prussia these were local, or at most provincial, connections which still had to be directed to all collective purposes by the central government of the state, whereas the aristocracy of Russia, however unorganized apart from the state, yet remained through the state a national aristocracy. Thus in the very same age that witnessed the aggressive struggle of aristocracies for national power and influence all over Europe, Frederick William I simply had no all-Prussian aristocracy with which to contend. When he excluded the aristocrats from central posts of civil administration and when he threatened them with his rights of "sovereignty," as he frequently did, it was precisely against their national ambitions rather than their local privileges that he acted. For the rest, the preferred position he gave them in his regional administration and in his peasant army and the full police powers over the peasantry that he permitted them on their estates indicate the successful juncture of the unified Prussian state with the fragmented Prussian society.

When the son—soon to be known as Frederick the Great—whom Frederick William had misunderstood and mistreated ascended the Prussian throne in 1740, he set about reversing the peculiarities of his father's position, and in respect to war, aristocracy, and western culture, put Prussia into the mainstream of European life. But the individuality of the historical and social pattern which had been forged in the first third of the eighteenth century persisted: in Prussia internal integration would precede aggression and the aristocracy would remain politically reliable and socially preferred as the primary channel between king and country.

GREAT BRITAIN

The society and politics of early-eighteenth-century Britain were closer to those of its continental contemporaries than the distinctive qualities which we have learned to associate with the island kingdom would lead us to believe. The lead in wealth over France and the Netherlands was achieved only during the eighteenth century itself. Urbanization and industrialization, together with the concomitant social traits of self-restraint and orderliness, became predominant only in the Victorian era of the nineteenth century. Parliamentary government, with its corollaries of a cabinet system, a prime minister, and the sovereignty of an elected House of Commons, was a nineteenth-century development, while the separation of powers, so famous in constitutional theory from the time of John Locke, is generally deemed to have corresponded to British political reality neither then nor ever after. The British society and polity, in the early eighteenth century, was violent in temperament, aggressive in disposition, rural in primary occupation, oligarchic in structure, conservative in the aims and royalist in the initiation of policy: it resembled, in short, one or another of its rivals across the Channel.

And yet there were gradations of national distinction, even beyond the obvious factor of geographical insularity, that foreshadowed the special role that Britain would play among the eighteenth-century powers. By the end of the seventeenth century, two of its economic developments were crystallizing into social effects that gave a peculiar slant to the British version of the common European social hierarchy. The extraordinarily large share of overseas trade in the British economy, together with an improvement of agricultural techniques, promoted the general increase of wealth, of domestic commercial and industrial activity, and of the enterprising spirit that would establish Britain's economic primacy by the end of the eighteenth century. These developments, moreover, combined with the new infusions into the aristocracy from the political convulsions of the seventeenth century to create an uncommon strand in the British governing class and in its relations with the lower orders. Although still based upon the ownership of land, the predominant section of this governing class was not only itself favorably oriented toward and actually participant in the mobile life of commerce but also joined in a *de facto* political alliance with the commoners of the mercantile community.

It was this ambiguous position of Great Britain on the periphery of the European world, at once sharing and modifying its characteristic institutions, that was given permanent shape in the legislation and conventions established in the period between the Glorious Revolution in 1688 and the resignation of Robert Walpole in 1742. Even the circumstances under which these fundamental arrangements were worked out reflected the combination of insular and European elements in the British social and political structure. For the much-touted "Britannic constitution" of the eighteenth century, usually not understood at home, misunderstood on the Continent, and prized as a model in both arenas, emerged both as a settlement of the local revolution and as a response to Britain's international involvement, first in the continental wars against Louis XIV and then in the competition with the European colonial powers. Under these general conditions, the particular British forms which this constitution enshrined developed under conditions common to all the great states of Europe. ·

The Revolutionary Settlement (1689–1714)

The revolutionary settlement that was gradually worked out between the Declaration of Right of 1689 (legalized as the Bill of Rights) and the Septennial Act of 1716 marked the start of a political continuity which has persisted to this very day. It set up what looked like an inimitable constitutional pastiche. The constitution itself was a mystifying blend of law and of conventional devices to make the law work. The law of the constitution, moreover, was passed in the way of ordinary legislation and was formally indistinguishable from regular revocable statute law. Although its chief pillars—the Bill of Rights, the main clauses of the Act of Settlement of 1701, and the Septennial Act of 1716—soon came, in what has since been characterized as the English fashion, to be especially reverenced as clauses in the unwritten constitution, it was never decided whether their special status was one of irrevocable fundamental law or of revocable contract between country and monarch.

The one clear political result of this mélange of prescription and convenience was the general consensus on the supremacy of Parliament. Four crucial governmental activities were subordinated to acts of Parliament: accession to the Crown (Declaration of Rights and Act of Settlement), elections (Triennial Act of 1694, replaced by Septennial Act of 1716), war and peace (a corollary in practice of Parliament's exclusive power of taxation), and—most important—the determination of what was and what was not subject to legislation and therefore to Parliament (Bill of Rights)—in legal parlance, the decisive jurisdiction over jurisdictions. But with this one generally comprehensible fact of parliamentary sovereignty, clarity ended. Parliament was not a thing but an abstraction, and when it came to giving practical effect to its theoretical preeminence the new British constitution began to seem like the obscure reshuffling of the ingredients in a peculiarly British political recipe.

Parliament had been—and still was—composed of three independent and equal organs—King, Lords, and Commons—each with a different root in the nation and with a different function in Parliament. Although composed by these three organs, moreover, Parliament could not be simply defined by them, since both King and Lords also exercised governmental functions outside and independent of Parliament. The essence of Parliament was thus not that it was a body with three organs but that it was a definite relationship among three authorities insofar as they were organs of it. The relationship which linked them was the law-making function, but beyond this function and beyond Parliament the king possessed the supreme executive and the Lords the supreme judicial power. It was because the King and Lords had extra-parliamentary functions and Commons did not, that the Commons became the chief spokesman of parliamentary claims in general and tended to be especially identified with Parliament.

This structure, with its mixture of functions in at least two of the three governing organs, antedated the Glorious Revolution. Although, moreover, the revolutionary period helped to identify as legislative, executive, and judicial, functions which had not been so classified before, still the subsequent changes in constitution did not separate in substance the powers

that it segregated in name. The revolutionary settlement did not rationalize the actual distribution of powers by assigning one kind of power to
each organ. Rather it distinguished, by name and in law, between the
powers that were exercised jointly and the powers that were not,
labeled the joint powers legislative, raised these joint legislative powers
to superiority over any and all of the powers exercised by the same organs
separately, shifted a few crucial powers from separate to joint exercise, but
for the rest left the traditional mélange of powers in each constitutional
organ as it had been. This meant that in the very process of establishing
the supremacy of Parliament as the seat of the joint legislative power, the
revolutionary settlement not only retained the mixture of powers in King
and Lords that tended to confuse legislative, executive, and judicial functions but compounded the confusion by conferring on the legislative power
a preeminence and a supervisory capacity that permitted incursions by
Parliament from its legislative base into executive and judicial functions.

Thus the King exercised both his exclusive prerogative and his joint parliamentary powers, and the line between them was tenuous indeed.
Although royal prerogative was now primarily executive and parliamentary
power primarily legislative, the prerogative still extended to such legislative
acts as the convocation, prorogation, and dissolution of Parliament; and the
Parliament of which he was a part acquired the power to fix the limits of
the sphere within which the exercise of the prerogative was, by definition,
unlimited. The House of Lords exercised both its exclusive jurisdiction as
high court of appeals and its share in parliamentary power, but here too
the line was hard to draw in view of the persistent tradition of the whole
Parliament as a "high court" for the declaration of the common law and
the protection of rights under it. The House of Commons, finally, coupled
with its share in parliamentary legislation its old judicial right to impeach
(with the approval of the Lords) the King's ministers and its new *de facto*
executive power, which stemmed from its legislative initiative in money
matters and from its legislative rights over foreign policy, the standing
army, and the conduct of war. Nor were mixtures of powers in the three
organs of government simply historical anachronisms. They were essential
to the functioning of the eighteenth-century constitution, for they were
rooted in the independent origins and powers of King, Lords, and Commons outside of Parliament—in the fundamental law of succession, the
prescriptive right of a hereditary council, and the electoral power of the
national community respectively—origins and powers which were the bases
of their mutual equality inside of Parliament.

This unwieldy structure made sense in its negative and parochial function of preventing a recurrence of the despotisms of either the King or the
Commons which had seemed so imminent during the seventeenth century.
But by the same token it seemed to run counter to the centralizing tendency which characterized the rising states of the late seventeenth and early

eighteenth centuries. The appearance, however, was deceptive, for if the legislation of the revolutionary settlement had as its primary goal and result a balance of powers that resolved a peculiarly English conflict, this same legislation also had a countervailing tendency toward the concentration of powers in response to the general European trend in this direction. And the conventions that made the laws work reinforced this tendency. Here indeed is the real meaning behind the apparently pedantic insistence on checks and balances rather than separation of powers as the underlying principle of the eighteenth-century British constitution. Whereas separation of powers would have meant divided sovereignty, checks and balances actually meant joint sovereignty. As the *Annual Register* would later summarize the system: "The impulsion, the soul . . . of the British government depends on the harmonious understanding and cooperation of all its members."

The fundamental laws of the revolutionary settlement laid down the practical basis for such cooperation by the simple device of making each of the parliamentary organs dependent upon the others. Thus not only did the dynasty owe its existence to an act of Parliament but the King was made dependent upon the houses of Parliament even in his lawful operations by virtue of the new parliamentary monopoly over the taxing power and because of the limits which the legal requirement of septennial elections placed upon the King's control over the House of Commons. Parliament itself, on the other hand, continued to owe its operational existence to the King and his prerogative, for within the limits set by the Septennial Act it was at his discretion that the Lords and Commons were convoked, prorogued, and dissolved. Thus was created a legal circuit of dependence in which each organ could fulfill its own functions only with the assistance or toleration of the others.

Within this framework of law the set of practices which hardened into persistent conventions tended overwhelmingly to be those which harmonized the operations of the three national authorities into one parliamentary sovereignty. Although these conventions assumed the precise forms which they were to hold through the eighteenth century only after the accession of the Hanoverians in 1714, they had their origins and received their characteristic unifying tenor in the wartime conditions accompanying the reigns of King William and Queen Anne between 1689 and 1714. Six important practices which were to become tacit clauses in the eighteenth-century British constitution originated during this period. The one tendency comon to them all was the conversion of divided powers into a single governing system and the assignment to each member of its own function in the activity of the whole.

First, to the King went a monopoly not only over the execution of policy but also over its initiation. The King chose and dismissed ministers, like the rest of his "servants," at his discretion, and the King's government made policy within the limits of legislative approval and financial support by Parliament. These royal functions were consolidated by William III, who insisted on keeping in his own hands military and foreign policy as well as the executive means to administer it. They became standard under the weaker Queen Anne, when, despite the monarch's personal frailty, they were sealed by the formal repeal, in 1705, of the Commons' attempt to subjugate the royal advisers through parliamentary control of the Privy Council.

Second, to the Commons went the great preponderance of the parliamentary legislative control over royal policy. The same war that confirmed the King's initiative in policy and administration expanded the Commons' legal right to initiate money bills into a general power to approve policy. The length and intensity of the war not only bred the habit of annual Parliaments to vote supplies but gave to Commons the lever to use this right as a means of expressing approval or disapproval of policy and to extend this right by a degree of parliamentary control over the expenditure of all revenues from extraordinary taxation—a continuously growing area of finance that came to include the entire military and naval budget after 1697. This *de facto* distribution of functions could, and occasionally did, lead to friction between King and Commons, but its actual effect tended more toward the complementarity than the opposition of powers. This was indicated by the actual evisceration of the monarch's discretion in the convocation of Parliament and by his (or her) surrender after 1708, in practice, of his parliamentary right to disapprove legislation.

Third, the right of the king's "placemen"—*i.e.* officeholders—to election into the Commons assured royal influence in the deliberations of that House and provided a solid core of Commons majorities in support of the King's governments. This relationship was worked out the hard way between 1692 and 1716 in a tug-of-war between the members of the Commons and supporters of the King's government. Of the sixteen bills introduced into the House during this period to assure the independence of the Commons by eliminating or significantly restricting the placemen eligible to sit in that House, only four became law—and these provided for enough exclusions (particularly of the lesser revenue officers) to prevent the Commons from being swamped by the beneficiaries of royal patronage but not enough to prevent the Commons from being continuously susceptible to management by government. However much an abuse this influence which the King's government could exercise within the House of Commons through patronage might appear, it actually operated through the eighteenth century as one of the sinews of British collective power.

Fourth, the system of royal influence in Parliament worked as well as it did essentially because it operated through still another convention that muted the potential conflict over it: the role of the Lords in mediating between King and Commons. Surprisingly, in view of their apparent eclipse during the seventeenth-century conflict between King and Commons, the Lords first established their claims to independence by playing an important part in the Glorious Revolution and then by asserting their parliamentary equality vis-à-vis both King William and the Commons. Then, with its own position thus reasserted, the House of Lords benefited from the need for a unified joint sovereign which the wars against Louis XIV demonstrated. This need stimulated practices which made the House of Lords both the reservoir of the King's ministers and the channel through which the ministers could influence elections to the House of Commons. For it was because of the Lords' influence over the boroughs (which elected almost three fourths of the members of the House of Commons) that the King's government, usually composed of coalitions among the great families in the Lords, could count on a majority in the Commons at the start of every new Parliament.

Fifth, the replacement of the Privy Council by the "cabinet" (alternatively called "cabinet council") as the monarch's chief advisory organ on policy was an extralegal development called into being by the new requirements of activity and efficiency in the central government. Ultimately it assisted in bringing about the collaboration of the houses of Parliament with the government. The existence of an unofficial group of advisers labeled "cabinet" or "cabinet council"—referring to consultations in the King's private chambers—went back to the earlier Stuarts, but only under the pressure of war did William III make frequent resort to it and did Anne institute it as a regularly convoked body. It was distinguished from the unwieldy Privy Council not only by its smaller numbers but by the exclusive focus on governmental function rather than on the traditional mixture of status and function as the criterion for attendance. Behind the shifting membership dependent on the royal discretion, it tended to be composed particularly of officeholders. Its orientation toward effective government was demonstrated both by its relegation of the Privy Council to largely honorific duties and by the emergence, already under Queen Anne, of a small inner cabinet constituted by the leading ministers to make decisions that the large cabinet simply endorsed.

To be sure, under the last Stuarts and throughout the eighteenth century this cabinet was a far cry from the modern institutions that have developed to associate the executive with the legislative powers in parliamentary systems of government. The eighteenth-century cabinet had no recognition—or even mention—in the law, no definite membership, no collective tenure or responsibility, no formal connection with political parties, and no dependence upon a prime minister beyond the informal influence which the leading minister might exercise, as a first among equals, upon the King, to whom each minister remained directly and individually responsible. As an unofficial body that smacked of cabal, moreover, the cabinet continued through the eighteenth century to be mistrusted by Commons, which saw in it an extralegal device for removing royal policy-making from parliamentary scrutiny. But if the eighteenth-century cabinet did help, in these respects, to keep the King's government independent of Parliament, it also contributed, in other respects, to their collaboration—a contribution that received reluctant recognition in the grumbling Commons' evasion of any fundamental challenge to the cabinet after that house gave up on its attempt to control the Privy Council in 1705. Behind this restraint lay the tacit acknowledgment by the Commons that the decisive role played by the heads of governmental departments and agencies in the cabinet rendered that body indirectly accountable to the Commons as the parliamentary organ that appropriated the money for those departments and agencies. The rise of the cabinet to executive preeminence thus furnished another occasion for the mutual cooperation of government and Parliament.

And finally, the distinctive shape assumed by the British party system in the wartime Parliaments of William and of Anne surprisingly abetted the harmonious relationship between monarch and Commons which it superficially seemed destined to frustrate. The Whig and Tory parties had risen during the factional strife of the restoration and were perpetuated after 1688 by the competition for preferment, the advocacy of different alternatives for the dynastic succession, and the conflict over war and peace before Utrecht. Each of these parties was based upon a combination of general principles, private loyalties, and personal ambitions which tended to work at cross purposes within each group and hence to moderate rather than to intensify party divisions. Thus, on questions of political principle, an undeniably fundamental opposition divided the Tories' belief in the divine right of kings, nonresistance to royal authority, and strict conformity to the established Anglican Church (High Church), from the Whigs' inclination toward parliamentary monarchy, resistance to royal transgressions of the law, and a latitudinarian or Low Church. And yet in practice the Tories' fidelity to the Church of England nullified their reverence for the sanctity of monarchy so thoroughly as to make possible the cooperation of their great majority with the Whigs in the crucial political actions against the Catholic Stuarts: the Glorious Revolution of 1688, the Act of Settlement of 1701 (prescribing the succession of Anne and the Hanoverians), and the actual acceptance of the Hanoverian George I in 1714. Again, the evolution of most Tory groups into the peace party and of most Whig groups into the war party under Queen Anne did not prevent the Tory Marlborough from collaborating with the Whigs for the further prosecution of the war or some Whig groups from collaborating with the Tory minister Robert Harley, Earl of Oxford (1661–1724), in the conclusion of peace.

Indeed, cutting clean across the Whig-Tory division and weakening its impact was the cleavage between the Court and Country parties, rooted primarily in the varying degrees of influence which the various members of Parliament had on the disposition of offices and favors by the Crown and its appointees. The Court party consisted of those, Whig and Tory alike, with actual or potential access to such offices and favors through their ties with ministers or other high officials. The Country party consisted of those, Whig and Tory alike, who were either gentry essentially independent of the Crown's influence or "out" politicians and their satellites with a policy of mobilizing opposition to get back "in."

The net result of these overlapping opinions and interests was a party lineup that formed, dissolved, and re-formed from issue to issue and from ministry to ministry. The bitter parliamentary debates and pamphleteering polemics that gave the illusion of a struggle between fixed party organizations actually used party labels as straw horses with which to dignify or brand the momentary position of an evanescent group, while in usual fact members of both major parties were temporarily aligned on either side of the dispute. Neither Whig nor Tory nor Court nor Country, in short, had any party organization, any party discipline, or any party program. Each was a party only in the sense that individuals so classified themselves by virtue of habitual political dispositions and/or associations. William made a deliberate policy of mixing Whigs and Tories in his ministries of the 1690's, an indication of their consensus at that time on the basic issues of the revolution and the war. Even when, in the following reign, the combination of Queen Anne's political indolence with the tendency of Whigs and Tories to divide on the issue of the war led ultimately to the all-Tory ministry of 1710–1714, the peculiar flexibility of the British party system served rather to abet than frustrate the support of the Commons for the government's peace policy. Beneath the surface of vociferous party squabbling, the mutual hostility between the two leading Tory ministers, Robert Harley and Henry St. John, Viscount Bolingbroke (1678–1751), was perhaps more serious an obstacle to forceful government than the conflict of parties. The government used the party conflict to its own advantage: Harley could attract the support of Whig groups to the ministry while the feud between Whig and Tory segments of the opposition kept them from joining forces against the ministry.

It is obvious that the function of any party system is to keep government accountable and thereby in restraint, but parties are also practical means for organizing support behind governments in a parliamentary regime—and it was this latter function that prevailed in Britain between the Glorious Revolution of 1688 and the accession of George III in 1760. The most telling evidence of this function was the fundamental attitude toward party as such held by the public figures—including party men—of the period. Party was universally denounced as "faction," connoting seditious conspiracy against the king. The British thus found themselves in the apparently paradoxical position of living with parties whose validity they rejected. But the anomaly is only apparent, and the explanation demonstrates the state-building orientation of the early parties. For parties were accepted as a means of identifying the actual or potential supporters of the King's government, and they were rejected as a means of grouping the opposition to the King's government. Only later in the eighteenth century, with the growing recognition of society's independent role as a source of political power, would the development of a "loyal opposition" permit the full acceptance of the idea of party.

Social Basis of the Settlement

These six unifying mechanisms, ensconced in the practice of the new parliamentary regime during the two and a half decades of war following upon the Glorious Revolution, outlasted both the martial influence and the dynasty under which they had been devised. Their longevity can be attributed in part to the British successes in the military and colonial competition with France and Spain, but institutions do not long draw their vitality from past achievements, and these unifying conventions had more persistent roots than the revolution and the wars that first helped mold them.

These practices could survive both the peace and the new dynasty that came to Great Britain in 1714 because they were the political expression of a social alliance whose members were to remain for more than a century fundamentally agreed on the forms and objectives of the British state. Behind the unified sovereignty of Parliament was the concord of the nobles, gentry, and propertied middle classes whom Parliament represented. By the terms of their accord, the nobles and gentry made up the governing class, supported by the consent of the propertied middle classes and oriented toward the pursuit of interests common to all three groups. These interests were a compound of political order and commercial enterprise, a compound that made for parliamentary unity since it blended a conservative reverence for authority with a progressive cast of policy. Hence there was a consensus on the vigorous prosecution of colonial acquisition, of overseas trade, and of wars against colonial and commercial rivals; on the studied neglect of restrictive mercantilist regulations (save the Navigation Acts that protected the British carrying trade); and on the toleration of Protestant dissent alongside an established Anglican Church. What made these interests common was the convergent effect of three social factors: the participation of all propertied classes, privileged and commoner alike, in the commercial net extended by the growing international trade and stimulating in its turn the capitalization of both agriculture and industry; the infusion of enterprising and progressive recruits into the aristocracy not only from the process of economic growth but from the shrewd management of high public office; and finally, the crucial mediatory role of the gentry in eighteenth-century British society.

Of these social factors the role of the gentry was perhaps the least obvious and the most far-reaching politially. These "gentlemen," or "squires," as they were alternatively called, occupied a fruitfully ambiguous position between the aristocracy and what we should call the middle class (in eighteenth-century parlance "the middling sort"). The gentry possessed no privileged status by law, but they did possess a privileged status by virtue of social prestige. Linked to the aristocracy by their common interests as estate owners, their common rights as landlords, and the reciprocal claims of gentle clients and noble patrons, they were at the same time linked to the middling sort by their common legal position as commoners, by the commercial and professional occupations of their younger sons, and by their common interests as local oligarchs—the gentry defending for the counties the same kind of investment in autonomy as the burghers defended in the towns.

Despite the many instances of parochial pride, expressed in resentment of the titled nobility and arrogance toward all of ungentle birth, the gentry supplied the cement in the British social structure. They represented the commoners of the realm in the House of Commons, and dominating that House, collaborated with the nobility in the governance of Britain. Moreover, not only did they embody, on the national level, the social consensus that made the parliamentary system work but they also manifested the invisible ties that forged the national and local authorities of Britain into a powerful unified state without the obvious clamp of a centralized bureaucracy. Because the same social group that dominated the most influential organ of the sovereign Parliament also supplied the justices of the peace who dominated the local government of Britain, the levels of government were tied together by the bonds of common interest, of common outlook, and, often enough, of common kinship.

But this social accord that formed the basis of British power was not independent of the political factors that were making for the centralization of other European states. War, for example, was a powerful and continuing influence on the modern English industrial society which began to emerge in the eighteenth century. This was a matter not simply of military stimulus to the economy and of additions to the colonies but of the cohesion worked upon British society by the common hostility to the French enemy and by the growing accord on the primacy of commercial interests as the mainspring of national power.

What distinguished Great Britain from its continental competitors, then, was not so much the obvious difference between limited and absolute sovereignty—since this difference was quite deceptive in terms of effective political power—but rather the difference between a state run by an alliance of social groups and states run by officials who mediated between social groups. Not, to be sure, that British society was immune to the popular disorders by the underprivileged, endemic to Europe during this era, but in Britain—unlike France, for example—the concord of all propertied classes sufficed to reduce such disorders to evanescent mob riots without definite goal or effect.

The social alliance forged in Britain by the Glorious Revolution and the subsequent wars against France proved to be a more permanent fount of unity than the more purely political instruments of continental absolutism. In the two and a half decades of comparative peace that followed upon the Peace of Utrecht, Britain shared in the aristocratic resurgence that affected so many European countries but not in the retrenchment of centralized power that marked this resurgence in states like Russia (after the death of Peter the Great in 1725), France, Sweden, and the Netherlands. Certainly the initial signs seemed to presage a crisis in the British government as well. The accession of the new Hanoverian dynasty in 1714 stimulated the activities of the "Jacobite" party, a small group of High Tory lords, squires, and Catholics committed to the claim of the Stuart James III upon the British succession. The Hanoverian preference for the Whig aristocracy, moreover, initiated nearly half a century of Whig ministries which seemed destined to turn Tories into Jacobites and dynastic feud into civil war and which, moreover, put into the saddle precisely the section of the aristocracy most suspicious of central power and most jealous of its own rights, privileges, and—above all—property.

But the signs were misleading. When rebellion for a Stuart restoration was attempted in Scotland by the stubborn James (the "Old Pretender," 1688–1766) in 1715 and by his infinitely more charming son "Bonnie Prince Charlie" (Charles Edward, the "Young Pretender," 1720–1788) in 1745, they were joined in both cases by a few of the Scotch lords and clans still smarting over the unwanted union of 1707 with England. Agitation by a minuscule Jacobite sect which persisted throughout the half century simply had the unintended effect of reconciling moderate men to the reign of the Hanoverians and the preeminence of the Whigs. As for these Whigs, despite their theoretical suspicion of authority, their actual domination of both the government and the houses of Parliament resulted in the peacetime consolidation of the war-born conventions that had knit the organs of the British state into an effective sovereign power.

Under the Hanoverians (1714–1748)

The tone of the approximate half century covered by the reigns of George I (ruled 1714–1727) and George II (ruled 1727–1760) was set by the Whig country gentleman, Robert Walpole (1676–1745), by whose name, indeed, the era is now known. Both out of office and in, he confirmed the conventions which limited the range of opposition and put a premium on a governing consensus. When he was excluded from government during the Hanoverian settling-down period he initiated the pattern, which was to persist through the century, of minimizing principle and of organizing the out-groups, Whigs and Tories alike, into a joint opposition to Whig ministries for the simple tactical purpose of creating a nuisance and so blackmailing their way into ministerial offices. Walpole's period in opposition (1717–1720) coincided, moreover, with the first of the deep-

Sir Robert Walpole directing a cabinet meeting. *Painting by Joseph Coopy. British Museum, London.*

seated rifts between king and crown prince that were to be a recurrent feature of the Hanoverian dynasty and were to have two important effects upon British constitutional practice.

With the first of these effects Walpole had little to do: after the King's rift—perhaps even more characteristic of royal than of ordinary families—with his son, the future George II, George I established the precedent of the king's absence from cabinet meetings, less because of his ignorance of the English language in itself (the usual reason cited) than because of the advantage his ignorance would have bestowed upon his hated bilingual son at such meetings. The second political effect of the royal feuding, however, Walpole did help to initiate: the gravitation of the opposition leaders to the household of the crown prince, with the effect of emphasizing the role of personality rather than principle in the opposition and resulting in the formation of a kind of shadow government for the next reign. Here was the beginning of the notion of a dynastically loyal opposition.

But it was in his long tenure of governmental leadership, from 1721 to 1742, that Walpole left his chief unifying impress upon British politics. The nature of this impress mirrored the combination of traits that made up his political personality. For Walpole, like Britain itself, was not so much an integral personality as a composite character that blended generally familiar purposes with distinctive ways of realizing them. Forceful, self-confident, avid of both wealth and power, skilled in the acquisition of the one and the conservation of the other, Walpole was as feared, mistrusted, and intrigued against as the leading minister of any contemporary autocracy. And yet, country gentleman on the make that he was, his conception of his own interests so abetted his unquestioning faith in the British constitution as to make the art of managing people and interests the characteristic instrument of his power.

Walpole sounded the keynote of his regime on the very occasion of its establishment: in his handling of the crisis attendant upon the bursting of the "South Sea Bubble." The South Sea Company, which had been chartered in 1711 nominally as a commercial corporation with a monopoly on trade in the South Seas, had actually functioned as a kind of investment trust, and early in 1720 its directors proposed to use the national debt for this function, issuing stock in exchange for government securities which would, in turn, form the basis for further capitalization in expectation of the profits from the South Sea monopoly. Persuaded by the prospect of a cost-saving refunding of the national debt and by the liberal gifts of stock in the right places, Commons approved the scheme, and aided by the apparent magic of credit exhibited during the successful late war, by the fever for quick gain following hard upon it, and by the Company's encouragement of buying on margin, the stock rose from 130 to over 1,000 before running out of fresh buyers and collapsing in September, 1720. The crisis that followed was more serious politically than economically, for the resentment and bitterness stemming from lost fortunes were directed at the King's government and indeed at his very household, and Walpole's solution of it, which was his springboard to power, was characteristically political as well. His financial proposals may have helped somewhat in the reestablishment of confidence but in fact stability was recovered without the necessity of their application.

What made Walpole the indispensable man was his resolute management of the question of responsibility, for at the expense of his own popularity he spared the King and the King's associates and threw to the wolves only those participants in the scheme who were minimally necessary to satisfy Commons' thirst for revenge. On this basis, as the only public figure who could hold King and Commons in harness, he was appointed by the King and accepted by the Commons as the First Lord of the Treasury and Chancellor of the Exchequer in April, 1721, the official posts from which he exercised what even then was occasionally and unofficially called the office of "prime minister" for the next two decades.

It is true enough that Walpole himself rejected the appellation of prime minister and that, as commentators on eighteenth-century Britain have cautioned *ad nauseam*, he lacked much of what the office of prime minister now connotes: he had no tenure independent of the King's favor; he had no official authority over the appointment, dismissal, or conduct of other ministers; he found no use for the cabinet as a formal vehicle of collective consultation and decision. But the one essential function of a prime ministership which he did provide was the concentration in one minister of the responsibility for achieving unison between King and Parliament.

Walpole was a royal favorite, not only because of his varied services to the Crown starting with the South Sea Bubble, but because of his assidu-

Mass anger and bitterness in London in 1720. *William Hogarth's caustic view of the effect of the "South Sea Bubble" on London life and morals.*

ous cultivation of the intelligent Princess Caroline (1683–1737), who was liked by her father-in-law, George I, and as Queen after 1727, revered by her husband, George II. Walpole built a reliable machine by putting his own men into as many influential governmental posts as he could reach. By 1733 he had even persuaded the King to purge the ministry in which he was legally only a first among equals, and thus Walpole did succeed to an unprecedented degree in excluding opposition from the ranks of the administration. Just as intense, finally, was his management of the Commons. He refused a peerage in order to retain his seat in the Commons. He organized a steady—although not infallible—majority through the artful blend of patronage for his faction with the deliberate display of the country squire's plain and blunt rusticity to attract the independent gentry into the ranks of his sympathizers.

The governmental policy of the Walpole era was similarly calculated to avoid offense, to avoid strain, to placate all interests, and thus to avoid the irritation of any social grievance that might disturb the collaboration of government and Parliament, a collaboration that was henceforward to be the necessary basis of any leading minister's secure possession of power. Hence Walpole's policy was simple: to keep the peace, to encourage trade, to reduce taxes—and "to let sleeping dogs lie." Not, of course, that Walpole followed this policy simply because of his overriding concern with maintaining himself in power. He was compulsively for efficiency in administration and against the extravagance of war. He believed in economy and peace, and he associated his political destiny naturally with them.

For Walpole's opponents, similarly, the desire for power did not exclude genuine considerations of policy. Their indiscriminate attacks all along the personal and political front had indeed their envy of Walpole's power as their one consistent element, paralleling the centrality of Walpole's ambition in his own makeup; but just as he associated his interests with the British interest in peace, so they connected theirs with the British interest in economic, and if need be military, competition with France and Spain.

The intimate union of private and public interests which thus came to characterize British political life was a sign of the close and direct relations that subsisted between British society and the British state. The state both reflected and shaped the common interests of the society, and the Walpole era served to show that the unifying institutions of the state worked as well in peace as in war. It created the British system which guaranteed the cooperation of the organs of sovereignty on the basic issues and reduced political conflict to the status of personal rivalries as long as consensus on the fundamental issues persisted. But by the same token, this system could and did raise these rivalries to the status of political conflicts requiring a new orientation of all the organs when the consensus on the issues changed.

Down to the accession of George III in 1760, the issue which determined the preponderance of personalities or principles in the amalgam of British politics was precisely the question of war and peace, and in terms of it the fall of Walpole was a demonstration of the workings of the British political system. Centered first in the ministry and then, after its exclusion from there during the early 1730's, in the House of Lords, the opposition to Walpole had always been vociferous enough, but it had also been localized and largely personal as long as the governing classes in country and town had remained content with the prosperity that accompanied Walpole's peace policy. But as impatience with this policy grew, aggravated by commercial conflict with Spain, the opposition, born along by the unifying force of the war issue, spread through the several organs of government.

First, in 1739, Walpole was forced to accept a declaration of war against Spain—subsequently known as the War of Jenkins' Ear for circumstances too obscure to detail—when support for it extended into both the Commons and his own ministry. Then, when his halfhearted prosecution of the war instigated patriotic fervor and factional hostility to combine against him in a fundamental challenge to his regime, Walpole came up against an opposition that was well entrenched in the royal family—by courtesy of Frederick, Prince of Wales (1707–1751)—and in the Lords, and that by 1742 attracted a majority in the Commons. Even the continuing favor of George II could not save him: both King and minister had to yield to a new government that could harmonize the three governing organs in the waging of the Spanish war and its extension to the European continent through participation in the War of the Austrian Succession.

The regime that replaced Walpole's was a precise response to the combination of personal and political issues that had unseated him. The Pelham brothers dominated the British government for the next dozen years, Henry (c. 1695–1754) as policy maker and Thomas (better known as the Duke of Newcastle, 1693–1768), as Whig party manager, until Henry's death in 1754. Their tenure shows that Walpole's was more than an individual achievement, for without his forcefulness they still led a government which proved stable for the same reason that his had—because like his it harmonized King, Lords, and Commons. They had been, indeed, members of Walpole's government, and Henry, at least, acknowledged himself Walpole's disciple, but the conditions of the regime differed sufficiently from his to reveal the existence of a political system independent of the accidents of personalities and capable of accommodating changes in policy without crippling divisions.

Henry Pelham was as unassuming and ingratiating as his predecessor had been arrogant and feared, and yet the conventions of government worked as well for the Pelhams as they had for Walpole. The Pelhams' eminence was grounded both in the judicious use of political mechanics—that is, in the careful management of patronage and connections—and in the fidelity with which their policy of limited war reflected the attitude of the ruling classes. The martial enthusiasm of these classes still came from an inchoate feeling of where British power and profit lay rather than from a clear and persistent perception of Britain's national destiny as world trader and colonial power—William Pitt (1708–1778) had this vision, but his was still a voice crying in the wilderness, hated by the King and isolated in the Commons—and it was therefore a fickle enthusiasm that flagged at the point of hardship and sacrifice. The curtailed military commitment and the inconclusive Peace of Aix-la-Chapelle in 1748 which were the hallmarks of the Pelhams' policy raised no widespread opposition because, unsatisfactory as they were generally sensed to be, they conformed to unreflective British sentiment that was still but one stage removed from Walpole's pacifism.

Not until the outbreak of the Seven Years' War in 1756 and the accession of William Pitt to ministerial office a year later did there arise a permanent consensus on the direction of the national interest that could stand the test of all-out war. It was at this point, when the unifying force of government had organized society into a self-conscious unit, that collective initiative passed from the state into the society, ending one historical age and initiating another. For the accession of George III in 1760 followed hard upon the rise of Pitt to national leadership, and the conflicts that marked the new reign were important not because of the old party politics they perpetuated but because of the new social participation they inaugurated. And so, its version of state making completed, Great Britain passed, together with its western European neighbors, from the political into the social phase of eighteenth-century civilization.

Part II

THE PHILOSOPHERS, 1687–1789

CHAPTER 5

The Social Context

Historical dates are conveniences to mark the temporal relations of events. Historical periods are conveniences to mark the temporal relations of groups of events. Dates are, by and large, especially appropriate to the history of men's politics, since men have directed their political interests and desires to the performance of particular actions in definite times and places. Periods are, by and large, especially appropriate to the history of men's social and cultural pursuits, since what is essential to them is embodied in persistent institutions and attitudes that are constituted by whole sets of related actions. To choose a specific date as a division between two periods is thus doubly misleading if it makes historians forget both that the sequence of political events has usually continued through the critical date without a noticeable break and that changes in social and cultural orientation are too gradual to be bound by any singular dates. If, therefore, we choose the middle of the eighteenth century as its watershed, we must do so with the full realization that in politics not only did this midpoint obviously signify no fundamental shift in the domestic regimes of the European powers but it did not even alter the tendency to general warfare recently resumed in 1740, and that in society and culture the trends toward economic growth and intellectual ferment characteristic of the second half of the century were evident as well in the preceding generation.

But if due regard be had for its function as a rhetorical device, then a date—the year 1748—may be singled out as a dramatic way of marking the reversal of the proportionate weights of politics and society in determining the direction of European history. For two events of this year—one political and the other cultural—marked the intersection of a political development that was losing its former autonomy and a social development that was acquiring a new focus. The Peace of Aix-la-Chapelle, inconclusive as were its substantive provisions and short-lived as was the peace it sealed, marked the end of the significant dynastic wars triggered by crises of succession: when continental military conflict was resumed in 1756 it was preceded by a reversal of alliances—the so-called Diplomatic Revolution—which brought the old rivals, Bourbon France and Habsburg Austria, into coalition against Great Britain and Prussia and thus announced the shift from prescriptive monarchy to collective interest as the main guide to policy. In 1748, too, the Baron de Montesquieu published his *Spirit of the Laws,* a work which focused the diffusive thought of the Enlightenment upon the problems of social and political organization and thus announced the corpus of influential works in the field of public affairs that would spearhead the rising demand of a mobilized society for a reformation of the traditional ways of thinking and of doing.

From about mid-century on, then, the tone of European life gradually altered. The game of international politics went on and the domestic institutions of public order held firm, but the rules of the game were insensibly amended and the domestic institutions were pushed into an alternation of defensiveness and accommodation as the social pressures for change grew in intensity, crystallized into definite forces, and began to occupy the center of the European stage. Let us consider first the factors of social mobility that were growing through and around the stable arrangements of the traditionally organized European society, and then go on in subsequent chapters to the intellectual groups and ideas that articulated this mobility, to the new style of politics that was a response to it, and, finally, to the prerevolutionary movements of social and political protest that were the harbingers of a new age.

No economic revolution preceded the political revolution that ended the eighteenth century. During the entirety of the period with which we are concerned—that is, until 1789—by far the greater part of the European population lived, and saw no option but to live, in the same kind of corporately organized, hierarchical society that they and their forebears had inhabited since the reestablishment of religious and civil peace in the seventeenth century; and for the vast majority of men this pattern of stability held for all regions from the Urals to County Kerry. Throughout Europe, in progressive Great Britain as well as in retrograde Russia, most men were still undertaking the significant activities of their lives as members of time-honored associations which channeled these activities along the lines of well-tried custom and imbued these men with the values of the security that is attached to familiar routine. The model existence for which men strove was still to have a rich variety of protective institutions—ideally, a separate institution for each function of life. However distinct from one another in function or membership these institutions were supposed to be—like the organs of the human body to which they were still so often compared—they shared important qualities: they were bound by tradition; they were addicted to ritual; they were organized on the basis of privilege both in their internal structure and in their external relations with one another. For the guarantee of their rights in law and social custom (including the rights to political representation, where such rights were recognized), men were still grouped in a hierarchy of "ranks," "orders," or "estates," as they were variously called. For the pursuit of their occupations they were still subject in varying measure to the regulations of guilds, manors, or peasant communes. For the guidance of personal and social life, local corporations retained a far-reaching autonomy, and they continued to sanction the rules that were administered by local authorities who were powerful precisely because of the corporate tradition they administered: oligarchs were the heads of municipalities, gentry of counties, lords of villages, and in their exercise of controls they were joined by the bishops and local clergy of the established churches, who still registered the great events of personal life, sponsored the social entertainments, and articulated the public conscience.

The reality, undoubtedly, was not nearly so harmonious or stable as this model. In the first place, the neat allocation of separate corporations to separate groups and functions had never worked without friction in practice, and particularly in the second half of the eighteenth century the overlap and the competition between different corporations pursuing the same function, between complementary corporations pursuing presumably complementary functions, and between different groups in the same corporation, were exacerbated. Thus the merchants of the burgher estate and the progressive landowners of the noble estate fought over wholesale trade and rural manufacturing. The lay aristocracy came increasingly to dispute the local influence of the clerical aristocracy, in a campaign favored by the growing toleration, in fact more often than in law, of dissenting churches and by the ensuing competition between ecclesiastical establishment and dissent. And within the churches, the gulf between higher and lower clergy grew apace.

But there was also a second disturbance of corporate tradition. Distant authorities, as we have seen, had been encroaching for centuries on the judicial, financial, economic, and ecclesiastical autonomy of the local corporations, and this tendency continued throughout the eighteenth century. Responding in part to the supralocal administrative activities of the ever more numerous officials working and traveling for the central agencies and in part to the extra-corporate economic activities of merchants and factors who ignored guilds to set up their branches or their domestic industries among the rural cottagers, increasing numbers of people were escaping the traditional corporate institutions.

It is indeed the series of changes in the wonted way of doing and looking at things that makes up the history of the second half of the eighteenth century and that will be our chief concern, but these changes can only be understood if we keep always in mind the integrated structure and the static ideal of the society which contained the activities and retained the allegiance of most Europeans until the end of the Old Regime. This image of a corporately organized and traditionally motivated European people is obviously important both as the constant backdrop against which all changes must be measured and as a reminder not only that the agents of change were a minority, as agents of change usually are, but that in this case they were a minority who did not, until the explosion which ended the Old Regime toward the close of the eighteenth century, succeed in altering the fundamental rules by which men actually lived.

There are, however, two other reasons that are perhaps not so obvious but that also make the remembrance of what did not change in the eighteenth century important for the explanation of what did. First, the active minority that spread the seeds of change, whether in the policy of governments, in the pattern of trade, or in the realm of ideas, did what they did and thought what they thought in full consciousness of the predominantly static society upon which they were operating, and neither their deeds nor their theories are comprehensible without awareness of this valid consciousness of theirs. Second, the persistent commitment of most Europeans to their wonted ways and their familiar values meant that in response to the dislocations engendered in these ways and values of life by the proponents of change the conservative leaders were themselves galvanized into action to defend the social establishment. The actual course of change in the later eighteenth century makes sense only in light of the knowledge that it was powered not only by those who wanted change but also by those who unwittingly and unwillingly contributed to the process of change through the novel means they chose to fight it.

For a portrayal of Europe in the second half of the eighteenth century, then, let us turn first to the economic and social relationships which show the factors of stability and mobility in their due proportions.

POPULATION

The eighteenth century witnessed the takeoff of the population explosion that has continued to our day, surging powerfully against all social barriers in its path. Although the absolute numbers may be unimpressive by our standards, the proportional increase during this initial stage was great enough to overflow the dikes that had been constructed for a less densely packed humanity. Population figures for the eighteenth century are as unreliable as their explanation is uncertain, but their basic tendency seems clear enough: the population of Europe increased considerably, and the increase was markedly greater in the second half than in the first half of the century. According to one plausible estimate, the increase for the century totaled about three fifths, from around 120 million to around 190 million, with two thirds of the increase coming after 1750. The cause of the increase is even more uncertain than its extent. Historians now reject the older explanation of this "vital revolution" in terms of a falling death rate attributable to improvements in the practice of medicine and in sanitation, for these improvements were themselves limited in kind and restricted in incidence. The most probable explanation would seem to be a falling death rate explicable by the retreat of the age-old scourges of man—pestilence, devastation, and hunger—because of ecological changes noxious to the plague-bearing rat, the more disciplined conduct and limited depredations of eighteenth-century warfare, and the acceptance of hardy new crops like the potato as staple items of mass consumption. But a case has also been made for a rising birthrate in localities where a traditional tendency toward early and prolific marriages was given an unprecedented boost by the waning of natural calamities in the eighteenth century.

Although the causes of the population rise may still be debated, there can be little doubt that its effects were far-reaching. Population pressures increased the demand for goods and thereby initiated the chain reaction which stimulated trade and expanded the capitalization of both agriculture and industry. The expansion of the labor supply, especially in such favored areas as Britain and the Low Countries, led to the development of intensive agriculture and of urban labor reservoirs for industrial growth. But in less favored areas, the increase in population resulted in rural overpopulation that forced the subdivision of small farms to the point of agrarian crisis, and created an oversupply of wandering artisans who became tinder for popular uprisings in town and countryside alike. But however diversified its precise economic effects, the constant growth in the numbers and the density of Europe's inhabitants during the eighteenth century had a uniform social effect: whether it pushed people from the family farms into the labor pools of the countryside, from the countryside into the cities, or from the home country into the colonies, everywhere it upset established customs and began to orient men toward change rather than stability as the dominant way of life.

TRADE

International trade, for some five hundred years one characteristic activity among many in the undulating kaleidoscope of European life, broke from its duly assigned mooring to become a second major force for economic change. Not, of course, that its incidence was evenly distributed. The growth of international commerce in the eighteenth century occurred mainly in overseas trade, with direct effects upon the great maritime and colonial nations, Great Britain and France, and with diminishing but perceptible effluence, mediated largely through these nations, into the rest of Europe. Although the statistics for trade are almost as inadequate as they are for other eighteenth-century economic activities, some notion of the

The extension of the European market economy, in which Great Britain led the way during the eighteenth century, was based largely on water transport, both at home and abroad. *Above: The Duke of Bridgewater canal in England. On the opposite page: Merchant adventurers of the East India Company in the Far East.*

orders of magnitude involved may be gleaned from such estimates as the fourfold increase in French overseas trade and the fivefold increase in the carrying capacity of the British merchant fleet during the course of the century.

The importance of international trade in European life is evident not only in the rise of the British-French commercial rivalry to the status of the single most important issue in international politics but perhaps even more clearly in the great leap which both of these powers took over such former maritime and colonial competitors as the Netherlands and Spain. For both declining powers, the relative insulation of their international economies from their domestic economies now became a comparative disadvantage. The Netherlands did continue to play an important role in European overseas and transit trade, and Spain retained its colonial system, but for both powers the stagnation of their development in relation to their own past and the decline of their competitive position in relation to their chief rivals testified to the changed role of international trade. Amsterdam, indeed, remained the center of international finance and the Netherlands the chief source of the world's capital during the eighteenth century, but since the Dutch tended increasingly to invest in the more vital economies of other countries, they themselves contributed an international movement of capital to the process of economic development in the industrialized nations. The expanding orbit of international trade came to include Scandinavians, Prussians, Russians, and other new or rejuvenated actors on the maritime mercantile scene. Their entry increased the competition in international commerce, but the economic effect which world trade had on them was limited and the social effect correspondingly different from that in the more mobilized societies of the west.

Great Britain and France, on the other hand, shared a distinctive combination of economic traits: both had a colonial basis for their foreign trade, and both felt the domestic effect of this commerce. But the precise pattern of the trade and consequently of its effects differed for the two countries. By 1789 not only was more than half of the British trade with areas outside of Europe, in comparison with France's one third, but the character of the commerce itself varied. British commerce consisted in general of the importation of raw materials in exchange for manufactured products, as indicated by the intensity of its trade flow with the North American colonies, a relatively prosperous market for manufactures, and with the Baltic region, a source of grain and naval stores. French trade involved mainly the transshipment of foreign raw materials and the export of French natural products—especially wine and spirits—accompanied by only a modicum of cloth manufactures, as was attested by the large role played in French commerce by Spain, Italy, and the Levant—areas with their own handicraft industries and a low effective demand for industrial imports. For the British, consequently, overseas trade contributed substantially to the demand for increased production and for materials to be used in production. By the last third of the century these demands were preparing the change of economic system we know as the Industrial Revolution. In France ever-expanding sectors of the society—aristocrats, peasants, merchants, bankers, and the professional classes—were caught up in the movement and dislocations of a commercialized economy, but without the alterations in economic organization needed to resolve the resulting tensions and insecurity.

Without the direct stimuli of colonies and overseas trade in massive proportions, the other large European nations fell behind Britain and France both in the affluence and in the mobility of their societies. Still, even the less advanced countries experienced the indirect effects of a modest commercial growth stimulated by the oceanic powers, which in conjunction with the direct effects of a population increase and the international political ambitions of the ruling classes, did have consequences for the mainland societies. Essentially, these consequences were of two kinds: first, influential, albeit small and isolated, groups of merchants and landowners were absorbed into the larger network of interlocal exchange; and second, the rulers of these countries adopted economic and social policies geared to the growing material bases of power in the leading mercantile states.

Both these kinds of continental economic development were visible in the pattern of urban growth, for the cities in the underdeveloped sectors of Europe that rose to international prominence in the eighteenth century were themselves of two types, corresponding to the two channels of economic stimulation. First, there were cities like Hamburg, Frankfurt, and Geneva, which through their position on the sea or on the great rivers became transit centers for the exchange of Dutch, British, and French goods and money for inland products. Second, there were the expanding cities of Vienna and Berlin, both of which increased in population to well over 100,000 in response to the demands of the royal court, the administration, and the military for the most modern goods and services. Small wonder that the cities of Europe, capital and provincial, became centers of prosperity, culture, and power that exceeded even the great urban concentrations of the Italian Renaissance.

INDUSTRY

The spurs from a growing population and a ballooning overseas trade combined to shake unprecedented numbers of Europeans out of their wonted routine and into the kaleidoscopic world of the distant marketplace. To assay what this change meant for the way in which such men earned their livelihood, let us make clear first what it did not mean. There was no "Industrial Revolution," in the proper sense of the term, during the eighteenth century. The Industrial Revolution refers to the rapid series of economic and social events that enthroned mechanized production as the determining factor in the material life of Western society. This drastic shift of economic control from the directors of natural and manual power to the managers of invested capital would, when it came, involve both the change from machines as isolated, *ad hoc* laborsaving devices to mechanization as a general process transferable to all branches of the economy, and the initiation of a self-sustaining chain reaction through which the comparative advantages of machines would continuously create the industrial and urban social conditions and attitudes favorable to their own extension.

The eighteenth century witnessed only the first of these two steps, and it witnessed this introductory phase, moreover, only in Great Britain. Not even in Britain did the second step occur, which would turn technological change into a permanent economic and social revolution. The Industrial Revolution, in short, was a product of eighteenth-century economic and social conditions, but the mechanization they sponsored did not react back upon the economy and society to consummate the revolution until well into the next century.

Because the conditions for the Industrial Revolution first appeared in late-eighteenth-century Britain, this island kingdom may be seen as the most advanced, and therefore the clearest, representative of the commercial system that still dominated the economic development of all Europe. For the inventions that initiated the economic transformation to the industrial era were British not because only the British were inventing or because invention was a different kind of activity in eighteenth-century Britain than it was in Europe then or had been in Britain before—it remained a product rather of practical craftsmanship than of theoretical science—but because Britain experienced in greater degree the factors of economic mobility that were affecting Europe as a whole, and responded in ways that became different in kind. Thus the British inventions of the latter eighteenth century were economically distinctive because here the commercial pressures for increased supplies were so pervasive and the relaxation of social and political bonds was so general that the inventions dovetailed in an economic series altering whole processes of production.

The most obvious factor making for the comparative advantage of the British was their leadership over the rest of Europe in the rate of population growth and in the expansion of international trade—elements directly relevant to the expanded market for textiles which was the primary stimulus for technological innovation. The apparently insatiable demand for cloth led to a contagious imbalance which stimulated inventions all along the production line. The comparative efficiency of cotton weaving over spinning, which had been reinforced by John Kay's flying shuttle of 1733, created the challenge that was answered by James Hargreaves' spinning jenny (1765), Richard Arkwright's water frame (1769), and Samuel Crompton's mule, a combination of jenny and water frame (1779). The consequent efficiency of yarn production, in turn, called for the mechanization of weaving, introduced gradually with the improvements upon Edmund Cartwright's first power loom (1787). The need for a reliable metal from which to make these precise machines led to the exploitation of coke smelting, after 1760, to produce the pig iron that went into the new tools. The need for mechanical power to drive them was filled by James Watt's version of the steam engine (1769), whose distinctive contribution was to extend the applicability of this engine from mining, where it was originally used, to all kinds of industry—particularly to textiles.

But if its superlative rise in population and foreign trade made Britain representative of the most obvious dynamic tendencies in Europe as a whole, the peaking of industrial change in Britain was also conditioned by other circumstances, which were apparently distinctive to the island kingdom. Yet these too, upon closer examination, turn out to be expressions of tendencies real but latent in the rest of Europe. They were also tendencies that were products of a long-established economic organization, however revolutionary their potentialities ultimately proved to be.

Even the distinctive insular geography of Britain—the small, compact land mass indented by the long, serrated shoreline—was in economic terms the most felicitous locale for the water transportation that for centuries had been the lifeline of European trade and was now exploited for commercial purposes as never before. Behind the industrial leadership that Britain was beginning for the first time to assume in Europe lay British leadership not only in oceanic and coastal trade but in the improvement of rivers and the construction of canals. The development of land transport, which was to become so signal a force in nineteenth-century economic growth, was not, interestingly enough, a prominent factor during the eighteenth century. Although there was some improvement in the building and maintenance of British roads, they remained in the hands of local turnpike trusts, and the heightened activity of these authorities after mid-century was unfortunately accompanied by corresponding increases in neither efficiency nor coordination. The most notable advances in road building were made in France, where, by the last quarter of the eighteenth century, a special corps of officials, trained at a technical School for Bridges and Roads, constructed and reconstructed some 25,000 miles of state-controlled highways. The French roads, like those of the German states which used them as models, undoubtedly contributed to the growing scope of the market economy on the European continent, but it should be remembered that none of these countries broke through to any decisively new stage or level of industrialism in the eighteenth century. The crucial physical channel of economic growth remained what it had been for centuries—the waterway—but simply exploited now to an unprecedented degree.

More peculiarly British and more apparently germane to the new industrialism was the complex of qualities associated with the British political and social system—a complex which derived from the abstractly antithetical but practically complementary connections of unity and individual liberty in Britain. By virtue of the early centralization of the British state, traditional local authorities raised no effective barriers to the movement of goods, men, and resources and hence to the formation of a national market equipped with a rapidly specializing division of labor. The effect was not only the absence of such obvious deterrents as local tolls but also the emphatic relocation of industry into the countryside, where capitalist entrepreneurs operated unencumbered by the restrictive regulations of municipal corporations and the old guilds. At the same time, the parlia-

A scene from *The Rake's Progress. Engraving by William Hogarth.*

mentary defense of property rights, manifested as early as the Patent Law of 1624, which undoubtedly encouraged the industrial inventions of the next century, led after the Glorious Revolution to the deliberate neglect and atrophy of mercantilist controls (with the exception of the Navigation Acts) and thus to a *de facto* reign of economic liberty.

Favored by this political climate, moreover, the relative fluidity of the relations among the classes not only offered incentives to the enterprise of energetic men with social ambitions but also had economic effects which redounded directly to the national demand for increased production. In the countryside the agricultural "revolution," which standardized crop rotation, fertilizing crops, and new fodders in the service of increased yields and calculated profits, was associated, to be sure, with such scientifically and commercially minded noblemen as Charles ("Turnip") Townshend (1675–1738) and Thomas William Coke of Norfolk (1754–1842), but it was also predicated upon the flexible economic and social structure of British farming. The enclosure acts, whereby an aristocratically dominated Parliament sanctioned the reorganization of scattered strips and unproductive commons into consolidated holdings, thereby encouraging the capitalization of agriculture and the raising of rural rents, accelerated an agrarian system which operated not through the direct exploitation of unitary estates by the aristocracy but through a system of long-term leases to middle-class farmers with whose interests the aristocracy associated itself.

On the urban side, the pattern was analogous. In the commercial and financial centers, as in the mushrooming industrial towns, the patriciate of inherited wealth and the oligarchy of established municipal families were at once threatened and replenished by enterprising traders, workshop owners, and professional people whose numbers and prosperity grew with the national economy.

The growth of a larger and richer middle class and the growing incidence of its upward mobility into the governing class meant not only an increase in the effective domestic demand for goods but a qualitative change in the goods that were now demanded in the market. Whereas international trade had traditionally been dominated by the luxury items called for by the tastes of a segregated court and aristocracy and their mimics among the local oligarchs, the spread of wealth and the opening of the aristocracy both to recruitment from below and to styles of a more popular kind began to make articles of mass consumption staple items of commerce and consequently of industrial production for market. The most spectacular and far-reaching of these shifts was the growing tendency of cotton to replace wool and silk as the chief material of textile manufacture. In part this change was a matter of economics and technology: the cotton supply was the most flexible in response to demand and cotton fiber was the most adaptable to mechanical spinning. But whether as cause or as effect, a change in social mores and standards of taste accompanied the shift. As the century wore on, silks and heavy brocades gave way to muslins as the preferred cloth of aristocracy and middle classes alike, and with it the materials of dress yielded to the subtler criterion of style as the mark of class distinction.

Nor was this development an isolated phenomenon. The propensity of the well-to-do in all classes to use wallpaper instead of woven tapestries, and their inclination to surround themselves with fine furniture made from plentiful overseas woods, were also obvious signs of the expanded market that was being created by an enlarged upper class, an increasingly prosperous and ambitious middle class, and the pressure on production exerted by their numbers and converging tastes. In the case of some foodstuffs—such as coffee and sugar—what had been items in the luxury trade of the sixteenth century penetrated even below the middle-class level to become items of mass consumption and demand by the end of the eighteenth.

Clearly, then, the political liberality, the social fluidity, and the material prosperity of the British scene created an economic demand and favored a technological response that proved in the event to be qualitatively different from contemporaneous tendencies on the Continent, since only on the island did they crystallize after the turn of the century into an Industrial Revolution, while on the Continent this revolution came later, the product as much of British influence as of native development. And yet, however distinctive the British origins of the distinctive British Industrial Revolution may seem in retrospect, they constituted, during the eighteenth century, only the most advanced stage of a general economic growth that in varying degrees and covert forms was affecting the whole of the European world.

The similarity in kind, albeit not in degree, of British and continental economic growth can best be understood if we illustrate the limits upon the former and the achievements of the latter. The statistics, approximate as they are, reveal a Britain only on the turn toward a new industrial system. In the 1780's Britain's production of iron was still smaller than France's. Even by the end of the century there were only some five hundred of Watt's steam engines in use, producing about 5,000 horsepower and reflecting an industrial structure still largely dependent upon water-power, upon the traditional woolen textiles as much as the revolutionary cottons, and upon the cottage and the workshop rather than the factory. Continental industrial growth, on the other hand, albeit spotty, was perceptible enough to make most contemporary observers unaware of a qualitative difference between the economic systems of the island and the mainland. France and the Austrian Netherlands (the later Belgium) were older industrial centers whose steady advance during the century seemed to keep approximate pace with Britain's, and at least in Russia and in Austrian Bohemia new industrial areas sprang into European prominence, eclipsing the more modest and artificial service industries that were mushrooming in the expanding capital cities.

In the French case, industrial production doubled, and most of the characteristics of the British economic growth were in evidence as well: extension of industry into the unregulated countryside, atrophy of controls both by guilds and by central mercantilist regulation, application of technological invention to economic processes (particularly in the silk and mining industries), and the beginnings—especially in the 1780's—of industrial concentration into large plants. By 1789, indeed, only the French necessity for using British machines in the cotton industry and the French weakness in coal deposits could have presaged the drastic lag which that nation was about to experience vis-à-vis Britain, and at that time the position of cotton and coke as the bellwethers of an Industrial Revolution was not yet clearly recognized.

Russia in the eighteenth century developed into one of the great industrial powers of Europe. As in its renewed industrialization at the end of the nineteenth century, the distinguishing trait of the Russian development was its concentration, both in plant and in region. Factories devoted to non-metallurgical manufacturing tripled in number between 1760 and 1800 (from about seven hundred to two thousand) and were grouped mainly in the Moscow area and the Urals. The latter, indeed, now became one of the great industrial regions of the world, for it was also the main seat of Russian metallurgy, the most important branch of Russian industry. As late as 1800 Russia was still the world's leading producer of pig iron, although there were already signs then of the stagnation, accountable to technological inertia, that was to last far into the nineteenth century. Even in the palmiest years of the eighteenth century the relatively limited proportions of industry in Russia were exhibited in the continuing role of agricultural raw materials as the chief Russian export and in the prevalence of metals over finished manufactured goods among the industrial products it did export. But lopsided and convulsive as its economic development may have been, the agricultural exports of flax, hemp, and—after 1780—wheat to western Europe, and of pig iron particularly to Britain, in exchange for finished manufactures made Russia an important factor in world trade and oriented a significant sector of the Russian economy to produce for and to purchase from distant markets.

Thus wherever industrial advance occurred in eighteenth-century Europe it took on a roughly similar pattern: it responded to increased demand stemming from interregional and overseas trade; it took the form primarily of an expansion of domestic industry into rural areas where traditional controls were weak, and secondarily of the growth of large plant units in the separate industries and locales where the supply of labor and power permitted; and it applied technical improvements piecemeal to the industrial process without transforming the character of that process.

THE IMPACT ON SOCIETY

Just as European economic growth in the eighteenth century can be viewed as a single economic process that varied significantly in its proportions from country to country, so too can the social facet of this growth—that is, the relations of the groups that engineered it to the groups that suffered it—be seen as a common social process whose variations from state to state hardened into the distinct nations of the European community.

The chief protagonists of commercial and industrial development were the middle-class merchants who assumed more and more the function of industrial organizers as the increasing supplies of raw materials and the expanding markets for finished products drove manufacturing into the suburbs and countryside where labor was plentiful and corporate modes of industrial organization were weak. Economically ancillary but socially crucial were the secondary agents of industrial growth: on the one hand, the artisans and the peasants who rose to the status of small-scale entrepreneurs in their own workshops, and on the other, the titled landowners whose estates became the locus of larger-scale industrial enterprises. Frequently entailing the paradoxical use of serfs as workers to assure labor discipline in modern, profit-oriented factories, such enterprises ranged from the food-processing, mining, and iron industries of the Russian nobility to the larger textile mills of the Bohemian aristocracy.

But both economically and socially the countervailing tendency toward the preservation of the old ways was far stronger on the Continent than in Great Britain. In France the guilds, however limited in their economic functions by public administrators and private entrepreneurs, persisted as a pervasive conservative influence and even increased in number as the government continued to profit from licenses for them. In Russia the notable rise of factory production shaded but did not categorically alter the preponderance of peasant handicraft and the local market in the Russian industrial picture. In both nations, moreover, even the middling sectors of society, which included the prime agents of economic change, responded to the change differently than in Britain. Where the British entrepreneurs in industry and the wholesale trades tended increasingly to set the aggressive tone for the bulk of the middle classes and ultimately for the most influential groups in the society as a whole, their French and Russian counterparts remained, in varying ways and degrees, isolated even within their class. In France, the bourgeois continued typically to yearn for status, either through investment in landed property and hence a claim on a place in the aristocracy or urban patriciate, or through investment in government obligations and acquisition of the perquisites of the leisured *rentier*. Despite the increased role of Russian merchants in both trade and industry, the active traders and industrialists among them were such a minuscule part of the urban communities that the municipal delegates to Catherine the Great's Legislative Commission of 1767 themselves complained of the paucity of merchants in their ranks and proceeded unwittingly to back their complaint through the passivity of their own behavior in the Commission.

Among the traditional groupings of the continental European population the negative response to economic growth went beyond such inertia to overt counter-action. These groups not only set limits to the dimension of change upon the Continent but triggered reactionary movements against it. The most spectacular and the most fateful of these movements was the so-called "feudal reaction" in France, where from mid-century, noble estate owners responded to the economic pressures of rising world prices by searching out old titles and seeking to enforce both manorial claims against the peasants and political immunities against the crown. Ultimately, in the portentous spring and summer of 1789, two other groups representing the conservative dimension of French society—the peasants and the artisans—rose against the campaign of the aristocracy to pass the cost of economic and social change on to the French masses.

In Russia, similarly, the most important social developments of the latter eighteenth century were reactionary movements of the traditional groups. By the reign of Catherine the Great—that is, from 1762—the Russian nobility acquired, with a decisive assist from the state, for the first time the legal status and the corporate consciousness of a caste such as had existed in western Europe since the Middle Ages. The aristocracy exploited its new legal status to extend its judicial, police, and seignorial powers over the serfs at the cost of the governmental protection formerly accorded these wards.

Pugachev in chains. *Drawing from a contemporary pamphlet designed pointedly to show readers the grim end awaiting any "rebel and traitor."*

The other prominent conservative group—the peasantry—responded in its own fashion to the new mobility in Russian affairs with the most radical of countermovements. The Pugachev rebellion of 1773 was the most widespread of eighteenth-century peasant revolts. Starting as a political rebel on the southeastern frontier of European Russia, Emelyan Pugachev, himself a Don Cossack, appealed first to a mixture of outlying groups—Russian Orthodox Old Believers, Ural Cossacks, and other ethnically non-Russian tribes—who resented the recent encroachments of the central government, but then, masquerading as a wrongfully deposed Peter III (who had actually been murdered in 1762), he raised the banner of social revolution, promised freedom and land to the peasants, and enlisted a host of private landed and factory serfs in a large area of southeastern Russia. The revolt was crushed and the retribution terrible, but it gave spectacular notice of the pattern which agrarian revolts in Europe would take until the middle of the nineteenth century in response to the ever-deeper penetration of an exchange economy. The virulence of the peasant movements stemmed from the triple stimuli that triggered them. However local the substantive issues behind it were and however untypical of western Europe the Russian tendency toward the extension of serfdom in the eighteenth century may have been, the Pugachev rebellion was representative in its accumulation of grievances: first against the state as an agency of change; second, against progressive sections of the aristocracy which caused dislocation in the countryside by bringing capitalistic enterprise to it; third, indirectly against the exchange economy and directly against the regressive sections of the aristocracy which recoiled from this economy by tightening their hold on the peasantry.

In sum, the social response to the spreading effect of the exchange economy in Europe was divided between the minority in all classes who joined the merchant pioneers in advancing it and the majority of all classes who passively or actively resisted it. But it must be emphasized, to understand this response aright, that this distinction between a progressive and a reactionary response was an economic and social, but *not* a political distinction. No more in the eighteenth than in the previous centuries of the early modern era was there the consistent lineup of social and political interests to which we have become accustomed from subsequent experience. Thus Pugachev's revolt was politically radical and socially conservative. Obversely, enterprising businessmen, particularly in Britain and France, continued to support governments which, whatever their political complexion, favored the trading interest.

The primary reason for the discrepancies between the social and the political lineups in the eighteenth century lay indeed precisely in the ambiguous relationship between society and government. The authoritarian regimes of the eighteenth century were not simply reflections of the dominant social group or tendency. Because the stability of these regimes was based on the resources they could mobilize from the whole society to meet the ever-present threat of war abroad and on the pressure they could exert among the groups of the society to meet the still-present threat of disorder within, governments required both social mobility to generate force and social hierarchy to control it. Typically, then, governments swayed from one side to the other of the social structure they sought to straddle, in response to the changing pressures of external security, internal order, and domestic lobbyists. The politics of the various social groups, in turn, often depended more upon the direction of governmental policy at any particular moment than upon any consistent attitude toward politics dictated by their abiding social interests. Government was relevant to the social classes because it required their support and because the policies it adopted affected their destinies, but government was also independent of its social base because of the specifically political dimension—external and internal security—in its policies. In addition to the various estates and classes, then, government must be considered an independent factor in the society of eighteenth-century Europe.

SOCIETY AND GOVERNMENT

Like the relationships of the classes to one another, the policies of governments varied greatly from country to country and yet, especially during the second half of the eighteenth century, manifested an increasing similarity that reflected the common European scope of the economic and social development with which these policies were designed to deal. However dissimilar in forms and however varied in specific policy, European rulers and officials tended increasingly to favor the process of industrial and commercial growth, not only in the obvious forms of financial subsidies, tax privileges, public sponsorship and public ownership of manufacturing and trading enterprises, and the like, but also in the creation of a freer environment for the prosecution of private undertakings. Thus in some measure the freewheeling atmosphere provided by the commercially interested and property-minded parliamentary sovereign of Great Britain marked the extreme point of a tendency in more modest evidence elsewhere. In country after country on the continent of Europe, the apparent incongruity of their absolute monarchies with constitutional Britain was softened by their adoption of economic policies comparable to the growing liberality of the island kingdom.

The favored field for the relaxation of controls was—as might be expected from the most expansive of the century's economic activities—the field of commerce. But not all trade was equally subject to liberalized economic attitudes. Curiously enough, in view of the enormous increase in the volume and attraction of foreign trade, it was internal rather than international commerce that was the chief beneficiary of the new policy. Aside from a slight moderation of their trading monopoly with their West Indian colonies by the French in 1784, the only notable steps toward international free trade were the Franco-American Treaty of Amity and Commerce of 1778 and, more importantly, the Anglo-French commercial treaty of 1786.

The common factor of France's participation in all these arrangements would seem to argue the prevalence of liberal commercial ideas in that country, and indeed from 1750 to the 1780's an influential school of economic reformers called the Economists, led by an administrator, Vincent de Gournay (1712–1759), and a court physician, François Quesnay (1694–1774), did have considerable effect in French official circles. But if their ideas made possible the tariff reductions that rendered the Anglo-French commercial treaty so noteworthy, they were not primarily responsible for its actuality. The French, indeed, were the initiators of the treaty, but for a political reason—to seal the peace of 1783 with Britain—and it was opposed by French industrial groups who feared inundation by British manufactures. The British negotiator, William Pitt "the Younger" (1759–1806), was an authentic disciple of Adam Smith and does seem to have been moved by the perception of the benefits of free trade for Britain, but he stood almost alone and succeeded in having the treaty ratified rather through his general influence than through any generally favorable response to this policy.

Governmental attempts at liberalizing internal trade were much more widespread, and where they took place had much stronger backing, than on the international stage. The best known of these attempts is associated with the idea of *laissez-faire*, but the policy had a far broader base than this explicit doctrine. In 1774 Anne Robert Jacques Turgot (1727–1781), long a friend of the Economists and recently appointed Controller-general of France, enacted the domestic free trade in grain as part of a far-reaching general program of liberal economic reform, an enactment that was then frustrated along with Turgot and his program. But in fact this kind of measure had a more positive career in the latter eighteenth century than the spectacular rise and fall of Turgot indicated and a more hybrid character than its association here with a general economic liberalism connoted. The positive attitude toward freer internal trade was indicated even in this context, for a successor of Turgot as Controller-general, Charles de Calonne (1734–1802), renewed his declaration of free trade in grain during 1787.

But it was the removal of barriers to domestic commerce elsewhere in Europe, where the influence of liberal doctrine was not so strong, that revealed more accurately the kind of pressure behind the free-trading policy. By edicts of 1753 and 1762 Russia abolished internal customs barriers throughout its dominions, and in 1775 the Habsburgs did the same for their crown lands (only Hungary and the Tyrol were excluded from the single-customs territory). The Russian enactment showed governmental responsiveness to pressures from merchants and market-minded nobility; the Austrian revealed the antithetical form that the relations between international and internal free trade could take in the eighteenth century. For the Habsburg decision to enlarge the Austrian domestic market was taken as a deliberate counterweight to the decision to maintain the prohibitive tariffs on foreign goods that obviously handicapped Austrian exports.

Thus the realities of eighteenth-century commercial policy belie the simple opposition that Adam Smith (1723–1790), like his fellow Scotsman David Hume before him, found between the system of economic freedom which he advocated and the set of restrictive practices which he saw all around him and to which he affixed the systematic label of mercantilism. Undoubtedly the school of liberal British economists whose ideas Smith synthesized and the school of French Economists, who coined the term *laissez-faire* for the policy of non-interference, did think in terms of a disjunction between desirable liberty and existing controls. It is true too that these ideas did invade the councils of governments in this oppositional form and set off conflicts between liberal and restrictionist officials; the younger Pitt in Britain, the economic reformers in the French administration, and the liberal young Prussian bureaucrats who expressed a rising discontent with the protectionist policies of Frederick the Great are cases in point. But the fact remains that the most characteristic effect of liberal economic ideas in the latter eighteenth century was not to replace but to redefine mercantilist practice, and this explains the pattern of domestic free trade behind a mercantilist tariff policy.

The theoretical mechanics of this pattern can be seen in the distinctive character of the doctrine that was the most influential vehicle of economic liberalism on the Continent. Physiocracy, the name attributed in the nineteenth century to the subgroup of Economists who followed François Quesnay, flourished particularly in the sixties and seventies of the eighteenth century. As the label indicates, the Physiocrats believed in a natural economic order that should be inviolable by government and to this extent shared with the general run of economic liberals the general faith in the beneficence of *laissez-faire*. But at the same time the particular emphases of the Physiocrats that distinguished them from other economic liberals were such as to permit more easily the modulation of this faith into a mercantilist framework. For the Physiocrats, a corollary of the primacy of the natural order in economics was the status of the soil as the sole source of wealth and consequently of agriculture as the sole producer of value. Exchange was important to them, to be sure, but not as a criterion of wealth. For the physician Quesnay and his disciples, the economy, like the individual human, was a body, and exchange was the means by which wealth, produced originally from the soil, circulated naturally through it. Hence the Physiocrats tended to emphasize production more than trade and because of this emphasis seldom carried their subscription to free trade beyond the national frontier. Neither Catherine II of Russia nor Joseph II of Austria found any great problem of consistency in fitting an endorsement of Physiocracy into general policies of mercantilist regulation. It simply contributed to the more liberal redefinition of mercantilism which removed intermediary units between the state and the individual.

The tendency toward the relaxation of economic controls in the second half of the eighteenth century extended to the process of production as well as to trade. In its application to production, indeed, the policy of relaxation ran directly afoul not only—like trade—of the traditional intermediate authorities but also—unlike trade—of the mercantilist central bureaucracy. On the issues of industrial and agrarian liberty, then, can be found both the bitterest conflict of reformers against guilds and aristocracies and the greatest tension, within governments, between the proponents of individual enterprise and of the supporters of centralized direction. Neither type of struggle had a decisive result in the form of dramatic and categorical transformations of policy all along the economic line, but the cumulative effect of the innumerable skirmishes was definitely toward a greater freedom of production, if freedom is taken in its eighteenth-century connotation of individualism. Here again Great Britain was the model of a process shared more inchoately by the rest of Europe. The British liberalized economic conditions tacitly and practically, with little change in literal law and institutions, and yet in this unspectacular style they showed the way to European reformers all along the productive front, detouring around the guilds, converting the British aristocracy from lords to property owners, and deliberately neglecting the governmental regulations for industry still on the books from the previous centuries.

On the Continent the scope of the changes in policy was more modest. The reformers tended to have more success against the intermediate corporate authorities than against the mercantilist officials of the central bureaucracies, and even their successes against the traditional corporations were often nullified in practice. But while the scope of economic liberty was much narrower than in Britain, in the economic fields for which the policy was adopted it was much more clearly marked by definite legislation which made it an explicit social issue. Even the rulers and bureaucracies of Russia and Austria, two of Europe's most underdeveloped areas, sought to impose the conditions of economic mobility upon their largely static societies by legal fiat. More typical were the miniature states, intermediate between the western and eastern wings of Europe both in geography and in the sociopolitical spectrum, which enjoyed liberal reform that was the resultant of action taken by enlightened governments and by spontaneously stirring social groups. In western Germany and northern Italy, the economic vitality of yesteryear had become routinized, but the towns, the burghers, and the free peasantry which had once worked these flourishing economies remained in institutional being. Here the measures of progressive governors reflected their awareness of latent social possibilities that needed to be mobilized for economic growth. In the margravate of Baden, in Piedmont-Savoy, and in the Austrian-dominated Italian territories of Lombardy and Tuscany, hereditary bondage was abolished, free trade in grain was established, and the introduction of crop rotation, the use of fertilizer, and the division of common pastures—all steps toward the commercialization of agriculture—were officially sponsored under the explicit aegis of Physiocratic doctrines. In Baden, the government of the enlightened Charles Frederick (ruled 1738–1811) frankly expressed its liberalizing intention of teaching its subjects "even against their will how to manage their own business." In Piedmont-Savoy, distinguished by an exceptional degree of freedom, government policy under King Charles Emmanuel III (ruled 1730–1773) reflected this condition by proceeding to abolish the real as well as the personal obligations of the servile past—that is, the traditional dues owed by the peasant not only for his person but also for his land. Again, in Tuscany, with its strong Florentine industrial history, the Grand Duke Leopold (ruled 1765–1790, subsequently Leopold II of Austria) proceeded to abolish the guilds in a modestly successful attempt to rejuvenate Tuscan industrial life.

Thus, whereas in eastern Europe governments were striving to create the social agents of economic growth, in western Germany and northern Italy governments encouraged an existing minority of enterprising social agents to stimulate economic growth.

In France, to complete the continental spectrum, there was an even balance between governmental initiative and social pressure that reflected the comparatively even balance between mobile and static elements within the society itself. These forces were more evenly matched in France than else-where in Europe, and this fact helps to explain both the French represent-ative position as arbiter of a common European culture and the greater intensity of the political and social crisis in France which brought the Old Regime to its close. To this crisis we shall return in our final chapter.

SOCIETY AND ENLIGHTENMENT

Thus did the domestic policies of the various European states run the gamut between molding and reflecting the crucial relationship between the conservative defenders of the social establishment and the enterprising promoters of a dynamic economy. Since, as we have seen, the govern-ments' interest in the new resources of power was always circumscribed by the constant concern for the preservation of internal order and of the privi-leged classes without which this order appeared inconceivable, the states' acknowledgment and encouragement of the economic and social agencies of change remained limited, indirect, and diffuse. The most substantial and crystallized expressions of this change were neither economic, nor social, nor political—they were cultural. What was new and distinctive in European society was defined primarily in its intellectual works, and only subsequently, through politicians educated in these works, did governments assume the distinctive eighteenth-century form of "enlightened" absolu-tism and did society begin its distinctive eighteenth-century development toward political revolution.

The culture of the Enlightenment was the most articulate product of the new social dynamism in its confrontation with Europe's inherited social torpor. Because the social confrontation was European in scope, so was the span of the Enlightenment. Because the relative strength of the active and passive opponents in the social confrontation varied from region to region, the function of intellectuals in the cultural movement did too, ranging from the production of Enlightenment in Britain and France to the various degrees and ways of consuming it in central and eastern Europe. And because the philosopher, in his eighteenth-century role as a worldly intellectual, was the most self-conscious and influential spokesman for the new society in its relations with the old, he became its uncrowned king, a partner ultimately in a kind of diplomatic correspondence with the crowned kings of Europe.

CHAPTER 6

The Worldly Philosophers, 1687-1776

AROUND THE MIDDLE of the eighteenth century the proponents of the intellectual movement which took its name from their proclaimed dedication to the cause of "Enlightenment" became the representative social leaders of the party of change and the dominant figures in the culture of the whole European society. This development was the joint result of a social process which now found its focus in the Enlightenment and of an intellectual process which had equipped the Enlightenment for both its social role and its cultural hegemony.

We have already examined the ingredients of the social process. Out of it there grew an active minority of men committed to social mobility but forced by the external pressure of traditional institutions and their own loyalty to the fundamentals of hierarchy and authority in those institutions to invest their cherished desires and values in the malleable realm of ideas and to see themselves most faithfully represented by intellectual brokers. This social environment furnished the external conditions which influenced the developing thought of the Enlightenment, and explains its popular reception. Like the Italian humanism of more than two centuries before, the European Enlightenment of the eighteenth century was essentially a movement of urban culture. The restless profusion of its ideas; its positive orientation toward change; its attraction for a whole intellectual hierarchy of innovators, diffusers, and popularizers; its sense of community, which gave to its protagonists an *esprit de corps* among themselves, a continuing rapport with a growing audience, and a practical social reference for their intellectual endeavors: these qualities of Enlightenment culture grew out of the tempo and integration of city life.

But the social environment does not entirely explain the ideas themselves. For these ideas also had their own intellectual base, and their development had its own intellectual momentum. From this base and this development we can plot the course of the Enlightenment which made it socially relevant by mid-century and socially effective subsequently. This inside story of the Enlightenment's worldly philosophers is our next assignment.

The Enlightenment was not, of course, born in 1748, although it became predominant on the European scene at that point; and it was not the only considerable cultural movement of the century, although intellectual historians have frequently enough labeled the whole era with its name. Its life was coterminous with the period of this volume. It was conceived with the publication of Newton's *Principia Mathematica* in 1687 and born—insofar as any movement within the continuous development of ideas in Western civilization can be said to be "born" at all—with the coincident publication of John Locke's *Essay Concerning Human Understanding* and his *Two Treatises on Civil Government* in 1690. It finally died, after a lingering illness, in 1789, when the French Revolution scaled the alienation of its social support and the disruption of its intellectual identity.

Made up of as many fiercely independent virtuosos as it was, the movement was organized in no definite institution and subscribed to no uniform doctrine, but it did develop a real, if intangible, supra-individual identity in which its members came to participate and which took on a life of its own. In this sense we may feel justified in applying an organic analogy to its career. It can be viewed, then, in three stages: a protracted childhood in which, until the middle of the eighteenth century, it defined itself internally by the gradual coalescence of separate perceptions into a characteristic outlook and externally by self-assertion against competing outlooks; a period of maturity in which it extended its unified outlook across the board to all kinds of natural and social reality, achieving thereby a comprehensive and powerful integrity with an enormous comparative advantage over its intellectual competitors; and finally, a period of querulous and troubled old age, in which family discord fed the recovery of former competitors and the growth of new ones.

The intellectual identity, cultural preeminence, social impact, and hence the historical role of the Enlightenment date from the second stage of its development in the latter half of the eighteenth century. But if the Enlightenment was the central cultural movement of the century it was far from the only one, and we must go back into the earlier half of our period not only to trace the elements that composed it but also to take note of its rival cultural movements at a time when they were still recognizable, before they were blurred by the blaze of the triumphant mature Enlightenment.

ORIGINS OF THE ENLIGHTENMENT, 1687–1715

Every cultural movement is both a development of and a reaction against a precedent cultural movement. The Enlightenment was no exception, but of the two dimensions the proportion of filial dependence upon the dominant science, philosophy, and jurisprudence of the seventeenth century loomed uncommonly large in its origins. The continuity is visible in some of the labels affixed to the two cultural eras. Around the middle of the eighteenth century, Etienne Bonnot de Condillac (1715–1780) and Jean Le Rond d'Alembert (c. 1717–1783), two of the keynoters of the Enlightenment, coined and diffused, respectively, a formula for comparison of the Enlightenment with the rationalism of the seventeenth century. The similarities between the two movements are all the more striking for the contrast they intended. Even at their most filially impious, they could make only the tenuous distinction between the "spirit of systems" and the "systematic spirit" to epitomize the difference between the cognate movement of the seventeenth century and their own. Subsequently, historians have added to the ambiguity by denominating the period of either the "age of reason," at their discretion. And when we list the generic qualities in the two phases of rationalism there is a striking degree of overlap. Both were secular in their emphasis, natural in their focus, scientific in their models, mathematical in their methods, individualist in their criticisms, and lawful in their constructions.

For the original impulse of the Enlightenment we should look to its fathers, men who grew up in the seventeenth-century world and never entirely outgrew it but who, in the generation from 1687 to 1715, added the special touches from which the Enlightenment took off. This generation produced the patron saints of the Enlightenment—Isaac Newton for science, John Locke and Gottfried Wilhelm Leibniz for philosophy, and Pierre Bayle for a little bit of everything, critically considered. These shining lights presided over what has been called a general "crisis of the European mind"—a crisis fed by political and sectarian conflict, the accumulation of scientific experience, the growing awareness of the larger world outside Christian Europe, and a resultant skeptical habit of mind.

"Crisis" is probably too strong a word to use for the Enlightenment's setting—though any historian worth his salt can find a cultural crisis wherever he has a mind to find it—for the doubts prevalent around the turn of the eighteenth century rarely extended to the fundamentals of religion and society. But with the ever greater attention paid to realities that did not fit any of the inherited systems, the final stages of seventeenth-century thought did produce the transition and the challenge that eventuated in the Enlightenment.

What, then, were the emphases of these late masters from the "century of genius"—as historians have labeled the seventeenth century—and what did their busy little successors do with them in the first half of the eighteenth century?

The first of the transitional emphases in the late seventeenth century was the shift in the center of gravity from general principles to particular facts. The dominant mode of thought in the seventeenth century, represented by Bacon, Descartes, Hobbes, and Spinoza, had validated both principle and fact by ruling out theological dependence in the knowledge of

Gottfried Wilhelm Leibniz.
*German philosopher, math-
ematician, jurist, historian,
and pioneer of the Euro-
pean Enlightenment.*

either, but in the absence of an ordaining divinity, these thinkers had
given priority to ordering principle. Without surrendering the joint character of the framework, the generation that closed out the century tended
rather to focus on the particularity and plurality of reality and on the
empirical sources and inductive methods of knowing it. Thus Newton's
famous "rules of reasoning in philosophy" accepted the uniformity of
nature and of nature's laws but the distinctive element in his recipe was
the decisive role he attributed to specific phenomena as the basis of knowledge; to observation, analysis, and experiment as the means of processing
them; and to the descriptive nature of all general laws. Again, in spite of
rejecting the innate "clear and distinct ideas" which Descartes had deemed
the general ordering powers of the mind, Locke retained the notion of
"ideas" as the constituents of mind, but he insisted upon their origin in
specific perceptions of external objects and in specific mental operations
upon them. Even Gottfried Wilhelm Leibniz (1646–1716), high-flown
speculator and proponent of a preestablished universal harmony that he
was, made his most striking contributions through his notion of "monads,"
the mutually independent and incomparable basic units of reality which
reflected the universal order in a wholly individual way, and through his
"law of sufficient reason," a special logic of probability designed especially
to give a firm foundation to *factual* truth. Finally, in Pierre Bayle, whose
Historical and Critical Dictionary (1697) was to be a treasure chest of uninhibited information and skeptical judgments for the Enlightenment,
there was a large, rich, encyclopedic corpus of knowledge whose apparently
simple strain of critical rationalism actually covered a deeper tolerant faith
in the beneficent multiplicity and variety of natural and human creation.

Second, along with the shift in emphasis from general reason to particular facts, the generation at the turn into the eighteenth century likewise shifted its preferred fields of knowledge. Where the prime generations of the seventeenth century had systematized all fields of knowledge from natural science to politics with the connecting cables of metaphysical universals, the last generation submerged metaphysics, minimized system, and focused on the released branches of academic and intellectual concern. Both Locke and Bayle extended their condemnation of dogma to a condemnation of metaphysics, theological and secular alike, on the ground that authentic knowledge of this kind was beyond the capacity of the human mind. Locke, the most influential philosopher of the age (the influence of Leibniz, who published little, was indirect and belated), and Newton, its most influential scientist, embody the dissolution of system: after a century in which such double-barreled geniuses as Giordano Bruno, Galileo, Descartes, Hobbes, Spinoza, and Pascal had coupled science and philosophy in inseparable combinations, we find that Locke evinced little science and Newton a most naïve and confused philosophy.

Nor was this separation of the talents entirely fortuitous. Locke shifted the task of philosophy entirely to the investigation of how we know (epistemology), a concentration appropriate to the empirical approach but hardly conducive to scientific theorizing. Scholars, indeed, are still trying to fit the rationalism of Locke's natural-law political theory into the empiricism of his epistemology without much success, and the most notable philosophers of the half century that followed, Bishop George Berkeley and David Hume (again, Leibniz excepted), were—like Locke—British, empiricist, predominantly epistemological and not notably scientific. In science, analogously, Newton shifted the emphasis from mathematics, the most philosophically adaptable of the seventeenth and eighteenth-century sciences, to physics, where the greater attention to the real plurality of observed phenomena diverted men from the abstractions of philosophy in its traditional metaphysical mode. Both from our point of view and from that of his eighteenth-century successors, to be sure, Newton's achievement consisted in his miraculous synthesis of physics and mathematics, but he put the greater historical momentum into physics in two different ways: first, his emphasis upon its autonomy and upon its indispensability to mathematical laws was far greater than was that of the mathematical physicists who preceded him; and second, his equivalence of physics and mathematics undermined the belief in the absolute sovereignty of mathematical law and initiated the commitment to its necessary immanence in the facts of the actual world. It followed consistently from Newton's impulse that his great eighteenth-century successors in the world of science were distinguished for the laws and processes they discovered in the physical and life sciences and for the theories they formulated in these fields. Among these men were Joseph Priestly and Antoine Laurent Lavoisier in chemistry;

Joseph Black and Count Rumford in heat physics; Luigi Galvani, Alessandro Volta, and Charles Coulomb in electricity; Carl von Linné (Linnaeus), Denis Diderot, Georges Louis Leclerc de Buffon, and Jean Baptiste de Lamarck in biology.

A third late development of seventeenth-century culture was the extension of the critical spirit from theoretical to practical affairs. The main line of seventeenth-century intellectuals had criticized and revised the foundations of institutions rather than the institutions themselves; the last generation continued to accept both the new foundations and the old institutions, but shifted the onus of criticism to the specific operations of those institutions. Thus the church and the state became targets of intellectual discussion in the decades around the turn of the eighteenth century, but for their specific policies rather than their fundamental structure. On the church, both Locke and Bayle treated particular religious affiliation as a matter of indifference, and emphasized the nefarious moral effects of intolerant clerical practice. On the state, we have already had occasion to take notice of the particular complaints levied by Vauban, Boisguillebert, and Fénelon against the policies of Louis XIV (see pp. 71–72). Perhaps even more telling was the selection evident in the immediate reception of Locke's work on government. Men chose to see in it, not its principle of popular sovereignty or its assertion of the right of revolution, but its defense of private property and its validation of lawful as against arbitrary government—a reception which converted Locke's legacy, at least temporarily, from a model of political theory into a model of constitutional law.

A final important change of late-seventeenth-century thought, consistent with its substantive trend toward the tangible and the concrete, was perceptible in the appearance of a new level of discourse, geared to popular reception and translating the specialized language of the narrow circle of seventeenth-century scholars and thinkers into the common language of men of letters and their educated public. The popularizer who more than any other figure of his century set the tone for the century of the Enlightenment to follow was Bernard de Fontenelle (1657–1757). In works like the *History of Oracles* and *Dialogues on the Plurality of the Worlds,* both published in 1686, he put the insights of the new science and its philosophical implications relating to the lawfulness, the self-sustaining order, and the autonomy of nature, into a gracious and entertaining form which helped to make the revolution in cosmology a conversation piece. More important perhaps, the style in which he diffused seventeenth-century thought carried with it a subtle change in point of view: by presenting its results as matters of common sense he gently dismissed the metaphysics it had prized and exalted the self-evident truths of everyman's reason. With his sure touch for the dramatic issue, finally, he presented the achievements of his century in the eye-catching guise of a victorious duel: he turned what had been the purely literary feud of "the Ancients and the

Moderns" on the comparative values of ancient and contemporary tragedy into a celebration of the intellectual progress registered by the naturalism and the rationalism of the "century of genius" beyond even the highest points of past human attainment.

It was the unprecedented progress in human culture achieved by the intellectual pioneers of the seventeenth century that popularizers like Fontenelle proposed to disseminate. In England, Joseph Addison (1672–1719) and Richard Steele (1672–1729) made this campaign into an explicit program, when they published *The Spectator* daily in 1711 and 1712, with the avowed aim of bringing "Philosophy out of closets and libraries . . . to dwell in clubs and assemblies."

THE ORTHODOX REVIVAL AND THE CULT OF SENTIMENT, 1690–1740

Accompanying these final modulations of seventeenth-century rationalism in the generation that spanned the break between the centuries, two cultural tendencies of a quite different order also made a successful transition from the seventeenth century into the new era. These tendencies—religious orthodoxy and the cult of feeling—would live through the transitional generation to form the competitive cultural background against which the young Enlightenment would grow during the first half of the eighteenth century.

Despite the threat of naturalism and pantheism from the main line of seventeenth-century philosophy, religious orthodoxy had shown a formidable intellectual as well as ecclesiastical vitality in at least two of the three established Christian confessions—the Catholic and the Calvinist. And despite the threat of total regulation by the aesthetics of seventeenth-century classicism, the poetry and drama of imagination, passion, symbol, and wit had ignored, strained, or broken through the classical "unities" to create the powerful literature of Milton, Racine, and Dryden.

Occasionally, as the brilliant figures of Milton and Pascal illustrate, the two extra-rational cultural tendencies that were rooted in religious piety and in human emotion had met in creative union, but such junctures were rare and smacked of individual heresy. In general, orthodoxy had prevailed over feeling in the seventeenth century. Piety was dominated by dogmatic conformity that either repelled or subordinated spontaneous emotion just as it rejected the autonomy of reason and made it dependent. The force of feeling and imagination was diverted into the orthodox service that produced at its best the Lutheran hymns of a Paul Gerhardt (1607–1676) and at its worst the excesses of heresy hunting and witchcraft. There was not yet, in the seventeenth century, sufficient trust in the authenticity of man's imaginings or in the reliability of his feelings to do without the direction and control of them. Appreciation did grow for the cultural function of these human powers in the immediate perception of reality and in the creation of art, but within a framework set by faith or reason. By far the greatest cultural achievements of imagination and feeling during the seventeenth century—apart from the rare religious genius of a Milton or a Pascal—had come from the engagement of these faculties with the classical rules of reason, which gave them both support and challenge. The typical results of this engagement were what might be called indirect products of emotional and imaginative culture—Racine's tragedies of the noble passions and the address to "the passions and humors" of human nature in the penetrating satires of Molière and Dryden.

During the first half of the eighteenth century, these nonrational cultural currents not only maintained themselves but developed in directions that permitted them to live through even the subsequent triumph of the rational Enlightenment. These developments went essentially along two lines: first, religious orthodoxy adjusted itself to the vogue of a critical and practical reason through a combination of spirited defense in the name of tradition, shrewd appropriation of a rational dimension, and the wholehearted alliance with emotionalism. Second, the aspects of human culture rooted in the more feeling, imaginative, and intuitive faculties of men developed independent movements, both through the powerful role that emotions now began to play openly in religious piety and religious music and through the direct cultivation of a frankly sentimental literature to accompany the perfection of the satiric fantasy.

Types of Orthodox Revival

The religious orthodoxy which arose just before the turn of the century would provide fresh targets for the secular Enlightenment, but it also equipped churchmen with the means of their own preservation in this duel.

In their defense of organized churches against both rational criticism from without and "heresy" from within, the orthodox found their intellectual scope limited. But the vigor of their attacks against all presumed violators of the divine order betokened the continuing appeal of unbroken tradition. At the end of the seventeenth century Bishop Jacques Bénigne Bossuet (1627–1704), the official troubleshooter of French Catholicism, asserted against all comers the virtues of divine-right monarchy and Catholic hierarchy. He seems in retrospect a caricature of an intellectual today, but his exposition of the divine-right political principle, his scheme of providential universal history, and his analysis of Protestant sectarianism were contemporary enough to remain standard targets through much of the eighteenth century. One of his most spirited antagonists, moreover, was a kind of mirror image of Bossuet, confirming the persistence of his kind of institutional orthodoxy. The exiled Hugenot pastor Pierre Jurieu, whom we have already met as a critic of the aging Louis XIV, polemicized passionately for the nominal supremacy of the rights of free conscience over the authority of a persecuting church, as well as of a tyrannical ruler, but his insistence on assigning the protection of these rights to social and religious corporations, in a pattern reminiscent of sixteenth- and early-seventeenth-century Presbyterianism, and his savage attack upon Bayle for extending the defense of toleration and dissent beyond the interests of the true Reformed faith, confirmed the essential orthodoxy of his Calvinist position. As Bossuet perpetuated the intellectual defense of orthodoxy by associating it with the preservation of worldly order, Jurieu showed how to perpetuate it by associating it with the defense of personal liberty. In either case, they illustrated the continuity of conservative orthodoxy, of the Catholic or the Protestant variety, as an intellectual as well as institutional counterpoint of the Enlightenment.

A second kind of orthodoxy, which may be called moderate orthodoxy, became rooted in these decades around the turn of the eighteenth century by absorbing elements of the new science and philosophy into the traditional religions. The most striking Catholic influence along these lines was the subtle work of Nicolas de Malebranche (1638–1715), the Oratorian priest who argued persuasively and incessantly through some thirty volumes of writing and through years of edifying discourse in sundry aristocratic salons for the reconciliation of dogma and Descartes, faith and reason. Among Protestants, Leibniz strove for a similar kind of harmony by elevating both reason and religion above partisan considerations—that is, by making reason more inclusive than the Cartesians did and by making theology more ecumenical than either the Catholics or the Protestants were wont to do. Although he himself remained rather a philosopher than a theologian and was suspect to both confessions, his influence in the eighteenth century went into German Protestant as well as into European secular thought.

The British branch of this modernized Protestant orthodoxy also received its main impetus around the start of the century. The much-maligned Latitudinarians became the dominant party within the "established" Anglican state church—the original "Establishment"—as it was reconstituted by William III after the Glorious Revolution and perpetuated by the Hanoverian Whigs after 1714, but despite the frequent indictment of them for worldliness and superficiality they did produce an intellectual defense which diverted into orthodox clerical channels much of the fashionable deism characteristic of the British Enlightenment. In both the sophistication and profundity of their sermons and treatises they fell far short, to be sure, of the Cambridge Platonists, who had woven a delicate mesh of mystical faith and reason after the Restoration of 1660. For the Latitudinarians' reason was simple and common-sensical rather than architectonic and all-embracing, and their faith tended to be trimmed rather to the reasonable requirements of the moral practical life than to its assumptions and its source. But many of the Latitudinarians had studied with the Cambridge Platonists, and if they vulgarized the exalted rationality of the latter, Latitudinarian bishops like John Tillotson (1630–1694) and Edward Stillingfleet (1635–1699) did diffuse reasonableness, a tolerant spirit, aversion to dogma, and an ethic of social responsibility into commonplaces of the British official and educated classes.

A third kind of orthodoxy, finally, which we may term reactionary orthodoxy, also took new forms in this transitional generation and so could remain a definite, if recessive, cultural factor through the eighteenth century and beyond. The characterization of "reactionary" is meant, for this religious context, not in any pejorative sense but literally, to designate the point of view that would undo existing ecclesiastical arrangements in favor of an earlier model of establishment. For the distinctive attitude of the reactionaries was their rejection not simply of secular trends—for this was also true of the orthodox conservatives—but of the moderate adaptations of orthodoxy as well, even when such adaptations were built into the official established churches.

The two most spectacular examples of clerical reaction in this sense were the British Nonjurors and the Russian Old Believers. The Nonjurors were some four hundred Anglican clerics who accepted deprivation from their offices rather than take a new oath of allegiance to the revolutionary monarchy of William and Mary. Their original motivation was undoubtedly a mixture of politics and conscience rather than defense of distinctive principle, but in the debate that they initiated during the 1690's they asserted a principle that made them the vanguard of the High Church party within the Church of England and hence of anti-official orthodoxy in the eighteenth century. The principle was the spiritual independence of the Church, and on the basis of it, High Churchmen initiated such running disputes as the Convocation controversy, from 1697, on the right of the clergy to its own regular assemblies and the Bangorian controversy of 1717 on the corporate rights of the Anglican church vis-à-vis both individual judgment and temporal authority. Because it deemed the undogmatic and unritualistic temper of Low Church Latitudinarianism to be tainted by the politically motivated toleration of dissent, the High Church party developed its institutional defense of the Church into an assertion of literal doctrine and strict observance of ritual.

The origins of the Old Believers go back before our period to the mid-seventeenth-century reaction against Patriarch Nikon's revision of traditional Russian ritual and liturgy to conform with the sources of the Orthodox Church in the light of Greek scholarship. But it was only after 1700, when Peter the Great abolished the remnants of ecclesiastical autonomy, and like the British, associated the established church with the rational attitudes of political administration, that the cultural strain of Old

Belief took its long-range form. As the participation of Old Believers in Pugachev's revolt shows, they came to represent and to symbolize the inchoate attitude of all those who would have no truck with modernity.

A final variety of religious reaction was represented by French Jansenism. Certainly it was not as clearly reactionary as the others we have considered, but the eighteenth-century Jansenists in France showed an explicit connection between religious piety and social reaction which was obscure in the purer examples of traditional religiosity. In its origins and early career, as we may recall (see pp. 20–21), Jansenism had been a kind of Puritanism within the Catholic Church, with a logical rigor in its theology of God's omnipotence, a moral vigor in its principle of man's total commitment to God's prescriptions, and an uncompromising·honesty in its penetration into human frailty which had made it a pervasive intellectual and cultural force in the seventeenth century. But after the joint papal and royal persecution of Louis XIV's last years, this movement for a reformation of the spirit tended to become, in the eighteenth century, a respectable ideological cover for sundry social and political tendencies of a reactionary kind. Its theological and moral fervor faded into an institutionalized Gallicanism (advocacy of the French national church against the Jesuits' championship of papal authority), and as Gallicans, the Jansenists became associated with the various groups in the disgruntled Church hierarchy, the lower clergy, and the aristocratic *parlementaires,* who found in Jansenist Gallicanism a pious common front for organizing opposition against centralizing tendencies within the monarchy. There was, of course, nothing reactionary in Gallicanism itself, but in the hands of these partisans the Jansenist attitude tended to become a kind of aggressive fundamentalism, directed against what was progressive in their opponents—against the Jesuits' addiction to learning and accommodation to secular culture, and against the monarchy's policy of equalizing the burdens of taxation. It is hardly surprising to find that through this development what had been inspiring in the seventeenth century became obscurantist in the eighteenth, when Jansenism became associated, not with a philosopher like Blaise Pascal or a dramatist like Jean Racine, but with mob delirium, the relentless pursuit of Jesuits, and the preservation of aristocratic privilege.

Types of Emotional Culture
Essentially independent of religious orthodoxy, and as the future was to show, even more dangerous a rival to the reasonableness of the Enlightenment, the cultural movement which we may call—for want of a better term—emotionalism also took a new lease on life in the transition from the seventeenth to the eighteenth century. But if both the transitional form and the subsequent history of this movement are to be understood, we must fix precisely—as contemporaries did not—its ambiguous

relationship with religion. For one main type of it still took a religious form and through much of the eighteenth century was judged to be as traditionally dependent as always upon dogma and church when in actuality the relations of the emotions with religion were being completely transformed.

Toward the close of the seventeenth century a movement arose which deemed the emotional way of reaching the truth more important than the definition of the truth to be reached. With this shift in emphasis, emotional*ism* was born. Alienated from religious orthodoxy by the orthodox emphasis upon the defined truth and upon the habitual means of apprehending it, repelled from rationalism by the rationalists' intellectual approach to passion, will, and intuition, and yet unready to declare the sovereignty of the emotions, the protagonists of the emotions turned to revivalist religion as their appropriate vehicle. Quietism in France, Pietism in Germany, and Wesleyanism in England became its chief social forms, the music of Bach and Handel its chief aesthetic expression.

Quietism, a development of the highly charged Spanish mysticism associated with St. Teresa and formulated by Miguel de Molinos (1640–c.1697), became influential in the France of the 1690's, thanks mostly to the sympathy of Archbishop Fénelon. It was typical of emotionalism in its indifference to dogma and ritual and its stress on the most fervent degree of love as the only way to union with God. It was less typical in its focus on passive contemplation, inward segregation of the spirit, and self-destruction of the individual will. The vogue during the age of Enlightenment itself of the Swedish mystic Emanuel Swedenborg (1688–1772)—"dreamer of emotion," as Kant was to call him—indicated that mysticism did indeed remain an alternative in the emotional void left by orthodoxy and rationalism.

But it was not with the mystics that the future of emotionalism lay. The transition between religiosity and the autonomy of the emotions was represented rather by the kind of evangelical movement pioneered by the German Pietists and continued by the English Wesleyans (a common function that permits us to label both as "pietists" in a general sense). No more than any other intellectual current of the eighteenth century was pietism as simple or uniform as our label would imply. Thus mysticism, persistent in the German religious tradition from medieval times and recently revived in the influential writings of the early-seventeenth-century mystic, Jakob Boehme (1575–1624), remained an essential feature in the Pietism of so prominent a leader as Count Nikolaus Ludwig von Zinzendorf (1700–1760), sponsor of the most influential of all Pietist foundations—the Herrnhut Community of the Moravian Brethren. Mysticism was, moreover, a factor in the development of most pietists, from the Saxon Jakob Spener (1635–1705), more than any other single individual the founder of the movement, to John Wesley (1703–1791), founder of the Methodist Church and pietism's most famous disciple in the English-speaking world. Mysticism contributed to pietism a spiritual alienation from the arid intellectuality of dogma and an emphasis instead on personal experience and on the emotional immediacy of faith.

But the pietists added two other essential traits which distinguished their movement from mysticism and made its ultimate impact that of a general cultural force rather than merely a particular religious sect. These traits were individualism and activism: pietists were individualistic in that they regarded the religous experience as essentially personal, and they were activist in their encouragement of good social works as the only authentic expressions of piety. Such features obviously created tensions with the self-abnegation and inwardness that were other pietist values, and indeed, in their respective emphases on the transcendence of personal spirit and the immersion in communal practice, individualism and activism did not comport perfectly with each other either. Thus pietists were torn between the outer passive acceptance of a Lutheran or Anglican church and of a secular world from which they were spiritually and emotionally alienated and the inner challenge to penetrate the church and the world actively with congregations of the true faithful and with beneficent foundations of missions, hospitals, schools, workhouses, and orphanages.

Because such divisions of conscience were not threats to an original consistency but were built into the very essence of pietism, they help to account for its far-reaching historical influence and importance. For they reflected the impulse of men to reassert the ancient integrity of faith in terms appropriate to a dawning new age by withdrawing the individual soul from dependence on this world but then giving it practical effect in this world. However inconsistent from the points of view of dogma or reason, the living otherworldly faith and the living worldly deed became one in the immediacy of men's feeling for God and man. Thus the pietists fixed on human feeling as the decisive faculty in faith that could renew itself in an individualistic and practical age, and the moving and enduring qualities of Methodist hymns still attest to the fruitfulness of the new emphasis. Pietism could compete with the Enlightenment because it offered an independent alternative direction for the ideal individualism and the real worldly activity drawn by both movements from the atmosphere of their common century.

Pietism was, indeed, to outlive the Enlightenment as an identifiable cultural force. Like the early Enlightenment, it took root in the last decades of the seventeenth century and spread well into the forties of the eighteenth. But the form which it took during this period—small conventicles within the established Protestant churches of Germany and England—proved unstable, and this instability, combined with the cultural preeminence and intellectual attractiveness of the mature Enlightenment,

Handel conducting an eighteenth-century orchestra and chorus.

reduced the movement temporarily to an obscure and subterranean existence during the middle decades of the century. But then, in the seventies and eighties, as the Enlightenment began to unravel, pietism found the three forms in which it became a permanent cultural force. In England, by virtue of its revivalistic appeal to large masses of working people it had organized a myriad of independent Methodist churches. In Germany, it exercised a less crystallized but a culturally more pervasive force. Within the established Evangelical church it was asserting the validity of natural human feelings in the rejuvenation of faith, and through its influence on theologians like Friedrich Schleiermacher (1768–1834), German Pietism would prepare the way for cultural modernism in the Protestant church. And beyond the church, the Pietist influence would help to launch the creative movement in thought and the arts associated with the giant figures of Goethe and Schiller and dedicated to exalting the role of spontaneous emotion in the freedom of the individual.

What the pietists achieved in religion and contributed to literature, composers like Johann Sebastian Bach (1685–1750) and George Frederick Handel (1685–1759) were achieving in religious music and contributing to secular music. Both these composers worked during the first half of the eighteenth century to deepen the emotional life of church and society by combining the natural human feelings expressed through Italian musical forms with the themes of Protestant piety. Bach concentrated on the emotional expansion of church music, Handel on the Protestant infusions into worldly musical forms which established the oratorio to give a new freedom to choral drama. The pattern of their musical influence, like the sermons and literature of pietism, outran their own generation and their own categories. For the legacy of Bach too was submerged in the mannered music of the middle decades, but then, toward the end of the century, his influence joined that of Handel to inspire Joseph Haydn (1732–1809) and Wolfgang Amadeus Mozart (1756–1791) with the added dimension that gives their later music its most profound emotional appeal.

The sovereignty of the emotions that pietism prepared did not come to full fruition until the Protestantism and the romanticism of the nineteenth century. In the pietism of the first half of the eighteenth century the validity of human feeling was still balanced by the validity of traditional faith and church. But there was another area of culture in which, during this same period, the emotions were recognized in their own right. For the modern novel was born then precisely as the mode of analyzing human character through the depiction of an individual's sentiments and as the mode of communicating the insight through the deliberate appeal to the reader's sentiments.

Early in the century Jonathan Swift's *Tale of a Tub* (1704) and *Gulliver's Travels* (1726) had applied the seventeenth-century satiric tradition to the novel form and demonstrated the capacity of that form to make narrative coherence derivative from the power of imagination and fantasy. But it was in the decade of the 1730's that the novel of "sensibility" and with it the cult of emotionalism came into being. "Emotionalism" is an inexact term for the set of attitudes that holds the combination of passion, feeling, intuition, and will to afford an immediate access to reality superior to that attained through either the graduated steps of discursive reason or the self-denying leap of blind faith. Its appearance as an influential cultural movement apart from religious faith and independent of rational control was most prominently associated with the publication of the tremendously popular *Pamela*, by Samuel Richardson, in 1740; but this work was a representative rather than a unique cultural product, for it came on the heels of other novels in the same genre. Pierre de Marivaux's *Marianne*, published from 1731 in eleven volumes (but still left incomplete), and Antoine Prévost's more famous *Manon Lescaut* (also 1731) probed inexhaustibly, like *Pamela*, the feelings of the heroine—in each case, characteristically, the protagonist was a sensitive and articulate female—feelings that were stimulated by the conflict between instincts and morals.

The emphasis upon feeling as the most integral and authentic faculty of the individual and upon the articulation of it as the most genuine kind of communication between individuals swept through Europe and threatened to drown the continent in a sea of tears. The connection of the sentimental novel with the emotional underground that later emerged strongly in the preromanticism of Rousseau's *Nouvelle Héloïse* (1761) and Goethe's *Sorrows of Young Werther* (1774) is obvious, but what may not be so obvious is the positive influence it had upon the Enlightenment

Samuel Richardson. *His sentimental and moralizing effusion
initiated the literary form of
the modern novel.*

as well. Marivaux, to be sure, was hostile to Voltaire and the Enlightenment in general, and the tongue-in-cheek attitude toward Pamela's vapor-
ings which Henry Fielding put to work in *Joseph Andrews* (1742) smacked
strongly of the Enlightenment's aversion to excess. But men of the
Enlightenment as critical as Denis Diderot and Samuel Johnson admired
Pamela precisely for its "sentiment," and hence the literary cult of feeling
confirms the dual relationship of religious and emotional cultural tendencies in the first half of the eighteenth century with the contemporary
Enlightenment: they furnished it with a target against which the Enlightenment sharpened its critical reason, but they also supplied it with an
appreciation of human emotions as morally sanctioned forces in a providential natural order. With due moderation, the emotions and the moral
order alike were taken into the fabric of Enlightenment thought.

THE EARLY ENLIGHTENMENT, 1715–1748

Since several cultural tendencies persisted and developed during the
period, it is clear that when the hundred-year span from the end of the
seventeenth century to the end of the eighteenth is called the Age of
Enlightenment—as it usually is—the title is meant not as a summary
of the century's culture but as a judgment of what was dominant
in it and most characteristic of it. The labelers have only followed the
self-congratulatory judgment by the protagonists of one definite cultural

movement among many when these advocates named their whole century the *siècle des lumières* after the light of knowledge which they themselves purported to bring their benighted fellowmen. Pursuant to this label these advocates—and many historians after them—tended to distort the movement, attributing to it both an internal consistency and an exclusive cultural influence which it did not in fact possess. The advocates and their movement require historical definition before we can even begin to talk about them.

The most numerous and most prominent of the advocates were grouped under the label *philosophes,* but the literal reference of the term in the eighteenth century to the philosophers of the French Enlightenment did not give its full meaning, for both "French" and "philosophers" must be understood in a special way. Because the French forms of the Enlightenment dominated Europe, we can speak of its devotees as *philosophes* whether they were French or not, in recognition of the international vogue of the French fashion in culture; but we must also remember, then, that there were national distinctions among the *philosophes.* More important, the *philosophes* were philosophers in a distinctive sense, for they lacked some of the most obvious traits which we have come to associate with philosophers and they obviously possessed traits which we have come to dissociate from philosophers: the *philosophes* were addicted neither to contemplation, nor to abstraction, nor to logical consistency, nor even to the inquiry into pure ideas and their mutual relations; the *philosophes* were, on the other hand, committed to the application of ideas to social criticism, and to political change. But if they appear to be closer to twentieth-century intellectuals than to twentieth-century philosophers in these respects, they were nonetheless philosophers both in the loose eighteenth-century sense of the term and in the fundamental sense of the term generally. For the *philosophes* asked the basic questions about God, man, and nature; they sought behind effects for their causes; and they looked through phenomena for intelligible realities that underlay them. The *philosophes* combined the vocations of philosopher and intellectual which would be separated later, and they could combine these vocations simply because they felt that the most fundamental ideas were necessarily applicable, communicable, effective, and socially relevant, and that there existed no valid pure idea to be thought or separable basic reality to be analyzed. The *philosophes* admitted variety and shrugged off illogicality not because they abjured philosophy, but because of the malleable character of the world they philosophized about.

The Enlightenment was a movement which actually first assumed an identifiable form between 1715 and 1748, and then only as a loose collection of like-minded individuals, engaged in the most various kinds of intellectual enterprises but associated through mutual recognition in the common task of turning the philosophies of secular reason and natural sci-

MAJOR FIGURES OF THE ENLIGHTENMENT

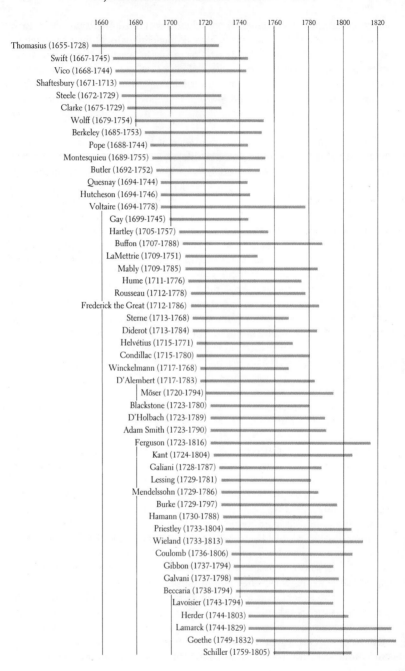

ence into a real cultural force competitive with contemporary orthodoxies and the emotive arts. Not until the intellectual generation of 1748–1776 did these protagonists of Enlightenment develop the organized communication and doctrine which endowed them with a comparative unity among themselves and a clear preeminence over their cultural competitors. And even this halcyon phase was short-lived, yielding to the unraveling of the Enlightenment itself and to the cultural pluralism which featured the last quarter of the eighteenth century.

But when the *philosophes* are not regarded as a closed party and their Enlightenment as an intellectual monopoly the movement can indeed be considered as the central cultural theme of the eighteenth century. The variations in internal organization and consistency among the *philosophes* were the chief expressions of the relationship between cultural innovation and society in the eighteenth century. Competitive cultural movements, orthodox and enthusiastic alike, oriented themselves during the same century primarily according to the threats and possibilities offered by the Enlightenment at any particular time. For both the social and the intellectual history of the eighteenth century, then, we are directed to the successive stages of Enlightenment culture.

The early Enlightenment first took identifiable shape amid the changed conditions of cultural production which followed upon the passing of the Stuarts, the death of Louis XIV, and the clearing of the strife-torn atmosphere associated with both sets of royal personages. The stimulus and focus of creative endeavor shifted from the patronage and entourage of kings to the educated groups in the society at large. In both France and Great Britain, the development of wealth, leisure, and self-confidence in the middle classes coincided around 1715 with a significant reduction in the cultural influence of royal courts (owing to the death of Louis XIV and the accession of the Hanoverians, respectively), and with a shift of aristocratic culture from royal to popular standards of taste. It was precisely in France and Britain that the social organizations of intellectual life were most advanced and the early Enlightenment most concentrated. Its characteristic channels of communication were academies (capital and provincial), salons, journals, books, pamphlets, and unpublished manuscripts and correspondences, all serving at this juncture primarily a "republic of letters" within the limited circle of intellectuals by providing forums for the exchange, debate, and mutual clarification of their ideas. The literary forms in which these citizens of the republic of letters communicated were equally various; they included the formal treatise, the informal essay, poetry, drama, the novel, and literary criticism. The typical protagonist of the Enlightenment worked in several of these genres. It was part both of his new self-image as representative of the society at large and of his pragmatic approach to affairs of the mind that he adhered to no academic protocol but wrote in whatever form would attract the widest interest, be most appropriate to his subject of the moment, and act with best narcotic effect on the official censors of church and state.

The content of the new Enlightenment culture was determined in part by these conditions and in part by the intellectual ingredients which the previous, turn-of-the-century generation had left floating free and which the early *philosophes* now sought to fuse into a relevant world view. From this purely intellectual point of view, the early Enlightenment may be seen as a movement which accepted the primacy of nature, law, and reason from the legacy of seventeenth-century classicism and rationalism but modified the meaning and the direction of these principles by applying to them the critical and empirical emphases added by the generation of Newton, Locke, and Bayle and the passionate moral individualism drawn from the memory of seventeenth-century religious and aesthetic dissent. The *philosophes* combined these cultural strands, moreover, in the context of the worldly concerns and opportunities opened by their own generation of comparative peace and prosperity. The metaphysical rational order which men of the seventeenth century had made the basic character of reality receded to the status of unspoken and even unconscious assumption as the function of reason itself changed for the men of the new Enlightenment. From the dispassionate explanation of natural reality and of man as part of natural reality, reason became the weapon of a fighting creed aimed at the mastery of nature for the sake of a wiser and better humanity and against competing orthodox or emotional—that is, "fanatical"—creeds. As the function of reason shifted, so did its character. As its function shifted from the construction of a stable and necessary order of nature to the demonstration of the freedom of individuals and of the orderly mutual relations which they could construct for themselves on the model of nature, reason became more concrete, more flexible, more utilitarian, more commonsensical, more libertarian, and more dynamic.

The mechanics of this transition from the rationalism of the seventeenth century to the reasonableness of the eighteenth was more evident in the early Enlightenment of the more stagnant and traditional national societies than in the more mobile Atlantic societies like France and Britain, where the break with the past was sharper and more deliberate. In Germany, for example, representative figures of the early Enlightenment such as Christian Thomasius (1655–1728) and Christian Wolff (1679–1754) carried enough of the past with them, both in their social position as intellectuals and in their theoretical position as thinkers, to expose the seventeenth-century scaffolding of eighteenth-century Enlightenment. Both were professors, thereby prolonging the social distance and academic flavor of seventeenth-century thought into eighteenth-century Germany in contrast to the literary tone of the Enlightenment in the west. Thomasius, moreover, developed his pattern of Enlightenment thought during the first two decades of the new century by combining the influences of seventeenth-century rationalism, Lockean empiricism, and German Pietism, thereby commuting between the Pietist values—freedom of conscience, individuality of faith, and the duty of pious charity—and corresponding secular principles—freedom of expression, moral primacy of individual happiness, and a commonsense rationalism as the guide from individual to social interests. Nonetheless, he always retained a Pietist spiritualism and indifference to institutions that was quite uncharacteristic of the western Enlightenment.

A bit later, in the second quarter of the century, Christian Wolff performed an analogous service for the rationalization of the German Lutheran tradition when he developed a philosophy that went far to reconcile the tensions between faith and reason in the direction of reason. Where Leibniz had complicated reason to make it harmonious with faith, Wolff appropriated the secular and homogeneous notion of reason from the recent doctrines of natural law and accomodated faith to it. Thus he stimulated the rationalist movement in German Protestant theology that would be known as Neology and he contributed to the philosophy of the Enlightenment the ultimate goal of human "perfection" as the secular equivalent of salvation. But for all his substantive contributions to the culture of the Enlightenment, Wolff's addiction to metaphysics, and the scholastic aridity of his writing, held him apart from the men of the Enlightenment proper, not only because his style resembled rather the heavy tradition they attacked than the graceful mode they espoused but because it indicated his persistence in a contemplative posture apart from the earthly reality in the midst of which they would frolic.

But if the lethargic societies of central and southern Europe best reveal the historical conditions of the early Enlightenment, the volatile societies of France and Great Britain produced versions of it which most clearly reveal its essential contemporary features. It is not easy to get at what these were, for at this early stage the partisans of the French and British Enlightenments were many and frequently obscure; no rank order of talents or prestige had as yet developed to weave threads of influence through the intellectual maze; a good number of the contributors to the Enlightenment mentality were, at this early stage, like Alexander Pope with his ambiguous religiosity, intellectual hybrids; and their fields of literary endeavor were various and disconnected. The multiplicity and diversity of its products must indeed be accounted a characteristic trait of the early Enlightenment, but it had certain common traits as well—traits which were consistent with its variety.

In order to select those traits of the early Enlightenment which were most relevant to the history of the Enlightenment as a whole we may focus, for our illustrations, upon the early thought of figures like David Hume (1711–1776), Charles de Secondat, Baron de Montesquieu (1689–1755), and François Marie Arouet, known as Voltaire

The young Voltaire. *The look of the man —acerbic, proud, and intelligent—parallels the tone of his work. He was obviously every inch a king—of the* philosophes.

(1694–1778), whose intellectual development spanned the early and mature stages of Enlightenment. When so considered, the distinctive functions of the early Enlightenment were, first, the frank acceptance and dissemination of the critical and empirical points of view which had been proposed in special contexts by the generation of Locke and Newton; second, the construction of a general intellectual framework of physical and human nature within which new theories of the world, man, and society, at once realistic and reasonable, could be subsequently developed; and third, the preliminary and piecemeal application of the new combination of practicality and rationality to particular events, works, and activities.

The New Reason

In their diffusion of the critical and empirical ideas which they took over from the preceding generation, the early *philosophes* took two paths. The more obvious device was the popularization of their intellectual patron saints, such as Voltaire undertook in his open adulation of Pierre Bayle and his epitomes of the ideas of Locke and Newton in his *Philosophical Letters* (1734) and his *Elements of the Philosophy of Newton* (1738). Their more original device was to identify the skeptical, practical, limited kind of reason which they adopted from the previous generation, and to match it deliberately against any metaphysics, whether of faith or reason, in a way which had not been dared by their predecessors. This shift from the older juxtaposition to the newer opposition of faith and reason and of different kinds of reason to one another was first prepared in the crucial field that intersected science and philosophy. Known to the seventeenth and eighteenth centuries alike as "natural philosophy," it became the arena, after the turn of the century, of a bitter intellectual feud between Cartesians and Newtonians on the metaphysical versus the empirical derivation of natural laws. The prevalence of the Newtonian view by mid-century spelled victory for Voltaire's prescription to "let the facts prevail" and consequently for the *philosophes'* address to particular kinds of knowledge as the materials of rational truth.

The same kind of emphasis then made its appearance in philosophy itself. Although the orthodox Anglican clericalism of Bishop George Berkeley (1685–1753) places him in general outside the Enlightenment, the subjective idealism which he developed to show the derivation of all knowledge from the operation of the mind upon its sensations rather than from any logical structure in the external world was actually a radical empiricism and reflected the spirit of the age. But it was David Hume, an authentic *philosophe* and the most original philosopher of the age, who made the most throughgoing application of the new attitude to reason. He wrote his *Treatise of Human Nature* (1739–1740) to show that "the experimental method of reasoning" reduced all certain knowledge to sense impressions, demeaned all rational connections among such impressions to associations based on fortuitous psychological habits and social customs, and therefore posited an empirically derived "science of man"—consisting primarily of "moral philosophy" and history—as the necessary basis of the whole corpus of science and philosophy. Hume's *Treaties* went too far for his colleagues among the *philosophes*, since his extension of skepticism from metaphysical to all rational coherence among things struck at the assumptions they tacitly held. But they chose rather to ignore than to refute it, and he remained a *philosophe* in good standing—indeed, the most popular Briton in the camp of the Enlightenment—because his rigorous empiricism and his hypercritical use of reason simply carried to an extreme the particular emphasis of the early Enlightenment. The *philosophes* did not mean all the negative things they said about Descartes, for they carried with them more of his principles of a rational order than they knew, but they could accept Hume, even if they could not respond to him, because their early impulses were as critical as his. And Hume himself followed a common practice of the early Enlightenment when his skepticism turned him from philosophy to history. Scholars once held that this development of Hume's marked a frightened retreat from the consequences of his own philosophical position, but it is now generally agreed that he was consistent both with himself and with his age when his rejection of "refined reasoning" in the abstract left him free to pursue the actual varieties of human behavior in his quest for uniform principles of human nature.

David Hume. *He was both a formal philosopher and a* philosophe, *a comparatively rare combination in the eighteenth century.*

The New Framework

In the place of the rejected supernatural order and metaphysical unity which had for so long supported men's thinking about the world and man, the *philosophes* now built a new platform of basic principles which would be more appropriate to their immediate concern with man's life in this world and from which the rethinking about it could be launched. Their favored intellectual fields for this purpose were natural religion and morals. Declared independent of their traditional theological and metaphysical tutelage, both fields now became arenas of primary principles and served together as the mold for the worldliness, the hedonism, and the humanism which were henceforth ingrained in the Enlightenment.

In the field of natural religion the most characteristic innovation of the early Enlightenment was deism, the antitheological movement which took the form of "natural theology." Deism may be narrowly construed to signify merely the theology that holds God to act exclusively through the invariable laws He has established in the natural creation and that holds men to know God exclusively through the natural reason which understands those laws. Certainly deism meant this kind of natural theology in the eighteenth century–but it also meant something more. It meant an anticlericalism which mounted a frontal attack on every ecclesiastical dogma, ritual, practice, and influence presumably directed against the rational autonomy of the individual layman. Deism originated in Britain as a natural theology, and for the forty years of its prominence there—between 1690 and 1730—its theological character as a religion of natural reason undoubtedly continued to prevail. But even in Britain this classification fails to convey the tone of the tendency. John Locke's *Reasonableness of Christianity* (1695) furnished the fundamental arguments of the movement, but there was an essential difference between Locke's cautious endeavor to reconcile reason with revelation and the work of authentic deists like John Toland (*Christianity Not Mysterious*, 1696) and Anthony Collins (*Discourse of the Grounds and Reasons of the Christian Religion*, 1724), who attacked the unreasonableness both of dogma and of Scripture itself. Indeed, Christian though they claimed to be, the British deists not only submitted revelation to the rational judgment of the ordinary individual but resurrected the anticlerical tradition of attributing dogmatic and ritual error to priestly deception and exploitation of the laity.

In the British case, to be sure, the anticlerical motif was countered by the constitutional moderation which was only now beginning to form part of what would come to be considered the British national character. Criticism of institutions remained subordinate to the assertion of the individual's autonomy within them, and consequently the impetus of deism was absorbed after 1730 by the respectable and tolerant reasonableness of Latitudinarian Low Churchmanship. It was in France that deism had its fullest, broadest, and longest effect, for here it was not only the central theological position in the whole intellectual community of *philosophes* but it included, as an equal emphasis, a virulent attack on every institutional aspect of Christianity.

The caustic criticism which the French *philosophes* mounted on Bible, doctrine, church, and clergy alike under the aegis of facts perceivable by everyman and of rational notions conceivable by everyman distributed the deist impact along a wider front and gave it a different cultural function from its counterparts either in Britain or in Germany, where it was limited by and large to the depreciation of revealed theology in favor of natural theology. In France, the theology of deism was joined to a anticlerical *an* campaign because in France, Catholic dogma had been indissolubly associated with a church which furnished common symbols and linkages for the social and political establishments. The struggle for natural religion against organized religion thus epitomized the general struggle for a larger individual liberty against the constructions of traditional institutions.

The representative function of religion for the protagonists of the early Enlightenment revealed an essential fact about the movement at this stage: the *philosophes* specialized in religion because religion afforded a peripheral approach to social reality at a time when the *philosophes* felt drawn toward this reality but could afford only an indirect path to it. There were several reasons for the detour. Circumstantially, the censorship in countries like France, sufficiently effective during the first half of the century to make the copying and clandestine circulation of unpublished

Charles de Secondat, Baron de Montesquieu. *The aristocrat who showed the* philosophes *the way in history, literature, and political theory, but was never considered one of them.*

manuscripts an important means of intellectual communication, was more politically than clerically sensitive. Tactically, the *philosophes* could achieve more consensus among themselves in their arguments against established religion than on any other topic. Thus despite the differences in their temperaments, styles, social status, and political loyalties, Montesquieu and Voltaire agreed on their common deism, while Hume, whose philosophy undermined the invariable laws and necessary connections so prominent in the rational faith of the *philosophes*, yet proved himself one of them by virtue of his essay on the implausibility of miracles (written in 1737 and published in 1748) and his sketch of *The Natural History of Religion* (first published in 1741 and, expanded, republished in 1757), which he designed precisely to show positive religion as the social effect of human foibles.

But political censorship was hardly a consideration in Great Britain and the Netherlands during the first half of the century and even in France would prove porous during the second half. Consensus among the *philosophes*, moreover, virtuosos that they conceived themselves to be, was not deemed a goal worthy in itself of a deliberate tactic. Behind the circumstances and the tactics of the *philosophes'* focus on religion during the early Enlightenment were crucial assumptions internal to their thinking. The early *philosophes* agreed that their shared antipathies—unexamined belief, blind obedience, unearned privilege, ignorance, superstition, intolerance, fanaticism, "enthusiasm"—had their common denominator in organized religion because they believed themselves to be the harbingers of a new age that was called first to settle accounts with the preeminently religious culture of the past by attacking its still-potent ecclesiastical residues in the present. More important, the *philosophes* concentrated on religion because their own ideas were, at this stage, concerned less with changing things than with changing the way of looking at them. For this, the relocation of point of view from the next world to this seemed decisive.

The *philosophes'* early concentration on attitude rather than on substantive theory paralleled the contemporary position of the mobile social groups of which the *philosophes* were a part. They too were altering the standards of a preponderantly static and agrarian society from its periphery, before they penetrated it. Hence the chief burden of the *philosophes'* message during the first half of the eighteenth century, conditioned in part by the apparent impenetrability of social reality and in part by their own stubborn faith that once turned toward its appropriate objects in the things of this world man's unfettered reason would do the rest, was the call for men to discard the dogmatic and ecclesiastical shackles upon free thought as the indispensable first step to any freedom whatsoever. In the two most characteristic writings of the age—Montesquieu's *Persian Letters* (1721) and Voltaire's *Philosophical Letters* (1734)—the intellectual leaders of the early Enlightenment gave an archetypal form to this message: through the indirection of an exotic model—Persia and Britain, respectively—they used the deistic principle of a universal standard implanted in nature and in man as the basis of a moral critique aimed at the fundamental institutions of French thought and society.

The second main foundation of Enlightenment culture, consistent with the deistic focus on man and this world, was humanitarian ethics. Relatively neglected in the seventeenth century, when it had tended to become merely derivative from the various combinations of the old religion and the new science, in the early Enlightenment human morals became an independent and central area of inquiry. With nature now deemed to be the only source of moral as well as of physical laws, and with the conscience now deemed as fully a part of nature as the rational order of things, the knowledge of this world became as much a matter of moral as of physical science. Since, moreover, God was deemed manifest exclusively through the laws of His creation, moral inquiry, as the probe of the laws for man's conduct implicit in this creation, assumed a new independent function in relation to religion itself. Not only had the divine rules for the good life now to be discovered in the created nature of man to replace those that had been derived from or at least guided by the prescriptions of special revelation, but morals now even acquired a positive religious function, since the only authentic worship of God lay in the knowledge of and the voluntary obedience to the fundamental laws of human nature.

Early-eighteenth-century moral philosophy, then, was simply the obverse side of deism, taking the same natural and rational view of man as the

deists had of God. Consistently with deism, too, the new morality emphasized a general point of view rather than systematic ethical doctrine, and it
was addressed rather to individuals for their reformation than to social or
political authorities for their reform. Hence it was concerned not so much
with what men should do but with the angle from which they should look
at what they should do. The chief common prescriptions in the moral
teachings of the early Enlightenment, consequently, were designed more
for the orientation than the direction of men: the norms of human behavior must be secular in origin; they must aim at man's earthly well-being;
they must include happiness, in the sense of both material and spiritual
satisfaction, as an indispensable part of earthly well-being.

In these three instructions on how to devise a humanitarian morality we
have the gist of what was common to the moral philosophies produced during the early Enlightenment. Specifications for such a morality abounded,
of course, but none achieved a classic formulation and none commanded
consensus, for in morals as in religion it was rather at the foundations
than the structure of ideas that the members of this generation worked
They were blocked from further construction in part by their preoc-
:upation with clearing away the inhabited ruins that blocked moral
enewal and in part by their own subscription to a secularized version of
riginal sin. For if the typical *philosophe* was optimistic—a term reputedly
coined in this period—about the moral possibilities of natural reason in
humans, he was not optimistic about human nature's will to exercise that
reason. Hume was, as usual, far more extreme than his friends among the
philosophes when he declared flatly that "reason has no influence on our
passions and actions" and that, consequently, "moral distinctions are not
the offspring of reason." But such representative *philosophes* as Voltaire,
Montesquieu, and even the young Jean Jacques Rousseau (1712–1778)
similarly qualified their confidence in the potentialities of rational man
with their acerbic insights into the actual tyranny of his self-seeking—and
worse, his stupidly self-destructive—impulses. They did not regard natural
impulses, passions, or self-interest as evil in themselves, but they did
consider these drives denatured and demoralizing when they were divorced
from reason and hence from the balance of nature.

The plurality of acceptable natural principles and the difficulty of harmonizing them led the first generation of Enlightenment moralists to
insist rather on the common ground occupied by such secular moral principles as naturalism, individualism, utility, happiness, and benevolence than
on systematic ethical formulations of the problematical relations among
them. Only the Britsh, conformably with their pioneering position in the
definition of deism, began early to distinguish among the new worldly
principles of morality. No more than anyone else in the first half of the
eighteenth century did they develop coherent moral doctrines, but they
did give definition to moral principles that would later be elaborated into
doctrines.

The moralists of the early British Enlightenment developed, in memorable form, the ideas that would become the building blocks of the three main moral theories of the eighteenth century. At the very start of the century, in a series of writings collected in 1711 as *Characteristics of Men, Manners, Opinions, and Times,* Anthony Ashley Cooper, Earl of Shaftesbury (1671–1713), esteemed as the "virtuoso of humanity," prepared the way for the intuitive or "sentimentalist" type of moral theory with his notion of a "natural moral sense," which impelled men to acts of benevolence and social beneficence through an innate affection for and sympathy with their fellows. The Reverend John Gay (1699–1745) published the first clear but implicit argument for utility as a moral principle (he had the idea but not the name) in his *Dissertation Concerning the Principle and Criterion of Virtue and the Origin of the Passions* (1730), where he declared happiness, defined as the achievement of pleasure and the avoidance of pain, to be the necessary and valid end of all human actions, which must therefore be assessed as means toward this end. The theologians Samuel Clarke (1675–1729) and Joseph Butler (1692–1752), finally, propounded the two standard versions of a morality based upon natural reason. In lectures of 1705, later published under the title *A Discourse Concerning the Unchangeable Obligations of Natural Religions and the Truth and Certainty of the Christian Revelation* (1706), Clarke based moral principle on the recognition of the "Fitness and Reason of Things," which were for him eternal principles of order in nature analogous to the propositions of mathematics. In his ethical discourses (published 1726), Bishop Butler, one of the great English moralists of the century, cast doubt on the rationality of nature as a whole, but he propounded instead a morality of "conscience," which he identified with "the principle of reflection" in the nature of man.

Each of these moral ideas would be taken up and developed into ethical and political doctrine later in the century, and the culture of the Enlightenment was characterized precisely by the simultaneous addiction to all three principles—sentiment, utility, and reason—and to the preservation of a balance among them. In proportion, indeed, as they were to fall out of balance toward the end of the century, the Enlightenment would dissolve as an identifiable cultural movement. But in the early Enlightenment they appeared typically and openly in combination with one another.

Indeed a chart of intellectual influences for this subject and this period in Great Britain would show a remarkable crisscrossing pattern. Protagonists of all three principles alleged their debt to John Locke, and both Shaftesbury and Gay, indeed, claimed to be his disciples. The objective rationalist, Clarke, taught the subjective rationalist, Butler, who in turn taught Hume, who first identified "utility" as an explicit moral principle. Hume took from Butler the rational conviction that morals are grounded in the constant principles of human nature, and he added to it the influence of Francis Hutcheson (1694–1746), who combined in himself the sentimentalist morality of Shaftesbury and the notion of its assessment by the utilitarian criterion of "the greatest good of the greatest number"—a phrase which, incidentally, Hutcheson coined. Nor was Hutcheson an eccentric in this respect. By the middle of the century Shaftesbury was deemed to have clothed utility in idealistic form of a moral sense, and the "Scottish school" of moralists, which included such well-known figures as Hutcheson, Hume, and Adam Smith, all characteristically united the morality of sentiment with the morality of utility. The role of reason in this ethical syndrome was, to be sure, more subdued in the early Scottish school than it was in the contemporary moralistic hedonism of Montesquieu and Voltaire in France or Thomasius and Christian Wolff in Germany. But even in Britain the moralists of the early Enlightenment sought to make a rational connection between the moral sense of individuals and the utility of society that was the object of this moral sense.

Thus the precocious formation of different schools among the British moral theorists of the early Enlightenment merely articulated what was implicit in the vaguer moralizing on the Continent: that the principles of self-interest, sympathy, utility, conscience, and reason were compatible enough to form a self-sufficient natural basis of moral doctrines. This early British ethical development also forecast what would be an essential quality of these moral doctrines during the mature Enlightenment: each would be a combination of these natural qualities, and even when they were ranged against one another—as the doctrine of utilitarianism would be against the doctrine of rational natural rights, for example— they would differ rather in the priority of the ranking than in the exclusive preference for one over another of the generally accepted moral principles.

The New History

The final common feature of the early Enlightenment lay at the other end of the intellectual spectrum from its formulation of appropriate general principles of natural religion and morality: the *philosophes* also applied themselves to the appropriate illumination of all kinds of specific realities—physical, psychic, and aesthetic alike. They described and explained gadgets and customs; they wrote and interpreted literature and art. To each thing and activity they brought their own combination of delight in detail and insistence upon rationalizing; from each thing and activity they took an added confirmation of the universal validity of their approach.

Examples of this particularizing tendency in the early Enlightenment can be taken from many fields, but perhaps the most revealing was its writing of history, since the deprecation of the *philosophes'* attitude toward history has been an important feature in the misunderstanding of the Enlightenment, and the disregard of the historical writing produced during its early stage has been an important feature in the distortion of the *philosophes'* attitude toward history. The great works of Enlightenment history would come, to be sure, in its mature stage, but they would build on the interest and the particular slant of the ideas invested in the lesser productions of the early stage. Just as the large works of interpretative and "philosophic" history would form a consistent part of the systematic and encyclopedic pattern which characterized the mature Enlightenment after 1748, so the more specialized and heterogenous interest in history which prevailed before mid-century was a contribution of the dispersed and particularized concerns inherent in the early Enlightenment.

The writing of history in the early Enlightenment contributed, indeed, more to the culture of the Enlightenment than to the discipline of history. Notable advances in the historical discipline were made during the period, it is true, but not by representatives of the Enlightenment. These advances were made by representatives of traditions that antedated the Enlightenment, and they were made in the three different kinds of historical study that were appropriate to the respective defenses of these traditions.

On the level of historical method, Benedictine monks of the Congregation of St. Maur in Paris, whose predecessors had advanced the critical study of documents in their seventeenth-century editions of ecclesiastical sources, extended their new techniques during the first half of the eighteenth century to the publication of authentic editions of sources for the study of the national and provincial history of Christian France. Nor was this extension of critical methods into secular history merely a local achievement. It was paralleled in Italy by the collections of the Maurist disciple Lodovico Muratori (1672–1750), whose edition of Italian historical sources earned him a reputation as the "father of Italian history."

If the clergy's urge to restore both the ecclesiastical and the political sources of a more religious past thus fertilized historical method, the impulse of kings and resurgent aristocracies—and of their literate minions—to buttress their respective claims with the sanctity of original right or long usage fed into a second kind of historical advance: the vogue of a constitutional history that put continuity into history through the persistent themes of a monarchical or aristocratic constitution undergoing processes of development or degeneration. The two outstanding exemplars of this history were the embittered and reactionary Count Henri de Boulainvilliers and the versatile royal agent and pensionary, the Abbè Jean Baptiste Dubos (1670–1742). Boulainvilliers' *History of the Ancient Government of France*, published posthumously in 1727, was a coherent history of the French constitution from the aristocratic point of view, unified by its theme of an original political power rightfully accruing to the French nobility as heirs of the Franks, but gradually eroded by successive generations of usurping kings. Dubos countered with his *Critical History of the Establishment of the French Monarchy in the Gauls* (1734), where he argued for constitutional continuity from the Roman emperors to the Frankish kings and thence to the modern kings, leaving no place for any autonomous Frankish right of conquest or, consequently, for any inherited aristocratic authority based on it.

The third and final level of history effectively worked during the first half of the eighteenth century was a philosophy of history produced not merely outside the Enlightenment but explicitly against it in the service of a competitive cultural tradition. The *New Science* (1725) of Giambattista Vico (1668–1744) revitalized the Christian Neo-Platonic tradition which had been strained through the Italian Renaissance, and which was in this work turned against rationalism in the Cartesian mode. His "new science" was an idealistic philosophy that incorporated history into his description of the irreducible multiplicity, the inimitable dynamism, and the essential autonomy of all living things. The only law of nature that pertained to men prescribed the organic pattern of development from infancy through old age as the common process which each organism experienced in its own way, realizing thereby a universal principle truer to life than the abstract universals of the mathematical reason common to seventeenth-century philosophy and eighteenth-century *philosophes* alike. If Vico thus invoked the history of nations, subject to a common pattern of natural growth but each realizing the design of Providence in accordance with its individual genius, to reconcile the cyclical and providential principles of philosophy, history in its turn acquired a developmental pattern that rooted it in the fundamental reality of things. Vico had no immediate influence, to be sure, on the contemporary early Enlightenment against whose rationalistic ancestors he overtly directed the substance of his philosophical history, but like the monastic progress in historical method and like the traditionalists' development of constitutional history, Vico articulated eighteenth-century tendencies toward the appreciation of individual things and of general processes within the time of this world which were also operative in the early Enlightenment and which were reflected more inarticulately in its historiography.

For the most part it was only later that the *philosophes* would make deliberate use of this threefold achievement by non-Enlightenment historians—as Voltaire would of Dubos' French history, for example, or as Herder would when he merged Vico's organic approach to the development of nations with the late Enlightenment's cosmopolitanism to create a polyphonic history of humanity (see pp. 232–34)—but the early Enlightenment did lay the foundation for the later enrichment of Enlightenment history. The representative writers of the early Enlightenment perpetuated the critical approach and the addiction to sources which had characterized their spiritual godfathers, Bayle and Leibniz, at the very beginning of the century, and they went beyond these forebears to develop a new sense of the importance of history and a concern for its connection with what they called "philosophy." They tended to express this sense and this concern rather in writing *about* history than in writing history itself, for, as with their interests in morals, the writers of the early Enlightenment were more engaged in establishing a point of view than in working it out through substantiated doctrine. The most famous of these programmatic pronouncements was undoubtedly Lord Bolingbroke's definition of history as "philosophy teaching by example," dating from the 1730's, when he was writing his *Letters on the Study of History,* and its fame rests on its faithfulness in typifying the age. By the end of the same decade Voltaire was beginning to write the *Essay on the Manners and Spirit of Nations,* for whose introduction he would later coin the term "philosophy of history," and Hume was publishing the *Treatise of Human Nature* and preparing the essays "Of the Study of History" (1741) and "Of the Rise and Progress of Arts and Sciences" (1742), which together laid the basis for the concept of history as a source of knowledge about human nature and of principles for human action—a basis which his later historical works would attempt to substantiate.

The actual history that was written from such points of view during this period tended simply to illustrate this approach to history as a casebook for the study of the universal principles of human nature. The best-known historical works of the period are probably Voltaire's *History of Charles XII* (1731) and Montesquieu's *Thoughts on the Greatness and Decline of the Romans* (1734), and both only faintly adumbrate the qualities through which their later works, Voltaire's *Age of Louis XIV* (1751) and Montesquieu's *Spirit of the Laws* (1748), would dominate the fertile historiography of the mature Enlightenment. Voltaire's earlier work lacked the historical depth, accuracy, and breadth of his later; Montesquieu's work on Rome was more traditional (in the humanist tradition of moral commentary on a classic theme), more imprecise, and more mechanical in its application of causal principle than his later study of the historically developed spirit of modern nations would be. And yet the earlier work of each man did prepare the way for the later. Voltaire's *Charles XII* was an integrated literary work, permeated with a unity at once moral and aesthetic; Montesquieu's *Romans* showed a coherent development and eventuated in a single moral on the need to adapt attitudes to circumstances.

In its scattered but programmatic works of history the early Enlightenment manifested the same general pattern as in its works of theology and morals. In all these realms the *philosophes* tested their rational faculty on sample issues of this world and made it an efficient means of separating the things that made sense and brought satisfaction from what did not. Equipped with this faculty as a cutting tool and with the raw materials of nature they had separated out from the dross of Christian tradition, the *philosophes* were ready by mid-century to carve out whole sets of ideas in conformity with their own bent.

THE MATURE ENLIGHTENMENT, 1748–1776

The change from the early to the mature stage of the Enlightenment may be dated with a precision not often permitted by the gradual changes in cultural fashions, for the mature Enlightenment both began and ended with clusters of characteristic intellectual events. The publication of Montesquieu's *Spirit of the Laws* in 1748 marked the advent of a series of remarkable works which signalized a new direction within the Enlightenment, and the coincidental appearance of Adam Smith's *Wealth of Nations*, Edward Gibbon's first volume of the *Decline and Fall of the Roman Empire*, and Gabriel Bonnet de Mably's *On Legislation* in 1776 marked a final concentration of important works along this line. The same terminal year, moreover, witnessed two events which, while not themselves intellectual, drastically altered the political circumstances in which the intellectuals wrote and thereby transformed the atmosphere in which the mature Enlightenment had flourished: the outbreak of the American Revolution and the fall of the reforming philosopher-minister, Turgot, from power in the French government combined to terminate an era of comparative stability and hopefulness and to bring into prominence the social and political turbulence that were helping to create other cultural styles and directions in the last quarter of the eighteenth century. But in the intervening third quarter of the century the Enlightenment came into its own as both the best-organized movement of European society and as the dominant theme of European culture. The two functions were related, because the informal organization of intellectuals into a "republic of letters," dedicated to the communication and the communicability of ideas, also helped to organize the exploratory reasonable principles of the early Enlightenment into the explicit, crusading, rational doctrines of the mature phase.

The Republic of Letters

The juncture of intellectual and aesthetic talents that produced the finely finished doctrines of the mature Enlightenment was encased in virtuosos of such varied temperaments as to cast doubt on the compatibility of their ideas and on the integrity of the Enlightenment as a unified intellectual movement. Certainly the works that were written during the mature Enlightenment have become classics of the major national cultures of Europe, and the authors they have immortalized evinced the social and personal waywardness of genius. Most of them, to be sure, had their social origins in what would now be called the respectable middle class and in mobile sectors of the aristocracy once removed from this middle class, if we may so classify Montesquieu's, Condillac's, and Mablys' descent from the judicial nobility, d'Alembert's knight-sired illegitimacy, and d'Holbach's probably imaginary German barony. But if these origins predisposed them toward the life-style of the urban burgher, the ways in which they actually lived were extremely varied. Diderot and Lessing eked out precarious livings as free-lance writers. By astute financial management of his income from plays and patronage Voltaire succeeded in building up a small fortune, which he used to enjoy the life of a country squire at his estate in Ferney. Hume, Gibbon, and d'Alembert lived comfortably on inherited annuities. Rousseau admired and envied the burghers of Geneva, but he himself lived the life of a vagabond: rootless, poor, dependent for both psychic and material subsistence on the favors of sympathetic women.

Nor are there overt signs of a joint personality for the *philosophes.* There was almost as large a distance between the willfulness of a Voltaire and the steady amiability of a Hume—"the good David"—as between the fastidious aesthetic tastes of the German critic, Wieland, and the grossness of the French physician, La Mettrie, who was reputed to have eaten himself to death. Nor should the cool irony so often associated with Voltaire, nor the passionless placidity reputed in Gibbon, nor the punctiliousness of Kant, by whose daily routine the citizens of Königsberg were said to set their clocks, be taken as representative of the typical personality of the rational *philosophe.* For even if we dismiss the countervailing capricious beneficence of Voltaire, the intense classical commitments of Gibbon, and Kant's persistent enthusiasm for the French Revolution, we must still reckon with the traits of the mercurial Diderot, that incessant fount of movement, ideas, and sentiments, who rarely kept an appointment, and—in a different vein—with those of Lessing, the anticlerical clergyman's son who spent a lifetime pursuing the Holy Grail of human perfection.

And yet, after all these varieties have been acknowledged and the inference drawn that they are undoubtedly connected with the diverse emphases in the doctrines of the Enlightenment—their lesser or greater radicalism, their lesser or greater rationalism, their lesser or greater materialism, their lesser or greater optimism—the fact remains that there were general features common to the *philosophes* and that these too affected their doctrines. The concentration of *philosophes* in the upwardly mobile propertied classes truly indicates their posture in favor of reform rather than revolution—in favor, that is, of an ordered society which would give due recognition to talents such as theirs. Personally, too, there were the rough outlines of a general personality which underlay the obvious individual differences. For one thing, the *philosophes* were, as a rule, restless seekers after the truths and goods of this world. Indeed, the very variety within the mature Enlightenment is explicable by the energy with which the *philosophes* pursued the different dimensions of earthly experience, and they were joined in the common desire to penetrate the reality of the here and now, calling on nature's God or man's history as auxiliaries in this enterprise.

The mature *philosophes* shared a persistent need for threads of meaning

Voltaire (hand raised) presiding over a dinner-meeting of *philosophes*. *Diderot is on his left; d'Alembert in the left foreground.*

with which to hold together their sundry experiences and make some textured sense of them. This need was a prime source of the sociability which was the most prominent of their common traits. For the *philosophes* formed a close social group and were in continual communication with one another. Aside from their voluminous correspondences, they met often and talked incessantly. The leaders of the Scottish Enlightenment—David Hume, Adam Ferguson, William Robertson, Adam Smith—were often with one another at home or with their French counterparts on the Continent. Hume and Gibbon were also accepted in the Parisian circles, where weekly attendance at salons like Madame du Deffand's and Baron d'Holbach's identified the international society of *philosophes* that might then be invited to the court of their own king, Voltaire, in Ferney or to the court of the Prussians' king, Frederick, in Berlin. The taste for one another's company which was displayed by the men of the Enlightenment was an indication of something more fundamental than the positive approach to pleasures of the world and the awareness of their own common intellectual identity—although both these indications were certainly true of them. What it indicated in addition was their conviction that experiences and ideas must be communicable and discussable to be authentic. This meant that they must be capable of being formulated in the sequential language of rational discourse, and thus behind the sociability of the Enlightenment lay the urgent requirement that the realities which it appreciated in all their variety must yet be arranged in patterns which revealed the principles common to them. When the *philosophes* drummed Rousseau out of the Enlightenment because he withdrew from participation in their club, they revealed the intellectual implication of their personal congeniality: it was both a channel and a symbol of the rational connections which gave purpose in this life to the experiences of this life.

The domination of the mature Enlightenment by *French* intellectuals favored both its communication with the society at large and the rational linkage among its ideas. The shift from the earlier British cynosure to the headquarters in France—and particularly in Paris—entailed special consequences both for the dissemination and for the intellectual character of the movement. The diffusion of ideas from their intellectual progenitors to the educated public went further in France than anywhere else in Europe, and the practice of writing for an extended reading public endowed the French Enlightenment with its special qualities of universality and social awareness which explain its preeminence in eighteenth-century European culture.

The French comparative advantage in the communication of ideas was in part a matter of intellectual institutions. Publication replaced the circulation of manuscripts as the chief means of distribution for the French Enlightenment after 1750, when the duties of chief censor were assumed by Chrétien de Lamoignon-Malesherbes (1721–1794), who was to prove himself more a friend than a judge of the *philosophes*. The salons of Paris and the academies of the French provinces, though far from French monopolies, outdistanced their British, German, and Italian counterparts in the intensity and the continuity of the intellectual interchange provided by the salons and by the breadth and progressiveness of intellectual interests evinced by the academies. The French, morever, showed a special predilection for the art of correspondence, and the tendency to circulate ideas in the form of epistolary exchanges showed, like the French addiction to incessant intellectual conversation, the new emphasis upon communicability. And in France, finally more than anywhere else on the Continent, "authorship," as a contemporary French directory of writers opined, "is a profession now, just like the army, the magistracy, the Church, and finance." As men of letters came increasingly to depend on it for their status they tended increasingly to produce a widely marketable commodity.

But none of these institutions—neither a moderately free press, nor a liberal choice of avant-garde salons and coffee houses, nor auxiliary urban centers of Enlightened culture in the provinces, nor the publication of intellectual correspondence, nor the free-lance writer—was exclusively French. Indeed, the persistent currency of the weekly general periodical in Great Britain and Germany—some hundred and fifty of them were in British circulation by 1750—indicated a mode of communication in which the French remained at a comparative disadvantage. It was, then, not only the techniques of communicating ideas but also the social structure of communication that lay behind the superior liquidity of French ideas both in the society of France and in the culture of other countries.

The French men of letters had a special place in their society that spurred them to produce and publish ideas with the widest possible appeal, a place that "engaged" them—to use a twentieth-century term for an eighteenth-century relationship—in the pressing concerns of the society. The leaders of the Enlightenment in France as elsewhere in Europe were middle-class in orientation, but the French middle class had a distinctive position which made its relations with the classes above and below at once more continuous and more problematic than anywhere else in Europe. Through the far-flung bureaucracy and the flourishing institution of purchased offices the middle class was connected with the court; through the bourgeois sixteenth- and seventeenth-century judges who sired the eighteenth-century nobility of the robe it was connected with the aristocracy; through the recruitment of wholesale merchants and members of the free professions from the ranks of the shrewder peasants, master artisans, and small traders it was increasingly connected by the prosperity of eighteenth-century France with the laboring mass of French society. More than in any other continental state, therefore, the aristocracy was infected by middle-class standards of value and taste and the masses of peasants and artisans shared in the fierce devotion to individual property-holding that was an extension of the middle-class way of life.

As part of this wide-ranging middle class, the French *philosophes* were encouraged to comport themselves as representatives of the whole society, and they were confirmed in this generalized character of their outlook by the absence of a traditional status or particular function specially appropriate to them in the society. In Germany, the representatives of the Enlightenment were often university professors or state officials. In Protestant lands generally, they were frequently clergymen. But in France none of these traditional callings diverted the *philosophes* from their image of themselves as free-lance intellectuals of the entire society. Many of them did take holy orders and carry the title of *Abbé*, but as the strictly secular writings of the *Abbés* Condillac, Mably, Morelly, and Raynal indicate, the affiliation was rather an avenue to higher education and patronage than a serious condition of an intellectual career. Again, the institution of patronage—at the royal court, in the houses of the aristocracy, and at the pleasure of the plutocracy—was still very much alive in France, as in the rest of Europe, but in France its spirit was transformed: the competition for *philosophes* was keen, the responsiveness of royal favorites and of nobles was apparently unlimited, and the advantage was on the side rather of the patronized than of the patron. These social ties served, then, not to constrain the ideas of the *philosophes*, but only to augment their effects. Although very few tried, like Diderot, to support themselves through their writing or editing, the protagonists of the French Enlightenment did in fact assume the self-appointed trusteeship for the whole society that we associate with the independent profession of letters.

The particular position which the French *philosophes* held within the middle class also helped the diffusion of what they wrote. The members of the French middle class had long been torn between the assertion of their own practical, rational, and worldly values and the desire to rise into the aristocratic echelons of the hierarchy they by and large accepted. The characteristic resultant of these two drives had been such hybrid social forms as the official aristocracy, in which middle-class aspirants were ennobled either by service or by purchase, and the patrician *rentier*, who patronized progressive culture in the cities and cultivated progressive agriculture in the countryside. By the mid-eighteenth century, however, both these outlets for middle-class ambition were being frustrated by the nobiliar reaction, ironically led often enough by middle-class converts of an older generation. In this situation, the bulk of the middle class was left in a state of embittered but impotent bewilderment. The intellectuals assumed the leadership of the class, using the flexibility of ideas to assert the bourgeois blend of criticism within the establishment and fundamental loyalty to it at a time when this mixture of attitudes frustrated definite action by the rest of the class. The French *philosophes* thus were in the anomalous position of writing on behalf of the whole society and at the same time castigating large sections of it for chronic abuses—governments for their inequities, aristocracies for their gratuitous privileges, and the masses for their servility. And yet this kind of anomaly, appealing at once to the capacities of men to love and to hate, has ever had the widest appeal.

This position of the French *philosophes* was, in relation to the intellectuals of the other European nations, at once distinctive and representative—that is, it was distinctive precisely because it combined tendencies that were one-sidedly manifest elsewhere. With their British counterparts the French intellectuals shared the wide social base and the consequent orientation of their writing toward the practical and social application of their ideas, but they did not entirely share in the transcendence of caste, the unbalanced empiricism, and the general tone of moderation that segregated the insular intellectuals as a group from the rest of Europe. With the intellectuals of the European countries to the south and east, the French *philosophes* shared the hatred directed toward the upper classes and the half-fearful, half-pitying contempt directed toward the lower, the combination of impatience with and dependence upon authoritarian government, and the tension between pride in themselves as an aristocracy of merit and their proclamation of equal citizenship as a general principle. But in the more progressive social context of France, the *philosophes* there directed this message rather to rational individuals everywhere

than to a narrow political or professional elite. Their writing thus combined practical and doctrinaire motifs with a common human touch that
was the envy of mid-eighteenth-century Europe.

The shift from the British to the French models that marks the
transition from the early to the mature Enlightenment helped to solidify
the differences in the intellectual features of the two stages. The British
vogue in Europe had reflected and focused qualities that were at once
characteristics of British thinking and caricatures distorted by the impossi-
bility of reproducing on the Continent the conditions and the references
of this thinking. Thus the skepticism and naturalism in deism that fed the
Latitudinarian church tendency in Anglicanism became anti-Christian on
French soil and a sectarian Protestant theology on German, during the
early Enlightenment. For the mature European Enlightenment of the
middle decades, the French inspiration had a more homogeneous effect. It
exhibited the shortened distance between the conditions of those who
made the cultural models and those who followed them, and it reflected
the universality built into the French mode of thinking. In contrast to the
empirical and relativistic emphasis of the insular British tradition, which
necessarily changed when it was applied elsewhere, the French articulated
their experience with a sense of form and a crusading zeal that made their
ideas travel very well indeed. The absorption of British practicality into
French universal doctrines is a simple way of viewing the essential balance
of the mature European Enlightenment.

In addition to these social forms of the mature Enlightenment, which
organized its ideas for the purpose of communicating them, its spokesmen
also developed characteristic intellectual forms of organizing its ideas,
for the purpose of impressing a unifying mold upon their various experiences. Two of these intellectual forms, in particular, were characteristically
employed toward this end.

First, because the *philosophes* appreciated the variety of real things and
real people as much as they did and also sought to organize them under
flexible principles, many of them looked to an aesthetic unity as the best
way of composing the idiosyncrasies of actual life into forms which bore
meaning. But theirs was an aesthetic unity of style that wove together
real things and ideas rather than the aesthetic unity of imagination that
exalts things to a reality above ideas. For the mature Enlightenment was
not an especially fruitful era for literature proper. The age of Swift and
Pope, of Marivaux and Prévost had just passed, and the time of Schiller
and Goethe, of Burns and Blake was still to come. Now the dictators of
style, like Samuel Johnson in England and J. C. Gottsched in Germany,
reigned supreme; it seemed an age rather of prescriptions for literature
than of the creations of literature. The hiatus may well be only apparent,
an implied tribute to the men of the Enlightenment, so many of whom
blended belles-lettres into formal thought. But whether by their merit or

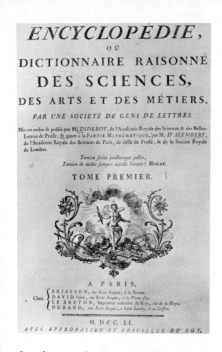

ENCYCLOPÉDIE,
OÙ
DICTIONNAIRE RAISONNÉ
DES SCIENCES,
DES ARTS ET DES MÉTIERS,
PAR UNE SOCIÉTÉ DE GENS DE LETTRES.

Mis en ordre & publié par M. DIDEROT, de l'Académie Royale des Sciences & des Belles-Lettres de Prusse; & quant à la PARTIE MATHÉMATIQUE, par M. D'ALEMBERT, de l'Académie Royale des Sciences de Paris, de celle de Prusse, & de la Société Royale de Londres.

Tantùm series juncturaque pollet,
Tantùm de medio sumptis accedit honoris! HORAT.

TOME PREMIER.

A PARIS,

Chez
BRIASSON, rue Saint Jacques, à la Science.
DAVID l'aîné, rue Saint Jacques, à la Plume d'or.
LE BRETON, Imprimeur ordinaire du Roy, rue de la Harpe.
DURAND, rue Saint Jacques, à Saint Landry, & au Griffon.

M. DCC. LI.
AVEC APPROBATION ET PRIVILÈGE DU ROY.

Title page of Diderot's and d'Alembert's great *Encyclopedia*, Volume I (1751). *Financed by subscription—five thousand subscribers were to pay almost two hundred dollars each for it—it had a tormented and tenuous career before the seventeenth and final volume was published in 1772. The royal approval, noted at the bottom of the title page, was withdrawn under pressure of Jesuits, Jansenists, and parlements in 1759, and only the liberal counterpressure of the uncensorious official censor Chrétien de Malesherbes and Madame de Pompadour, as well as the circumlocutions of the* philosophes *and the quiet internal censorship of the printers, enabled it to be completed.*

by chance, the literary lull redounded to their advantage, since it minimized competition with their hybrid products in the popular market. An appreciative Voltaire could say of a work as apparently technical as the *Discourse on the Grain Trade* by the Italian economist, wit, and favorite of the Parisian *philosophes*, "Abbé" Fernando Galiani (1728–1787) that it was a delightful blend of Plato and Molière!

Second, from 1748 on, the *philosophes* focused their diffuse interests on systematic publications in the grand manner. The most far-reaching of the new enterprises was Diderot's and d'Alembert's preliminary work on the *Encyclopedia*. They transformed the original plan for a translation of the mechanically organized Chambers' *Cyclopaedia* into the novel project of collecting—in Diderot's words—"all the knowledge scattered over the face of the earth" and of presenting it so as to dispel all illusions, include "the most essential details ... of each science and every mechanical and liberal art," expose the general principles connecting them, and direct the whole corpus to the end of making men "more virtuous and happier." By the time this new approach to human knowledge—at once critical, comprehensive, ordered, and useful—was announced to the public in Diderot's *Prospectus* of 1750 and d'Alembert's *Preliminary Discourse* of 1751, an impressive succession of other publications had also announced the new intellectual era that was under way.

In the interim no less than seven pioneering works had appeared, opening up various areas of human concern and initiating their reinterpretation in the light of the new skeptical, practical and commonsensical attitude. Hume's *Concerning Human Understanding* developed the standard proofs for the derivation of all knowledge—including both belief and reasoning—from experience. This philosophical primacy of perceived things in all the variety and multiplicity of their existence was applied by Hume himself, in the same work, to the disproof of miracles; by Condillac to scientific method in his *Treatise on Systems*; by Diderot to the psychological relativism of his *Letters on the Blind*; by David Hartley (1705–1757), in his *Observations on Man*, to the association of ideas as the only valid way of connecting diverse sensory perceptions; by Georges Louis Leclerc de Buffon (1707–1788) to the evolution of the individual forms of living nature in the preface of his *Natural History*; by Montesquieu to the order of society and politics in his *Spirit of the Laws*; and most stridently, by Julien Offroy de La Mettrie (1709–1751) to the materialistic doctrine of man in his *Man a Plant*, the climax of the trilogy whose earlier volumes, *The Natural History of the Soul* (1745) and *Man a Machine* (1747), had already scandalized Europe and caused their author to be exiled from his native France.

It is true enough that Hume's one-sided empiricism and La Mettrie's equally one-sided physical and mechanical determinism were neither typical of the Enlightenment nor compatible with each other. It is equally true that Montesquieu's aristocratic reverence for intermediate organs of government and his stress upon the ecological justification of political variety aroused the suspicions of the other *philosophes*. But what was common to this concentration of publications around mid-century was, at this stage, more impressive than what divided them: they proclaimed man's concrete experience of the world to be the test of their ideas about it, and stipulated that the ordering of this world, both in science and in politics, must follow from, rather than be imposed upon, the actual arrangements of its autonomous individual constituents. In field after field of knowledge they proceeded to work out the new views resulting from the assignment of reason to the linkage of things. The common emphasis, in short, was on the primacy of "facts" and on the subsequent role of reason in showing their "inner connections."

The program for a new knowledge and a new ethic that would dispense with beliefs and ideas prior to the actual experience of this world was, in itself, nothing new. As a program it had already been promulgated by Newton and Locke at the end of the previous century, and as a general approach it had already permeated the early Enlightenment. And yet, around the mid-century mark something novel was undoubtedly developing within this line of thought. The recognition of a new stage at this point in time is not simply a product of historical hindsight. The most representative figures among the *philosophes* were all aware, with Diderot, that "if one looks attentively at the middle of our century, . . . it is

A chemical laboratory, from the Diderot and d'Alembert *Encyclopedia. This illustration exemplifies the* philosophes' *intense interest in experimental science.*

difficult not to see that in several respects a most remarkable change has taken place in our ideas, a change which, by its rapidity, seems to promise a greater one yet." What marked this "change" at mid-century was the application of the "new method of philosophizing" to all kinds of actual issues—"from the principles of the secular sciences to the bases of revelation, from metaphysics to matters of taste, from music to ethics, from the scholastic disputes of theologians to affairs of business, from the rights of princes to those of the people, from the natural law to the discretionary laws of particular nations." What was novel at mid-century, then, was the progress from the sketchy program of the early Enlightenment to the actual reinterpretation of human knowledge in the clear light of a definitely perceived natural reality and to the actual revision of human ideals in terms of the primacy of individual freedom. Given the variety of the applications in which the *philosophes* actually invested their characteristic mode of thought and given their distaste for organizing the various applications of thought in the form of total systems on the model of Aquinas' *Summa Theologica* or even of Descartes' strict recipe of deductions from a few clear and distinct ideas, they had to find indirect ways of expressing their systematic spirit. They found these ways both in the coherent form of their writing and in the unifying function of their ideas.

Aside from the obvious device of loosely structured encyclopedias—the revealing subtitle of Diderot's great *Encyclopedia* was *Systematic Dictionary of the Sciences, Arts, and Crafts*—the *philosophes* used two other devices to organize their experiences in the light of an acceptable systematic spirit which would fall short of the spirit of systems they rejected. One consisted of the deliberate application of the same approach by the same thinker to many different fields of knowledge. D'Holbach was, as usual, too rigid and mechanical to be entirely typical when he wrote, in quick succession, a *System of Nature* (1770), a *Social System* (1773), a *Natural Politics* (1773-1774), and a *Universal Morality* (1776)—works which became notorious precisely for their attempt to apply a single doctrine of natural order to the whole range of human experience. But, again as usual, d'Holbach's system was an extreme development of a tendency generally characteristic of the mature Enlightenment. However more flexible a Voltaire, a Diderot, a Lessing, a young Rousseau, and a Prussian Prince Frederick may have been as they moved nimbly among the fields of philosophy, popular science, ethics, political theory, aesthetics, philosophical and sentimental novels, poetry, and even—in the cases of Rousseau and Frederick at least—musical composition, for each of these *philosophes* too the various fields of cultural endeavor received the consistent impress of the intellectual personality who spread himself among them.

The alternative unifying device of the mature Enlightenment was the vogue for single works on general subjects, since such subjects inevitably called for the all-inclusive and consistent arrangements of many ideas. This was the era in which the sense for the variety of all life and the sense for its inherent meaningfulness—the two intuitions which produced the blend of realism and of reasonableness that are associated with the Enlightenment—combined to produce works in the grand manner and on great themes, works in which the universal principles of reason were invoked to order vast reaches of human experience. Thus the most notable of the century's cosmic histories of humanity—a genre which we now label "philosophical history"—were penned in this middle period. Turgot's lectures on the "progress of the human spirit" (1750), Rousseau's anthropological history of the human species in his *Discourse on the Origins of Inequality* (1755), Voltaire's attempt at a genuinely universal history in his *Essay on the Manners and Spirit of Nations* (1756), and Adam Ferguson's *Essay on the History of Civil Society* (1767), became models of the Enlightenment's characteristic attempt to recognize the actual vagaries of nature's most fickle creature and still to interweave a rational pattern among them. Even when they set their sights lower than the heady vistas of all humanity, the men of the Enlightenment opted for large canvases. The first fifteen volumes of Buffon's *Natural History* (1749–1767), Samuel Johnson's epoch-making *Dictionary of the English Language* (1755), Voltaire's immortal *Candide* (1759), the first volume of Gibbon's ambitious *Decline and Fall of the Roman Empire* (1776), and Adam Smith's merger of ethics, sociology, and economics in his *Wealth of Nations* (1776) were outstanding examples of fundamental intellectual achievements in single works.

Whether in this form of a single work combining many interests or in the other form of a single set of ideas spread across several works, the *philosophes'* devices for organizing a variety of intellectual innovations in uniform molds made their doctrines irresistable to those groups in eighteenth-century society who would control change by embarking upon it from the security of a new intellectual order.

In addition to its social forms of communication and its intellectual forms of expression, the republic of letters developed two distinctive points of view in its approach to thought at the time of the mature Enlighten-

Contemporary illustration accompanying the initial tribulation of Voltaire's mock-comic hero in his satirical novel, *Candide* (1759). *Caught by the baron in the act of experimenting with the cause-effect relationship on the body of his daughter pursuant to Voltaire's version of the Leibnizian principle that "an effect cannot possibly be without a cause . . . in this best of all possible worlds," Candide is expelled into the series of misadventures which demonstrates the absurdity of any metaphysical system when applied to the vagaries of physical and human nature.*

ment, and these too helped to make the period a watershed in the history of European culture.

First, the *philosophes* made social relevance a constant touchstone of all their thinking. The realm of social and political relations was an arena particularly appropriate to the blend of rational and empirical principles characteristic of the mature Enlightenment. For those who achieved a satisfactory blend in the primary realms of moral or natural philosophy, the application to society and politics meant a pragmatic confirmation of their logical achievement. For those who were not so satisfied with the logic of their moral or scientific blend, the social and political realm played an even more crucial role. Attention to social and political conditions which by their very nature were common to whole groups of men provided a practical kind of unity for the social and political theory of the Enlightenment when its principles could be unified in no other way. Thus the principles of reason (or law), of utility (or happiness), and of passion (or sentiment), which were recognized by the men of the early Enlightenment and developed into full-fledged doctrines by the men of the mature Enlightenment, were either synthesized abstractly and then applied to society and politics, or left separate in theory and synthesized in their application to society and politics.

Whichever way was chosen, the result was a fruitful juncture of devotion to moral ideals and attention to social realities that produced the classic political theories of the Enlightenment. By proceeding in the first way, Montesquieu worked out the theory of constitutions in his *Spirit of the Laws*. Priestley and Paine the theory of liberal democracy in the former's *First Principles of Government* and the latter's *Common Sense*, Helvétius and d'Holbach the politics of the right to happiness in the former's *On the Mind* and the latter's *Natural Politics,* young Edmund Burke the idea of party in his *Thoughts on the Present Discontents,* and Adam Smith the policy of *laissez-faire* in his *Wealth of Nations.* Equally fundamental were the achievements of those who approached politics in the second way and found in the practical organization of civil society a cohesive force that made their political theory the most unified sector of all their ideas. Thus Hume's political essays and political history, Diderot's political articles in the *Encyclopedia,* and Rousseau's *Social Contract* were the most notable cases of works by men who saw in politics the rational calculation of means to connect the passions of individuals with the welfare of the society and who thereby invested their political theories with a unity of reason, sentiment, and utility that their philosophies did not otherwise provide. But, either way, the social and political emphasis of the mature Enlightenment helped to spread its influence, for through its social analysis and political critique its characteristic principles were brought home to the literate nonintellectual citizenry in terms most relevant to their actual experience.

In its second distinctive point of view, the mature Enlightenment marked a fundamental break and a new departure not only from the early Enlightenment but in Western thought generally: liberty replaced order as the dominant value toward which thinking was directed. No more than in any other intellectual revolution did this change mean an absolute metamorphosis, as if men had been exclusively preoccupied with order before 1750 and would be exclusively preoccupied with liberty thereafter. Order had been preeminent among the social values, including liberty, in the sense that it had furnished the constant point of reference with which all other values, especially liberty, had to be rendered compatible. Now the priorities were reversed: men's freedom became the issue of primary concern, and the continuing respect for order in the organization of both thought and society became subservient to the concern for liberty, for which order was to provide the necessary but external condition.

The new liberal faith was held by all types of *philosophes.* The sober d'Alembert pontificated that "liberty of thought and action alone is capable of producing great things." The passionate Denis Diderot (1713–1784) caught the spirit of the age perhaps even more faithfully when he recognized the logic of naturalistic determinism and the convenience of enlightened absolutism but broke through time and again to exalt the faith which was his primary commitment: "The child of Nature abhors slavery; intransigent foe of every authority, he is shamed by his yoke, he is outraged by constraint; liberty is his desire, liberty is his call." From this appeal of the man who came closest to being everybody's *philosophe* it was but a step to the radical Rousseau, in this context a reliable son of the Enlightenment, and his famous opening of the *Social Contract*:

Denis Diderot. *The most mercurial, the most original, the most iridescent, and probably the most representative of all the* philosophes.

"Man is born free; and everywhere he is in chains." And from here there was a direct connection with the careful and moderate Immanuel Kant (1724–1804), who declared that behind the rigorous logic of his philosophical *Critiques*, behind his demonstration of a necessary order in nature and an imperative law in morality, lay the simple lesson taught him by Rousseau—how to use thought for the purpose of "establishing the rights of humanity." Often, indeed, the *philosophes* despaired of human liberty. They despaired of achieving it or of the use that some men would make of it. Often they qualified their concept of liberty, to make it easier of attainment or safer to use. Often they devoted more attention to the prescriptive laws of nature and the obligatory laws of absolute kings which they felt to be the necessary prerequisites of freedom than to the elucidation of the freedom itself. But freedom it was that remained the ultimate end of their thought and their propaganda.

In the final analysis the social and intellectual conditions of life in the mature Enlightenment's republic of letters left their deepest mark on the substantive doctrines which the *philosophes* developed under their influence. For the doctrines, like the conditions, were shaped by the continuing effort to associate the varieties of experience in ways that made unified sense. In the generation that followed the intellectual innovations of the late 1740's, the *philosophes* developed doctrines that bridged the extremes set forth at the start of this generation. Between the limits set by Hume's skeptical empiricism and La Mettrie's dogmatic rationalism, the mature Enlightenment developed a whole host of hybrid positions. The variety of its philosophical doctrines was paralleled, indeed, by a similar scattering of its political positions, ranging from the pragmatic conservatism of a Hume through the radical democracy of a Rousseau to the utopian communism of a Morelly. The assignment of such labels as empiricism, rationalism, conservatism, democracy, and communism to the mature Enlightenment indicates its range and its flexibility, but for its characteristic ideas—the ideas that give it a distinctive identity in the history of Western culture—the Enlightenment must be considered not from the point of view of these alternative philosophical and political categories, but rather from the point of view of the doctrines which the *philosophes* invented to connect them. These unifying doctrines were their chief concerns. For the *philosophes* believed, in varying proportions, in the whole variety of basic positions opened up by their dismantling of orthodoxy, and they were distinguished in their heyday precisely by the doctrines which they devised to make combinations of positions rational which were not in themselves rationally compatible. The doctrines of the mature Enlightenment bridge such opposite categories as fact and reason, utility and ideal, authority and liberty. These hybrid doctrines, being of the same kind, could themselves be fitted together into rigorous systems, juxtaposed in compatible patterns, or at the very least discussed within a common universe of discourse. If we line up the most characteristic of the doctrines elaborated during the mature Enlightenment according to the fields which they represented—religion, psychology, ethics, politics, and history—we should be able to sense the harmony underlying the variegation of its accomplishments. Religion, ethics, and history were interests carried over from the early Enlightenment, but now they were related to one another through the new interest in psychology and politics, and they were themselves developed from statements of abstract principles to definite religious, ethical, and historical doctrines.

Religion

In the field of religion, the earlier emphasis upon the autonomous sphere of natural theology gave way to the doctrine of anti-Christianity. Not, of course, that deism or the other early forms of rational theology died out at mid-century. They spread from Great Britain into France, where they prominently framed the thinking of *philosophes* as various as the older Voltaire and the young Rousseau. When deism reached Germany, earnest "neologists" of much assiduity and little fame painstakingly reinterpreted Protestant dogma according to the dictates of reason. But for the Enlightenment as a whole, this kind of theologizing, while still being diffused and still operative as intellectual background, was no longer in the forefront of the *philosophes'* attention nor was it the kind of thinking about religion which attracted their most original efforts. What was more prominent as an explicit concern and more characteristic therefore of the mature Enlightenment was the anti-Christian campaign epitomized by Voltaire's battle cry: *Ecrasez l'infame* ("Crush the vile thing"). Anti-Christian doctrine became Hume's main interest during the decade of the

1750's. He wrote but did not publish his skeptical credo in *Dialogues Concerning Natural Religion* (finished in 1751, but published posthumously in 1779). And he then did publish his anthropological explanation of religion in *The Natural History of Religion* (1757).

The same preoccupation became Voltaire's obsession in the decade of the 1760's, when he bitterly castigated clerical persecution and enshrined his anti-Christianity in the immortal pages of his *Philosophical Dictionary* (1764). In this decade also d'Holbach carried the same crusade to another battlefield when he blamed the priests for the faulty education of men that diverted them from the happy and beneficent paths of nature. In the 1770's, finally, Gotthold Ephraim Lessing (1729–1781) developed, under the stress of sectarian opposition, the doctrine of universal toleration that, in his famous play *Nathan the Wise* (1779), reduced Christianity to but one of the several valid ways in which religion has served the moral perfection of human nature.

In its effects, then, the anti-Christian doctrine of the mature Enlightenment served to ally the various tendencies of the *philosophes'* thinking—skepticism, rationalism, humanism, and materialism—against a common orthodox enemy. But the shift from the earlier reinterpretation of Christian dogma to the rejection of Christian doctrine and the abomination of Christian churches came from a deeper source of Enlightenment thought. What this source was may be recognized from what was common to the two main forms taken by the anti-Christian doctrine. As a representative work like Voltaire's *Philosophical Dictionary* demonstrated, anti-Christianity could take the form either of explicit criticism of ecclesiastical beliefs and practices or of belligerent argument for the entirely secular and naturalistic basis of such crucial subjects as the soul, freedom of the will, and virtue, which had been favored topics of Christian exegesis. The first of these forms of anti-Christianity was an anticlericalism that had passed a decisive stage beyond the anticlericalism of the early Enlightenment: where the anticlericalism of the early Enlightenment was a criticism of ecclesiastical practice and dogma as a perversion of churches, the anticlericalism of the mature Enlightenment, particularly in its French version, was a criticism of ecclesiastical practice and dogma as the noxious essence of churches. The second, subtler from of the anti-Christian campaign was the more pervasive and the more influential of the two. Thus the *Encyclopedia*, which was certainly designed in large measure to exclude Christian revelation as a source and Christian theology as an explanation of human knowledge, executed this design primarily by ignoring the Christian God and, in Diderot's words, making "Man ... the center around which everything revolves."

But common to both forms was the single impulse of the *philosophes* to give their ideas a practical form. The twin themes of the *Encyclopedia* were articulated with cumulative emphasis as its seventeen large volumes of text and eleven volumes of plates rolled from the presses between 1751 and 1772. These themes were the self-sufficient rational unity of all human knowledge and the usefulness of the mechanical arts and crafts that were derived from it. But between these two themes—between the general principles that explained natural reality and the practical arts that enabled men to live in accordance with these principles—neither the Encyclopedists nor the mature Enlightenment which they epitomized could find a sure and positive way. For the practical arts required, like any kind of human action, incentives that were other than the incentives to theoretical knowledge, and the *philosophes* were never able to show satisfactorily why men did not act in accordance with a natural knowledge apparently open to all, or how man could act in accordance with the dictates of nature and still retain the autonomy of his will. But what the *philosophes* could not show positively they insisted all the more on showing negatively. That is, they could show how the knowledge of secular nature was congruent with the freedom of the secular will only by showing how both principles were equally opposed to Christianity, which had certainly succeeded in linking knowledge and will with a supernatural connection. The insistent logic of their anti-Christianity was this: things that are opposed to joined things must be joined themselves. The *philosophes* sought to demonstrate the connection between the unreasonableness of Christian dogma and the tyranny, at once vicious and unhappy, of its institutional effects. Through its rejection of both sectarian dogma and clerical institutions the anti-Christian doctrine of the *philosophes* forged a link, however negative in form, between the theory and the practice of the Enlightenment.

Psychology and Ethics

In the psychology of human nature, the *philosophes* promulgated the related doctrines of sensationalism and associationism, which for more than a century would dominate the discussion of how men derived their ideas. The standard works in this field were Condillac's *Treatise on Sensations* (1754) and Priestley's tendentious abridgment of Hartley's *Observations on Man* (1775), each of which developed an earlier limited idea into a comprehensive doctrine of general application. Condillac took as his starting point his own *Essay on the Origins of Human Knowledge* (1746), which was a popularization of Locke's theory on the derivation of knowledge from both sensation and reflection. But when he popularized it, he changed it by simplifying it. Condillac now traced the construction of knowledge as a continuous process starting from a single root in sensation and developing it into a richly ramified structure wherein perceptions, ideas, and passions were all simply different ways in which sensations combined, dissolved, and recombined into new sensations.

Where Condillac stressed the analysis of experience into particular, mutually negotiable realities, Hartley and Priestley made an explicit and independent doctrine out of the synthetic aspect of the process—they made the association of ideas the essential process in the construction of knowledge and considered what went into the association to be secondary. Hartley tied his original notion of association to a physiological theory of "vibrations" in the sensory nerves to explain what the primary units of experience were that first got associated. Priestley restated Hartley without the theory of vibrations and thus made the law of association an independent natural law of the human psyche applicable to any operation constructing a more general out of a more particular level of truth.

These compatible emphases in psychology—on particular sensations and on the natural law of association—passed into the foundations of morals to support an analogous combination of values there. In the field of morals, the *philosophes* developed the doctrines of utilitarianism and of naturalism as compatible modes of relating pleasure and principle, passion and control, self-interest and social welfare—in short, what is and what ought to be. The doctrine of utilitarianism originated during the mature Enlightenment precisely as an intellectual device to connect the apparently discordant values in each of these pairs. Just before the mature Enlightenment, Hume had announced the "principle of utility" as a human motive actually involved in men's moral ideals and social values but not rationally connected with them. Just at the end of the mature Enlightenment, Jeremy Bentham's *Fragment on Government* (1776) would isolate utilitarianism as a total and self-sufficient theory and would disconnect it from any larger natural order. In between came the mature Enlightenment's invention of the utilitarian doctrine which combined the principles of utility and of natural law. In this form the doctrine stipulated a rational connection between the individual's interest in the pleasurable effects of his actions for himself and his commitment to the pleasurable effects of his actions for the whole society. This rational connection was considered to be grounded in universal laws governing all natural reality.

The classic formulation of the utilitarian doctrine appeared in *On the Mind* (1758), by Claude Adrien Helvétius (1715–1771). It was applied to law by Cesare Beccaria (1738–1794), in his influential *On Crimes and Punishments* (1764), and to politics by Joseph Priestley (1733–1804), in his *First Principles of Government* (1768). Basing his ethics on Condillac's psychology, Helvétius reduced all morality to various forms of the individual's desire for pleasure and abhorrence of pain, just as Condillac had reduced all knowledge to the various forms of particular sensation. Since in Helvétius' doctrine all pleasures were equivalent in quality, all men were equally capable of moral acts. Each of these acts, moreover, contributed to both the utility of the individual and the utility of the society by virtue of the same Newtonian natural law that harmoniously ordered individual bodies with the force of gravitation. The connection between private interest and social benefit broke down only when faulty education obscured the recognition by reason that they were necessarily associated by nature. In this event the legislator had to supply laws as the means of re-educating the unfortunate.

In admitted dependence upon this basic utilitarian position of Helvé-tius, which invoked the lawmaker as the awakener of men to the natural order of things, Beccaria worked out his utilitarian juristic doctrine. He based the validity of penal law on its conformity with the natural law which "like the force of gravity... makes us always tend toward our well-being," and through its natural law the sole valid function of penal ordi-nances is the deterrent use of punishment to confirm the natural tie between individual and social pain. Priestley pioneered the broader political application of utilitarianism when he made the utilitarian criterion—"the good and happiness of the members, that is, the majority of the members of any state"—the supreme principle of political action, grounded it in the "natural rights" of every individual, and associated it with the natural right of popular revolution against governments that fail to promote the good of the majority.

For the mature Enlightenment, in general, utilitarianism was a doctrine with which to bring into reasonable connections all the great forces that moved men upon this earth, and to exclude as meaningless and illusory what could not be so connected. The utilitarians accepted the whole range of realities—from the passions of individuals, through the rational interests of the society, to the compulsory edicts of governments—but they accepted only those passions, those interests, and those edicts whose results could be related to one another through the operation of a general law of human nature.

All the *philosophes* were utilitarians in some degree, for they all com-bined the beliefs, characteristic of the utilitarianism of that vintage, that actions should be measured by the happiness they brought and that this measuring by results was sanctioned by its origins in the authority of nature. Moral utilitarians were thus moral naturalists as well, just as those who made nature the source of virtue also insisted on its useful effects. Yet the distinction between utilitarians and naturalists—between the *philo-sophes* like Helvétius, Beccaria, and Priestley who stressed utility and those like Diderot, Rousseau, and Adam Smith who stressed nature—was more than a mere difference of emphasis. It was also, and more impor-tantly, a difference in the principle that connected natural origins with happy results. For the utilitarians the natural warranty of happiness was a general law, discovered by reason either directly in nature or indirectly through the state. For the naturalists what guaranteed the congruity of self-interest and the social good was not the lawfulness but the variety and creativity of nature; it implanted the complementary impulses of "egotism" and "compassion," as Rousseau called them, in the original composition of man and sponsored their reciprocal and compatible interaction in all unobstructed moral acts. In this form naturalist moral doctrine took its place alongside utilitarianism as a separate, but related, moral doctrine of the mature Enlightenment.

Politics

From utilitarianism and naturalism in ethics it was but a short step to the articulation of constitutional and democratic doctrines in politics, and of liberal and socialist doctrines about society. The ethical, political, and social doctrines, indeed, were often identical, appearing as ethics when viewed from the angle of the individual and as political and social theory when viewed from the angle of the group. Political and social doctrines in the Enlightenment thus served the same function as psychological and moral doctrines—they served to distinguish the kinds of institutions and practices that could be put together into reasonable combinations from those that could not, and to show the principles of their combination.

But social and political ideas played a special role in the general synthesizing function which characterized the doctrines of the mature Enlightenment. Ideas about society and politics had a peculiarly ambiguous status with the *philosophes*. On the one hand, the active interest of the *philosophes* in them, starting at least from the publication in 1748 of Montesquieu's *Spirit of the Laws*, is undeniable, and not without cause have modern political movements traced their ideological roots to them. On the other hand, these same *philosophes* were often not very systematic in their theorizing, and there is a curious kind of absentmindedness in their political writings—as if they were aiming at something else, that was not political. In part, the explanation lies in the *philosophes'* distinction between society and the state and in their tendency to concentrate on the former, which they regarded as the organization of what was natural, moral, and essential in the relation of man to man, and to depreciate politics to the status of a necessary evil, contingent upon the will of the society and assigned the menial chore of protecting society from its unnatural defectors. The importance of this political function varied, to be sure, with the degree of restraint deemed needful for the human species, but common to the Enlightenment as a whole were both the judgment of the negative character of politics in respect to the essential human values of liberty and brotherhood, and the relative neglect of the political function in favor of the concern with the general relations between the individual and society. Thus the *philosophes* subordinated politics both to individual freedom and to social morality. Montesquieu, Voltaire, the *Encyclopedia,* and British liberals like Priestley, Richard Price, Adam Smith, and Thomas Paine, all exemplified this tendency, whether through the French emphasis upon the social "spirit" behind laws and politics or through the British emphasis on the primacy of civil over political liberties.

But what must still be explained is the political interest that led the men of this same Enlightenment to advance the first modern theories of such influential political doctrines as government by law, the separation of powers, popular sovereignty, the "night-watchman" state, and the welfare state. However secondary in value politics may have been for the *philosophes*, they fully recognized its inescapable necessity for the implementation of their primary values. Primary for them were the rights of individuals and the benefits of voluntary association, but because they were interested in results and were realistic enough about the actual moral disposition of their fellowmen to doubt their voluntary attainment, the *philosophes* turned sporadically and fruitfully to political compulsion as the means of calling men from what they were to what they should be—or more precisely, in terms of the Enlightenment notions of human psychology and ethics—to recall men from their unintelligent private diversions to the recognition of their true social nature.

Hence the most fruitful political doctrines of the mature Enlightenment were those that proposed permanent institutional channels for directing men's self-interest toward social morality. The *philosophes* approached politics through the idea of law, since they deemed the laws of the state to be embodiments of the moral law, adjusted to men as they are and equipped with the power to make them act as they ought. Montesquieu introduced the conception of a moral connection between nature and politics by recognizing fear, honor, and virtue as the operational moral principles "which necessarily flow from the nature of things," underlying the laws of all despotisms, monarchies, and republics respectively. Subsequently, writers as different as Helvétius and Rousseau approached politics through an analogous moralizing function of the law. Helvétius appealed to the "Legislator" to enforce the order of nature by associating public pain with unsocial acts, and thereby make men virtuous. Rousseau took an opposite tack when he denied the derivation of the law of the state from any law of nature, but he too saw in the law of the state and in the "Legislator" who initiated it the expression of the general will that turned natural into moral liberty.

The separation of powers, similarly, became a widespread and fundamental doctrine of Enlightenment political thinking because it was developed as the way to make a practical possibility out of a fundamental principle. Once more the initiation of the doctrine goes back to Montesquieu, who believed it was realized in the British constitution. Certainly, as has often been pointed out, his recognition was a distorted one, since the tortuous and intricate historical growth of mutual checks in Great Britain was a far cry from the categorical separation of legislative, executive, and judicial powers that Montesquieu claimed to see in it. But the distortion is precisely what made his doctrine of their separation so influential, since thereby seemed at once rational and real, general and specific. An accurate transcription of British practice would hardly have been transferable to any other situation, but in Montesquieu's version, it became a political incarnation of the cosmic balance of forces in the Newtonian structure of the natural universe. In this form of a constitutional balance of powers, paralleling the gravitational balance in physical nature, the age-old principle of mixed government was transmuted from a mere political preference into a basic constitutional doctrine which expounded the only valid way of guaranteeing and controlling the natural liberty of man. Thus did the doctrine pass through Diderot and d'Holbach into the *Encyclopedia*, and along with the individual freedom which it secured from violation and from license, became the characteristic political tenet of the Enlightenment.

Not nearly so widespread or characteristic for the Enlightenment itself, but momentous for the ages that followed, was the third political invention of the eighteenth century's middle decades, the modern doctrine of democracy. The emphasis here must be on the "modern," for two reasons. First, the name of "democracy" was not assigned to this invention of the mature Enlightenment until the revolutionary final two decades of the century. Second, this nameless mid-century doctrine of what would later be called democracy was a different kind of theory from the traditional ideas of democracy which the Enlightenment inherited and welded together into a new product.

We may distinguish three separate concepts associated literally or equivalently with the older notion of democracy. As a descriptive term for government by the people—that is, by the whole body of citizens—democracy had been used since the ancient Greeks as one of the valid pure forms of the state and as a constituent of mixed governments. Second, the derivative notion of popular sovereignty had been used since the ancient Romans as a legal concept to affirm the validity of those states that recognized the people as the possessors of the ultimate governing power, whatever the form of the government and whoever actually exercised this power. Third, the right of popular revolution, as asserted since the sixteenth century and embodied in John Locke's classic *Second Treatise of Civil Government* on the eve of the Enlightenment, validated the occasional assumption of the governing power by the people, whoever the possessors of sovereignty might be, in order to restore some fundamental, suprapolitical right of the people.

Common to all three traditional strands of the democratic principle was the age-old separation between the actuality and the ideal of political power. As a regular form of government, democracy had been deemed primarily a practical device best fitted to secure good government for civil societies in certain kinds of circumstances—notably those of small city-states. As the legal principle of popular sovereignty, democracy had been etherealized into an invisible sanction of visible political power. As a revolutionary ideal, democracy had been limited to sporadic moments of destructive efficacy. This traditional separation of the democratic actuality from its ideal, even among those who acknowledged its validity, had taken on added depth and meaning because it reflected a more basic separation in the tradition of political thinking–the separation between the origins and the ends of political authority. On the one hand, whether viewed as instituted by God, modeled on the hierarchical organization of nature, or authorized by contract, the origin of governments had been deemed a response to a practical need for order, varying according to the local circumstances of that need. But once originated, governments had also been deemed, on the other hand, to be a positive means to a higher good of the community than the mere preservation of order—a higher good that was variously identified as salvation, virtue, or welfare. Thus the form of government depended on its geographical, anthropological, and historical origins and was independent of the higher end of the community, which could be either approached or violated equally by any of the valid forms of government. For traditional political thought, in other words, the sanctity of the end blessed government in general and occasional revolutionary acts of popular sovereignty in particular, but it did not bless any particular form of government—not even democracy.

The political writers of the mature Enlightenment continued tradition in their literal notion of democracy as one of several valid forms of government—and as a not particularly favored form—but they prepared the way for modern democratic theory in their development of an implicitly democratic doctrine of consent. To be sure, the idea of consent too had a traditional history that paralleled notions like democracy and popular sovereignty in that the consent of the governed had been deemed historically fortuitous, occasional, or extra-governmental—but in any case politically inessential. Thus consent had been specified as a general factor in the origin of some governments, or as a particular factor in legitimating a government's power to abridge private rights by taxing property when this power was considered beyond the proper political sphere of government. But it was primarily through the convergence of these separate ideas of consent into a single doctrine associating the popular source of government with its sacred role in protecting individual rights that the *philosophes* created the pattern for the subsequent reworking of all the traditional notions of democracy into modern democratic theory.

The most transparent testimony of what happened to the idea of consent in the eighteenth century was its incorporation into Rousseau's doctrine of the general will, as he developed this doctrine in his *Social Contract* of 1762. Now it is perfectly true that by this date Rousseau was estranged from the *philosophes* and was well started on his "preromantic" path to the supersession of the Enlightenment. It is true too that the *Social Contract* was the least influential of his works during the eighteenth century. A final caveat to the democratic implications of Rousseau's general will for the Enlightenment was his own refusal to associate it literally with democracy: the general will was, in Rousseau's view, the foundation of valid law for all governments, but he viewed "democracy" in age-old terms as merely one of the many possible legitimate forms of government—the one particularly suited to small states. But after all these reservations have been made, the fact remains that Rousseau's doctrine of the general will set forth the cardinal principle on which democracy would be founded and that in respect to this principle he represented the undiluted extreme—the limiting case—of what was common to many of the *philosophes*.

The fruitful new principle that underlay the doctrine of the general will was the conversion of popular consent into a continuous and fundamental factor in government. This principle followed from three connected postulates. First, individual consent was not only prepolitical (that is, a condition for the installation of a regime or ruler) or occasionally political (that is, an agency for the deposition of despotic rulers) but permanently political, contributing to every valid act of government. Second, this continuous efficacy of political consent was grounded not so much in variable rights of custom or considerations of utility as in the fundamental rights of man that made the daily exercise of political consent a series of basic moral acts necessary to all governments. Third, the function of this permanent and fundamental political consent was to organize the free expressions of individual wills for the purpose of protecting the freedom common to them all; consent thus connected the origins and mechanics of government with the purpose of government and made the liberal ideal a determinant not of the results, as of yore, but now of the structure and operation of governments.

In Rousseau this new function of consent, which made the democratic principle the essential bridge between the actual conditions and the moral potentialities of man, was particularly clear from the two successive steps into which he analyzed his doctrine of the general will. By the first step, the general will is *formed* out of the free and actual decisions of all the participant individuals, living in a state of nature and driven by their natural needs to participate in a political community. Thereby they initiate the general will of this community into which every individual deposits all his insecure and instinctive natural rights for the purpose of confronting the similar rights of his fellow humans and distilling from the social interaction rights that are equal, certain, rational, and moral. By the second step, the general will *operates* in political communities through the virtual consent of the individual citizens. This is expressed both in the original sanction of the general will, which continues to serve as the measure of every political action, and in the will of the "people," who—usually in the form of majority voting—in every state realize the general will through their exclusive right to make laws. Rousseau did not call this model state a democracy because he identified "government" with the executive power and in this changed setting admitted democracy along with the other traditional forms of government as circumstantially variable agents of the constant legislative power of the people. But however abstract his notion of the general will and however much he doubted the fidelity of actual laws to it, Rousseau's doctrine did establish political consent to government as an essential act of moral freedom for every individual, and it did prescribe a continuing function for popular sovereignty in the making of ordinary laws. Thus he invented a democratic theory that made the continuous participation of all citizens in the exercise of political power a fundamental right of man and an essential activity in the realization of the good life.

In the specifics of his doctrine Rousseau stood alone. He was the only figure in his age to come so close to the literal democratic principle by combining absolute political equality, legislative sovereignty, and positive morality in the idea of consent. But the core of his achievement—the exaltation of political rights to an essential status among human liberties—was shared by many of his eighteenth-century contemporaries. Diderot advanced the notion of a general will before Rousseau, and Kant adopted it after Rousseau. For both Diderot and Kant it was part of a moderate design for a mixed government predicated on the limitation of active political rights to men of property. Others expounded the point of the new doctrine of political consent even when they avoided the notion of a general will, with its possible encouragement of strong and willful government. Thus in Great Britain the succession of political crises starting with the exclusion of the regularly elected John Wilkes from the House of Commons during the 1760's and climaxed in the issue of the American colonists' right of consent to taxation during the early 1770's spurred a whole group of political writers to include political liberty—that is, the right to hold public office or to be represented by those who do—among the inalienable natural rights of man. Joseph Priestley, Richard Price, Thomas Paine, and Major John Cartwright were the most prominent of these moralists turned political doctrinaires. If they were unlike Rousseau in their assessment of political society as a necessary evil and their restriction of political rights to the minimal function of securing other rights, they were like Rousseau in their grounding of these political rights in the "natural equality of mankind" and in holding that political rights were indispensable to all the other rights of mankind.

But practical as their political stimulus was and doctrinaire as their political language may have been, the British radicals ultimately, like the French, shied away from consistent democratic theory. Indeed, in the very distance they kept from it we may glimpse the characteristic contribution of this era to the subsequent formation of this theory. Only for Cartwright and his few followers did the political rights required by the equality of men mean equal political rights—that is, universal suffrage. Only for Paine did such rights mean the rejection of the independent rights of king and lords. For Priestley and Price alike the apparent inconsistency between the democratic principle and the moderate program was deliberate: they held both that "every government in its original principles, and antecedent to its present form, is an equal republic" in whose parliament "every man by natural right will have a seat" and that in the present forms of the state the political liberty of all individuals is neither necessary to nor sufficient for the civil liberty of these individuals. Thus they validated any political system that included a responsive representative organ.

This ambiguous insistence upon political equality as a fundamental principle with a persistent but impractical relevance points to the essential features of the incipient democratic doctrine promulgated in the middle decades of the eighteenth century: it was a doctrine not of democracy as a *form* of government but of democracy as an *end* of government. The mid-eighteenth-century radicals insisted upon the original equality of political rights not as a reason for an actual equality in the exercise of political rights but as the reason for requiring that political power be exercised for the sake of all men's equal rights. This first version of the modern democratic principle, in other words, grafted a political dimension onto men's fundamental liberties for the purpose of insisting that these liberties be respected by the state not as a matter of policy, but as a matter of right incumbent upon governments by their very constitution. Kant's later formulation of what we might call a "subjective democracy" was a precise expression of this Enlightenment position: all men should obey only those laws to which they "could have given consent."

Neither in Kant nor in his radical predecessors did this kind of constituent democratic principle confer on every individual a right to participate in the actual exercise of the political sovereignty that was bound hereby to cherish his rights in all other respects. But still the *philosophes* did draw from this principle one conclusion that went beyond the question of what political power was being exercised for and had bearing on the question of who should exercise it. However indifferent they may have been to precise forms of government, they were adamant on some role for the "people" in it. Since by the "people" they meant the collective association of ordinary individuals, the original political rights of the individual became the basis of the actual political rights of the "people." These actual political rights became in turn the popular basis of representative assemblies, however constituted. Through this conversion the original political rights of individuals were absorbed in the collective organs of the state and participation in these organs was no longer a matter of individual right but of utility in protecting the "people's" collective rights. This device for absorbing the political rights of the individual permitted the assignment of a democratic foundation to such oligarchic representative organs as the eighteenth-century British House of Commons and allowed for the typical *philosophes'* recommendation of a limited suffrage. Thus representative assemblies were secured a new positive function in the assertion of fundamental rights, and the democratic principle, duly camouflaged by the principle of representation, was built into the foundation of respectable institutions.

Society

The crucial notions of "people" and of "civil society" that permitted democratic principles to be connected with elitist politics lie behind the two other doctrines originated by the mature Enlightenment: the doctrines of *laissez-faire* and of socialism. We are used to thinking of economic liberty and collectivism in terms of the mutual opposition that was their most obvious relationship and that would govern their immediate future as theories and as movements. But equally important for the understanding of the Enlightenment and perhaps also of the ideas' mutual accommodation in our own time was the common attitude toward society that made these doctrines the twin products of the same conditions in the same era.

The concomitant appearance of the first modern socialist and *laissez-faire* doctrines was more than mere historical coincidence. The pioneering works of both schools appeared first in France during the same decade—the 1750's—and they shared prominent congenital tendencies. *The Code of Nature* (1755) of the mysterious Abbé Morelly attempted to bring the old dream of a communist society down to earth as a contemporary practical program. Three years later François Quesnay published his *Tableau Economique* (*Economic Model*), the *laissez-faire* treatise that has caused him to be called the "founder of economic science." Indeed, as we have seen, Quesnay and his followers labeled themselves "Economists," but their intellectual connection with their contemporaries is clearer from the label "Physiocracy"—that is, "the government of nature"—which would subsequently be affixed to their doctrine.

The differences between these initial socialist and *laissez-faire* doctrines were clear enough. First, for the socialists private property was the root of all evil; it was the cause of inequality, avarice, vice, and misery. For the Physiocrats private property was the basis of natural right and the guarantor of liberty. Second, the socialists had an ambiguous doctrine, they were themselves isolated and obscure, and their subsequent influence was tenuous and sporadic. The economic liberals, on the other hand, formed a genuine school, had an immediate impact upon educated laymen and policy makers alike, and initiated a continuous tradition that soon developed into the dominant school of political economy in Europe.

The comparative alienation of the socialists from their society is abundantly clear from a few salient personal facts. Despite the occasional strictures of a Diderot or a Rousseau upon private property—strictures indicating that at least a vague tendency toward socialism responded to something real in the contemporary society—there were only two recognizable proponents of socialism during the Enlightenment and neither of these was prominent in the eyes of his contemporaries for this doctrine. Nothing was—or is still—known about the Abbé Morelly save that he was the author of the socialistic *Code of Nature*, and indeed for years the mistaken attribution of this work to Diderot denied him even this shred of identity. Gabriel Bonnet de Mably (1709–1785), whose *On Legislation* of 1776 transmitted Morelly's socialist doctrine to the generation who made the French Revolution, was certainly visible enough and popular enough in his day, but his socialism was such a mixed and unstable set of notions that it was not socialism he was visible and popular for. He was a humanist with a passion for Plato's *Republic*; he was a secularized prophet and pessimist who preached that man's fall from his original life of harmony among equals to the sinful state of self-seeking avarice, greed, and dominion made it impossible for him to recover the "community of goods and equality of conditions" necessary to the good society; he was an ascetic who counseled respect for private property and abstention from its fruits as the virtues appropriate to the fallen condition.

Undoubtedly Morelly was more optimistic, more hedonistic, more practical, and consequently more relevant in his socialist doctrine—his *Code of Nature* advanced an explicit "model of legislation" for the actual establishment of a true community of property and of citizens—but in him too the mechanical insistence upon equality, the economics of the public storehouse, the local and pyramidal basis of social organization, and the undiluted collectivization of all aspects of life seem rather reminiscent of traditional utopias than relevant to the new large-scale society aborning. Even the terms "socialism" and "communism," terms appropriate to movements of this society, were not used by these eighteenth-century precursors, but were coined more than a half century later. The frequent use of these labels to characterize their doctrines is thus an anachronism not only semantically but substantively, in that the eighteenth-century doctrines manifested neither the progressive economic connotation of the more general term "socialism" nor the radical political connotation of the more restricted term "communism." And yet both terms have been and are still retroactively applied to Morelly and Mably, to indicate that behind the obvious retrogressive features of their moralism and their utopianism there lies a new idea of social progress which links them with the modern movements to come.

The relationship of the free traders to late-eighteenth-century society was obviously closer, for no such obscurity, ambiguity, or delayed effect qualified their function. The Physiocrats were a genuine "school" of intellectuals, wholeheartedly committed to the pioneering doctrines of their schoolmasters—Quesnay and his chief collaborator, Victor Riqueti, Marquis de Mirabeau (1715–1789), who contributed the *Theory of Taxation*

(1760) and *The Rural Philosophy* (1763) to the Physiocratic canon and was the father of the Count Honoré de Mirabeau of French Revolutionary fame. That the Physiocratic principle of economic liberty struck a responsive chord was signalized by the attraction of faithful disciples like Pierre Du Pont de Nemours (1739–1817), who coined the term "Physiocracy," and Paul Pierre Mercier de la Rivière (1720–1794), whose *Natural and Essential Order of Political Societies* (1767) developed Physiocracy from a tool of economic analysis and a principle of economic policy into a complete social doctrine. It was signalized too by the organization of its own journal (the *Ephémérides*), by its demonstrable impact upon more influential figures who were disciples of a kind (such as Turgot and Adam Smith), and by its self-conscious promulgation of the label—*laissez-faire*—which would continue to identify the doctrine in its subsequent versions down to the present day.

But the patent differences between the two contemporaneous doctrines should not obscure the common traits which make them complementary indications of what was happening in mid-eighteenth-century society. Of these common traits, three stand out as particularly revealing.

First, and most important, the proponents of both doctrines saw society as a prime reality of nature, equivalent to any other reality of nature and ordered directly by its laws. What was novel in this emphasis was the finality it attributed to society as a self-enclosed process with its own structure and its own purpose: society was conceived to be a constant and reciprocal relationship among all the individuals who composed it, and this relationship was considered real, valuable, and permanent in itself rather than, as heretofore, intermediate in the ultimate formation of a political or ecclesiastical authority out of individual persons or families. From this point of view, when the Physiocrats found the natural basis of society in the economic laws governing the circular flow of goods and services among individual producers and consumers and when the socialists found the natural basis of society in the essential law of equality governing the daily relations of all individuals, both were stressing the orderliness, the meaningfulness, and the self-sufficiency of the ordinary social relations among ordinary individuals. The recourse by both groups to nature for the ground of social laws, whether of economic exchange or of communal harmony, was impelled by the conviction that only the sanction of nature could confer value on a uniform relationship among essentially independent individuals and by the confidence that this approach to society as an extension rather than a modification of nature would make social phenomena susceptible to the same kind of scientific treatment and control as other natural phenomena. Quesnay's analogy of the economic process to the circulation of the blood, and Morelly's explicit allusion to the mechanics of the "moral attraction" provided among men by nature were but literal references to a natural science that was generally deemed applicable to society. It was now,

Adam Smith. *Founder of the classical school of political economy and pioneering theorist of the free-enterprise system.*

in this context which witnessed the application of the methods and laws of natural science directly to society, that economics was invented as the form of human activity closest to nature.

Second, and more surprising, the progenitors of both these doctrines that were to flourish with the inception of an industrialized society were protagonists of none of the groups or branches of economic activity that were generating this society. Physiocrats and socialists alike went so far as to favor agriculture, the most conservative of economic activities. The Physiocrats explicitly found it the only source of economic value, stigmatizing commerce and manufactures equally as "sterile," while the socialists assumed a static, unspecialized, consumer-dominated economic mentality that had for centuries been associated with the predominance of agriculture. Even progressive economists like Turgot, his friend Vincent de Gournay, and Adam Smith, all of whom differed from the Physiocrats in admitting the productivity of trade and industry, put no special stress on these activities or the classes that performed them and that would espouse the doctrines of these very economists. Adam Smith's labor theory of value was designed, not to favor industrial producers, but to indicate the productivity of every economically active individual, whatever his activity. He meant to emphasize the equality of all classes in the exchange process as opposed to the Physiocrats' notion of the agriculturalists' superiority, which he deemed inconsistent with general economic liberty, and he meant to emphasize the economic creativity of the individual human being as opposed to the Physiocrats' focus on nature's impersonal creativity in land, which he deemed a lopsided view of nature. But having justified trade and industry in theory, Smith balanced his position by making it quite clear that in practice he mistrusted merchants and masters of industry and as a matter of fact trusted both the agriculturalist and the old-fashioned journeyman to assess their interests more rationally and therefore more in accord with the national interest.

Whatever the variations among these economic and social doctrinaires, then, it seems clear not only that they did not come out of an industrial society but that they did not speak to one. They spoke for and to no special classes at all, since the traditional groups they favored were actually unprepared to engage in the competitive economic process or the collective social process the doctrinaires prepared for them. Thus the progressive agrarian capitalism espoused by the Physiocrats found so few takers that by the 1770's the school as such was in decline, leaving its doctrine of *laissez-faire* as a detachable economic model to be carried on by less definitely committed observers. Even Adam Smith's version of the model became a real social force only when a later generation of theorists transformed his assumption of the harmonious interests of all producers into conditions of inevitable competition favoring the industrial entrepreneur.

The failure of eighteenth-century collectivists and individualists alike to recognize the proletarian and bourgeois interests with which their doctrines would some day be joined reflected not the absence of perception or foresight but the presence of a definite and distinctive stage in the development of European society. They analyzed a society in which all groups, new and old, were entering into the orbit of an exchange economy and thus into a kind of relationship that rendered every individual both indispensable to and dependent upon every other. It was not a new economy or a new society that they saw, but rather the homogenization and the emancipation of the old. It was not any particular social group, but society itself, that was now deemed autonomous, for it supplied its own power and its own direction. Individuals in society provided the former; the nature of society the latter. Thus each of the main doctrines afforded two crucial concepts, one for each function: the Physiocrats proclaimed *laissez-faire* and the natural order; Adam Smith the division of labor and nature's "invisible hand"; the socialists the equality of all individuals and the benevolent harmony of human nature. It was this attribution of initiative and value to the social process as such, rather than to any specific dynamic group in it that reflects and helps to explain the diffuse nature of the actual social movements in the second half of the eighteenth century.

The third of the features common to the individualistic and collectivist doctrines of the mature Enlightenment was one that pertained to its constitutional and democratic doctrines as well: the whole of the political, social, and economic theory of the period was practical without being practicable. The critical problem implicit in the political dogmas of the mid-eighteenth century and illuminated by its economic and social doctrine was simply this: the same principles that were advanced as the real truth of how things actually worked functioned mainly as ideals that had still, in some unspecified way, to be realized. What was new about the separation of powers, popular sovereignty, free trade, and socialism in the eighteenth century was the claim that they manifested the actual force of nature in men's social arrangements—and yet in each case they were paired with antithetical political and social institutions, such as political authoritarianism or private property, which made the doctrines seem more like utopian visions than fundamental truths.

Much has been made of Montesquieu's double inconsistency—first, in misinterpreting the British mixed government in the doctrinaire terms of the separation of powers, and second, in juxtaposing this combination, exalted as the illustration of the only guaranteed liberty, with an analysis of France as a lawful monarchy whose whole sovereignty devolved from the king. But there must have been a rationale behind the inconsistency, for it was not personal to Montesquieu. The common subscription of a Voltaire, a Diderot, a Helvétius, and even a d'Holbach to both the constitutional separation of powers and the political cooperation with enlightened autocrats indicates a problem intrinsic to the constitutional and political thinking of the Enlightenment. The vacillation which we have seen in the radical group, moreover, between a belief in the democratic principle behind all governments and a pluralistic standard of effective governmental forms is another expression of the same kind of problem. The doctrines of *laissez-faire* and socialism bring this problem to a head and point the way to its solution. They bring the problem to a head because their analyses of men's economic activities and property relations were clearly attempts to bring natural philosophy to bear upon the most concrete and practical of all human interests, but these doctrines were at the same time abstract, simplistic, and utopian models separated from the inconvenient complexities of economic and social existence. Like the ideal of constitutional government and the principle of consent, they too required political action from outside the economic and social process before they could become the economic and social realities they claimed to be.

The key to this paradox between a practical kind of human ideal and the reliance upon an extraneous means to make men practice it can be found in an analysis of the frank Physiocratic defense of "legal despotism" as the political regime most appropriate to the antipodal liberal economics of *laissez-faire*. In the form given the notion of legal despotism by its chief proponents, Mercier de la Rivière and Du Pont de Nemours, it referred to the necessary despotism of the natural law, which imposed itself on men with "the irresistible force of truth" and which could be expressed only by a corresponding "personal despotism." Their explicit argument that the "despotism" of a natural order which prescribed the economic freedom of the individual could be administered only by a hereditary monarch and not by the individuals (or their representatives) who were the prime agents of this natural order revealed the three chief assumptions of eighteenth-century political and social theory:

First, the realistic quality of this theory consisted in the incorporation of material considerations within the thought but not in the consideration of how to get this thought into practice. Thus we must distinguish, when we assess these doctrines, between the earthiness in their ideas and the applicability of their ideas.

Second, the self-proclaimed practicality of Enlightenment political and social thinking entailed the further distinction between the practice of men within an established order and the practice of men required to get an order established. In the correspondence of a Voltaire or a Diderot with such "enlightened despots" as Frederick the Great, Joseph II, or Catherine the Great, as in the later political doctrine of a Kant, the ambiguous relations between constitutionalism and enlightened absolutism in Enlightenment thought are clarified into a call for the autocrats to create the conditions for a constitutional regime which could then become an operative reality on its own.

A third and final assumption of eighteenth-century political and social thought, following in turn from this distinction between the *de jure* independent social process that would maintain justice and the *de facto* political agency required to institute a reign of justice, postulated a fundamental ambivalence in the attitude toward the individual, whose liberty was deemed on the one hand essential to the movement of the social process but on the other hand inadequate, because of its partial function within the society, to the direction of the social process as a whole. The corollary of this ambivalence was the distinction between the freedom of individuals, whether singular or in combination, as the essential goal of collective action and the authority of institutions as the contingent sponsors of collective action. Thus whether the rights were those of Rousseau's democracy, the Physiocrats' *laissez-faire*, or Morelly's equal share in the communal property, they were conceived to be not in conflict with, but on a different level from, the visible rights of governments. Democracy, *laissez-faire*, socialism, were all, for the men of the Enlightenment, guiding ideas for those who happened to be in power.

The relationship between the liberal ideal and the practice of politics varied, to be sure, from country to country. In Great Britain, as befitted the vitality of its commercialized society and its representative form of government, the connection was closest. Not only did the political views of such prominent writers as David Hume and Sir William Blackstone (1723–1780) attempt simply to rationalize the existing constitution, but even the radicals associated their doctrines with actual movements for British parliamentary or American colonial reform. In France, as befitted the gaps between the absolute state and the society and the divisions within the class-torn society itself, the gulf between theory and actuality was far wider. Writers proposed their doctrines of a just constitution and a free society as counsel which the competing ministerial and aristocratic authorities should apply as the goals toward which their respective policies would tend.

In Germany, Austria, and Russia, finally, where the gap between active autocrats and passive societies was greatest, the doctrine of a just constitution and a free society was all but divested of any reality, whether present or future, and was assigned the status of a figurative and unattainable ideal of autocratic policy. The typical forms of political and social writing in central Europe were not political, social, or economic theory as such, but jurisprudence and Cameralism. These were theories that treated the fundamental questions of the state and the economy within the framework of the government and its policy. Through the influence of Christian Wolff, perpetuated during the mature Enlightenment through no less a publicist than Frederick the Great, the proper constitution of the state was made to consist in the proper policy of the ruler. Despite some direct borrowing of Physiocratic ideas by German officials the characteristic form of economic theory continued to be Cameralistic. The two outstanding mid-eighteenth-century Cameralists, the German Johann Heinrich von Justi (1717–1771) and the Austrian Count Josef von Sonnenfels (1733–1817), were both adept at turning the Enlightenment's liberal goals of individual and social welfare into canons of efficiency for the guidance of the monarchical administration.

But behind these national variations the common features of doctrine and the common assumptions of its role remained, and from them we may draw a composite sketch of the political and social theory characteristic of Europe's mature Enlightenment. By virtue of their very nature, men become real human beings only when they collaborate as free individuals with their fellows in a free society. Because individuals are nature's primary agents they are capable of acting freely within a free society, but because they are presently misguided and inevitably partial they are incapable now of instituting and ultimately of guaranteeing the generality of the rules for the operation of such a society. Enlightened by the *philosophes* in the understanding of the general laws of a free society, the political authorities (or "Legislators," as the *philosophes* preferred to call them) must use their traditional monopoly of social force to institute such a society and participate in its permanent guarantee. Once instituted, the free society is maintained by the harmonious activity of the free individuals within it and by the constitutional balance of social representatives and political authorities to prevent excesses both of individual rights and of governmental power. And as long as such a society has not been instituted and does not yet exist—a contingency which tallied, for almost all the *phi-*

losophes, with their contemporary situation—governments must prepare the way for it by making what would be the reality of this society the present ideal of governmental policy.

Philosophical History

Like the religious and ethical doctrines of the mature Enlightenment, the historical focus of the period further developed an interest already characteristic of the preceding phase. Like the practitioners of these other fields too, the historians of the mature Enlightenment gave substance to what had been only a program and a framework, but here the substance was not memorable doctrine but immortal monuments of historical literature.

Not, to be sure, that the *philosophes* showed themselves averse either to discussing the idea of history or to working out their favorite ideas in history—they were too fond of ideas in general and too conscious of their own educational mission to avoid either of these didacticisms. In Voltaire's historical prefaces—particularly in the 1756 introduction to the *Essay on the Manners and Spirit of Nations* which he entitled "The Philosophy of History"—the Enlightenment view of history received its authoritative formulation. Such formulations, indeed, became so much the style that when toward the end of the age the German philosopher and historian Johann Gottfried von Herder wanted to attack the rationalism and the pragmatism of Enlightenment history he published a counterformulation under the title *Another Philosophy of History for the Education of Humanity: Contribution to the Many Contributions of the Century* (1774).

But more characteristic of the mature Enlightenment's idea of history than this programmatic philosophy of history was the "philosophical history" which sketched the general history of humanity in order to prove the reality of one or another principle of human nature by demonstrating its role in furnishing rational coherence to the course of human history. Voltaire's *Essay on the Manners and Spirit of Nations* was the most famous of these philosophical histories, with its renunciation of the traditional historical focus on political leaders and western Christian culture and with its affirmation that all men everywhere were the subjects of history and that their struggle for rationality was the unifying principle of history. Turgot's lectures of 1750 on the "progress of the human spirit," with their stress on innovation as the force and progress as the principle of the human species, and Adam Ferguson's *Essay on the History of Civil Society* of 1767, with its stress on the role of social instincts in the origins of organized society and on the role of the civic virtues in its preservation, indicate that Voltaire's was not an isolated performance. None of these cases of what came to be called "theoretical" history was itself a notable work of historical literature (although a forerunner's status has been accorded Voltaire's for cultural history and Ferguson's for historical sociology), but together they did contribute three features to the modern idea of history. First, there is a connectedness and a meaning in human history that comes from something constant and fundamental in men themselves. Second, not only the politics and wars of kings but all kinds of activities of all kinds of men can have significance for the understanding of human nature and therefore for history when they serve as authentic ingredients of the moral "spirit" that connects the historical actions of men. Third, such coherent actions are not only to be found in history–they are the only authentic history. Actions that are trivial and unconnected, like the traditional political chronicles, are not historical and should remain beneath the notice of an historian.

Not the abstract statement of these principles, however, but the actual historical works in which they were applied have proved to be immortal in Enlightenment historiography. Voltaire's *Age of Louis XIV* (1751), Hume's *History of England* (1754–1762), William Robertson's *History of the Reign of the Emperor Charles V, with a View of the Progress of Society in Europe from the Subversion of the Roman Empire to the Beginning of the Sixteenth Century* (1769), and Gibbon's *Decline and Fall of the Roman Empire* (1776–1788) can be said to mark the beginning of modern historical literature. Previous histories had been valued, and have been valued since, for the religious or political points of view they served, for the historical sources they collected, or—as accounts of contemporary events— for the historical sources they themselves were. Now, for the first time, historical commentaries on a grand scale sought both to record and explain broad swaths of a definite human past from a point of view that was designed both to understand this past and to relate the historians' present to it.

These historians were all *philosophes* in good standing, representatives par excellence of the Enlightenment, and as such they have all been indicted for an unhistorical bias at least as great as that of the tendentious predecessors they attacked. It is undeniable that the attitudes which they brought to bear upon history did limit what we have come to consider a genuine sense of history. Their operative notion that not only human nature but human motivation was constant in all ages; the exaltation of the rational principle that led them to exclude the recalcitrant detail as trivial and to deprecate ages, institutions, and men of faith as noxious; their actual persistence, despite their pretensions to the contrary, in concentrating on politics as the representative strand of cultural history: these characteristic features of the Enlightenment world view that have made for its unhistorical reputation were undoubtedly visible in even its premier historians.

But in the great histories of the period these features were combined fruitfully with other equally characteristic features of the Enlightenment— notably, with its addiction to scientific method, its attention to the specific

Edward Gibbon. *Author of* The Decline and Fall of the Roman Empire, *the greatest historical work of the eighteenth century.*

identity of any particular fact, its skepticism toward traditional truths, its fascination with the human psyche, and its awareness of the social context in which it saw its politics. Thus Gibbon's ideal of "the philosophical historian" who selects from "the vast chaos of events" the facts "that dominate the general system" and arrives thereby at "the general causes" which "change the face of the earth" is to be judged not by the statement itself but by the historical function he makes it play. Outstanding in *The Decline and Fall*, far overshadowing the occasional errors, the intrusive anti-Christianity, the aristocratic preferences, and the curious modernity of Gibbons' ancient Romans, is the blend of vast canvas with precise scholarship, of panoramic composition with the startling clarity of every detail. In an early description of his historising, Gibbon revealed his desire always to immerse his ideas in his historical materials, an immersion characteristic of all Enlightenment thought. However, his judgment that in the final analysis "we must be careful not to make the order of our thoughts subservient to that of our subjects" was equally characteristic of Enlightenment thought. And so it is that through the awesome research, the colorful drama, and the majestic style for which *The Decline and Fall* is justly celebrated, Gibbon wove a fine mesh of narrative coherence, composing all kinds of variations on a fundamental theme—the destruction of "the solid fabric of human greatness"—and fulfilling his grand purpose of connecting "the ancient and modern history of the World."

In their lesser ways the other notable historians of the mature Enlightenment manifested a similar blend of the qualities that made the movement the sire of modern history. Political as was their emphasis and distorting as was their preference for the ancient and modern over the medieval stages of Western civilization, they too avoided the extremes of compilation and of theoretical exposition. Voltaire and Hume organized historical events around the patterns of nationality, while Robertson prefaced his detailed narrative history of sixteenth-century Europe's most ambitious emperor (the Habsburg Charles V) with a comprehensive survey of the tendencies which converged into the "one great political system" characteristic of modern times. Thus did the Enlightenment's concern for general principle become, in the practicing historian, the attention to a cohesive historical process within which each event had its place.

Far from representing a soft spot in eighteenth-century thought, the best history produced by the mature Enlightenment reflected as faithfully as any other field of its culture the attitude that would become its legacy to Western civilization. This attitude engendered a profound respect for the reality of every natural and human fact that played a role in a larger structure of meaning; and conversely it taught men to look for the general principles which make up the framework of meaning only in the fabric of facts and to trim this fabric in accordance with the nature of the facts. It was a delicate balance that could last only as long as facts and principles were in equipoise and as long as all facts and principles that were respectively incompatible were excluded from consideration. But the nostalgia with which men still hearken back to this age that has recently and admiringly been labeled the age of "humanity" signalizes its unforgettable, if evanescent, success in reconciling the most fundamental of human desires: to give the individual a stable identity and to discover the unity which associates individuals in common enterprises and gives to the life of each its direction and its meaning.

CHAPTER 7

The Unworldly Philosophers, 1770-1789

ORIGINATING AT the very height of the mature Enlightenment as a kind of fugal counterpoint to it, a new cultural movement gradually arose to dominate the last third of the eighteenth century. Not, of course, that the Enlightenment simply disappeared. The familiar figures and their disciples did continue to spread illumination in their wonted way. The giants of the mature Enlightenment—Voltaire, Diderot, d'Alembert, Mably, Gibbon, Wieland, and Lessing—continued to write well into the decade of the 1770's, and in some cases, the 1780's. When they fell silent, their message was taken up by a host of lesser figures—such as the radical historian Guillaume Raynal in France, the rationalistic systematizer of utilitarian morality William Paley in Great Britain, and the Enlightened journalists August Ludwig von Schlözer and Christoph Nicolai in Germany. But the movement no longer possessed, in these protagonists, its wonted flexibility, its creativity, and its power to attract the best of the new intellectual talent. These qualities passed in part to a radically opposed group, which is now usually called "preromantic," who abominated everything the Enlightenment stood for. But an even more critical sign of the decay of the Enlightenment may be seen in the identities of the other groups who succeeded the *philosophes* in dominating the cultural life of the last third of the century: they were heirs of the Enlightenment, and their development into cultural independence demonstrated the incipient disintegration of the parent movement.

The soul of the Enlightenment and the force of its typical doctrines inhered, as we have seen, in the flexible balance which the *philosophes* poised between variety and unity, individuality and generality, reality and meaning, experience and purpose, movement and stability, pleasure and principle—equivalent but antithetical values which they had to keep adjusting within the natural realm once they had excluded a supernatural realm. Since it was rather the balance and the communication maintained by the *philosophes* among these diverse factors than any homogeneous lineup of compatible factors that was the essence of the mature Enlighten-

Beatrice addressing Dante from the Car (Purgatorio, Canto XXIX). *Painting by William Blake, the British mystic, artist, poet whose revulsion against the rationality and the practicality of the Enlightenment betokened the dawn of another cultural era. National Gallery, London.*

ment, the cultural movements which succeeded it in the last third of the century could be powered as much by men who deliberately upset the balance by espousing the supremacy of one or another of the Enlightenment's own values as by men who espoused the supremacy of values outside the entire syndrome of the Enlightenment.

Thus the passing of the Enlightenment should be seen not as a simple mechanical case of petrifaction and reaction, but as an articulated cultural process in which developments from the Enlightenment provided a linkage between the Enlightenment itself and the revulsion against it. This polyphonic structure of the post-Enlightenment exhibits a cultural pattern far more integrated than the usual mechanical image of Enlightenment action and preromantic reaction indicates. Not one but three kinds of intellectual movements between 1770 and 1789 were putting an end to the Enlightenment and embalming its remains for the edification of posterity. First, what has been called the "radicalization" of the Enlightenment was actually the one-sided development of its rational ordering principles into the rigid systems of atheism, determinism, and inevitable progress, represented by such figures as d'Holbach, Laplace, and Condorcet. Second, what has been erroneously included in the reaction against the Enlightenment was actually the one-sided development of its individualizing, liberalizing, and dynamic principles into the utilitarian, sentimental, idealistic, naturalistic, and evolutionary creeds represented by such figures as Bentham, Rousseau, Kant, Godwin, and Lamarck. Third, the authentic revolt against the Enlightenment was actually a rejection of the *philosophes* and all their works on behalf of individual, anarchic, and demonic powers entirely outside the Enlightenment syndrome. Represented by the German school of *Sturm und Drang* ("storm and stress"), by organicists like Burke, and by mystics like Blake, this revolt was a preromantic movement of an aesthetic character, but it did appropriate ideas from the sentimental, classical, and dynamic offshoots of the Enlightenment for its intellectual content.

The age which was dominated in thought by this three-pronged cultural movement was an age which was dominated in action by the eruption of revolutionary situations in many of the European states. The development out of and against the Enlightenment may be seen as a kind of cultural revolution which peaked in anticipation of the subsequent political and social revolution in France. The detailed consideration of the three strands of this intellectual revolution will show the first forms taken by the typical revolutionary parties of modern times: the party that desires a radical execution of the systematic order promised by the Old Regime; the party that desires a radical execution of the freedom promised but compromised by the Old Regime; and the extreme party that wants no part of the Old Regime and would inaugurate an age categorically new.

But if this cultural revolution that climaxed the Old Regime anticipated the forms of modern revolutionary practice, and if it helped to prepare men's minds and their spirits for what they would do with political and social revolution after it came, it is also important to realize that the one revolution did not in fact cause the other. We must investigate all three parties of the intellectual revolution to understand the exclusively intellectual resolution that they gave to social tensions and the free field that they left to the more material and tangible interests of men in the initiation of the political and social revolution of 1789.

THE NEW RATIONALISM

Most closely akin to the Enlightenment and frequently characterized by posterity as its radical phase, the rigorous rationalism that flourished in the last quarter of the eighteenth century was actually a successor movement. The heirs of the *philosophes* resolved the tensions of the Enlightenment in the name of Enlightenment, but in a way that belied it. They reconverted its delicate "systematic spirit" into the rigid "spirit of systems" by developing its logical, rational, necessary facet at the expense of the individual, the experimental, and the voluntaristic.

The nodal figure in the transition from the flexible reasonableness of the *philosophes* to the intransigent rationalism of their successors was the Baron Paul Henri d'Holbach (1723–1789), author of the fashionable

Joseph Priestley. *British chemist, physicist, theologian, and democratic political theorist.*

Christianity Unmasked (1767), participant in the intellectual enterprises of the *philosophes*, and host at one of their liveliest salons. From 1770 to 1776 he published, under various pseudonyms, the series of volumes on natural and moral philosophy which developed the characteristic Enlightenment notions of reason, nature, utility, and humanity into a simple and unbending atheism, materialism, and fatalism. "All is in order in nature, no part of which can ever vary from the certain and necessary rules which issue from its inherent essence."

This renewal of dogmatic materialism earned d'Holbach refutations from such stalwarts as Voltaire and Frederick the Great, among others, but his viewpoint was increasingly shared by that intellectual barometer of the age, Denis Diderot, and independently, by that provocative blend of scientist, theologian, and philosopher, Joseph Priestley. In themselves, materialism, determinism, and even atheism—d'Holbach and Diderot were obviously atheists—were not anything new for the Enlightenment. At least La Mettrie and Helvétius had been of a similar persuasion in their conception of nature without bringing the Enlightenment to a final crisis. What gave these doctrines their lethal force in the last third of the century was their association with ideas of man's freedom and their influence in turning these ideas into radical dogmas. D'Holbach, Diderot, and Priestley all elaborated doctrines of moral or political liberty alongside their doctrines of natural necessity, and the logical rigor of the latter carried over into the former, subordinating the familiar Enlightenment notion of a moderate constitutional freedom to the categorical rational principles of an infallible general will or an unqualified and homogeneous law of nature. However modest their practical recommendations remained, the uncompromising statement of these underlying principles gave to the political doctrines of d'Holbach and

Priestley and to the moral protests of Diderot a radical tone that differed essentially from the reasonable aura of the Enlightenment. Thus, d'Holbach shared the general inclination of eighteenth-century Europeans to depend on the established rulers for the initiative in political and social reform, but his subordination of politics to the uniformity of his natural law gave a sweeping quality and trenchant tone to his demands for the removal of specific restraints and abuses. Similarly, both Diderot and Priestley shared the eighteenth-century intellectual's suspicion of the masses and tended to trust only the propertied middle classes with political rights, but once again the equal subordination of all individual things and men to their rigorous notion of natural law endowed their moderate political proposals with a radical egalitarian overtone that announced the onset of the post-Enlightenment era.

The emphatic rationalism to which d'Holbach, Priestley, and the later Diderot were the transitional figures had, like them, both a scientific and a political tendency.

The notable scientists of the post-Enlightenment era confirmed its tendency, if not to materialism specifically, at least to the rigorous rationality represented in the resurgence of mathematics. The mathematical determinism which Pierre Laplace (1749-1827) developed in this period grew ultimately into what is probably the most extreme and the most famous formulation of it ever penned: "An intellect which at any given moment would know all the forces that animate nature and would know the mutual positions of the beings that compose nature—if this intellect were vast enough to submit its data to analysis—could condense into a single formula the movement of the greatest bodies of the universe and that of the lightest atom. For such an intellect nothing could be uncertain; and the future, like the past, would be present before its eyes." Joseph Lagrange (1736-1813), Laplace's contemporary of equal mathematical genius, was impelled by the same faith in predictability on the basis of universal natural law to write his classic, *Analytical Mechanics* (1788), which abstracted from the physical and geometric (that is, spatial) properties of matter and turned the science of matter in motion—the science of mechanics—into a purely rational discipline, a perfect system of mechanical laws deduced from a few simple formulas through a sequence of differential equations.

It was in this same period, moreover, and under these same intellectual auspices that Antoine Laurent Lavoisier (1743-1794) reorganized chemistry into a modern science—notably in his *Elements of Chemistry* (1789)—essentially by quantifying and systematizing it. He reduced the phenomena of combustion to a "simple principle" ("the oxygenic principle"). He undertook a "new arrangement of chemistry" in which he recommended less attention to assembling facts and observations, and more attention "to classifying them" and to locating them in the proper

Luigi Galvani's experiments with frogs (1780). *Along with Alessandro Volta and Charles Coulomb in the same period, Galvani demonstrated the continuity of electrical current and contributed thereby to the substitution of physical for moral connections in nature.*

"part of the whole to which they pertain." He reformed the nomenclature of chemistry in conformity with "natural logic," that is, with "the natural order in the succession of ideas." By making precise experimentation and quantitative observation the basis of primary principles in a logically integrated chemistry, Lavoisier resolved the former tension between the uniformity of natural law and the multiformity of chemical phenomena in favor of the natural law. Nor was his pattern of resolution an isolated one: his contemporary Charles Coulomb (1736–1806) was performing an analogous service for the science of electricity when he worked exact measurements into "Coulomb's law" of electrical attraction on the Newtonian model. These scientific developments embodied an essential quality of the neo-rationalism which helped to dissolve the intellectual synthesis of the Enlightenment: the appreciation of particular realities and the importance of observing them precisely—values which the men of the Enlightenment had endowed with an autonomous status—were still acknowledged by the post-Enlightenment rationalists, but now they were integrated into overriding rational systems of natural law.

The characteristic note of the 1770's and 1780's in the human sciences—i.e., in the literature on human nature, society, and history—has often been defined as "radical," and in terms of emphasis, passion, and thoroughness in criticism of existing abuses the characterization undoubtedly fits. But in terms of intellectual content, this kind of writing is better understood as the social and political component of the new rationalism, imparting to the study of society a systematic quality which generalized the individual liberties of the Enlightenment in a way that was analogous to the contemporary scientific emphasis on generalizing particular observations. Like this scientific emphasis, the new social and political rationalism was in many ways continuous with the Enlightenment and was regarded by protagonists and antagonists alike as an integral part of it, but, again like the scientific emphasis of the age, it manifested a runaway universalism that actually betokened a growth out of rather than within the Enlightenment. There were, moreover, personal connections between the two branches of the new rationalism. The Marquis de Condorcet (1743–1794), one of the most prominent of the social rationalists, not only was an able mathematician but explicitly replaced teleology with science to ensure the strict lawfulness of human progress. Again, *The Philosophical and Political History of European Settlements and Trade in the East and West Indies,* whose ever more daring revisions between 1770 and 1780 made it a popular reservoir for radical sentiment and turned its presumed author, Abbé Guillaume Raynal (1713–1796), into an exile from his native France, was actually a compendium by Raynal of conversations and contributions from several sources, most notably from d'Holbach's salon and Diderot's pen.

The historic function of these so-called radicals, indeed, was not to develop new revolutionary ideologies, but rather to put a new emphasis on the drastic opposition of the Enlightenment's familiar social and political doctrines to contemporary social and political practice. The radicals were closely attuned to the agitated social and political scene of the 1770's and 1780's, and their writings registered their sympathy with the agitators— with the Americans, the British parliamentary reformers, and the anti-aristocratic French pressure group around Turgot. These sympathies took the form of a sharper tone, a more sweeping criticism, a more categorical condemnation, of established church and state than ever before, as the intellectuals became impatient with the compromise of rational principles and asserted them in ever greater purity. Thus the notorious radicalism of Raynal and his cohorts—as of the aging Voltaire—was directed primarily at the church on behalf of reason, and the rise of Freemasonry during the last decades of the Old Regime confirmed the hardening of anticlericalism into a rationalist dogma. When they did turn to practical policies, "radicals" like Mably (in his pro-American *Observations on the Government and Laws of the United States of America,* 1784), Richard Price (in his equally pro-American *Observations on the Importance of the American Revolution and the Means of Making It a Benefit to the World,* 1784), Joseph Priestley (in his utopian *Lectures on History and General Policy,* 1788), and Condorcet (in his essays of 1788 on the European relevance of the American Revolution) asserted the universality of the principles of natural rights for all men that underlay the American Revolution and the necessity of leveling European aristocratic institutions in the light of them, but they also were unanimous in limiting political rights to men of property, divided on the issue of a unicameral or bicameral legislature, and silent on the question of how the reforms would be realized. Only the future leader of the Girondin party in the French Revolution, Jacques Pierre Brissot de Warville (1754–1793), was a genuine revolutionary before the revolution, and in him it was a matter of an even more unqualified and systematic application of universal human rights than his like-minded contemporaries would face up to. In general, the swift pace, after 1776, of events they did not make left the radical rationalists further and further out of the real world they could not master.

For the most part, these political rationalists thus were prepared to welcome revolutions when they came (Raynal would not even do this), but they did not create the kind of doctrine that would start revolutions. None developed a program that called for popular political action, though all gave new emphasis to the people's right to political representation as an inviolable universal natural right that kings should grant or history realize—some day. Condorcet's formula made the attainment of civil liberty and social equality not, as formerly, the problematic issue of the struggle between personal utility and general law, but the inevitable, predictable product of the general laws that ensured the progress of humanity and the perfectibility of its nature. This formula, resolving the problem of freedom by making it a function of universal law, epitomized the physical and political rationalism that the dissolution of the Enlightenment deposited into the stream of European history.

THE NEW FREEDOM

A second principal legacy of the Enlightenment, similarly detached during the last third of the eighteenth century from its associations with the other principles of the mature Enlightenment, was the intense focus upon individual freedom and the effort to construct a system of values based entirely upon it. This tendency was intermediate between the radical rationalism that claimed to represent the Enlightenment and the preromantic revulsion aimed deliberately against the Enlightenment, and it combined characteristics from each movement. Like the rationalists, the new libertarians made predominant one of the values that had been balanced in the mature Enlightenment, and they hypostatized this value in order to resolve the tensions and frictions of its uneasy equilibrium. Thus they made primary the kind of human being that the *philosophes* had conceived—that is, one who found moral fulfillment in a social system. But like the preromantics the new libertarians rejected, as antithetical to individual freedom, the constant and universal kind of natural law that the Enlightenment had set up vis-à-vis the liberty of individual action as its controlling principle.

The result was a wholly distinctive program: the construction of a new kind of rational system, both in respect to the knowledge of nature and in the organization of society, that would realize rather than restrict the liberty of individuals. As the rationalists reduced liberty and particularity to logical functions of their rational systems, the libertarians reduced reason and society to moral functions of their individualistic systems.

One of the incongruities of European intellectual history is the number of eighteenth-century movements with some relationship to the Enlightenment that remained influential in the nineteenth century, when men were otherwise rejecting the Enlightenment. The explanation of the incongruity lies precisely in the way the Enlightenment dissolved during the last third of the eighteenth century. The movements in question—Bentham's utilitarianism, Rousseau's naturalism, Kant's idealism, and Lamarck's evolutionism—all developed from the individualistic libertarian strand of the unraveled Enlightenment, and hence they were historically both related to and independent of the Enlightenment itself. But there was an important historical distinction within this strand of movements—the distinction between those that acknowledged the Enlightenment as the source for their doctrines of individual freedom and developed beyond it unconscious of their departure from it, and those that came to revile the Enlightenment for its static and stringent laws of reason and developed beyond it unconscious of their debt to it. The founders of utilitarianism and idealism were in the first category; the progenitors of naturalism and evolutionism were in the second.

Bentham's Utilitarianism

The utilitarianism of Jeremy Bentham (1748–1832) grew naturally out of its eighteenth-century soil. The principle of utility had been announced in the early Enlightenment. The doctrine of utility had been developed in the mature Enlightenment. With all due and grateful acknowledgments to Hume for the first and to Helvétius, Beccaria, and Priestley for the second, Bentham worked the principle and the doctrine into the full-blown theory of utilitarianism, the main lines of which were laid down in works as early as his *Fragment on Government* (1776) and his *Introduction to the Principles of Morals and Legislation* (1789). Bentham has been adjudged an ambiguous intellectual figure. His utilitarian ideas, his analytical approach, and his reasonable tone all aligned him with the *philosophes*. But his starting point and his ultimate effect depended heavily upon his decisive rejection of their most cherished doctrine. The primacy of the individual-pleasure principle in the constitution of human nature, of the greatest-happiness principle in the ideal of society, of practical results in moral

Jeremy Bentham. *Founder of Utilitarianism.*

judgments, of *laissez-faire* in economics, and of a proper legislation in directing individual pleasure toward social morality—all these Benthamite ideas came straight out of the Enlightenment. They reflected not only its belief in individuals as the prime units of human reality but also its conception of the potentiality in these individuals for rational and ethical association. But in his categorical rejection of both the reality and the validity of natural law as a moral principle that guaranteed the harmony of individual and social utility, Bentham attacked the fundamental bond which the *philosophes* had used to assure this kind of association.

But this apparent ambiguity of Bentham's toward the Enlightenment disappears when Bentham is seen as one of the new libertarians who sought to free the utility-seeking individual from any a priori bondage, whether of privilege or principle, and sought only to erect a legal system based on the harmonizing of such individual utilities. Thus his fundamental convictions established the primacy of the individual: only the individual could judge what was useful to him; this judgment required the freedom to act upon it; the assumption of a priori, universal laws of nature was irrelevant and injurious to the freedom of this individual judgment. But he also erected an alternative rational system of measuring utility which he deemed consistent with individual liberty. He held that the rigorous deduction of a "calculus" of pleasures and pains to serve as the bond of a just and rational society was appropriate and salubrious for the freedom of individual judgment. Bentham thus built the self-interest of the individual into the common interest of the society through a set of moral and legal propositions which validated security and equality as well as civil liberties. Yet they remained for him derivative from individualism because they were constructed on the consequences of individual freedom rather than on the prescriptions of an a priori principle other than individual freedom.

Idealism

The German analogue of British utilitarianism was idealism, for it too had an important root in the liberal strand of the eighteenth-century Enlightenment and dominated its nation for almost half of the nineteenth century. It rose in late-eighteenth-century Germany and spanned the greatest age of thought and letters that Germany has ever known. "Idealism" in this context has both a specific and a general reference. Specifically, it refers to the philosophical position, dominant in these years, that made the world we know and act in primarily a product of ideas or mind. More generally, it refers to the cultural attitude, dominant in philosophers, men of letters, composers, and statesmen, that made the conscious infusion of spiritual ideals into neutral or refractory existence, both natural and social, the task of the generation. In its more general sense the German age of idealism was manifest in many branches of intellectual and artistic activity, and the function of the Enlightenment as an important root of German idealism is visible in each of these branches. In music, the development of both Haydn and Mozart from the melodious regularity and symmetry of their earlier works to the more moving, varied, and freely articulated mode of addressing the interior self of the individual listener in their quartets and operas from the 1780's, represent dramatic cases of the connection between the classic style of the Enlightenment and the style of spiritualized idealism in central Europe. This same connection is found in the more prosaic works of Lessing and Kant. In both, the relationship between the balanced reasonableness of the Enlightenment and the libertarian emphasis of early idealism was a matter of continuous growth and vital interaction.

Lessing, like Diderot, was one of the *philosophes* who initiated freelance writing as an independent, paid (usually underpaid) profession. Until the 1770's Lessing divided his efforts between collaborating with the leaders of the German Enlightenment in typical criticisms of the Christian establishment on behalf of reason and composing pioneer works of literature, literary criticism, and aesthetic theory in praise of individual dignity, sentiment, imagination, passion, and the individuality of the arts. In this latter line of his activity Lessing strained but did not yet rupture the orderly bounds of the Enlightenment. His epoch-making play, *Minna von Barnhelm* (1767), did indeed exalt the private honor and sensibilities of definite individuals, but it portrayed them in inevitable and equal conflict with the morality of society. In his *Laokoon* (1766), now a classic of aesthetic theory, he loosened the structure of aesthetics so as to provide for the individuality of each art form—especially for poetry in distinction from the plastic arts—but still within each of these art forms he insisted that

Gotthold Ephraim Lessing. *German playwright, literary critic, philosopher, and free-lance* philosophe.

universal criteria of beauty applied. He criticized the drama of Voltaire and declared the superiority of Shakespeare, but both on the contemporaneously acceptable grounds of fidelity to nature. Only in 1780, with the publication of his *Education of Humanity*, did the unflagging vigor, the passion for authenticity in any shape, and the elasticity of the rational impulse which had given Lessing a special place within the Enlightenment lead him beyond it. What had been a plea for toleration in *Nathan the Wise* now became a design for the internalization of the moral unity of mankind within each individual, to be realized by each in his own way.

Immanuel Kant, whose staid manner of life and placid career stood in marked contrast to Lessing's restless wandering and volatile spirit, traversed nonetheless a similar road to cultural immortality. Raised in the rationalism of Christian Wolff, the foremost philosopher of the German Enlightenment, Kant, like Lessing, spent most of his intellectual career in its service, revamping its framework of reason to sit more comfortably upon the variety of the realities it acknowledged in men and things. In the first—and the greatest—volume of his critical philosophy, the *Critique of Pure Reason* (1781), Kant took a fruitfully ambiguous stance precisely between the Enlightenment and a revolutionary position beyond it. On the one hand, he sought to save the Enlightenment's operation of reason as the unifying principle of human knowledge by defining the limits of the reality it could unify. On the other hand, he drastically shifted both the scope and the basis of this "theoretical reason" by excluding all but self-criticism and men's experience of nature from its proper field of employment and by making it entirely a common and necessary function of every individual's mind rather than, as previously, a correspondence between the mind and a natural or supernatural ordering principle outside the mind.

In the decade that followed, Kant moved definitely beyond the Enlightenment by developing an entirely different kind of reason to order the individualized kind of reality which was inaccessible to theoretical

Immanuel Kant. *Partisan of the Enlightenment who recognized its limits and went beyond them. Kant is frequently acknowledged as the most important Western philosopher since Plato. He shifted the core of human experience from something given to men from without to something that men help to make for themselves from the beginning.*

reason, but he never entirely gave up the connection with the Enlightenment, which now assumed a contrapuntal position in his thought. Indeed, in his smaller essays of 1784 he gave currency to the term "Enlightenment." He declared that "we do live in an age of Enlightenment" and he wrote a prescription for it: "Have the courage to use your own reason" (in his "What is Enlightenment?"). He also developed a theory of a rational progress toward freedom (in his "Idea for a Universal History") that has been deemed the epitome of the faith of the Enlightenment. But his major effort during this decade was expended in the construction of a system of "practical reason," a new kind of rationality that divorced the universal moral law from its familiar ground in nature and from its familiar source in man's knowledge of nature, and based it instead squarely on the ultimate reality of individual freedom by making it the necessary form of the direction the individual gave himself (chiefly in his *Critique of Practical Reason*, 1788).

At the very end of the decade which coincided with the end of Europe's Old Regime, Kant completed the final volume of his great philosophical trilogy. In it he worked his simultaneous commitment to and transcendence of the Enlightenment into a coherent pattern that both acknowledged its due place in the cultural future and led posterity beyond it. In the *Critique of Judgment*, published in 1790, Kant formulated this double-edged testimonial in two ways. First, this work climaxed the critical use of reason which his trilogy shared, as a general approach, with the Enlightenment, but it also announced the next stage of thought to be the construction of a "system . . . under the general name of Metaphysic"—a prescription for the future that the men of the Enlightenment could never have lived with. Second, in the substance of its argument the *Critique of*

Judgment asserted, just as the Enlightenment had, the validity of both natural laws and moral freedom and the necessity of finding a connection between them, but it revealed the growing tendency to go beyond the Enlightenment in satisfying this necessity. For Kant sought the connection in the judgment of individual things, and he found it in the artistic creation of men and in the self-directing organic forms of nature, both of which put the unity of reason in the service of the ultimate individuality of the free act. Only if the rational ideal of the Enlightenment is considered no longer as the goal but henceforward rather as the condition of human rights, according to Kant, is all of reality accounted for and does life have meaning. And with this step, he moved definitely beyond the Enlightenment and bore witness to its conversion from a movement into a heritage.

Naturalism

The propagators of naturalism in the last quarter of the eighteenth century exhibited a much more jaundiced view of the Enlightenment than did its loyal idealist sons, but they actually manifested essentially the same kind of legacy. The outstanding representative of the naturalist vogue was Rousseau, whose vociferous complaints against the rational universalism in the Enlightenment's view of nature obscured his own debt to the moral passion and individual freedom which the Enlightenment also derived from nature. The familiar interpretation of his development beyond the Enlightenment as a revolt against it seems confirmed by his personal estrangement from the *philosophes*. There is little doubt that he withdrew deliberately from their circle or that they considered him a "deserter" and poured contempt on him for his apostasy. But the character of the estrangement suggests not a complete separation but something rather more in the nature of a sibling rivalry. For Rousseau broke most directly and most violently with Diderot and with Voltaire, precisely the *philosophes* who influenced him most deeply in two of his most characteristic attitudes. Rousseau visited and was profoundly impressed by Diderot just before writing the *Discourse on the Arts and Sciences* (1750), whose theme of the contrast between the goodness of nature and the viciousness of artificial intellectuality was a favorite of Diderot's as well. Again, Rousseau acknowledged the shock that Voltaire's work on the 1755 Lisbon earthquake—"Poem on the Lisbon Disaster"—gave him, focusing his attention on the problem of evil that would henceforth bulk so large in his thinking and writing.

Rousseau himself claimed that all his works, from the beginning of his career to the end, were fashioned on "the same principle," but certainly he shifted his ideas of how to apply it. His break with the *philosophes* in the latter part of the 1750's—*after* his formulation of such characteristic attitudes as his exaltation of natural liberty against intellectual and social oppression in his discourses *On the Arts and Sciences* (1750) and *On the*

Jean Jacques Rousseau. *Tormented* ex-philosophe *who showed the limits of Enlightened values. Bust by Jean-Antoine Houdon. Louvre, Paris.*

Origins of Inequality (1755), and *after* his promulgation of the idea of the general will in the "Discourse on Political Economy" (1758), which he wrote for the *Encyclopedia*—symbolized the different way he would go to realize ideals which he had begun by sharing in good measure with his contemporaries. His rupture with the society of the *philosophes* was related to his conviction that the natural integrity of man was vitiated by the withdrawal of the rational faculty into a segregated realm of abstract communication, where it was associated with respectable society and divorced from action by individuals who would level this society. Rousseau continued to endorse the synthesizing ideas that the *philosophes* held to give men and things their order and direction—the reason of men, the laws of nature, the morality of society, and the deistic belief in a providential Creator—but he insisted on relocating them in the individual self and redefining them as the personal impulse, awareness, and conscience from which all social order must come. Consequently, Rousseau set himself the two-fold task of dramatizing the existing evils inherent in the artificial division of what should be united—instinct and reason, acting and thinking, individuals and society—and of constructing models of how the underlying nature of man could, were it not for psychic and social repression, develop reason, law, and society harmoniously out of the original instincts, liberties, and sovereignty of the individual. Since these tasks involved the dissolution of the loose and tolerant balance of the Enlightenment and the reorganization of its elements into a complex unity poised on its narrow individualistic and libertarian base, Rousseau's mature works mix values that were familiar to the Enlightenment with tendencies that modified them in a definite direction.

La Nouvelle Héloise (1761), a sentimental, moralizing novel in the popular tradition of Richardson's *Pamela* and Rousseau's greatest contemporary success, departed from the Enlightenment's standards primarily in its puritanical attitude toward sex, an attitude that seemed to square so ill with Rousseau's naturalism but that would be confirmed in the guilt-ridden obsessions of his *Confessions*. In contrast to the *philosophes'* compliant enjoyment of sensuality as an intrinsic boon of nature, Rousseau's rigidity in matters of sex typified a larger rejection, exemplified as well in the disapproval of theater which led to a break with d'Alembert, of sensory pleasures in principle and of any sophisticated art or science on the ground that they were diversionary, detached from the whole man, and obstructive of his freedom of action. In *Émile* (1762), Rousseau's educational treatise in the form of a novel, he followed a well-worn path when he proposed a regular scheme of secular education as the best means of conducting individuals to morality, but he departed from the norm with his thesis that moral education consisted not in the inculcation of rationality or sociality but in the simple provision of opportunities for the individual to be undisturbed in his natural growth into rationality and sociality.

The *Social Contract* (1762), finally, was typical in its exaltation of liberty as the source, contract as the sanction, law as the standard, and collective reason as the agency of the good society, but however familiar the political function of these ideas remained, in Rousseau they no longer had quite the same status or the same meaning as they did for his contemporaries. Liberty was no longer deemed a possession to be preserved, but was regarded as the continuing condition necessary for action of any kind; contract was no longer an instrument of obligation, but of self-elevation to social action; law no longer an eternal rule of nature, but the product of social action; reason no longer the capacity to recognize universal law or calculate public welfare, but the socializing faculty that gave every individual will an equal share in the general will to act. The meaning of these terms was conditioned by the purpose of the *Social Contract*: to show how every individual could enjoy the practical and the moral advantages of society and "still obey himself alone, and remain as free as before." Hence these terms no longer referred to a stable political order compatible with freedom, but to stages in a developing process driven throughout by freedom. The *Social Contract* was thus the complement of *Emile*: its "general will" was a higher freeeedom for all the individuals within a society, just as Émile's "conscience" was the higher freedom for all the faculties within the individual. In the human society as in the human psyche, freedom consisted in the never-ending interaction between the spontaneous variety and the self-controlled organization of all the elements in human nature.

It was precisely because Rousseau built a seamless continuum from the elemental drives of the isolated savage to the infallible moral will of the sovereign legislative power that he has proved so ambiguous, and has been invoked for causes ranging from primitivism to idealism, from anarchism to despotism. But this very ambiguity testifies to his historical role: he took seriously and simply the Enlightenment's commitment to both the freedom of individuals and the unity of their purpose, but where his contemporaries accepted the duality and mediated between the two, resigning themselves to compromise where need be, Rousseau strove for a total system of freedom.

Although Rousseau's major work was done well within the era of the mature Enlightenment, his positive influence began to tell only after this era had begun to wane, in the last third of the eighteenth century. This influence made itself felt in two directions. The more obvious and direct effect was on the preromantics (see pp. 228 ff.), who used his rejection of the stable rational framework of the Enlightenment to oppose the movement as a whole. Rousseau's own late development, indeed, intensified this line of influence. His *Confessions*, written in 1765–1770 but not published until the 1780's (the first part in 1782, the second in 1789), showed a derangement of his mind and his system in the direction of his exclusive absorption in the infinitely divided self so dear to the incipient romantics. In his lyrical and surprisingly serene *Day-dreams of a Solitary Stroller*, written a decade later, between 1776 and the eve of his death in 1778, he struck another preromantic chord by finally reconciling himself to himself in the immediate presence of nature. But the impact of Rousseau's work as a whole during the late eighteenth century was exercised in another direction. It was exercised on figures like Kant, William Godwin, and the notorious Marquis de Sade, heirs of the Enlightenment who confirmed Rousseau's position at its periphery through their own more patent transmission into identifiable cultural movements of the same kind of systematic freedom that he espoused.

Kant and idealism we have considered already (see pp. 219 ff.). Suffice it here to recall Kant's own acknowledgment that it was Rousseau who inspired him to devote his whole philosophical system to "establishing the rights of humanity." The bulk of both Godwin's and Sade's writings belong to the subsequent era of the French Revolution, but the formative intellectual experience of their prerevolutionary years remained with them always, and their works may stand as a kind of *reductio ad absurdum* of the attempt, so attractively ambiguous in Rousseau and so fruitfully dialectical in Kant, to construct a unitary system of freedom. Consequently, the intellectual process that was merely implicit in Rousseau and Kant became only too transparent in Godwin and Sade.

The very styles of the two *enfants terribles*—or more precisely, the defects of their styles—reveal the skeleton of their thinking. William Godwin (1756–1836), a chief transmitter of the Enlightenment to the British romantics, delivered his message on the sovereignty of the "feelings" or "affections" in essays of the most intellectual and casuistic cast, and he wrote melodramatic novels like *Caleb Williams* (1794) with avowedly didactic purposes in mind and in text. Sade, who has been elevated of late from the pornographic underground to the ranks of the pre-existentialists, alternated long sections of the most detailed and extravagant physicality with even longer sections of the most abstract and remorseless speculation on the meaning of it all.

The moral of what they taught was no more subtle than its style, for both Godwin and Sade deliberately took the idea of natural liberty out of its Enlightenment context and tried to construct unambiguous monistic systems upon it. Both espoused doctrines of extreme and unqualified individualism, and both used the idea of nature to make the sovereignty of the individual an absolute necessity by virtue of every individual's very constitution—Godwin by assigning to the individual the monopoly on universal benevolence, Sade by assigning to universal egoism a monopoly on the individual.

Godwin gathered the elements of his system in the 1780's, when he juxtaposed the natural individualism of Rousseau with the natural determinism of d'Holbach, but it was only after the shock of the French Revolution that he began to put them together in a system that would make the latter serve the former—that is, would make the order of nature furnish the underlying structure for the play of unlimited freedom among men. In his *Political Justice* (1793), Godwin compounded the negations of Swift, Hume, Rousseau, and his family tradition of religious dissent into a categorical doctrine of philosophical and political anarchism, seeing as human realities only free and independent individuals who seek happiness and who may not validly be limited in their search by any restriction whatsoever, whether its origin be in human authority, general law, or self-binding contract. Godwin's goal, indeed, was the return of men to the sovereign individualism of the state of nature, but he wanted to avoid the limitations which the Enlightenment had imposed via the educating role of the Legislator or the moralizing role of society. Godwin sought to set up this individualism neither as a mere ideal to be realized through other means nor as one of several values to be mutually accommodated, but rather as the underlying reality necessarily and exclusively corresponding to the nature of things. It is the mechanistic, tightly determined order of nature that makes all other kinds of order both superfluous and distorted, for when it is "unloosed from shackles," the mind of every individual must receive the "impressions" of this natural truth into itself, employ its reason to regard "all things—past, present, and to come—as links of an indissoluble chain," and expand itself to universal proportions accordingly. Thus through the primacy of reason Godwin had every individual recognize the absolute natural equality of all individuals and hence expand his local affections irresistibly into universal benevolence. Feelings, while still not primary, received now, from Godwin, a functional importance in thought that they had not heretofore had. As internal replacements for the institutional stimuli of state and society they provided a spontaneous motivation for the universalizing faculty of reason and thereby made the attainment of general happiness the monopoly of individual endeavor.

The Marquis de Sade (1740–1814) provided a mirror image of Godwin's paradoxical conversion of freedom into a necessary system, revealing the single intellectual process behind the opposite literal results. Where Godwin used the authority of nature to build a logic of humanity upon the principle of individual independence, Sade used the same authority to build a logic of solipsism upon the same principle. Most of Sade's works, like Godwin's, were written after the start of the French Revolution, but again like Godwin's the elements of them came out of the preceding era. These elements, revealed in the *Dialogue Between a Priest and a Dying Man* (1782) and in *Justine* (first draft completed in 1787), consisted of three categorical propositions. First, since every variety of taste and feeling derives "directly from the kind of organization we have individually received from Nature, . . . of whom we are the involuntary instruments," every action whatsoever is physically caused and morally justified (or more precisely, amorally justified) by "the designs of Nature." Second, Nature operates its designs exclusively through individuals who pursue their own happiness in their own way. "Egoism is Nature's fundamental commandment." Even "the philosopher" considers himself "alone in the universe; he judges everything subjectively; only he is of importance." Third, the individual's pursuit of happiness reduces itself to the immediate pursuit of sensory pleasure, which is, by Nature's fundamental decree, not only the basis but the final principle of moral philosophy: "Benevolence has nothing to do with Nature, . . . who never imbued us with any desire but that of satisfying ourselves at no matter what price."

Later Sade would develop his obsession with the absolute sovereignty of individuals entirely beyond Enlightenment views, coming to regard individuals as opposed to the claim of nature, and recognizing in them an autonomous force predominant even over nature and its pleasure principle. It is not this pre-existentialist position, however, but Sade's earlier naturalism that is the more historically revealing. Sade and Godwin, making into alternative systems of nature the principles that the Enlightenment had organized as natural complements—the individual's search for pleasure and the individual's capacity for benevolence—exemplify for the field of morals the pattern of the Enlightenment's passing and the character of its legacy. Those intellectuals who, toward the end of the eighteenth century, repudiated the ordering and unifying ethical devices which the Enlightenment had typified, such as the natural law and the moral sense, in favor of individual liberty, preached a freedom which bore one indelible mark of its eighteenth-century heritage: it was not sufficient unto itself but still required integration into rational doctrine for its definition and its meaning.

Evolution

The new combination of liberty with nature in the late Enlightenment, moreover, unleashed an intellectual force powerful enough to carry over even into natural science. It was reflected in the evolutionary doctrine and ideas of Jean Baptiste de Lamarck (1744–1829). In the 1770's and 1780's Lamarck developed the chemical and botanical notions which became preliminary stages for the theory of biological evolution he would announce in 1800. These notions he developed under the influence of Diderot's natural philosophy and Buffon's natural history, with their emphasis on the incessant flux of all nature and the infinite variety of all living things, and in explicit reaction against the static unities of mathematical reason represented by Priestley and Lavoisier. Certain basic assumptions of Lamarck's evolutionary theory stemmed from this one-sided appropriation of the dynamic and individualizing aspect of Enlightenment science together with the decisive dissociation from its physical mechanics: the assumptions, namely, of organic nature as an over-flowing life-force articulated into the great variety of individual organisms; of the individual organisms as the essential centers of life, whose activities toward their own perfection make up the fundamental process of nature; and of the organisms' capacity for change through appropriation of and adaptation to the resistant forms of inorganic nature.

But if Lamarck deliberately emancipated this living nature from what he considered the bondage of contemporary physical science by insisting

Jean Baptiste de Lamarck. *The French biologist who made the vitalist philosophy of nature scientifically respectable through the doctrine of evolution and the mechanism of the inheritance of acquired characteristics.*

on the categorical distinction between organic and inorganic nature (later to grow into the categorical distinction between the organism and its environment) and on the changeability of the chemical molecule (later to grow into the capacity for integral adaptation), he would not therefore emancipate it from all system. As in other fields of thought, the individualistic character of Lamarck's natural science was such as to drive him consciously into natural philosophy, and it was from this drive toward a rationale appropriate to the individualized life of his organisms that his theory of evolution developed. He chose, for his integrating concept, the idea of "systems" of organisms, by which he meant to signify the loose connection among individual organisms that comes from their parallel response to a common environmental condition. He hoped thereby to demonstrate the operation of an organized natural movement that would leave free its vital source in the autonomous individual organism. In the post-Enlightenment doctrine of evolution, as in the doctrines of utility, of the ideal, and of nature, the eighteenth century spawned the model for organizing a whole world view around one central idea, a model which would be followed in all the "isms" of the nineteenth century.

PREROMANTICISM

The third line of thought which rose to prominence in the last third of the eighteenth century stemmed from cultural traditions older than the Enlightenment and independent of it, rebounded to new life by publicly rejecting the Enlightenment root and branch, and developed into a modern movement by covertly taking from the Enlightenment whatever it could absorb. Associated especially with the names of Burke and Blake in Great Britain and of Herder, Goethe, and Schiller in Germany, the preromantics rejuvenated the emotional, pietist, and mystical currents that had retreated before the surge of Enlightenment. These currents gained a new force and a new direction from the growing impatience with the neat, balanced, limited world of the *philosophes* and from the surge of national passions that followed the association of this intellectual world with French hegemony. The favored medium of expression for preromanticism, consequently, was soaring aesthetics rather than rational exposition, and its habitat German and—to a lesser extent—British rather than the Gallic homeland of the "age of reason."

The common cry of the preromantics was for a kind of freedom and a kind of individualism that they claimed to be different from and greater than any liberty which the *philosophes* ever even imagined in their boldest dreams. The preromantics' deprecation of the Enlightenment's obvious commitment to human liberty in the name of liberty itself seems anomalous, particularly in view of their traditional background and the conservative future of the emotional and intuitional tendencies they represented. Thus the rebellious writers of the *Sturm und Drang* reverenced as their spiritual godfathers such intermediaries to a religious past as Johann Georg Hamann (1730–1788), who combined an abiding pietism with his revulsion against the "abstract" rationality of the Enlightenment, and Friedrich Gottlieb Klopstock (1724–1803), who caged his lyricism and his German patriotism within the confines of Protestant orthodoxy. Edmund Burke (1729–1797), despite a career devoted to original defenses of civil liberty, would end by becoming the model for the attraction of romantics to political reaction.

One of the keys to the kind of freedom exalted by the preromantics may be found in their radically distinctive idea, vis-à-vis the Enlightenment, of the individual whose freedom was in question. The distinction has been signified by the use of the term "individualism" for the Enlightenment's approach and of the term "individuality" for the preromantic approach. On the one hand, the Enlightenment had thought of individuals as essentially equal to one another, as essentially commensurable with one another in their fundamental interests, and as essentially needful of guarantees for the liberty that was common to them all, while the preromantics, on the other hand, thought of individuals as severally unique, as absolutely incommensurable with one another in any essential way, and as needing an escape from the shallow limits of common experience into the infinite depths of self-discovery. What defined preromanticism as an intellectual movement was not so much the revolt against the tyranny of formal rules in the arts about which they fulminated so furiously—for many of the *philosophes* had also fought this kind of regulation—but rather the deliberate identification of the Enlightenment with such formalism. The liberty that the *philosophes* based upon the individual's capacity to reason, to communicate, and thus to enjoy the rights of humanity was to the preromantics not liberty at all; it was the reduction of individuals to interchangeable "atoms," the denial to every person of what was truly individual in him, and his subordination to the rule or the law of reason that was supposed to be the common standard of all individual rights and judgments alike.

Where the *philosophes* identified freedom with the homogeneous and compatible rights of everyman, the preromantics identified it with the incomparable and unlimited rights of genius. Through their "cult of genius" the preromantics exalted not only the need, the right, and the capacity of the creative artist to break through all rules and barriers in the development of his aesthetic powers but also the rights and the powers of great men in any walk of life, who become individuals only by pursuing their own genius against the distorting and depersonalizing laws of the outside world. "Every individual human soul that develops its powers," wrote Friedrich von Schiller (1759–1805), "is more than the greatest of human societies," and both he and Johann Wolfgang von Goethe (1749–

Johann Wolfgang von Goethe. *A literary genius ranking with the greatest produced by any age in Western culture, Goethe epitomized the development of European classicism from the reign of the rules of reason and of balance in the arts to the perception of an ultimate aesthetic meaning and unity behind the acknowledged richness and variety of all life. (By the same token, however, Goethe's very gift for applying the vitality of concrete experience to the idea of the mind perpetuated the German disinclination to apply the ideas of the mind to the formation of concrete experience.)*

1832), during the 1770's and early 1780's when they participated in the flourishing stage of *Sturm und Drang*, developed this theme in the youthful dramas that they wrote and in the initial versions of their later, more famous dramas. From these years come Goethe's *Götz von Berlichingen* and *Egmont*, Schillers's *The Robbers*, and abortive versions of Goethe's *Faust* and Schiller's *Don Carlos*. They gave the world, in Karl Moor of *The Robbers* and the title figures of the other plays, unforgettable portrayals of "demonic" individuals—heroes driven by a ceaseless inner force to assert themselves beyond all human measure and against any social consideration. At this early stage of their growth, the heroic genius represented, for Goethe and Schiller, the only true freedom, since only the self-creating individual in this mold seeks to realize his freely chosen values in a world otherwise dominated by rules, routine, and practical necessities. The cult of genius was thus a kind of metaphor of the preromantic concept of individuality, signifying both its essential antipathy to any order or system and the inevitable elitism of its incidence.

The preromantic connotation of freedom in terms of an unconfined and aristocratic individuality had three corollaries. First, it supplied the context for the emotional emphasis that would become the most obvious feature of romanticism. That such an emphasis goes back to the preromantics is undeniable. Burke's *Philosophical Inquiry into the Origin of Our Ideas of the Sublime and Beautiful*—the early essay on aesthetics in which he exercised his most important influence on Europe until his writings on the French Revolution—persuaded German critics that both the sublime and the beautiful originate in the "passions," that "the influence of reason in producing our passions is nothing near so extensive as is commonly believed," and that, to the contrary, "the great power of the sublime, . . . far from being produced by them, . . . anticipates our reasonings and hurries us on by an irresistible force." Hamann taught Herder, a charter member of *Sturm und Drang*, that "nature works through the senses and the passions. Whoever mutilates these instruments of hers—how can he experience anything?" And Goethe himself, in his *Sorrows of Young Werther* (1774) drowned susceptible Europeans in copious tears of sentimental melancholy when he novelized a kind of mirror portrait of his heroic theme: the integrity and authenticity of the sensitive man of feeling, and his destruction, through his lack of a heroic genius, under the pressure of conventional society.

The preromantic stress on passion and emotion was undoubtedly spurred by the obvious hostility explicitly demonstrated by its progenitors against the rationalism of the Enlightenment. Since the *philosophes*, as we have seen, acknowledged the valid roles of passion and emotion far more than their opponents admitted, the emotionalism of the preromantics was in this respect an exaggerated partisan reaction against the guiding and balancing role that the *philosophes* did attribute to reason. But there was also a more essential and a more justifiable cause of the one-sided concern with passion and emotion than the mere squabble over the ranking of the human faculties. Passion and emotion were crucial to the preromantic idea of individuality, just as reason had been crucial to the Enlightenment idea of individualism. For the typical position of the preromantics was not that human action and ideas stemmed directly from sensations, emotions, and passions, but rather that they stemmed from the whole person—in Goethe's terms, "from all his united powers"—and what Hamann called "immediate feeling" and Herder "inner sentiment" was deemed the unifying force among these powers. The idea that the emotions supplied the psychic unity in a fragmented world was clearly a secularization of the traditional function of religious faith, and this secularization was a product of the competition with the secularized reason of the worldly philosophers. The preromantics revived religion as well, to be sure, but rather as an appropriate medium of the emotional life than as its final purpose. For them, the naturalized emotions now became an independent factor in the cultural life of Western man. Henceforward they would rival reason as the source of the internal unity that made a human being an authentic individual.

The second corollary of the preromantic commitment to individuality was the notion that the essential issues of life were fought out within the individual, who then proceeded to form the outer world in his own image. The vogue of Shakespeare in the Germany of the late eighteenth century was accountable not only to his obvious freedom from the French rules of classical dramaturgy but also to his focusing of tragic issues upon internal conflicts within the individual. Goethe's *Götz von Berlichingen* (1773) was the first of the German tragedies on a frankly Shakespearean model. It is no coincidence that it was precisely Goethe who made both a literary form and a philosophical doctrine out of the process of first localizing conflict and resolution in the individual and then showing how a plastic macrocosm (nature) is molded by the complete microcosm (the individual). In the England of Lawrence Sterne (1713–1768), his novel *Tristram Shandy* (1759–1767) and his autobiographical *Sentimental Journey* (1768) developed prose literature in a similarly subjective direction. Dispensing with both the objective moralization and the objective narrative sequence of the Richardsonian pattern, Sterne concentrated meaning and continuity in the individual protagonist's consciousness of events and circumstances that were casual and indifferent in themselves. In Hamann's dramatic summary: "Only our descent into the hell of self-knowledge opens our way to Paradise."

This preromantic corollary that made the individual an arena before he could become an agent had the immediate effect of withdrawing intellectual attention from political and social life. There was, to be sure, no inherent necessity in this withdrawal. To a man, the leading preromantics were abundantly aware of the conflict between their assertive individualities on the one side and the stagnant combination of conventional social morality and bureaucratic political absolutism on the other, and certainly the romantics would later use attitudes similar to theirs for all kinds of social and political positions. But in the period before the French Revolution the preromantics tended to feel themselves rather alienated from than engaged in their contemporary society. In part, undoubtedly, this passive alienation had to do with the comparative social immobility of the Germany which was the headquarters of the movement. But in greater part it reflected the original impulse of the movement to urge the segregation of those individuals who were great enough to receive and to master the varied experience from without before sending them out to infuse the great world with their genius.

If the mental set of the preromantics was such as to inspire no political or social doctrine, it did produce a third and final corollary of individuality that extended it beyond the human individual and was a harbinger of romantic political and social doctrines to come. In Herder's idea of the "nation" and in Burke's justification of "party" we may glimpse the original tie between the fundamental preromantic notion of the individual and the principled defense of group life over and above the individuals of whom the group was composed.

The early doctrine of the culture-nation—which Johann Gottfried von Herder (1774–1803) developed during the 1760's and 1770's—may be best understood in terms of the ideas of individuality proffered by two of its sources: Leibniz' monadology and Hamann's symbolism. The "monad"

Johann Gottfried von Herder.
Philosopher of nationalism.

was Leibniz' term for the metaphysical principle of individuality that made everything what it was. Because the monad lived and developed harmoniously in a world of monads it prefigured the capacity of the sovereign individual to be integrated into a group and yet retain his freedom. Because the monad applied not only to particular persons and things but also to any body, however complex, that developed its own potential in its own inimitable way, it could confer individuality as easily on collective as on personal bodies.

On this skeleton of the socialized and historicized monad, Herder hung his version of Hamann's intuitive symbolism, to emerge with the culture-nation as the primary unit of humanity. For Hamann, the only approach to human reality that could avoid the deadly distortions of abstract reasoning was the immediate intuition of linguistic symbols, particularly in folk poetry, for here the succession of concrete images brought men as close as they could come to the fleeting, elusive stuff of human reality. The feeling for language and literature thus became the key to the insight into humanity for Herder, who was concentrating, in the years that he was helping to found the movement of *Sturm und Drang,* precisely on these subjects—in his *Fragments on Recent German Literature* (1767) and *On the Origins of Speech* (1772). In Herder's hands, language and literature composed a single primary social power, shaping the attitudes of each people into a national culture that conferred an individual form upon its art, its religion, and indeed all its collective expressions. The nation as a greater individual was the immediate creation of nature, as the intimacy of the national languages and folk literatures with their direct perception of nature's evanescent reality attested, but it also was, for Herder, the natural expression of all the human individuals who were its members. Since the variety, complexity, and mobility of the natural world were such that individual persons could know it and assert themselves in it only through the common symbols created in collaboration with their neighbors, the nation was for Herder not only an individual in its own right from the point of view of nature in general but the necessary condition for the individuality of the human persons who composed it.

In the early version of his philosophy of history, *Another Philosophy of History for the Education of Humanity*, which he published in 1774 while he was still under the influence of *Sturm und Drang*, Herder gave special emphasis to the genesis of nations, when their collective personalities were first formed, and to their disparate but equal individualities, which were based upon the incomparable genius of each. In its origins cultural nationalism may thus be understood as a doctrine which applied the elitist ideas of unlimited freedom and incommensurable individuality to the mass of ordinary individual humans, whose capacities equipped them not for the creative freedom of the individual genius, but for a share in the creative freedom of the individual nation.

Others besides Herder were promulgating ideas of cultural nationalism during the last third of the eighteenth century, in contrast to the humanitarian cosmopolitanism inferred by many *philosophes* from the universal scope of reason in men. In two of Herder's like-minded contemporaries, the German historian Justus Möser (1720–1794) and the British parliamentarian Edmund Burke, the notion of culture was extended to emphasize institutional and constitutional rather than aesthetic forms, but the cultural idea of the nation as an immediate product of nature and the only permanent identity for the ordinary individual was at the basis of their constitutional nationalism and supplied what was new in it.

In addition to the cultural nation, the preromantics also created the modern idea of political party. They attributed to party, as to the nation, the personality and principles of a collective individual. Although Burke developed his classic formulation of the national constitution as "a partnership not only between those who are living, but between those who are living, those who are dead, and those who are to be born" only after the revolution broke out in France, he formulated his equally classic justification of party before that cataclysmic event. Party had for centuries been identified with faction and classified under sedition. The main ground for this condemnation had been the conviction that for each government, as once for each religion, there was but one true set of principles, which bound the sovereign and the individual citizens and which would be undermined by any other bond of political association. In the rare instances when the idea of party was defended, as it had been by Machiavelli, it was defended on grounds not of individual rights but of public effect—to wit, that the competition between parties prevents the tyranny of either. But Burke based party both on the right of individuals to combine for a political purpose and on the validity of making a "particular principle" the bond of their combination in a party. The political individual, indeed, had not only the right but the obligation to enter into such parties, for we must "model our principles to our duties and our situation" and so form "connections" which are the only means of carrying these principles into execution. From Burke's idea of party we glean the fundamental contribution of the preromantics to the modern theory of associations: the idea of a group as both an extension of its individual members and an embodiment of general principle. Hence it enables principle to be imposed on the individual without ostensible loss of his freedom.

It remains only to ask what was the actual role of the preromantics in the cultural life of the eighteenth century. Their own idea of that role, as we have seen, was that of a revolutionary opposition to the Enlightenment, and hence the inference has sometimes been drawn that a straight line of cultural development led away from the Enlightenment through the preromantics to the romantics proper, who emerged around the turn of the century to complete the revolution. But the inference is only partly valid. What went into preromanticism did not determine what came out of it. Although preromanticism originated in a revolutionary posture against every characteristic feature of the Enlightenment it did not maintain this position throughout its development. In fact, the preromantics, during the 1780's, manufactured their own brand of classicism. This classicism had its sources in the era before the French Revolution and was part of the legacy of the Enlightenment. Romanticism arose later, in the conditions produced by the French Revolution, and is no part of our story at all.

The assessment of the influences involved in the origins of preromanticism requires, like most historical assessments, a qualified rather than a categorical judgment. Undoubtedly, there were positive relations between the *philosophes* and the preromantics. Burke was impressed by Montesquieu and in his turn impressed Diderot. Moreover, the impact of Burke's aesthetics on the German *Sturm und Drang* was mediated through Lessing and Moses Mendelssohn (1729–1786), two figures variously associated with the German Enlightenment and otherwise *non grata* to this same *Sturm und Drang*. Herder studied in Königsberg under the early Kant as well as under Hamann and was influenced by the rationalist version of Leibniz that marked Kant's position before he developed his critical philosophy. As late as 1768 Geothe was under the spell of French culture and the Francophile influence of Christoph Wieland (1733–1813), before a transitional Pietist conversion and his meetings with Herder helped to usher in the *Sturm und Drang*. Rousseau was reprobated by Burke as the writer who put an emotional surcharge on the abstractions of the so-called age of reason: but Rousseau was also a powerful positive force in the development of Herder, Goethe, and Schiller alike. Wieland, who was too frothy, too hedonistic, too ironical, too French in his tastes to be generally respected by the preromantics, yet did affect them specifically through his contribution to the liberation of art from morals and was himself an appreciative connoisseur of Klopstock, Goethe, and Schiller.

But the specific contacts of the preromantics with the *philosophes* should not obscure the far more emphatic preromantic conviction that they were overthrowing simultaneously the tyranny of French civilization over German culture and the tyranny of the Enlightenment over creative freedom. The specific influences of the Enlightenment that helped to prepare the preromantic attitude were transmuted into building stones of a qualitatively different cultural attitude.

For the preromantic revolt was short-lived. Its instigators simply could not sustain the irresolution of the unlimited freedom or the loneliness of the absolute individuality in their initial posture. Herder, Goethe, Schiller—the three most prominent figures of the *Sturm und Drang*—all sought, during the 1780's, to organize ideas of a larger world in which individual men and nations would find appropriate materials and a unifying principle to provide substance and direction for their freedom. In his mature philosophy of history—the *Reflections on the Philosophy of the History of Humanity* (1784–1791)—Herder adduced notions of a common humanity and of the progress of nations toward its realization that were obvious reprises on Voltaire and the Enlightenment for the purpose of lending coherence to the aimless pluralism of his original nationalism. Ideas from the mid-century classical revival, stimulated especially by J. J. Winckelmann's excited confusion of the Greek aesthetic ideal with universal standards of culture as such, led Goethe to sketch a philosophy of nature which made the standards of art into the principles of reality and conceived the outer world to be a dynamic unity of spirit and matter serving at once as stuff, model, and form for the creative individual.

Schiller, finally, went through an analogous crisis during the 1780's. As Herder had found a world for the orientation of his sovereign individuals in a universal philosophy of history and Goethe for his in a pantheistic philosophy of nature, Schiller found a moral world for his in Kant's categorical imperative—that is, in the ethical realm created by the laws which every individual determines for himself. Insisting still on the primacy of freedom and on the role of art in synthesizing the sensual and moral natures of man into the wholly free individual, Schiller now learned both to define this freedom—*i.e.* as self-determination—and to give it form by equating morality with reason and making the rational harmony within and among individuals the measure by which freedom is assessed and the purpose to which art is directed. Thus in Schiller's *Don Carlos*, the spotlight put by the early draft upon the tempestuous hero who gives the play its title shifted in the final version (1785) to the humane and tolerant Marquis of Posa—now the central character, who, like the verse form of the drama, reflects the influence of Lessing's informed and principled *Nathan the Wise*.

The German preromantics not only were influenced by Enlightenment figures like Lessing and Kant but joined them in the same cultural movement, German classicism. This classicism was thus composed of two convergent currents—the men of the Enlightenment who detached the libertarian strand from it and developed a new kind of lawful order on this libertarian base, and the men of the *Sturm und Drang* who created a new kind of freedom and grafted on to it a rational order, taken from the Enlightenment and its heirs. This composite movement would later produce a Hegel and a Marx. Clearly, this classicism that was the last great cultural movement of Europe's Old Regime did more than merely complement the rationalist and libertarian movements. It was, together with the direct channel which links the witty, tolerant, critical, reasonable, socially concerned minds of the *philosophes* with ours, the other main conduit through which the civilization of eighteenth-century Europe passed into the contemporary world.

FROM THOUGHT TO ACTION

The balance of laws and movement, of reason and facts, of society and individuals, and of morals and politics in the thought of the mature Enlightenment came appropriately from the mid-century apogee of prerevolutionary Europe. For the society of this Europe was characterized by an analogous balance between the crust of political and social institutions that were still accepted and a movement of people from below toward levels of well-being, education, and self-assertion that was spreading from commoners to notables and producing a massive restiveness beneath the placid surface of public life. The intellectual movements of the post-Enlightenment era that arose during the two decades between 1770 and 1789 were also faithful articulations of their contemporary society. The impatience with unreasonable practices, the sense of incessant movement, and the idea of infinite freedom which were the chief solvents of the intellectual order represented by the Enlightenment had their counterparts in the local social and political unrest that began in this period to break through the institutional crust of the Old Regime.

But the interaction of thought and society was not only in the direction of thought. If the first product of the interaction was the intellectuals' translation of the social conditions in which they lived and wrote into the language of philosophy, science, and the arts, this crystallization was quickly followed by a reciprocal movement which brought this language to bear upon the concrete political and social development of the second half of the eighteenth century. The application of eighteenth-century ideas to political and social reality was carried out not by intellectuals, but by practical men who were the consumers of the ideas of the intellectuals.

There were two radically different kinds of such practitioners, corresponding to the two different stages in intellectual history of the late eighteenth century and to the two different kinds of society characteristic of the Atlantic and continental peoples respectively. The first kind of practitioners consisted of the enlightened monarchs of central and eastern Europe who sought to apply the intellectual pattern of the mature Enlightenment by finding a role for rational order and civic virtue in the welter of real interests that were their primary concerns. Both the sincerity and the result of this attempt are moot historical problems which will engage our attention, but it is clear that the ideas which the enlightened rulers professed to apply were the identifiable and integral ideas of the Enlightenment and that their political version of the Enlightenment dominated European public life until the 1780's, when another kind of practitioner rose to prominence. This second kind of practitioner of eighteenth-century ideas consisted of the notables and commoners whose use of the dynamic, radical, and libertarian tendencies spawned by the last phase of eighteenth-century culture initiated the movement toward social revolution among the Atlantic communities. With these practitioners the independent and formative force of ideas which had been cherished by all eighteenth-century intellectuals yielded to the role of ideas as supports of practical social interests and demands. Thus the rise of fundamental opposition to the kings coincided with the passage from philosophy to ideology, and it is no historical accident that if the origins of the joint movement against the kings and the philosophers can be found in the society and culture of the eighteenth century, its victory belongs to another era.

What follows, then, is the story of the men who sought to realize reason by grafting the intelligence of the *philosophes* onto the power of the kings and of the social movement that would ultimately topple both the detached philosopher and the ensconced king from their places in the traditional civilization of the West.

Part III

THE PHILOSOPHER KINGS

CHAPTER 8

Enlightened Absolutism

FOR SOME TWENTY-FIVE hundred years, when men dreamed of a better life they were caught between the hope that the better life would make men better and the fear that only better men could make a better life, and they looked to a single extraordinary figure, the philosopher king, who would break through the dilemma to improve men by his example and life by his power. He was to be a *philosopher* king because knowledge and virtue were convertible in the good life. He was to be a philosopher *king* because only a man whose force was independent of other men but yet acknowledged by them could have the leverage to initiate improvements which men as a whole were incapable of initiating and the coverage to make improvements which would be generally effective on the lives of men as a whole. Even the few periods and the few polities where republics had been preferred to monarchies contributed to the persistent ideal of the philosopher king, for in a tradition reaching from Solon to Helvétius and Rousseau the republican "Legislator" was assigned the power to impose the constitutional conditions of the subsequently good society and thus to fill the role of a constituent philosopher king. But in general, just as the model of the Greek and Roman republics had given way to the composite model of the Roman Empire and the Christian monarchy, so was the ideal of the temporary and dictatorial Legislator absorbed in the ideal of the permanent and legitimate philosopher king.

For the most part this ideal of the philosopher king remained only an ideal. The actual records of kingship afforded some examples of saintly kings who exemplified virtue, and even more of the knowledgeable kings who patronized scholarship and the arts—in the period around the beginning of the eighteenth century Louis XIV, the Habsburg Emperor Leopold I, and the Prussian Frederick I were cases in point. But there were indeed few philosopher kings who deliberately applied the principles of knowledge as means and the civic virtues as ends to a system of royal policy aimed at social improvement.

From around the middle of the eighteenth century, rulers who impressed contemporaries as belonging to this rare breed appeared in such a cluster as to indicate a remarkable convergence of the actual conditions bearing on kingship and the intellectual tendencies of contemporary philosophy—a convergence that made the marriage between the king of the realm and the queen of the sciences the most revealing political institution in Europe during the half century preceding the French Revolution. King Frederick II ("the Great") of Prussia, the Habsburg Emperor Joseph II of Germany and the Habsburg dominions, and Empress Catherine II ("the Great") of Russia were the outstanding examples of this combination by dint of the power and prominence of the states they governed, but the style of rulership which they modeled extended beyond them to become the dominant fashion for royalty in the second half of the century. The kings Charles III of Spain, Stanislas II of Poland, and Gustavus III of Sweden, the Habsburg Grand Duke Leopold of Tuscany (subsequently Emperor Leopold II), and a number of German princes—avid as ever to replicate the latest mode in European royalty—were all members of the set to which the collective label of "enlightened despotism" was later to be affixed. And where legitimate rulers were inadequately enlightened or despotic, there were leading ministers like the cultivated Prince Kaunitz in Austria, the doctrinaire Johan Struensee in Denmark, and the reforming Bernardo di Tanucci in Naples, to play an analogous role.

THE PROBLEM OF "ENLIGHTENED DESPOTISM"

But if the popularity of Enlightenment culture in some of the unlikeliest courts of Europe demonstrates beyond doubt the advent of a new vogue in government, it has also raised a serious question of what that vogue really was. Those who have called it "enlightened despotism" have tended to signify by the term a distinctive stage of absolutism, in which rulers responded to the changing social conditions of power and the congruent philosophy of the Enlightenment by making government into an unprecedentedly effective instrument of authority and by taking a deliberate interest in the civil rights and welfare of all citizens, thereby initiating a categorical extension in both the means and the ends of monarchical government. Some

But others have rejected the term precisely because they consider this implication of a new content as well as a new style in autocratic government to be a historical distortion. What has been called enlightened despotism, it is argued, was neither enlightened nor despotic. It was still simply absolutism as such, now adjusted to the particular tone of the later eighteenth century but essentially continuous in its forms and its goals with the absolutism that preceded it. The statements of principle, policy, or purpose that are usually taken as proof of a different, enlightened form of absolutism, these critics conclude, were, in respect of politics, either rhetorical or irrelevant: monarchs used the fashionable terms of the Enlightenment to rationalize irrational policy or to express cultural interests other than policy, but in either case such terms had, and were intended to have, little bearing on the realities of government.

Now obviously, if this were only a pedantic squabble among historians about the suitability of a label, it would be of little moment, since it does not matter whether the kings and ministers concerned are called enlightened despots or mere autocrats as long as we know what they thought and did. But the issue is worth attention because it underscores, as an issue, certain qualities about the politics of the age that are not accounted for either by the loose notion of enlightened despotism or by the undifferentiated concept of a general absolutism, taken separately. What is important, in other words, is not whether the absolutism of the later eighteenth century was actually independent enough of its past and distinctive enough from other forms of government to warrant its own label—what is important is to clarify the problematic historical reality that is reflected by the conflict in historical interpretations.

For the most part the clarification must come from the consideration of what kind of people the presumed enlightened despots were, what kind of policies they had, and what kind of measures they enacted. But before we enter into such an empirical accounting—into enlightened despotism from the inside, as it were—we must secure a certain preliminary clarification from an analysis of what is indisputable about the tendency as a whole—a view from the outside, as it were. Only from such a preliminary analysis will we know what to look for in the empirical investigation to follow.

Three general facts about the rulers who are usually classified as enlightened despots define the issue raised by the label, and by defining it, contribute to the understanding of culture and politics in late-eighteenth-century Europe.

First, each of the major rulers so labeled had a predecessor whose policies were similar to those of "enlightened despotism" but whose political personality and rhetoric have barred him (or her) from inclusion in the set. Peter the Great in Russia, Frederick William I in Prussia, and Maria Theresa in the Habsburg lands strove for and in large measure effected fundamental reforms in the direction of the centralized welfare state, the retrenchment of aristocratic privilege, and the legislation of a common state citizenship that their "enlightened" successors could in many ways only elaborate upon. Peter and Frederick William we have already met, and we can understand how, despite the constructive policies which created the basic institutions of the modern Russian and Prussian states respectively, the tyrannical brutality of the Romanov and the sanctimonious paternalism of the Hohenzollern would seem antithetical to the notion of an enlightened ruler in any of its usual connotations.

But lest we think the distinction merely a matter of chronology or of

Empress Maria Theresa of Austria. *The domineering Habsburg pride and willfulness, the keen good sense, the attractive and self-conscious femininity, the stern but kind motherliness — all the qualities which went into Maria Theresa's mode of governing—are apparent in this portrait of the aging monarch.*

personal character we have the later case of the Habsburg Queen Maria Theresa (ruled 1740–1780), intelligent, warmhearted, beloved by her subjects, contemporary of the enlightened Frederick, mother of and coregent with the equally enlightened Emperor Joseph, promulgator of the permanent reforms which modernized the Austrian empire—and yet, by common historical consent, no enlightened despot. Nor can it be argued that in her case the problem was one of despotism rather than enlightenment, for however benign her manner and however effective her arts of persuasion, the quality of "gentle violence" which was recognized as the epitome of her policies testifies to the inexorable force behind the soft tactics and establishes her place firmly in the ranks of the autocrats. Politically shrewd and self-willed, she knew how to delegate authority, when to bargain, and what limits were set to her power by her own femininity and by the disjointedness of her polyglot dominions. But within these limits she asserted all the prerogatives of sovereignty to effect the political and military reorganization of her empire's heartland.

As in the cases of her Russian and Prussian precedent state builders, Maria Theresa's governmental reforms were a direct response to a military challenge, and like them too the response entailed not only an administrative overhaul to increase revenue but more fundamental reforms in the direction of the equalization of taxable classes, general conscription, universal elementary education, state control over the established Church, and secularization of university programs. In Maria Theresa's Austria, as in Petrine Russia and Hohenzollern Prussia, the actual progress toward these goals was slow, halting, and still unequal in its incidence upon the privileged, but enough of a start was made in the direction of equalizing the conditions of citizens and of encouraging practical initiative in the individual subjects to indicate the conformity of such tendencies to the essentials of statecraft—enlightened and unenlightened alike—in the eighteenth century. Maria Theresa has been excluded from the group of enlightened monarchs not because of what her policies did in particular but because of what her political personality guaranteed they must add up to in general. She was badly educated, had a simple, orthodox Catholic piety, and cherished the benevolent but archaic attitude of a "universal mother" toward her peoples. The political relevance of these qualities in excluding her from the ranks of enlightened absolutists to which her measures and her favorite ministers, such as the enlightened Prince Wenzel Kaunitz (1711–1794) and Count Friedrich Haugwitz (1702–1765), might otherwise have entitled her, tells us something about the genre.

The uniform presence of effective and intelligent, albeit "unenlightened," reforming rulers in the immediate background of "enlightened despotism" goes far to delimit the problem of what was distinctive to this later-eighteenth-century version of kingship. It confirms the view of the skeptics that the association of the interests of the state with the equal protection of rights within the state had become ingrained in the tradition of monarchical sovereignty as such and that there was consequently nothing particularly enlightened about the endorsement of it by the so-called enlightened despots. Their differential qualities must be sought elsewhere.

The second preliminary observation which should be made about the general conditions of enlightened despotism has to do with its political and historical geography: it tended to characterize the states of central and eastern Europe and the states—like Sweden and Spain—well along in the decline from former greatness. Undoubtedly, the accidents of birth had much to do with this geographical distribution: Great Britain's George II and France's Louis XV were not interested enough, and their successors George III and Louis XVI not bright enough, to qualify. But however fortuitous the immediate cause, the historical effect was to locate "enlightened despotism" in states where the requirements of government, both to meet the contemporary challenge of international competition and to satisfy the contemporary standards of social justice, exceeded the material and moral resources of their comparatively retrograde or stagnant societies. Ministers like Turgot and the younger William Pitt, however cultivated and however authoritarian they may have been, denoted something other than "enlightened despotism" in late-eighteenth-century politics, not because they lacked the formality of a royal title, but because they represented and articulated, constitutionally or virtually, the positive claims of a whole mobile, middling sector of the society upon the state—a function for which a royal title would have been in any case irrelevant.

Thus factors of geography and of history limited "enlightened despotism" to those monarchies in which the ruler framed his goals and his policies in a language that far transcended the terms of any existing social interest or the claims raised by any combination of existing social interests.

The third general feature of enlightened absolutism that helps to define the character of late-eighteenth-century monarchy is the restricted sense in which its "enlightened" quality must be taken. We must accept the double meaning which inevitably inheres in "enlightened" here, for it refers—and is meant to refer—both to the general quality of intelligence and to the particular passion for the culture of the Enlightenment that are to be found in the enlightened rulers of this period. In itself the ambiguity is permissible enough, for if intelligence be taken in this context to mean the rooting of political judgments in broad secular knowledge then certainly the Enlightenment may be seen as a fitting cultural form of such a quality.

But perhaps because of the moral ends that have always been associated with philosopher kings, the connection of eighteenth-century monarchs with the philosophy of the Enlightenment has tended improperly to expand from their appropriation of its ideas of knowledge to their appropriation of its moral ends. Thus enlightened despotism has been interpreted explicitly to mean "benevolent despotism" and implicitly to mean liberal despotism, in reference to the humanitarianism and the individual freedom that were supreme values in the general culture of the Enlightenment. These are the connotations that have obscured the reality of eighteenth-century monarchy and have threatened to invalidate the whole concept of enlightened despotism. The fact was that universal benevolence and individual rights were endorsed by the rulers concerned, but not as *political* principles. "Enlightened despotism" in the benevolent or liberal sense is thus self-contradictory, for it refers to the principles by which the despots defined the limits of their utilitarian and authoritarian politics. What we must look for in "enlightened despotism" is not the political realization of the Enlightenment ethic or even of the liberal political doctrines that were the corollaries of that ethic. What we must look for is the entirely distinctive form taken by the Enlightenment when kings applied it as a theory of knowledge to the realities of human politics and as a theory of value to the context of human politics.

The Enlightenment was for politics, as for many other fields of eighteenth-century endeavor, above all a way of mastering reality. What has been called enlightened despotism thus mirrored the Enlightenment at large in its belief that knowledge is power. But it also resolved the Enlightenment's ambiguous relation of the real and the ideal by affirming in principle the gap that remained between the political utility the absolute rulers could achieve and the human values they could only profess. If, then, the term "enlightened," is justified for such rulers in the triple sense that they were devotees of Enlightenment culture, that they applied the materials and method of rational knowledge to statecraft, and that they made a political principle out of the *philosophes*' moral dilemma between the reality which they appreciated and the ideals which would transform it, the term "despots" is thereby unjustified. Absolutists these monarchs certainly were, for there was nothing in their "Enlightenment" to make them welcome or acknowledge in principle any limitation by other human agencies; but despots they were not, for they were enlightened enough to perceive both the actual limits upon the will of any government and the inherent limits of all politics. Enlightened despotism in the eighteenth century is a rhetorical hyperbole. Enlightened absolutism was a historical reality.

THE ABSOLUTIST PERSONALITY

Like the *philosophes* whom they read, hosted, and mimed, the enlightened absolutists were free spirits who uninhibitedly expressed their individual tastes and temperaments. But they also shared certain general traits of a collective personality.

Frederick the Great of Prussia (ruled 1740–1786), the first of the enlightened absolutists and the model for the rest, was an amateur philosopher, poet, musician, composer, and critic, a moralist and an aesthete who was also an implacable and indefatigable general in the field, a probing, hardworking administrator in chambers, and an energetic inspector of all the phases in all the locales of his subjects' lives. However powerfully he affirmed nature, culture, and humanity in general, he just as strongly denied men in particular. His occasional acts of spontaneous generosity were increasingly overborne by the suspicious, cynical, and domineering attitudes that peer out from the grim-faced portraits of his later years.

Where Frederick was a study in contradiction, Joseph II of Austria (co-regent 1765–1780, sole ruler, 1780–1790), on the other hand, seemed a model of simplicity. He was restless and impatient, driven by human sympathy, ambition, and a passion for logical consistency to the repeated anonymous travels among his people that sponsored the legends of the "Peasants' Kaiser," to his repeated international aggressions upon weaker powers, and to the remorseless execution of doctrinaire policies that ultimately called down revolution upon him.

Catherine II of Russia (ruled 1762–1796), in apparent contrast to both of these royal contemporaries, was notoriously fickle and opportunistic. By her own admission, she was a "starter" rather than a finisher of policies. But there was a pattern that ran through the variety of her initiatives. Certainly she had to tread more warily, as befit the fragile status of a German-born widowed sovereign in the rough court of the tsars. Nor was she helped by the circumstances of her accession. She had certainly usurped the throne from her own husband (Peter III) in 1762, with the assistance of the ever unreliable palace guard; she was generally believed to have conspired in his mysterious death immediately after the deposition; and she double-crossed the old-line nobility who had looked for a compliant regency after the event. Nor did she have even the modest philosophical and literary talents of a Frederick or the spontaneous human sympathies of a Joseph. But she was, for all that, at least as vigorous and even more versatile than they. Her voracious consumption of lovers showed a kind of zest for life that was shared by neither her Prussian nor her Austrian counterpart, but it was a passion that supplemented rather than replaced worldly interests they all did share. For Catherine too consumed the writings of the *philosophes*, corresponded lengthily with the intellectual suzerains of the movement, hosted them, and even wrote plays, stories, and an abortive Russian history in inferior imitation of them. Like the other enlightened monarchs, moreover, her taste for rational discourse and aesthetic composition dignified rather than inhibited the flamboyant expression of sentimental pity for the unfortunate and of indefatigable delight in the business of ruling.

From this amalgam of distinctive and similar traits in the enlightened absolutists the outline of a collective personality emerges. It is a personality that bears a marked resemblance to the possible pencil sketch of the Enlightenment's typical French *philosophe*, for whom, indeed, these monarchs shared an unstinting admiration and to whom they owned their chief

The price of power: Frederick the Great before (left) and after (right) the royal possession of it. *The facial contrast registers not simply the aging process but also the impact of dangerous experience and the traces of the iron discipline which he came to impose on others and upon himself as well.*

Emperor Joseph II of Austria, who overreached himself with egalitarian reforms in an aristocratic society. *After a painting by Drouais.*

cultural debt. The enlightened absolutists were given a collective identity by two primary features. They were all impelled by an insatiable cultural drive to know and experience what life in this world had to offer, and they were all equally impelled by the determinate political drive to assert their mastery over it. These teamed commitments found obvious expression in their preference for the Enlightenment, which gave intellectual form to precisely this double tendency.

Politics and Culture

But it was not merely this preference for the Enlightenment combination of politics and culture that shaped the rulers' distinctive personality. What did shape it most decisively was their resolution of the duality between politics and culture in a way that made of politics the rigorously and rationally organized core of their lives, around which they could afford to dispose their carnal, sentimental, and cultural interests freely. The long hours which without exception they devoted wholeheartedly to the business of state were reminiscent of the cherished administrative labors of a Philip II or a Louis XIV, but if the hours and working conditions of all the dedicated autocrats were similar whatever the generation of the autocracy, still the spirit of the labor was not. Monarchs of the earlier stage of autocracy, like Philip and Louis, doted on all the details of government from the mixed motives of suspicion and simple pleasure. They wished to know as much as possible about their realms and to resolve by themselves as much of their business as they could humanly manage because they feared resistance and mistrusted any delegation of their powers. But they also enjoyed administrative details for their own sake, so that it has been said of both Philip and Louis that despite their fearsome repute each had

Catherine the Great of Russia in 1769. *This portrait faithfully conveys the sense of her energetic and imperious disposition.*

the soul of a petty bureaucrat. Such motives were not wholly absent from the enlightened absolutists—Frederick mistrusted his officials and Catherine certainly had reason enough to fear sedition—but in general their immersion in the details of government was spurred rather by the conviction that the organization of these details by one rational mind was necessary to consistent policy and that consistent policy was also the only sound policy. For the enlightened monarchs much more than for their illustrious predecessors, in other words, the time and energy they devoted to the business of state were aimed not simply at the control but at the direction of social life. In the rulers' own existence as in their peoples' the work of state furnished a secure base for all the activities of man.

In Catherine of Russia, undeniably, the two collective traits of the enlightened absolutist personality—the passion for varieties of experience and the passion to master them—never jibed. The hardness of her policies was obviously and tragically separate from the humanity of her cultural professions—an incongruity which indeed earned her an unenviable repute as a hypocrite. But as the opprobrium itself shows, Catherine did succeed, however reprehensibly, in relating her sensual and cultural interests to the rational core of her politics. Even in her love affairs, uninhibited as she seemed in the bestowal of her favors, the political motif was rarely absent. Not only was she quite immune to influence by her lovers but as often as not she put them to good political use.

If Catherine's duplicity represents the tenuous extreme in the relations of the energy and the control that were the two poles of the enlightened monarchs' collective personality, Joseph represents the other—integrated—extreme. He has been called the political man par excellence precisely because all the notorious signs of his spontaneity—his impulsiveness, his impatience, his forcefulness, his passion for ideas, his quick sympathies—were harnessed by political ambitions and directed toward a political goal.

Both extremes meet in showing the preeminent power of politics as the organizing principle in the lives of the enlightened absolutists. Catherine and Joseph exemplify the different ways in which politics could organize culture, but neither exemplifies clearly the autonomy of the cultural impulse and its role in the personal syndrome. For this we must turn to Frederick the Great, whose character developed in a way that lay bare the inner relations of the traits common to but not so transparent in all the rulers of his ilk.

In his early years as king, from his accession in 1740 to the outbreak of the Seven Years' War in 1756, Frederick's interest in the humanitarian culture of the Enlightenment and his commitment to a politics of sheer power were equally strong and mutually independent in him. Perhaps the fierce duress with which his austere and orthodox father, Frederick William I, had broken the young, freethinking, and irreverent Crown Prince to obedience and public administration simultaneously was responsible for the original isolation of the political power-motif in Frederick. But whatever the cause, the approximate simultaneity (around his accession in 1740) of such ill-assorted measures as his rejuvenation of the Berlin Academy as a cultural center, his publication of the *Anti-Machiavel* as a handbook of the philosopher king for the direct application of morality to politics, and his unprovoked aggression against Austria for the conquest of Silesia set the pattern for the separate tracks his interests would follow for a decade and a half.

Not, of course, that there were no connections at all. Just before he invaded Silesia, Frederick did apply culture to policy by dismantling prior censorship of the press, decreeing religious toleration, and abolishing torture in penal proceedings. In the *Anti-Machiavel*, moreover, behind Frederick's enlightened provision for a rulership contract between ruler and people which sanctioned the ruler's obligation to govern for the happiness of his subjects he was careful to settle the enforcement of the obligation only on the conscience of the king and to include a goodly measure of military security and public order in the makeup of his subjects' happiness.

But the fact remains that until the Seven Years' War the mutual independence of Frederick's cultural and political interests was much more in evidence than their sporadic connections. When he played and composed for the flute; when he protected La Mettrie, or discussed and corresponded at length with Voltaire; when he wrote his own poetry, drama, essays, history, and joyfully belabored the works of others; when he filled his court and his Academy with the bearers of the contemporary French culture he loved so well: in all these activities he was enlarging himself and his kingdom by added dimensions that were only marginal to the necessities of politics.

But the trials of the Seven Years' War, which brought Prussia to the verge of apparent destruction at the hands of an encircling continental coalition headed by Austria, France, and Russia, tempered Frederick and merged the different strands of his character into one composite whole. Preyed upon—so he felt—by a pack of neighbors, and deserted—he was convinced—by his uncertain ally, Great Britain, Frederick, along with the state for which he was responsible, survived through a combination of luck (the dim-witted Tsar Peter III, who idolized Frederick, acceded to the throne and pulled Russia out of the war in 1762) and his own desperate perseverance. But in the process Frederick lost his earlier spontaneity, manysidedness, and confidence in the capacities of his fellowman. A plurality of interests was a luxury that neither he nor his state could henceforward afford, and his former inclination toward the intellectual liberties gave way to a new stress on practical controls. Yet his cultivation of iron discipline, both for others and for himself, did not mean the exclusion of cultural interests, but only their subordination to another kind of interest. He examined them carefully for their relevance to the safety of the state, which was now, in its turn, defined more broadly than before. The upshot was his growing commitment to a Stoic way of life, which made knowledge and the arts essential to the well-being of the state, valued them according to their contribution to the state, and made their cultivation for this political purpose a public obligation of the ruler.

Perhaps the clearest expression of this development was Frederick's changed attitude toward French culture. No longer did he acknowledge the French Enlightenment to be the model culture, and no longer did he seek out the French *philosophes* to grace his Berlin Academy. He came to deplore the radicalism of the French version of Enlightenment which he associated with d'Holbach, and he came at the same time to understand the importance of encouraging German intellectual participation in letters generally and in official cultural institutions like the Academy particularly. But these changes represented something new in Frederick's idea about the function of culture rather than in his idea of culture itself. For he remained a devotee of the Enlightenment that he had learned from the French and he continued to prefer their language as the cultural medium above all others. For the distinctive German literature and the new appreciation of the German language that were the great cultural events of his last two decades, Frederick showed no appreciation. What he recommended to the Germans was their development of the same kind of rational culture and standardized language from which he felt the French were latterly defaulting. This amalgam of cultural attitudes, whatever it may mean for the interminable subsequent debate on Frederick's German patriotism or his lack thereof to which it is often applied, does reveal a definite feature of his growth: the increasing tendency to see the political relevance of culture and to make political categories the organizing principles of cultural interests.

Theory and Practice

The crucial and complex relationship in Frederick between political and cultural or humanitarian concerns which were at once distinct and connected was shared by his fellow enlightened absolutists in whom the relationship was not so clearly articulated. For all of them, culture and humanity were intellectual and natural values transcending the state. But for all of them too the call to legislate the conditions for the progress of human thought and welfare combined with the need of their state for informed administration and popular support to make politics the center of their persistent commitments to culture and humanity. The same pattern, moreover, holds for the more familiar, but essentially derivative, problem of the relationship between the liberal and the authoritarian, the ameliorative and the power-seeking, strains *within* their politics. Here we return to the crucial issue of the relations between profession and deed, between ideology and policy, that is at the heart of the dispute over the authenticity of the "enlightened" in enlightened absolutism, but now, after our insight into the structure of the absolutist personality, we may hope to shed some light upon it.

Unquestionably, the "freedom," "rights," "welfare," and "happiness" of man which all the enlightened monarchs professed to have as their primary concerns were in fact frequently and deliberately violated by the oppressiveness of their bureaucracies and their studied neglect of social inequalities. Unquestionably, too, the principles which the enlightened rulers took, often literally, from the political theory of the Enlightenment—the principles of an original natural liberty, of government founded on contract, and of sovereignty limited by natural law—were frequently negated by the practical principles of power politics and the interests of state. But if we look closely at the absolutists' formal statements of their principles—at Frederick's early *Anti-Machiavel*, his *Political Testament* of 1752, his *Essay on the Forms of Government and the Duties of Sovereigns* of 1771; at Catherine's *Instruction* to the Legislative Commission of 1767; and at Joseph's assorted correspondence and memoranda—we can see that the discrepancies between their theory and their practice were not attributable simply to hypocrisy, for the discrepancies were prepared within the theory itself.

For Frederick, the contractual public powers which natural individuals transferred to the political sovereign, and which were recompensed by the security and welfare to be delivered by the sovereign to the citizens, were irrevocable and unaccountable. For Catherine, the explicit dependence upon the liberal principles and legal doctrines of Montesquieu and Beccaria, however borne out by her endorsement of human rights in the law, equality before the law, and definition of legitimate government by the law, stopped categorically short of endorsing the separation of powers or the political right of consent, and she deliberately revised her mentors in the direction of monarchical absolutism. For Joseph, finally, the self-appointed task of legislating "philosophy," however liberal in its orientation toward religious toleration, peasant emancipation, and equality of opportunity, tended to find its rationale more in the collective than in the individual welfare of his subjects.

Rather than a mere conflict of theory and practice in the politics of eighteenth-century absolutism, the tension between humanity and power which obscures its "enlightenment" may thus be seen as a feature of political personality infecting political theory and political practice alike. These monarchs endorsed the liberal principles of natural right, rulership contract, and the general interest because they were the only available sanctions for the secular service state in which they believed and the only available substitutes for the divine right of kings, in which, as the basis of the prescriptive political hierarchy and the religiously bound state, they just as energetically disbelieved.

The rulers needed this change in principles not because the worldly service of the community at home and abroad was a new function of authority, but because they now claimed it as the exclusive function of the state. Hence it required a correspondingly categorical set of secular, rational, and utilitarian principles. But however sincere the adoption of these principles, their use was definitely limited. They were used as the grounds of political obedience and as the purposes of policy, but they were *not* used as organizing principles for the state. Thus the liberal principles of freedom of thought and conscience, sanctity of property, and equal protection of the laws served to justify autocratic legislation, but the equally liberal principles of enforceable limits upon the monarch and representative participation in the legislative process were rejected for the constitution of the state.

The enlightened monarchs rejected these constitutional principles in part because they were as subject as anyone else to the general rule of Western politics that power is not relinquished spontaneously; in part because the socially static regions in which enlightened absolutism flourished generated comparatively little pressure for such relinquishment; in part because such pressure as did exist was aristocratic and corporate, claiming influence over or exemptions from rather than division of the state's power; and in part because the persistence of international rivalries made the continued concentration of political force a continuing responsibility of the ruler.

But over and above these general considerations of public order that conditioned the thinking of enlightened as well as unenlightened monarchs there was an equally important reason for the inhibition of liberal principles that was distinctive to the enlightened monarchs who professed

them: in the overwhelmingly agrarian and conservative social context of
central and eastern Europe, liberal principles could not be made operational without becoming self-contradictory. In this context the religious
liberty of minorities was deemed to violate the rights and sensibilities of
the orthodox majority; peasant liberation, to violate the property rights of
either the lords or the peasants themselves, depending on the disposition
of the land; the entrepreneurial freedom of estate owners, progressive farmers, and merchants, to infringe on the communal rights of peasants and
the collective rights of artisans. Hence the society could not, even in
theory, be vouchsafed the right of representative government without
importing the contradictory liberties into the very structure of the state.
For the enlightened monarchs, then, the maximum of human rights could
be achieved, even in theory, only by balancing the different kinds of rights
with an impartial measure that was not itself a matter of right and that
could command a larger consensus than right—in other words, with the
undiluted and undivided authority of the monarch to service the amalga-
mated rights of the community.

Hence when Frederick the Great epitomized the political theory of
enlightened absolutism in his famous description of the sovereign as "only
the first servant of the state," he revealed as much about the sovereign's
primacy which he did not emphasize as about the obligation to service
which he did. In this theory of enlightened absolutism, the variety of
individual rights required the unity of sovereign power, and the legal
obligations of ordinary citizens were enforced only by the sovereign's
supralegal *ethic* of responsibility. The enlightened monarchs justified
absolute political authority as the only common bond among the competing rights in a diversified society and as the only power that could,
by its very constitution, guarantee what was fundamental in these rights
from violation by any social force whatsoever.

We may conclude that the enlightened absolutist was identifiable, first,
by his espousal of intellectual interests and liberal ideas apparently indifferent to or at variance with the authoritarianism of his political calling, and
second, by his deliberate integration of this neutral or antithetical political
authority into his scheme of cultural and liberal values as their indispensable complement. Such a royal personality was especially relevant to the
Enlightenment because he shared with the *philosophes* the Enlightenment's assumption that men's material interests, including the benefits
of political power, were ultimately compatible with their ethical principles
—in Frederick's frank formulation that "the original principle of virtue is
interest"—and he also shared the Enlightenment's contrary insight that
men's actual prosecution of these interests was usually antithetical to
their ethical principles.

But the enlightened monarch did more than simply share in the culture
of the Enlightenment. Because he had to act where the *philosophes* only

wrote, he had to bring into confrontation the recalcitrant facts and the unrealized principles that the *philosophes* could acknowledge equally side by side. Hence he created a logic of facts to connect the actual facts he found in the world with the unity of principle that gave them meaning, and he assigned the working out of this factual logic to politics. In his accessibility to wide ranges of cultural experience and in his insistent tendency to conceive of political authority as a rational field of force which gave to this manifold experience a manageable pattern, the enlightened absolutist filled the void left in the Enlightenment by the *philosophes'* provision of an essential place for politics in the good society and their unpolitical reluctance to occupy it. The enlightened ruler was, indeed, the political *philosophe* par excellence.

But even if we grant to enlightened absolutism a distinctive psychic and ideological reality, the question of its political and social reality still remains. For it can be argued—and has been argued—that no such specific identity pertains to the actual measures and deeds of the putatively enlightened autocrats, who met problems, dealt with resistance, and embarked on practical policies that had far more in common with the traditions of absolutism than the principles of Enlightenment. For this issue of enlightened absolutism, which is important because it involves the whole nature of politics in the second half of the eighteenth century, we turn from what the enlightened absolutists thought to what they did.

CHAPTER 9

The Enlightened Absolutists Abroad

THE RECORD OF foreign affairs in the second half of the eighteenth century undoubtedly constitutes the most serious indictment of enlightened absolutism as a distinctive kind of government. If enlightenment is understood to include, as the typical *philosophe* certainly understood it to include, the explicit rejection of force, conquest, dynastic claim, interest of state, and balance of power in favor of reason, peace, international law, universal morality, and cosmopolitan unity, the foreign policies of the enlightened absolutists must be accounted infinitely more absolute than enlightened. For the eighteenth century has long enjoyed a reputation of stealth, duplicity, rapacity, and naked aggression in international relations which is second to that of no other century in Western history, save possibly our own, and the rulers most responsible for this dubious preeminence were precisely the most "enlightened."

In part, the special responsibility of the philosopher kings is a matter of rhetoric. They were more articulate than other monarchs, and they gave literal expression to some of the notorious maxims of foreign policy that have seemed to epitomize all that was unprincipled in the international practice of the age. "When one has an advantage," wrote the great Frederick rhetorically, "is he to use it or not?" The first rule of foreign policy, he wrote, is to "seize the favorable opportunity." As for "rights" in international relations, he deemed them "the business of ministers" to work up, not of sovereigns to wait upon, and his main concern with them was epitomized in his notorious cynical injunction anent the partition of Poland, that "when rights are not very good, they should not be set forth in detail." "Of all States, from the smallest to the biggest," he concluded grimly, "one can safely say that the fundamental rule of government is the principle of extending their territories.... The passions of rulers have no other curb but the limits of their power. Those are the fixed laws of European politics to which every politician submits." Joseph was more sententious, but Catherine spoke for the diplomatic and military orientation of all three philosophical monarchs with her succinct aphorism: "He who gains nothing, loses."

Again, the enlightened monarchs have been particularly associated with the generally unsavory character of old-world diplomacy by virtue of the simple fact that they dominated continental diplomacy in the second half of the eighteenth century, precisely when its moral prestige was at its nadir. The foreign policies of Great Britain and France, the leading Atlantic powers, where the accidents of royal character, the persistence of constitutional traditions, and the surge of an increasingly mobile society excluded enlightened absolutism, were alternately paralyzed and obsessed during this period by their overseas duel for colonial wealth and possessions, leaving the initiative in manipulating the European system of states to the great central and eastern European powers with the energetic, shrewd, and enlightened monarchs.

Not only the shape of continental war and diplomacy as a whole, finally, but the most influential—and notorious—events in it were the special work of the enlightened absolutists. The secretly prepared Diplomatic Revolution of 1756–1757 and the ensuing Seven Years' War, the one-sided Russo-Turkish war of 1768–1774, the cynical Polish partition of 1772, and the expansionist Austrian designs upon Bavaria which produced the War of the Bavarian Succession in 1778 and the German crisis of 1785 were the outstanding continental events of the half century. All of them were in the mold of foreign policy created by Frederick the Great's unprovoked seizure of Silesia in 1740, and like this pilot event all were initiated by one or more enlightened monarchs.

To confirm this correlation of the unprincipled side of eighteenth-century international politics with enlightened monarchs we may note that the British-American struggle and its ramification in Europe, the one notable conflict between nations involving principle at all, was the one prominent event with which these monarchs had least to do. It had to do with precisely those countries—Great Britain, the British colonies, and France—in which the culture of the Enlightenment was associated more prominently with the society than with the state. True enough, French policy was pursued primarily in the prosecution of the commercial and colonial rivalry with Britain and in conformity with the inveterate royal habit of encouraging the rebels of one's enemy, but the difference between the French government's attitude toward these goals and the attitude of the allied Spanish government, under the enlightened Charles III (ruled 1759–1788), toward the same goals in the same war confirms the difference between the moral ambiguity of traditional foreign policy and the definitely amoral cast of enlightened foreign policy in the second half of the eighteenth century.

The French foreign minister, Charles Gravier, Count of Vergennes (1717–1787), was a career diplomat with a fear of and vengefulness toward Britain that had become a French obsession after the Seven Years' War of 1756–1763 and with a respectable belief in American independence as a "weight in the balance of power." But he also had the liberal conviction that trade had superseded territory as the chief sinew of power. His was the famous declaration that "in the present state of the world commercial questions are political questions," and it was he who would be responsible for the free-trading Anglo-French commercial treaty of 1786, which would establish naval peace and commercial competition. These insights not only led him to see the war more in terms of intangible trade privileges than brutal conquests but also made him responsive to the French literate society in general—since its members were vocal proponents of these insights—and to its principled pro-Americanism in particular. It was, indeed, through his preparatory work with the Dutch party of republican Patriots that the Netherlands entered the war against Britain during 1780 in ostensible defense of the commercial freedom of the seas. It was through his initiative that in the same year Catherine the Great agreed to form the League of Armed Neutrality, in which she never did believe, on the same principle of neutral rights. Spain, on the other hand, whose dogged, heavyhanded, single-minded king was accounted enlightened precisely for the conformity of his policies with the great monarchs' of central and eastern Europe rather than for any similarity in cultural tastes or intelligence quotient, entered the war against Britain in 1779 purely and simply for the reacquisition of Gibraltar and Minorca and for the expulsion of the British from the Gulf of Mexico and the Caribbean Sea. Unlike official France, "enlightened" Spain was entirely unsympathetic to the American principles in the war, refused to ally with the former colonies, and granted them recognition only at the very end of the war.

PRINCIPLES OF FOREIGN POLICY

Let us stipulate from the start, then, that the foreign policies of the enlightened autocrats shared none of the Enlightenment's typically pacific and humanitarian principles of international relations. But there remains the question of whether there was anything distinctive in the way these sovereigns pursued the policies of aggrandizement for the home country and balance of power for everyone else which had long been the goals of monarchical foreign policy. As a matter of fact, their approach to international relations does show a constant tendency, common to all of themselves and different from their predecessors, that was not so much a reflection of as a contribution to the culture of the Enlightenment. This common tendency was composed by the combination of two persistent traits in the foreign orientation of enlightened absolutism.

First, whereas personal, dynastic, and collective considerations merged in the traditional canons of international statecraft, the enlightened monarchs distinguished among these strands and deliberately arranged them in a clear order of priority which recognized the collective interest as supreme, the personal interest as subordinate, and the dynastic interest as purely instrumental. Frederick the Great put as little store in the Hohenzollern claims to the Silesia he seized as in the Habsburg, and if he acknowledged princely "honor" or "glory" as a valid "principle" of foreign policy he also declared categorically that it must be "sacrificed" when "the safety and the greater welfare of the state demand it." Joseph was no less cavalier about the ancient Wittelsbach title to Bavaria. If he at first put forth a weak and hoary Habsburg claim to a part of that electorate, he ultimately sought to exchange the Austrian Netherlands for the whole of it, deliberately negating the reciprocal rights of dynasties and peoples in return for the "solid advantage" of an expanded Austrian heartland in central Europe.

The enlightened rulers believed, to be sure, in the superior merit of hereditary monarchy, but they believed in it rather for the orderly benefits it conferred than as something good in itself, sanctified by divine ordination or human tradition. The final measure of all political values and institutions, by which both dynastic right and individual princely honor must be assessed, was now deemed to be a single standard. The collective interest of the realm, joining the interests of ruler and people into a unity vis-à-vis other states, was now explicitly recognized by the rulers themselves to be *the* guiding principle of their policies. In Frederick's categorical terms: "The rulers must always be guided by the interest of the state. . . . The interest of the state is their law and is inviolable."

The interest of state was not only tangible and integral but also rational —and this rationality in foreign policy was the second distinguishing feature in the international attitude of the enlightened monarchs. The standard of state interest was rational not in the normative sense of conformity to a universal law or principle, but in the functional sense of its capacity to be calculated, compared, and logically linked with similarly analyzed interests of other states. Hence the tendency to view the interest of state in the quantitative terms of miles, souls, and wealth to be acquired. The Polish partition, for example, was viewed by all three enlightened rulers as the preservation of a numerical balance among the three eastern powers, and Joseph's own designs upon Bavaria were stimulated by his estimation of it as a precise equivalent for the irrevocably lost Silesia. Such considerations, moreover, were only the most literal expression of the objectivity, the regularity, and the uniformity that were deemed the general attributes of the interest of state. It was Frederick, as usual, who articulated this rational approach into appropriate maxims. "He whose conduct is best calculated," he wrote about the making of foreign policy, "triumphs over those who act with less consistency." An analogous view went into his prescriptions for the understanding of foreign policy, for he directed attention to "the fixed and lasting interests" of the various states and assigned to their "interplay" the rigor of "systems." By virtue of their commensurability, the respective interests of state permit the wise man to compare current events and, "observing the relations and similarities, ... to be able to know everything, judge everything, predict everything."

These two main tendencies in the foreign policies of the enlightened rulers—the organization of various partial interests within the community into the single standard of an exclusive state interest, and the possibility of connecting it rationally with the analogously perceived interests of other states—shared a common assumption. Both tendencies alike postulated a world of states that was constituted entirely by facts—by political and economic conditions, by contemporary events, and by the motives of statesmen that would produce new facts. There was no place in this realm for the universal qualities of human nature that referred to what man fundamentally *was* rather than to how men severally acted and that in other realms of human relations provided for the authority of universal law and humane moral principle over the real actions of men.

It was, indeed, precisely in their exclusion of laws and principles common to humanity from any relevance to relations among states that the enlightened absolutists diverged signally from the *philosophes* whose rhetoric they shared. When the *philosophes* spoke of the actuality of human behavior in the international arena they usually analyzed it into the same kind of naked self-interest that formed the basis of their royal readers' policies. Voltaire's cynical reference to occasion, custom, and force as "the only laws" and Kant's dour portrait of self-seeking men in an international jungle were typical of the *philosophes'* attitude toward international affairs, past and present. But where the *philosophes* condemned this actuality by measuring it against the reality of humanity and its universal laws, which they deemed as relevant to international as to domestic affairs, the enlightened absolutists accepted the same actuality as the only reality pertinent to international affairs and committed themselves wholeheartedly to it. Catherine gloried in intrigue, Joseph threw himself enthusiastically and continuously into project after project for the expansion of his dominions, and even Frederick, who alone lamented on occasion the evil ways of his peers that compelled him to lower himself to their level, ended by making "a sacred law" out of his necessity.

But if the rulers thus segregated foreign policy from the more general political and moral considerations which the disengaged *philosophes* held to be relevant to it, they did apply the characteristic intellectual approaches of the Enlightenment within the circumscribed sphere of international politics. Kings and ministers used the skeptical, empirical, pragmatic strand of the Enlightenment as a destructive weapon of the regional service state against the residual temporal and patriarchal bonds of an older Christian Europe, and they used the Enlightenment's typical balance of reason and fact to construct rational international arrangements of actual state interests. The combination of the critical and synthetic uses of reason in war and diplomacy, the fields of politics furthest removed from the humanitarian ideas of the age, demonstrates the status of enlightened absolutism as an authentic but autonomous branch of Enlightenment culture.

The enlightened absolutists displayed their characteristic patterns of foreign policy most distinctively in the Diplomatic Revolution of 1756–1757 and the first Polish partition of 1772, the two events which most clearly were the products of enlightened-absolutist initiative and which most decisively impressed the influence of enlightened absolutism upon the emergent forms of modern international relations.

THE DIPLOMATIC REVOLUTION OF 1756

The Diplomatic Revolution of the mid-eighteenth century comprises the three successive treaties which reversed the alliances binding France and Prussia against Great Britain, Austria, and Russia—multiple and ill-assorted bilateral alliances only a generation old at most, to be sure, but generally deemed to reflect an underlying international order hallowed by both nature and tradition, and confirmed by the War of the Austrian Succession (1740–1748). The three "revolutionary" treaties were: the Convention of Westminster (January 16, 1756), which joined Great Britain and Prussia in a nonaggression pact aimed at the neutralization of the German Empire to prevent any extension of the *de facto* Anglo-French war from its actual maritime and probable Dutch theaters; the First Treaty of Versailles (May 1, 1756), which bound Austria and France in a defensive alliance providing for mutual assistance in the event of an attack upon the European possessions of either by any power but Great Britain, pledged Austria to neutrality in the event of such an attack by Great Britain, and was supplemented by Russian adherence on December 31, 1756; finally, the Second Treaty of Versailles (May 1, 1757), concluded by Austria and France well after Prussia's Frederick initiated the Seven Years' War with his invasion of Austria's ally, Saxony, on August 29, 1756. This last treaty converted the Austro-French defensive pact into an offensive alliance looking to the dismemberment of Prussia, with explicit provision for the restoration of Silesia to Austria, in return for the ultimate transfer of the Austrian Netherlands to France.

That such instruments—two defensive agreements hopeful of sparing previous alliances and one offensive treaty that was a reflex of ongoing military hostilities—should register the impact of a revolution upon contemporaries and posterity alike is a matter not so much of their specific provisions as of their implications and effects.

First, the replacement of the old Bourbon-Habsburg rivalry with a Franco-Austrian alliance signalized the supersession of dynastic interests by reasons of state.

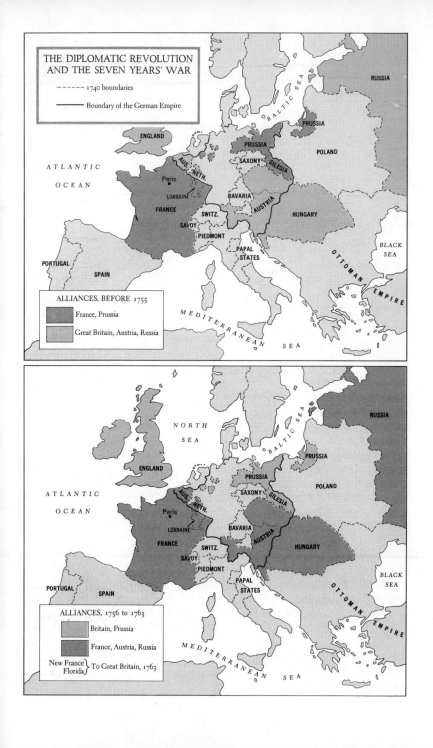

THE DIPLOMATIC REVOLUTION
AND THE SEVEN YEARS' WAR

‒ ‒ ‒ ‒ ‒ 1740 boundaries

———— Boundary of the German Empire

RUSSIA

PRUSSIA

ENGLAND

BALTIC SEA

ATLANTIC

OCEAN

Paris

LORRAINE

FRANCE

AUS. NETH.

PRUSSIA

SAXONY

SILESIA

POLAND

BAVARIA

AUSTRIA

SWITZ.

SAVOY

PIEDMONT

PAPAL
STATES

HUNGARY

BLACK
SEA

PORTUGAL

SPAIN

MEDITERRANEAN

OTTOMAN EMPIRE

SEA

ALLIANCES, BEFORE 1755

France, Prussia

Great Britain, Austria, Russia

NORTH

SEA

RUSSIA

ENGLAND

BALTIC SEA

PRUSSIA

ATLANTIC

OCEAN

Paris

LORRAINE

FRANCE

AUS. NETH.

PRUSSIA

SAXONY

SILESIA

POLAND

BAVARIA

AUSTRIA

SWITZ.

SAVOY

PIEDMONT

PAPAL
STATES

HUNGARY

BLACK
SEA

PORTUGAL

SPAIN

OTTOMAN EMPIRE

MEDITERRANEAN

SEA

ALLIANCES, 1756 to 1763

Britain, Prussia

France, Austria, Russia

New France }
Florida } To Great Britain, 1763

Second, the older balance of power, in which the Bourbon-Habsburg opposition had provided the pivots for a whole series of different regional balances in the various trouble spots of Europe, was replaced by a single system of five relatively equal powers (the old antagonists, France and Austria, and the old balance wheel, Britain, plus the two new arrivals, Prussia and Russia), whose general balance was affected by disturbances anywhere on the Continent.

Third, the diplomatic revision was associated with the violence of the Seven Years' War of 1756–1763, which executed with armed force the changes registered by the reversal of alliances and rendered them irreversible.

Finally, and most revealingly, the shift of alliances amounted to a revolution because it had its revolutionaries, men who perceived that the interests of their own parties—in this international case, sovereign states—could be advanced only through a radical change in the whole system of politics. The revolutionaries in this crisis were precisely the two most enlightened statesmen involved in it—King Frederick the Great of Prussia and Prince Kaunitz, the freethinking Austrian chancellor whose admiration for the rationalism of the French *philosophes* and confidence in his ability to organize international relations scientifically into a system of "political algebra" exceeded even Frederick's own. Their role in the Diplomatic Revolution of 1756–1757 reveals the persistent effort of enlightened absolutism to organize diplomacy into some kind of manageable system.

Their achievement is clear from the contrast with the unenlightened diplomacy of the age. At this very time three of the great powers of Europe suffered under myopic leadership—Britain under the painstaking but dull Duke of Newcastle, France under the divided counsels of a routine-bound official diplomacy and the sporadic, dynastically obsessed personal diplomacy of King Louis XV, and Russia under the impulsive Tsarina Elizabeth and Count Alexis Bestuzhev-Ryumin, her British-subsidized foreign-office chief. These powers vacillated between the familiar issues of the Low Countries, Hanover, and the Baltic, which continued to determine their basic policies, and the developing interests in overseas colonies and the continental borderlands of eastern Europe, which distracted their attention and rendered their policies indecisive. Prussia's Frederick and Austria's Kaunitz, on the other hand, grasped the import of the apparently peripheral oceanic and eastern European interests for the traditional alignments of the powers and brought both newer and older issues together to bear on their own struggle for supremacy in central Europe. Hence their seizure of the diplomatic and military initiative in 1756 was a matter not only of the highly touted "realism" of enlightened statesmen in foreign policy but of their ability to conceive of the whole constellation of international relations as a rational system in which each reality had its due place. In international politics as in intellectual life, the devotees of

The pious Maria Theresa with her Enlightened chancellor, Prince Kaunitz.

the Enlightenment were distinctive for the constancy with which they strove to connect their two ultimate passions—their passion for perceiving the facts as they were, free of any obscuring associations, and their passion for associating these facts in patterns manageable by reason.

Again analogously with intellectual life, there were different versions of the common enlightened approach to foreign policy, and the variations served to show the range of possibilities in Enlightenment principles. A comparison of the proportions of realism and system in the respective roles played by Kaunitz and Frederick in the Diplomatic Revolution demonstrates, in general, the joint addiction of both men to both principles as such, in contrast to the combination of illusion and incoherence in their unenlightened and passive contemporaries. But it will also show a difference of proportions which betokened a difference of method between the two men, and this difference clarifies the two alternate methods bequeathed by enlightened monarchy to the making of foreign policy; for it was the play and counterplay of Kaunitz's and Frederick's methods that made the Diplomatic Revolution.

It was a notable confirmation of the connection between the real and the rational in the practical as in the theoretical culture of the eighteenth century that in his rivalry with Frederick during 1756 and 1757 Kaunitz proved to be the more realistic precisely because his system was the more inclusive. His grand design, conceived back in 1749 and accepted as official Habsburg policy in 1755, organized the various Austrian interests into a logical sequence of priorities and organized the even more various interests of all the powers concerned into a system of Austrian foreign relations which could presumably account for every contingency. The recovery of Silesia and the concomitant destruction, through dismemberment, of Prussia as a great power were the supreme immediate goals to which all else was to be subordinated, not for the reasons of revenge, damaged dynastic pride, and outraged morality that were Maria Theresa's private incentives, but because the Austrian recovery of hegemony in central Europe was a necessary prior condition for the assertion of the other Austrian interests—in the east against the Ottoman Empire and in Germany and the west against the French.

To accomplish the immediate goals. Prussia had first to be isolated and then crushed by an encircling coalition. To achieve these conditions, in turn, a clear hierarchy of priorities was set up. Most important was Austria's complete freedom of military disposition and diplomatic maneuver, based on the financial independence born of internal reform. Next in importance was the detachment of France from the Prussian alliance, purchased by the promises of support for Bourbons in Poland and of their investiture in the Austrian Netherlands. Almost as crucial was the conversion of Russian friendship into active assistance. Lowest in priority was the retention of the British alliance that had worked so poorly for Austria in the last war (of the Austrian Succession).

From 1749 on, Kaunitz pursued all the lines indicated by this system, but by the summer of 1755 only the internal policy of achieving military independence through financial reform, administrative centralization, and the equalization of the tax burden was actually beginning to bear fruit. Then, precisely because he was looking for an enlarged framework of international policy that would be more appropriate to his large-scale planning than the frustrating bilateral crisscross of existing foreign relations, he perceived the real, if still subliminal, effect of the undeclared Anglo-French colonial war in expanding the arena of international relations and making possible more rational combinations among the pentarchy of great powers. He now intensified his wooing of France, artfully combining new and old appeals to the French fears of a British-organized continental coalition, to the official French mistrust of an upstart Prussian satellite, and to Louis' dynastic cupidity. At the same time he increased his pressure on the exposed British and pushed them to promise, in the Anglo-Russian convention of September, 1755, the subsidies which would make Russia an effective partner in a Habsburg-led continental bloc. With this large preset scheme, Kaunitz established a whole network of conditions that gave to each particular action of the powers a different reality and effect than it was intended to have. Only the Anglo-Russian convention proved abortive, because of Frederick's counteraction in concluding the Convention of Westminster with the British, but Kaunitz's system endowed this defensive agreement with an offensive effect upon the French and endowed the subsequent Franco-Austrian defensive pact of May, 1756, with an offensive effect upon Frederick, even anticipating, in the words of Count Georg Adam von Starhemberg (1724–1807), Kaunitz's ambassador in Paris, the impact of Frederick himself, as "our most effective helper" in activating the desired offensive combination of Austrians, French, and Russians against Prussia.

Kaunitz's comprehensive system of conditions evoked from Frederick the incisive analysis of politics which was, in turn, ever characteristic of *him*. He would separate a complex condition into its component issues and initiate immediate action upon the issue most vital and accessible to him, with a view to isolating and resolving it before its connections with other issues made it insoluble. For Frederick, political conditions as a whole could not be mastered, but they had to be understood as a whole so that they could be rationally analyzed into their constituent parts, which could be mastered. Thus, reasoning that the Anglo-French conflict gave both powers alike a real interest in disengagement from central Europe, Frederick signed the Prusso-British nonaggression pact of January, 1756 (Convention of Westminster), in the expectation that by localizing the Anglo-French war in the colonies, the seas, and the Netherlandish coastal areas where it belonged, it would remove Britain from the hostile coalition, undermine the financial capacity of the Russians to participate, and yet not violate his alliance with France. Again, Frederick's invasion of Saxony in August, 1756, which first made a matter of fact a reversal of alliances that had heretofore been a matter of opinion, was only in part a reflex response to his perception of Kaunitz's grand design against him, triggered by the dubious reports of his intelligence agents of preparations in Austria, Russia, and Saxony for an imminent concerted attack upon him. The very real and persistent obstacles still raised by the reluctant French to Kaunitz's offensive design before August had left Frederick with a choice of policies and indicate an additional cause outside the design that persuaded him to make the choice he did. This cause was Frederick's own model of action, and the outbreak of the Seven Years' War is best seen neither as the inevitable result of the diplomatic realignment nor as the fortuitous compounding of French and Prussian mistakes, but rather as the collision of two inflexibly rational systems of international relations—a collision that may well be viewed as the conflict of Frederick's analytic with Kaunitz's synthetic spirit within the Enlightenment syndrome.

For Frederick's unannounced attack upon Austria's ally, Saxony, was not simply a reflex reaction to Kaunitz's system but also a characteristic conclusion from his own chain of calculations. He came to the decision to strike when and where he did as the only valid inference from the conjunction of two of his long-cherished premises: that a hostile union could be countered only by anticipating the combination of its elements and mastering them piecemeal; and that the annexation of Electoral Saxony, with its productive industries, with its Catholic Elector's ties to Austria, Poland, and, through Poland, to Russia, and with the strategic threat of its long common frontier running up the extended western edge of Silesia and along the southern border of Brandenburg itself, was and had to be a persistent object of Prussian policy.

What was illuminating about Frederick's initiation of the Seven Years' War was his conviction that a particular Prussian advantage could be acquired through the dissolution of a general European situation into its manageable parts. Where Kaunitz would direct an entire system toward a particular claim as its necessary result, Frederick acted to break up the system on the principle that one should adjust one's claims to "the barometer of one's fortunes." So Frederick chose to attack Austria in Bohemia through Saxony rather than Austria in Moravia from Silesia because the former course seemed better calculated to attain his goal of isolating and defeating Austria before Maria Theresa's Russian and French allies could bring their concerted forces to bear and because like all wars for Frederick such a war would be worthwhile only if its costs were compensated by a permanent gain like Saxony.

Actually, the Seven Years' War achieved the goals neither of Kaunitz's synthetic nor of Frederick's analytic utilitarianism. The diversion of the French war effort to the colonial conflict against the British and the lack of coordination between the Russian armies, committed to the Baltic, and the Austrian armies, committed to Saxony and Silesia, ultimately frustrated the Austrian project of regaining Silesia and dismantling Prussia. But if Frederick did thus manage to save the integrity of his state by using his characteristic strategy of dealing separately with the coalition armies and his characteristic tactic of the oblique battle order which permitted him to concentrate his forces against a single isolated wing of the enemy, he also not only failed to acquire Saxony but came very close to complete defeat from the powerful, if sporadic, effects of successful coalition warfare. He felt, indeed, that only the Russian withdrawal from the war in 1762, occasioned by the accident of Tsarina Elizabeth's death and the accession of the admiring Peter III, rescued him from the increasingly effective encirclement.

For both Austria and Prussia, the Seven Years' War marked a decisive turning point. In 1765 Joseph II became German Emperor and coregent, with Maria Theresa, of the Habsburg dominions. Henceforward he joined Kaunitz in decision-making, and he helped to bring a new direction to Austrian policy, away from Silesia and from obsession with Prussia. Frederick, for his part, never forgot the terrible abyss of failure that the war had opened before him, and he now came to feel, as never before, the "uncertainty" that "holds sway in all operations of foreign policy."

But the failure of the Diplomatic Revolution to fulfill the requirements of either of the systems—Austrian or Prussian—which were jointly responsible for it did not mean the end of systematic foreign policy for the enlightened absolutists. So powerful was the tendency toward systematic policy for them that their response to failure was simply to adjust their systems to their experience. Frederick's became more combinatory, more synthetic; under Joseph's influence Austria's became more partial, more flexible. In conjunction with the parallel development of Russian policy toward a regional system under Catherine the Great, the convergence produced the first partition of Poland and therewith the origins of the eastern system that would play a dominant role in European history for the next century and a half.

THE FIRST PARTITION OF POLAND, 1772

The shock and disappointment which the course of the Seven Years' War brought to the expectations of its participants had the immediate effect not so much of reducing the scope of the great-power system, but of dismantling it temporarily in all its versions, traditional and revolutionary alike. Even during the last phase of the war itself international relations had been reduced to unilateral action and to exclusive bilateral arrangements. Despite treaties of mutual assistance which had bound the Russians and Austrians in February, 1757, and the British and Prussians in April, 1758, both sides during 1762 began separate negotiations in which allies were not consulted and their interests were not considered. The Anglo-French preliminary agreement of November 3, 1762, which provided for mutual withdrawal from the continental war, for Britain's retention of its mainland conquests in North America, and for its return of occupied West Indian islands and Indian bases to France and Spain (a belated belligerent since the British extension of the colonial war to the Spanish empire in January, 1762), became, with the later Spanish adherence, the basis of the final Peace of Paris on February 10, 1763. The separate Prussian-Russian peace of May, 1762, and the offensive alliance which Frederick negotiated a month later with his Russian adulator, the new but short-lived Tsar Peter III, were voided by the enforced abdication of the latter at the end of June (he was assassinated in his jail during July), but they set the stage for Catherine the Great's unilateral withdrawal of Russia from the war in July, and consequently, for the final separate Treaty of Hubertusburg of February 15, 1763, wherein Prussia and Austria (along with Saxony, the Austrian satellite), agreed to peace in central Europe on the basis of the *status quo ante bellum*.

The decomposition of the wartime alliances reflected, moreover, a growing awareness within each of the great powers of distinct long-range interests—an awareness which perpetuated the war-born pattern of segregated interests and independent initiatives, tempered only by limited bilateral arrangements, in the international relations of the postwar period. In both Great Britain and France the governing classes persisted in the conviction, which had disposed them to peacemaking, that maritime and colonial rivalry had become the primary issue of foreign policy and that it would be much more effectively pursued without the diversions of continental entanglements. This view led Britain to diplomatic isolation, and France to reliance on the Franco-Spanish Family Compact of 1761, with its provision for joint action by the Bourbon powers to satisfy their respective claims against Britain, as the mainstay of French foreign relations. Henceforward French continental connections, such as the entente with Austria and the support of Francophiles in Poland and Constantinople, were depreciated to the purely defensive purposes of maintaining a balance and preventing a diversion of French energies upon the Continent.

Prussia and Russia, similarly, focused their interests and commitments after the war. Frederick the Great inferred from that conflict the dispensability of the western powers and the indispensability of Russia to the defense of his scattered holdings in central and eastern Europe. At the same time Catherine the Great based her policies on the underpopulation of Russia and resolved to replace her predecessors' policies of European commitments and adventures with a policy of expansion into populous, contiguous Poland. This convergence of particular interests produced the Russo-Prussian agreement of 1764, which gave to Frederick the desired security of a Russian defensive alliance and to Catherine Prussian support for her unilateral diplomatic and military intervention in Poland, beginning in the same year, to secure the election of her former lover, Stanislas Poniatowski, as Polish King and to assert Russian hegemony over an unreformed Poland against the resistance of the conservative Roman Catholic Polish nobility organized in the Confederation of the Bar. Both Frederick and Catherine, significantly, opted for these limited benefits against broader alternatives—Frederick against his own expressed fears of Europe's contributing "to the rise of a people that may some day become Europe's own doom," and Catherine against the project of a Northern System set forth by her adviser Count Nikita Panin (1718–1783) to organize a multipower permanent military alliance to keep the peace in Europe.

Even the Habsburgs, whose spread of dominions across Europe from the Belgian coastline on the English Channel to the Turkish Balkan frontier continued to provide the real underpinnings for the comprehensive policymaking of their long-term Chancellor Kaunitz, contributed after 1763 to the international fragmentation that was the essential background of the Polish partition. Convinced of the necessity for a thorough internal reorganization and consolidation of the Habsburg dominions as a prior condition of any resumption of the diplomatic offensive, the Austrian authori-

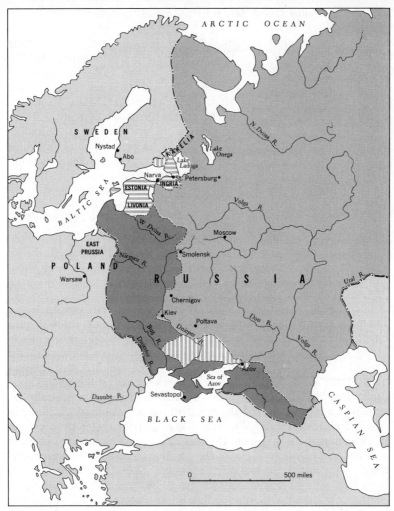

THE WESTERN EXPANSION OF RUSSIA UNDER PETER AND CATHERINE

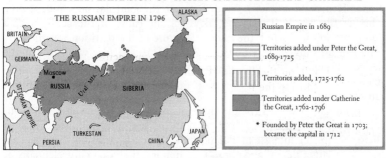

THE RUSSIAN EMPIRE IN 1796

Russian Empire in 1689

Territories added under Peter the Great, 1689-1725

Territories added, 1725-1762

Territories added under Catherine the Great, 1762-1796

* Founded by Peter the Great in 1703; became the capital in 1712

ties—including Kaunitz himslf—shifted their main attention from the diplomatic to the domestic systematizing of the "second reform period," as the decade following the Seven Years' War has been called in comparison with the first period, the years 1749–1756, with their less absorbing and extensive reforms. When Joseph II joined his mother, Maria Theresa, as coregent in 1765, not only did he collaborate wholeheartedly with his fellow devotees of the Enlightenment in the work of internal centralization and modernization but his own thirst for personal glory brought a force for unilateral action into Habsburg diplomacy that would henceforth rival its traditional passion for combinations. Characteristically, the one fruitful initiative of the Habsburgs in the decade after the Seven Years' War was the unilateral seizure of the county of Zips in February, 1769: a place—a Polish enclave in Hungary adjacent to Polish Galicia—and a time—during the confusion attendant upon the recently opened Russo-Turkish war of 1768–1774—that would make it a precedent for further partition.

The Eastern Crisis

The general context of the first Polish partition thus consisted in a European constellation which had each power pursuing regional goals either independently or with, at most, the passive support of one neighboring ally. In this disorganized situation the fortuitous eruption of the Russo-Turkish war—it started when the Turks panicked at the violations of the Polish-Turkish frontier by pro-Russian Polish guerrillas in defiance of official Russian policy—threatened to trigger a generally destructive chain reaction, and the first partition of Poland, in 1772, can be seen as a mutually concerted organization of particular interests to prevent it. More important—and more fruitful—than the still unresolved issues of who was primarily responsible for the partition and which motive—mutual greed or the anxiety to localize the Russo-Turkish war—was its primary cause were the two indubitable facts about the decision to partition: first, all the enlightened authorities embroiled in eastern Europe—Catherine, Joseph II, Kaunitz, Frederick II, and his similarly enlightened brother, Prince Henry (1726–1802)—contributed to the joint decision; and, second, whether the war in Turkey be taken for the cause or the occasion of a compensation in Poland, the essential feature of the partition was the resolution of an immediate crisis arising out of a particular war through the deliberate organization of the separate long-range interests of the three major eastern-European powers into a permanent common stake in the entire region.

The enlightened rulers of the three major powers, following a well-worn intellectual pattern of the contemporary culture they admired, resolved their conflicts of interest in Poland and Turkey by relating them as subplots in a larger design and thereby combining the discordant elements of each arena into harmoniously balanced parts of the expanded whole. The

Destruction of the Turkish by the Russian fleet at Cesmé in the Aegean Sea, July 1770. *This naval battle was one of the notable Russian victories over the Turks which made imminent the involvement of other powers and set the stage for the first partition of Poland.*

suggestions of each government for a Polish partition had been irreconcilable as long as they reflected the incompatible long-range interests of the three powers in the limited Polish context, but were reconciled in the fact of a concerted Polish partition when the expanding Turkish crisis created the possibility of a general eastern settlement deliberately aligning the unequal Polish interests of the powers into a system of equilibrium with the unequal Turkish interests of the same powers.

Only in 1771, when the conditions of policy making were drastically altered by the imminent spread of war, owing to Russian military conquests and the Austrian promise of armed support to the Turks, did the enlightened policy makers select from the various interests the common elements that would constitute an agreed scheme of Polish partition as the core of a general eastern settlement. Frederick, with most to gain in Poland and nothing to gain in the Ottoman Empire, was the first to recognize the combination which used the Ottoman war to make possible a Polish partition and the Polish partition to limit the Ottoman war. Taking up Catherine's playful suggestion of a three-power grab in Poland and turning it into a serious policy of collective security, he spent most of 1771 urging it upon both Catherine and the Kaunitz-Joseph team as a mutual compensation for what each must concede and as a reciprocal pledge for what both parties tacitly accepted in the Turkish theater. Frederick's pressure on Poland and the Austro-Russian negotiations on the Turkish war ran on side by side, and in October, 1771, Catherine on the one side and Kaunitz and Joseph on the other came to corresponding decisions on both issues: both sides agreed on the principle of a Polish partition among the three powers, and both sides agreed on the limits of a Turkish settlement that would realize Russian war aims on the Black Sea and in the Crimea, but not in the Danubian principalities.

By February, 1772, the details were worked out, but it took a Russo-

Cartoon illustrating the first partition of Poland in 1772.

Prussian *fait accompli* and six months more for the representatives of the political Enlightenment to persuade the old-fashioned Maria Theresa to sign up, against her avowed "inability to understand" how she could be urged "to imitate two other powers in the injustice of using their superior force to suppress an innocent victim on the dubious grounds of prudence and convenience," and against her avowed insistence on the contrary principle that "the rights of the prince are not different from the rights of any private man." But nonetheless consent she did, and the Austrians acceded to the treaty on August 2, 1772. The event had as an incidental by-product a rare confrontation of Christian and Enlightened judgments on the standards of European foreign policy. When Maria Theresa moaned that the treaty spread "a stain over my whole reign," Frederick made the dry response that epitomized the Enlightenment's view of Christian politics: "She cries, but she always takes."

Terms of the Partition

The instruments of the first Polish partition were several. What we think of as one arrangement was actually the joint product of three bilateral treaties, concluded by each possible pair of the partitioning powers with each other (in 1772); a declaration by the Russian ambassador in Warsaw endorsed by the ambassadors of the other two partitioning powers (also in 1772); and separate treaties concluded by Poland with each of the three partitioning powers and confirming the provisions of the prior treaties and the declaration (in 1775). This staggered pattern of treaty making is important because it formally sanctioned the joint stake of the three great eastern states in both the territorial and the political terms of the Polish partition.

Almost one third of the Polish kingdom's territory and one half of its inhabitants were divided among the three neighboring great powers, with each gaining what was required by its own long-range interest. Prussia took the smallest but strategically most vital section, the West Prussian districts that now connected East Prussia with the heart of the monarchy, and Ermeland, the large Polish enclave in the middle of East Prussia—a total area of some 14,000 square miles and 600,000 inhabitants. Only the isolated port of Danzig was left dangling in Polish possession, inviting toll wars and a future repartition.

The Russians received the sections of White Russia, Lithuania, and Livonia that gave them the coveted river courses of the upper Dvina and Dnieper, adding an area of some 34,000 square miles for the support of their western armies and more than a million and a half souls to their human resources.

The Austrian gain was the least vital of the three to the partitioners' interests, as they were then conceived, but compensated by being quantitatively the most impressive of all. The Habsburgs took Lodomeria and the old kingdom of Galicia on the northern slope of the Hungarian Carpathians and the district of Red Russia to the east of the kingdom, together an area of 32,000 square miles and 2.5 million people, including Lvov (renamed Lemberg), one of Poland's largest cities. Conformably to the Habsburg pattern of accumulation, the new acquisition formed a salient protecting Hungary from the new dominant threat in the east—Russia.

Less remarked than this massive transfer of land and people but perhaps even more subversive of acknowledged rights were the political principles explicated in the treaties, for these principles belied the formal guarantee pledged by the powers to the territorial integrity of the residual Polish kingdom and legitimated in advance the complete destruction of independent Poland that was not yet intended. The signatory powers justified their annexations as security measures necessary to protect their claims in Poland, and their own adjacent territories, from Polish "anarchy," and they confirmed the implications of this promise for further intervention by requiring joint participation of the partitioning powers in the preservation of the Polish constitution that was in fact producing the anarchy. Moreover, they legitimated such intervention in advance by forcing the Polish Diet itself to endorse not only the territorial transfers but also the constitutional intrusions.

Results of the Partition

However much the facts and principles of the partition may support the subsequent moral judgments of it as a piratical conspiracy against international law, an unconscionable oppression of Polish nationality, and a suicidal model for revolutionary destruction of monarchy, these judgments tell more about the ideals, the nationalism, or the nostalgia of the later generations who did the judging than they do about the partition that was judged. A clue to the political, rather than moral, meaning of the partition lies in the stark contrast between the indifference or even mild approval prevalent among its contemporaries and the righteous indignation that would obsess their descendants. The obvious disorder of Polish conditions to which so many men of the age referred in justification of the partition pointed clearly to what was positive in the policies leading to it and what was permanent in its results. The partition adumbrated the three pillars of the great-power system which, for better or worse, would bring a degree of order into the anarchic international relations among the several states of Europe.

First, the enlightened partitioners perceived the fundamental rule of the new international relations—the necessary connection between the concert and the balance of powers—and converted it from a pious principle into a literal and permanent reality. The political notions of concert and balance stemmed from very different roots, concert from the traditional ideal of an essential Christian community among the European temporal authorities and balance from the traditional practice of preserving their contingent plurality. These divergent origins would continue to foment illusions of a necessary antithesis between the concert and the balance of powers among the naïve and the unwary from the Holy Alliance of 1815 through the United Nations of the present. In actuality the European concert and the balance of its several sovereign states would be permanent complements and mutual dependents in the great-power system which would dominate world history from the mid-eighteenth to the mid-twentieth centuries. The outstanding statesmen of this system—Metternich, Bismarck, Churchill—would understand that a secular concert of powers could be united only on the common adjustment of their several independent interests and that these interests, conversely, could be kept in balance only through the concerted acknowledgment of each by all. Not only was the Polish partition of 1772 the first deliberate and categorical example of this combination, unmitigated by either the older rhetoric of Christian unity or the older fragility of emergency coalitions against a hegemonic power, but it created a settlement whose balance required a continuous tacit concert of the partitioning powers over the next century for its preservation.

The second important principle of the great-power system which the partition crystallized into an overt and unmistakable reality was the prescription that the approach to domestic issues—both of one's own and of other countries—be made in the context of foreign policy. To be sure, some of the ways of measuring internal political relations by the standards of foreign policy were centuries old. But in the last third of the eighteenth century this relationship entered into a new phase, inaugurated by the first

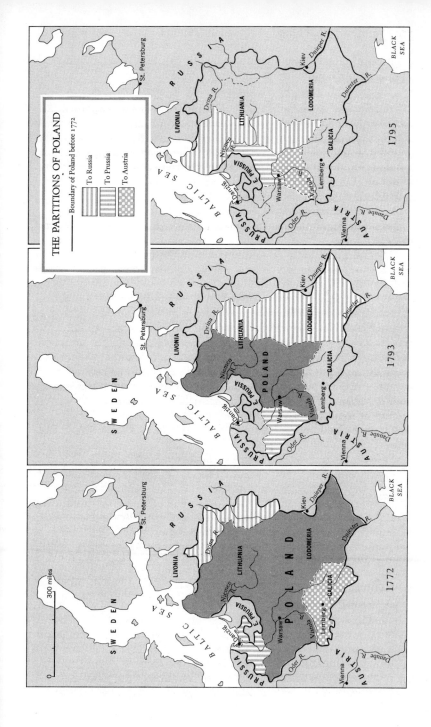

THE PARTITIONS OF POLAND

— Boundary of Poland before 1772

To Russia

To Prussia

To Austria

300 miles

1772

1793

1795

Polish partition. Where intervention by foreign powers into the domestic arrangements of other states had tended to focus on persons, religions, or specific policies, it now came to include constitutional change as a regular by-product of foreign policy. Thus the same enlightened absolutism which inaugurated the broad new use of constitutional politics for diplomatic purposes in the first Polish partition was also behind the struggle between Joseph II and Frederick II over the Bavarian succession, from 1778 to 1785. Here began the Austro-Prussian dualism in Germany that made the form of the German constitution both a function and an instrument of the two powers' respective foreign policies. Joseph's efforts to annex Bavaria inaugurated the Austrian policy toward Germany which regarded Habsburg predominance in a confederated Germany to be the indispensable central-European basis for the Austrian position in Europe as a whole.

When Frederick, in response, instigated the formation of a *Fürstenbund* ("League of Princes") in July, 1785, associating himself at first with the Electors of Hanover and Saxony and then with fifteen other German princes, Catholic as well as Protestant, for the preservation of the constitution of the Holy Roman Empire and of the rights and possessions of all its members, his pious pose as defender of the Imperial constitution and its "Germanic liberties" was a mere facade for his actual use of the Empire to retain the balance of Austrian and Prussian power in the European arena. The patriotic intentions that were widely attributed to Joseph and Frederick by respective contemporary admirers and a tendentious posterity existed only in the eye of the beholder, but the connection which these enlightened rulers did perceive between the constitutions of nations and the foreign policies of states would become a crucial ingredient in the later policies of men who did have patriotic intentions.

The third and most immediate contribution of the Polish partition to the European constellation was the cornerstone it provided for a separate eastern system of powers. The common stake which the three enlightened monarchs created in Poland was reinforced by the common interest to which the same rulers committed their states in Germany. By provision of the Treaty of Teschen, which terminated the War of the Bavarian Succession between Joseph and Frederick in 1779, Russia, as a mediating power, thenceforward shared the traditional position of France as guarantor of the German constitution, which had been legalized by the terms of the Peace of Westphalia (1648). But it was their mutual dependence in Poland that exercised the most continuous attraction in keeping the relations among the three eastern powers relatively compatible vis-à-vis one another and relatively unified vis-à-vis other theaters of international relations. Thus when Catherine and Joseph arranged the Austro-Russian entente of 1781, the one solid provision on which their vague assurances of mutual assistance were based was their joint guarantee of the post-partition situation in Poland. Even after the outbreak of the French Revolution, moreover, not only did the persistent eastern orientation of the three absolute monarchies at first grant to the revolution the three years of peace it required for its own consolidation but the revolution itself had the effect of strengthening the connections within the eastern system. Absolutist as they were, Prussia's Frederick William II (Frederick the Great's nephew and successor from 1786) and Russia's Catherine were at first too preoccupied with their conflicting ambitions in rump Poland to attend seriously to the French revolutionary menace. Then, the revolution in the west recalled them, and later the Austrians as well, to the basis of their joint power in the east. Linking Polish reformers with French "Jacobins" and Polish nationalism with revolutionary anarchy, by 1795 the eastern powers completed the partition of Poland among themselves.

Thus the foreign policies of the enlightened absolutists, cynical, opportunist, and materialistic as they were, bequeathed more to subsequent European history than their obvious contributions to the definition of the long-range interests of Prussia, Austria, and Russia and to the suppression of moral conscience and dynastic rights in international affairs. They exemplified the combination of balance of powers and concert of powers that alone would organize the separate state interests into a viable system of international relations, and they glimpsed the connection of internal constitutions with foreign affairs that would remain the key to statecraft through the next century. But their most fateful achievement was to create the basis for an eastern system of absolutist powers that would provide an international solidarity for the defense of political conservatism against the currents of change.

CHAPTER 10

The Enlightened Absolutists at Home

WITHIN THEIR OWN states the enlightened monarchs never questioned either the structure of absolutism or the priority of the military and economic power whose mobilization they recognized to be the indispensable domestic requirement of their competitive foreign policies. The connection of domestic and foreign policy spurred these vigorous, restless, and arrogant rulers to organize their resources for the increase of their strength, and to this extent it reinforces the view of enlightened absolutism as simply a more intelligent and efficient mode of exercising unlimited authority. But their deliberate focus of domestic policies upon the increase of governmental power explains these policies in the sense of determining their limits rather than in the sense of determining their substance within those limits. It explains, that is, why the enlightened monarchs did not undertake policies which might diminish power rather than how they chose the policies that they deemed compatible with it. Power, however beloved by them, did not automatically prescribe definite courses of domestic action to them. What did prescribe these courses were the rulers' specific ideas about the kind of things that made for power, the kind of things that were antithetical to power, and the kind of things that were indifferent to power, and the rulers' specific decisions to maximize the first, exclude the second, and accommodate the third. The contribution of enlightened absolutism to internal politics, indeed, was not only its reduction of politics to power but its redefinition of political power in terms of its relationship to the larger life of the community.

Hence the enlightened monarchs applied themselves vigorously to all of the three main fields of internal affairs—to the structure of administration and law that was the channel of power, to the forms of education and religion that separated what was political and accessible to the exercise of power from what was not, and to the social and economic policies that would reconcile the apparently discordant aims of increasing the resources available to the state's government and increasing the resources available to its citizens. Each of the three fields of internal policy revealed the same general idea of politics in a different way, and only when all these ways are taken into consideration does the whole enlightened idea of domestic politics emerge clearly.

The pattern of a unified principle amidst diversified practice characterized the progenitors as well as the fields of enlightened domestic policy. By reason of her sex, the physical difficulties of administering her vast territories, and the special political orientation of her aristocracy toward the state as the persistent source of its privileges as well as obligations, Catherine remained the most insecure of the enlightened monarchs and the most inclined toward placating the notables of her realm. Joseph represented the opposite extreme of a radical, leveling absolutism, not only because it fit his temperament to "approve nothing that was done before his time and by others," as his own mother, doting as she was, sorrowfully admitted, but more importantly because he started from the already considerable reforms enacted under her auspices by enlightened ministers.

Despite the domestic variations among the enlightened monarchs who ruled the great states, the aggregate internal policy of each was designed to complement the foreign policy which was so similar in all, and the common context of their international great-state status made the parallel features in their respective domestic policies more essential than the divergencies. The one fundamental difference of pattern, establishing another species of enlightened monarchy, concerned not these rulers but the progressive sovereigns of small states for whom international rivalry was not a constant condition of domestic politics. In the spontaneous and wholehearted patronage of the arts by Duke Charles Augustus of Weimar (ruled 1775–1828), in the categorical abolition of serfdom and the wide-ranging application of free-trade doctrine by Margrave Charles Frederick of Baden (ruled 1738–1811), and in the combination of strict neutrality in foreign affairs with economic liberalism, tax equalization, penal reform, and even a planned representative constitution by the Habsburg Grand Duke Leopold of Tuscany (ruled 1765–1790)—in all such reforming policies of small-scale rulers there was a sensitivity to practical needs that was relatively free from the continuous pressure for the maximal mobilization of economic and military power, and there was room for cultural, doctrinal, or humanitarian considerations that were relatively free from practical needs. Such rulers were indeed set off from like-minded sovereigns of the great powers.

The presence of such a benign species of enlightened monarchy in the eighteenth century had a significance that went beyond the blessings conferred upon the inhabitants of the individual states concerned. It showed a congruity of the moral and intellectual values characteristic of the Enlightenment with the practical politics of small and pacific communities that would help to perpetuate particularism in Germany and Italy for almost a century and minor states in Europe until our own day. But both in the

quantitative terms of effect upon the lives of men then and since and in
the qualitative terms of effect upon the basic issue of resolving the conflicting claims of power and freedom in those lives, the enlightened absolutism of the great powers was the more influential and the more problematical. What follows, then, is an inquiry into the main fields of the
domestic policies promulgated by this species of enlightened rulers, with a
view to elucidating the way in which they tried to resolve in actual fact the
problem of relating political power and human freedom.

GOVERNMENT AND LAW

The enlightened absolutists approached government as a single force
and civil society as a collective whole animated by government. In Joseph's
terms, government must be organized from top to bottom in accordance
with "uniform principles," and it must act "to unite the parts of the monarchy . . . into a single province, . . . a single mass of people all subject
to impartial guidance [and] . . . joined in a common enterprise." The
resulting state he called a "universe" (*Universum*), to characterize it as
a human world revolving around a common administration as its axis and
unified by the rule of general laws. The enlightened rulers contributed
both to the administrative unity of government and to the legal unity of
the state, albeit more tangibly to the second than to the first.

In the field of governmental institutions the enlightened absolutists
were at their least distinctive, for they made comparatively few structural
changes in the administrations which they inherited from their less cultured state-building forbears. What they added tended to build on the
centralizing, professionalizing, specializing, and bureaucratizing institutions
which they had received. But they did contribute a distinctive spirit and
a changed attitude toward these institutions which put government in a
different relation to the community than heretofore. Unlike the piecemeal,
ad hoc approach of their fathers, the enlightened autocrats viewed the governmental apparatus as an integrated whole in itself and as a deliberate
force for the integration of society at large. A representative example of
their comprehensive approach to government was their contribution to
modern bureaucracy. They were responsible for merging their sundry
officials into a homogeneous bureaucratic corps, with the spirit and the
character that would dominate the public life of their respective countries
into the twentieth century. They did not create their bureaucracies any
more than they created any other of the essential administrative institutions
which they used, but in the case of the bureaucracy their distinctive attitude
took perceptible form in the shape of a definite, long-range set of practices
and standards.

Identifiable "Frederician" and "Josephinian" traditions of civil service
would mark Prussian and Austrian officials for generations to come with

the obedience, probity, industry, impersonality, professionalism, officiousness, punctilio, and hierarchical sense for which Prussian and Habsburg bureaucrats would become notorious. The merit system in recruitment and advancement and the measure of performance by regular inspection were practices bequeathed to modern civil service in general by these demanding and ubiquitous royal founders of the bureaucratic ethic. In Russia, the professional bureaucracy did not develop into its definitive mold during the eighteenth century, as in Prussia and Austria, but Catherine's modernization of the service nobility's conditions of state service from a general and unspecified military and administrative obligation to a definite monopoly of local government did seal the junction of bureaucracy and aristocracy that would persist as long as the empire. The enlightened absolutists' suspicious resort to their own spies, spot inspections, and direct interventions as checks on the work of their regular administration gave a personal cast to the governmental apparatus that did not outlive their energetic persons. But even such capricious operations left a lasting residue in the tendency toward arbitrary behavior that would accompany the mechanical functioning of nineteenth-century bureaucracies.

The second result of the enlightened monarchs' deliberately unitary approach was the codification of the law of their respective states. In this sphere, these rulers did innovate, for their codes were not simply in the administrative pattern of infusing a new spirit into old institutions but were themselves new institutions. Both Frederick and Joseph directed the compilation of the law codes that would serve as unifying bonds for the Prussian and the Habsburg monarchies through the nineteenth century. Both monarchs prefaced the preparation of the codes with judicial reforms that established a centralized hierarchy of courts, separated from the rest of the administration (rigorously in the Austrian case, imperfectly in the Prussian), and an autonomous corps of trained and salaried judges to run them.

The legal amalgamations themselves included codes of procedure (Prussian civil procedure in 1781 and Austrian criminal procedure in 1788) and the great syntheses of substantive law that were initiated by the enlightened monarchs and finished after their deaths. The *Allgemeines Landrecht* (Prussian Law Code), a composite of civil, criminal, and public (*i.e.* constitutional) law prepared by Frederick in conjunction with his chancellor J. H. von Carmer (1721–1801) and the reforming jurist Karl Suarez (1746–1798) was completed and published under the more conservative auspices of Frederick William II in 1794. The first section of the Austrian civil code was promulgated by Joseph in 1786 but completed in 1812 under Francis I. The Austrian penal code, however, was published in full during 1787.

The primary purpose of all these codifications was to homogenize, over a statewide range, the myriad of local ordinances, Germanic tradition, and

Roman law that perpetuated the particularity of the sundry provinces in each realm. To realize this purpose the laws had to be not only mutually adjusted but rooted in and measured by a constant principle which made each collection of laws something more than and different from the sum of its parts. This principle, as prominent throughout Frederick's and Joseph's actual codes as in Catherine's *Instruction* for such a code, was the proposition, authorized by the self-evidence of natural law, that the inherent right of all men to pursue their own welfare can only be secured by the equal benefit and protection of the laws dispensed by a common sovereign to them as "free citizens of the state." Since the laws guarantee men's fundamental rights and since the sovereign is the source of these laws, the community of men formed by common subjection to the law is the most essential of human associations and the good of this community becomes both the general measure of the different rights and duties of its citizens in respect to one another and the general sanction of the equal obedience owed the sovereign.

Thus the law codes that were projected in Russia (the project of 1767 did contribute to the code enacted in 1830) and enacted in Prussia and Austria under enlightened auspices helped to translate into reality the enlightened rulers' integral attitude toward their states. The codes' anomalous mixture of custom and innovation, of humanitarian reform (such as the abolition of torture and the reduction of crimes subject to the death penalty) and the retention of serfdom, of declarations of equality and affirmations of caste privileges was now rationalized by a single standard which required each right and each privilege to be assessed by the general interest of the entire community and the general interest of the community to be defined by the only citizen in a position to make such a definition—the enlightened sovereign.

RELIGION AND INTELLECTUAL LIFE

The enlightened monarchs' approach to administration and the law organized their subjects into a coherent political body. Their approach to religion and intellectual life supplied this body with a soul. Their policies in these fields were such as to absorb a whole set of spiritual values into their system of political controls. Thereby they elevated the function of the state from providing the common welfare as the external political condition of a higher suprapolitical community to providing the common welfare as a primary ethical value produced by a political community independent of and at least equivalent to any other human community.

Political sovereigns had, of course, long exercised authority over the hearts and minds of their subjects, but along with the rulers of religious and social communities and without making such authority an essential ingredient of the state. They either had trimmed the state's role in ecclesiastical

Frederick the Great playing the flute at his palace, Sans Souci.

and intellectual issues down to the mere provision of an external temporal
order or had at most claimed for this role the political community's instrumental contribution to the higher general order in which all human communities shared and for the domination of which they all competed. The
enlightened absolutists now added a new spiritual dimension to the state
itself because they claimed for the state a monopoly over human order, in
both its utilitarian and ideal aspects. The principle of liberty, on the other
hand, they now assigned to individuals outside of their relationship to the
community.

Thus the blend of repression and toleration that was the hallmark of the
enlightened absolutists' policies toward churches, schools, and publications
was not merely an *ad hoc* mixture of authoritarian disposition, religious
indifference, and practical sense for the limits of the politically possible,
that it superficially seemed to be. It was also—and in terms of its permanent effects, more significantly—the function of the complementary relationship posited by the enlightened sovereigns between the state on the
one side, now definitely conceived as the exclusive locus of the principle of
unity among men, and men's consciences and minds on the other, now
definitely conceived as the locus of liberty among men. For the enlightened absolutists, the institutions of religious and intellectual life combined both sides: churches, academies, books, all had their unitary aspects
that made them part of the expanded function of the state, and they all
also had their spontaneous aspects that made them both independent of
the state and needed by it. Authoritarian and liberal principles thus joined
in the religious, as in the intellectual, policies of the enlightened monarchs.

Religion and the Churches

In the field of religion, the enlightened autocrats combined the extension of state control over the established church with the grant of toleration to dissident churches—a combination which, in terms of the principle of religious liberty, abridged the autonomy of the one while it affirmed the autonomy of the other.

The most definite sponsor of both policies, moreover, was the same ruler—Joseph II. Indeed, "Josephinism"—a term that originally referred to his reform of the law and would later be used to epitomize the whole tradition of rational bureaucratic absolutism stemming from Joseph—was a label which contemporaries generally applied to his ecclesiastical policy alone, and as the blend of authoritarianism and liberalism in the usual connotation of "Josephinism" indicates, its subordination of the official Catholic Church and its toleration of religious minorities were deemed by Joseph and his aides to be equally contributory to the central authority of the state. Joseph's specific measures along both lines, undertaken simultaneously during the 1780's, were such as to reveal the precise nature of the common political criteria behind the apparently divergent policies.

On the one hand, Joseph conceded the right of private worship and full civil rights to Protestants, Greek Orthodox, and Jews (the concession to the latter was a particularly rare expression of liberality for the eighteenth century). On the other hand, in contrast to this relinquishment of state controls, he notably extended the control of the state over the established Catholic Church. He prohibited all communications between the Pope and the Austrian Catholic Church without the sovereign's approval. He increased, by political decree, the ecclesiastical powers of the bishops and required them to take an oath of allegiance to the sovereign. He founded new Austrian bishoprics to replace the older politically uncontrollable jurisdictions of German bishops in Austria. He abolished pious lay brotherhoods and contemplative monastic orders, and transferred their properties to a "religious fund" administered by public authority for socially useful ecclesiastical purposes. He subordinated the other—teaching and charitable—orders to the local bishops. He prohibited religious processions and pilgrimages. He regulated Church ritual, sermons, and adornments, and ordered the supervision of clerics by bureaucrats to ensure obedience to the regulations. He assigned clerical education to "general seminaries" which would be established by the government and operated under the direction of governmental appointees to train priests to be "spiritual officials of the state." He validated civil marriage.

What unified these liberal and authoritarian measures into a coherent policy were the two political functions both kinds of measures shared. Both had the fiscal function of increasing taxable population and production, and both had the governmental function of attributing to the head of the state the determination of the respective rights of church and state.

Monks leaving
their monasteries
after Joseph II's
decree of 1781.

The Josephinians themselves propounded the practical connection in the government's joint authority to determine the rights and the limits of ecclesiastical activity: "Toleration helps to populate lands and make them rich; fanaticism degenerates into persecution and will depopulate and impoverish them."

But powerful as these political criteria were in the formulation of Joseph's ecclesiastical policy, they were not the distinctive elements in it. The assertion of the state's authority over the Austrian Catholic Church against the papacy had been persistent Habsburg policy since the Thirty Years' War, and under Maria Theresa, orthodox by religious disposition and intolerant by religious principle as she was, this policy had been expanded in practice to include creeping encroachments upon Catholic clerical preserves and tacit concessions to industrious religious minorities. During her regime, indeed, advocates of Jansenism—in its eighteenth-century German version of Febronianism, a doctrine rooted in the published argument of "Justinus Febronius" (pseudonym of Johann von Hontheim, 1701–1790), for the espiscopal constitution of the Catholic Church, the supremacy of general councils over the papacy, and the solidarity of national councils and temporal princes against papal domination—and of the Enlightenment had already collaborated tactically to further the anti-papalism, the anti-Jesuitism, and the ban on ecclesiastical extravagances that were immediate aims common to both kinds of advocacy. What was distinctive to Joseph's regime was the fusion of the two movements into an integral civic faith that joined the Jansenist belief in the autonomous, inner, religious springs of the moral impulse with the enlightened belief in the secular, rational, social organization of moral action. The result was a theistic political rationalism that sponsored a fundamentally new position on the state and its relations with religion. It meant the attribution to the state, in principle as well as in practice, of the final responsibility for men's supreme ethical task in this world—the realization of their common humanity, of their essential unity as brothers under God. In frank deference to the religious dimension of this new political function, the Josephinians called religion "a political matter" (*Politicum*), and Joseph described his own position to be "fanaticism for the state."

But of equal importance with this shift of the responsibility for the moral ordering of mankind from the old partnership of state and church to the exclusive sovereignty of the state was the state's new relationship to the church. For the Josephinian, not only religion as such but "theoretical religious doctrines" and "external rites"—*i.e.*, churches—were "indispensable" to the state because they supplied to social morality an essential spiritual ingredient that the state could indeed direct but not supply by itself. This function of the churches created a twofold relationship with the state. On the one hand, the state had to regulate and reform the churches to ensure the indispensable contribution of religion to the moral unity of the community for which the state was primarily responsible. Hence the Josephinians retained the commitment to an established Catholic Church, but on the novel ground that the overlay of church and state furnished the most appropriate arrangement for channeling the religious impulse into the moral service of the state.

But the religious impulse itself, on the other hand, was viewed by the Josephinians as a force independent of the state, and their insistence that the Catholic Church be "purified" was impelled not only by the idea of reorganizing it into a proper political instrument but also by the ideal of reforming it into a religious instrument of authentic piety. Joseph himself was a convinced Catholic. Indeed, his decree on toleration excluded deists, and a contemporary Swiss observer remarked in general on "the bigotry which is rooted deep in his soul." Joseph insisted that "religion must be strengthened not only by inspirations of the heart but also by outer ceremonies," and he limited the activities of the anticlerical Masonic lodges. His piety combined the urge to good moral works commanded by the Author of humanity with the rational forms of worship appropriate to stimulate them. Reason in the religious service consisted for him in a simple ritual which excluded the appeal to miracle, terror, sentiment, and unquestioning faith and included effective exhortations to good deeds.

The appropriateness of such a moral, social, reasonable, and practical piety to the collective service purposes of the state seems obvious enough. Actually, however, Joseph's piety pointed in two very different directions: if it pointed toward the state by virtue of its forms and its effects, it pointed toward the individual by virtue of its principles and its origins. He insisted that both the feeling for humanity and the rational knowledge of human rights were originally implanted by God through nature in all men. This individual ordination, for Joseph, was the religious source of the authority and the force behind the moral community of man organized by the churches and directed by the state. Hence he admonished the Protestant ministers of Vienna that "everyone should be allowed to pray and to sing in his own way," and he accompanied this admonition both with the additional prescription of definite rites and doctrines to prevent "Christianity from degenerating into a rational paganism" and with his covert hope that the political reform of Catholic rite and doctrine toward primitive Christian simplicity would bring a mass conversion of Protestants to a single official ecclesiastical organization. For Josephinians, this was a consistent position because it reflected their belief that the individual, the church, and the state were equally indispensable to the ideal of social service and unequally disposed to the realization of that ideal. Only personal piety could supply the incentive to social service; only the church could organize the pious intentions of individuals into the civic loyalties and the foundations for the relief of the poor and the handicapped that could make a reality of social service; and only the state could keep the church to this, its primary function. Through their political control of churches whose confessional identities they acknowledged the Josephinians thus extended the power of the state over the acts of individual wills that were themselves beyond the power of the state.

Neither for Frederick nor for Catherine was church policy as central a consideration as it was for Joseph. The combination of controls and toleration which they shared with him was much more exclusively external and circumstantial in character. Frederick's chief aim in the regulation of the Lutheran church was to prevent any excess of dogmatism and fanaticism from endangering the civil peace, and prominent among the incentives of his broad-gauged toleration policy were the old Hohenzollern motives of attracting able-bodied and able-minded immigrants and of keeping peace among the minorities at home while stirring turmoil within the majorities abroad. Thus he even granted asylum—and a base of operations—to the much maligned Jesuits after their expulsion from Portugal, France, and the Habsburg dominions led to the abolition of the order (1773) under duress by Pope Clement XIV (1769–1774).

Catherine's Orthodox policy featured most notably the definitive nationalization of all the properties of the Russian Orthodox Church and the conversion of its clergy into officials paid by the state. For the rest, she remained careful to recommend external observance of Orthodox rites and to respect Orthodox sensibilities, as befit the political motives of her nominal conversion to Russian Orthodoxy. Like Frederick, she practiced *de facto* toleration, justified it by reference to the civil peace of a varied population, maliciously extended it to the Jesuits, and suspiciously abridged it for the Jews.

But if Frederick's and Catherine's indifference to denominational religion represents an enlightened approach quite distinct from Joseph's desire to reform it, the divergence was overshadowed by what was common in the relations established by all three monarchs between their states and religion in general. All shared the view of churches as political institutions specializing in the adaptation of social ethics to the ignorance, superstition, and simplicity of the mass of their subjects. All shared too the conviction that authentic religious belief resided in individuals. Thus all three attempted to legislate religious toleration as an individual right, and in the case of Frederick's Prussian Law Code the belief in the individual basis of piety inspired an unqualified declaration of religious liberty: "Every inhabitant of the state must be granted complete freedom of conscience and religion."

The shared attitudes toward church and religion effected a common contribution by enlightened absolutism to the public consciousness of what a "state" was; the attitudes that were not shared revealed the alternative policies which states could adopt toward the social organizations and the individuals within them. By regarding the churches as extensions of the state, the enlightened rulers agreed in appropriating for the state the socialized organization of individual religious beliefs that were themselves beyond the reach of the state. Religion thus became the midwife of a new politics that not only *defined* what belonged to the state *in contrast to* what did not but also *justified* what belonged to the state *in terms of* what did not. Politics was now *defined*, not as one kind of human activity among others, but as the collective and orderly dimension of all human activities in contrast to the individual and libertarian dimension of all human activities that epitomized the extrapolitical in man. Politics was now *justified* by the complementary relations that the enlightened rulers posited between the collectivity of the politics and the individuality of the religion. They posited this affirmative connection between opposites in one or both of two versions. The deistic Frederick directed the state's power especially to the defense of individual conscience against the oppression of religion's social organizations—that is, churches; the Catholic Joseph directed the state's power especially to making individual conscience practically effective in the social organizations—that is, churches—that were the state's only connections with conscience. In either case, religion contributed to the development of a politics that could regiment for the practical purposes of the community the same human activity that it held sacrosanct as the ultimate source of its individual members' moral capacity for community.

Intellectual Life

The state's relations with secular thought under enlightened absolutism exhibited the same apparent incongruity and the same kind of underlying pattern as its relations with religion. Just as the apparent contrast between the political control over churches and the acknowledgment of free conscience reflected a division of function between the community's and the individual's role in effecting the moral good of humanity, just so the political control of institutionalized education and the acknowledgment of intellectual freedom should be considered as complementary functions of state and individual in a coherent approach by the enlightened rulers to the secular culture of European society.

For all their sporadic flurries of educational activity, the effective policies of the enlightened rulers in this field, as in the field of administration, remained within the framework set up by their absolutist predecessors and contributed rather a conscious spirit than viable institutions to it. The parallel between educational and administrative policies was not fortuitous, since the training of the citizenry, in Joseph II's terms, "to become fit for service to the state" was precisely the goal of education for the enlightened sovereigns, and consequently the features which they stressed in the scholastic arrangements which they found and extended were similar to what they favored in administration generally: they stressed what was authoritarian, utilitarian, and elitist. Joseph infused the Austrian school system particularly with the first two of these qualities. He worked with the model educational pyramid, ranging from compulsory elementary schools to the universities, which the Habsburg bureaucracy had organized under his co-regent, Maria Theresa, in the General School Ordinance of 1774, and was primarily responsible for the rigid regulation of books, courses, and teachers aimed at the elimination of individual discretion and at the production of civil servants. Frederick stressed the elitist principle in education because he believed that only the aristocracy was socially and morally capable of direct service to the state. Hence he was disinterested in the education of other groups, which he thought should be designed only to keep them in their economic and social stations; he focused his energies on the founding of academies for the sons of his nobility and neglected the execution of the ordinance worked out by Johann Hecker (1707–1768), his own school planner, to put enforcement and control by the state behind the general elementary-school system which had been initiated by Fredericks' unenlightened father, Frederick William I.

Only Catherine seemed to transcend the usual limits of absolutist scholastic policy and approach the exalted aims which the *philosophes* cherished for the education of humanity. Proclaiming the goal of education to be the production of a "new breed" of Russian, transformed not only as a citizen but as an "entire man," Catherine enacted resounding general decrees in 1764 and again in 1786. They were designed not only to rejuvenate the decayed and spotty system of primary schools which had been instituted by Peter the Great but to expand it into an unbroken national network of general education in both technical and humanistic curricula. But in fact, neither of these far-reaching measures was seriously applied, partly because of Catherine's fickleness in matters not directly affecting her own power, but mostly because of the limits imposed by administrative necessity and social privilege on enlightened absolutism. Hence her most effective activities in the field of education were the founding of engineering schools, the expansion of aristocratic Cadet training, and the concession of the nobles' right to organize their own schools—activities that conformed to the technical and elitist tendencies both of Russian education since Peter the Great and of contemporary enlightened absolutism elsewhere.

But the state-oriented educational policy of the enlightened monarchs should be viewed in conjunction with the socially oriented cultural policy which balanced it, for only together do they give an undistorted picture of enlightened absolutism's characteristic approach to intellectual life.

Certainly the enlightened rulers' political approach to culture shared a common authoritarian dimension with their approach to education. In part their cultural policy too was defined by the arbitrary modes of their government and by the ever-present criterion of clear and present political danger to authority. Examples of these limits were prominent enough, indeed, to have left the dominant impression that in the field of culture, as in education, religion, and constitutional rights, absolutism overbalanced enlightenment for the rulers in which they were combined. Frederick's misanthrophy led him to conclude in principle that "enlightenment . . . is a destructive firebrand for the masses" and to censor in fact the private communications and the publications of ordinary citizens and uncelebrated pamphleteers when they engaged in political criticism. Joseph was notorious for his utilitarian deprecation of the pure arts and sciences in favor of applied knowledge. To this philistine quality he added the studied policy, between 1785 and his death in 1790, of assigning censorship to the secret police and of intensifying the suppression of "books . . . which are calculated to undermine the principles of all religion, morality, and social order." His expulsion of the radical publisher Georg Wucherer, and the destruction of his stock of books in 1789 without due process of law, was only the most sensational instance of Joseph's increasing concern to suppress criticism and control public opinion. Catherine's restrictions on intellectual freedom were the fiercest of all. When she tried her hand at journalism, during the late 1760's, in the vainglorious enterprise of raising the level of Russian culture all by herself, she first pressured the humanitarian Nikolai Novikov (1744–1818) into suspending his journal because he dared to polemicize against her, and later, in 1792, she condemned him without trial to a fifteen-year prison term because he continued to criticize the government for its failure to help the needy. In her *Instruction* to the Legislative Commission of 1767 she recommended the abatement but not the abolition of censorship, and in 1773 she refused Diderot's request to permit an uncensored Russian edition of the *Encyclopedia*. Her most celebrated suppression, finally, was her prosecution in 1790 of Alexander Radishchev (1749–1802). A disciple of the French Enlightenment in its late phase of radical criticism, Radishchev was tried for his "diffusion of dangerous reasoning" in his famous *Journey from St. Petersburg to Moscow*, a trenchant and circumstantial indictment of Russian conditions.

controversial discussion.

ЖИВОПИСЕЦЪ

ЕЖЕНЕДѢЛЬНОЕ

НА

1772 ГОДЪ

СОЧИНЕНІЕ.

ВЪ САНКТПЕТЕРБУРГѢ.

Title page of a 1772 issue of the satirical journal *The Painter*, edited by Nikolai Novikov. *Catherine, at one stage a contributor, subsequently suspended the journal and jailed its editor.*

But important as all these prominent political limits on cultural free-dom were, they are quite misleading if they are not seen to be pre-cisely that—political limits on a cultural activity for which the mon-archs' own liberal policy was itself largely responsible. Frederick the Great distinguished sharply between the intellectual elite and the literate general public, recognizing an unprecedented freedom for the former as the pro-ducers of culture and persisting in the traditional controls over the latter as the politicizers of culture. Thus, immediately upon his accession in 1740 Frederick encouraged the growth of a periodical press, exempting its non-political organs from censorship on the ground that "if journals are to be interesting they should not be restricted." He proceeded, analogously, to reorganize the old Berlin Academy of Science into a broad-gauged Acad-emy of Science and Literature, to people it with free spirits from all over Europe under the lead of French *philosophes,* to load the Prussian univer-sities with representatives of the natural-law school of philosophy and juris-prudence, and to affirm the freedom of both the Academy and the univer-sities from censorship. Faithful to Frederick's notions of intellectual hierar-chy, the universities exercised a self-censorship over their members while the members of the Academy were subject to no censorship at all.

The same basic distinction was embodied in the Prussian Law Code that was drawn up under Frederick's inspiration: it provided, on the one hand, for the prosecution of public critics of state and church and of published authors of ideas endangering civil peace, and on the other, for the categorical distinction between external acts which could be punished and internal convictions which could not. Whether a published idea was an act or a conviction depended, apparently, on its position in the cultural scale between intellectual creation and social consumption. The failure of the Code to give fuller recognition to freedom of expression manifests the wary response of the aging Frederick to the radicalization of the Enlightenment whose dissemination he had himself sponsored.

For Joseph and Catherine too, their later reactions to radical opinions were built upon an earlier commitment to a liberalized regime of the press. In 1781, shortly after his accession, Joseph passed a law which went far toward the creation of a free press: it permitted public criticism, including criticism of the sovereign himself, and forbade only those publications that attacked public morals or religion as such. The result was a veritable flood of pamphlet literature, most of it even more rationalist, more freethinking, and more anticlerical than the government's policy. It was, indeed, the critical middle-class public opinion that the government's own liberality had spawned which triggered, in conjunction with a bloody Transylvanian peasants' uprising, Joseph's accelerating censorship and clericalism after 1785.

The young Catherine, similarly, could declaim that "nothing can bring me to fear a cultivated people," and despite her failure to amend the institution of censorship, she transformed its spirit to give Russia both an atmosphere and the materials of intellectual freedom, the like of which had never before been experienced in that nation. Catherine's concern in the 1760's was rather for the conditions of cultural creation than for the interests of political order. We must remember, she wrote, "the danger of debasing the human mind by restraint and oppression which can produce nothing but ignorance, must cramp and depress the rising efforts of genius, and must destroy the very will to write." The result of this attitude, undoubtedly attributable at least in part to Catherine's own pretensions as a writer, became apparent in the astonishing leap in the sheer quantity of published material. Whereas the decade before Catherine's accession had seen an average annual publication of a mere 23 books, the figure rose almost fivefold in the decade from 1761 to 1770, and finally reached an annual high of 366 in 1790 before Catherine's repression reversed the trend. Like Frederick, finally, Catherine revamped her capital city's Academy of Sciences to include literature and thus established an institutional link between the educational culture immediately useful to the state and the pure cultural activity external to the state but needed by it to feed its educational system.

Thus the relationship which the enlightened monarchs set up between state education and free culture paralleled their subscription to a system of state churches founded on freedom of individual conscience. The overlay confirms both the principled distinction they made between men's social activity that was subject to the state and the individual springs of this activity that were not and the complementary connection between them. For if the monarchs' exclusion of religious belief from political control could be accounted to indifference, their analogous exclusion of the intellect they cherished was certainly a matter of principle. The result of the enlightened absolutists' spiritual policies—ecclesiastical and educational, religious and cultural—was to give the state a categorical definition as the organized monopoly of collective authority and collective power and to give it a positive function in the realization of the individualized freedom that would henceforth be recognized as the fundamental principle of human activity beyond politics.

SOCIAL POLICY

Equipped with the enlightened absolutists' operational ideas of what the state was and of its relations with what it was not, we now possess the assumptions wherewith to simplify and to understand their social policy, that most controversial and ambiguous aspect of their regimes, which is almost incomprehensible without these assumptions. There was an apparent ambivalence in their treatment both of the agrarians—that is, of the intertwined claims of the landed aristocrats and the peasantry—and the burghers which requires an explanation in the context of their total approach to government and society if the place of enlightened absolutism in Western history is to be understood.

Lords and Peasants

The enlightened approach to the agrarian problem is particularly revealing because in the overwhelmingly agrarian society of central and eastern Europe lord-peasant relations were the primary social issues and because the ambiguities of policy in this field were equally visible on two different levels of enlightened absolutism. Not only were there the crucial discrepancies between the rulers whereby Joseph took measures to liberate the peasants, Catherine took measures to intensify their serfdom, and Frederick left their status virtually unchanged, but there were identifiable countercurrents within each ruler's policies.

The main thrust of Joseph's social policies was undoubtedly in the anti-aristocratic and pro-peasant legislation which ultimately earned him rebellion by the notables and veneration by the rural masses. In a whole series of decrees, starting with the famous November patent of 1781 and continuing throughout the decade of his exclusive rule, Joseph prosecuted what seemed to contemporaries a veritable agrarian revolution and what undoubtedly amounted to the most liberal peasant program of any regime before the French Revolution.

For the Habsburg dominions as a whole, the legislation emancipated peasants from the condition of "hereditary subjection"—that is, bondage to the soil—that was the residue of serfdom in the eighteenth century. This condition imposed two kinds of obligations upon the peasants, obligations which were, of course, the obverse of the manorial lords' legal rights. The first kind comprised the personal duties owed by the peasant to the lord as part of the obligations stemming from the former's attachment to the soil. They were particularly galling because they were reminiscent of the direct personal bondage of peasant to lord, the more oppressive form of serfdom which was no longer valid in the legal practice of eighteenth-century central Europe. Joseph simply abolished the most pressing of these personal liabilities that persisted in the servile property relationship: the peasant's obligation not to marry, leave his holding, or enter a vocation without the permission of his lord, and the peasant's legal incapacity to lodge complaints with the public authorities or bring suit in the state courts against his lord. The second kind of reciprocal peasant obligations and seigneurial privileges comprised the real dues stemming from the lord's blend of public and private rights in the land held by the peasants. Joseph prescribed renegotiation by lords and peasants under state supervision for some of these rights, such as the lord's milling and brewing monopolies; imposed limitations on others, such as the lord's hunting rights on the land (rights which, however, remained a seigneurial monopoly); and most important, converted the historical accumulation of assorted traditional, capricious, and servile dues on peasant tenures—customary rents and fees payable in varying dimensions and in both money and kind, and above all the hated compulsory labor services for the lord—into a single money rent amounting to 30 per cent of the peasant's gross income, divided between the state and the lord on the ratio of about 2 to 3.

The effect of the reform was to make the peasants affected by it free citizens and hereditary leaseholders, with rights to protection under the law, to freedom of movement and occupation, and to being charged a fixed and reasonable rent for the land they worked. The one obvious right that was denied them in this general legislation—the property right in the land that would make them its owners with free disposition over it—seemed promised for the future. On all demesnes immediately subject to the sovereign—dynastic, secularized, and municipal—the abolition of compulsory labor services without compensation and the easy terms granted for the peasants' full ownership of their tenures were both designed and taken by contemporaries to set up a model for the general legislation of the future.

Joseph's tax program, moreover—for him, as in general for the eighteenth century, the barometer of monarchies' social policy—anticipated a social regime of legally uniform equal property ownership on the land. Utilizing as his bases the population censuses initiated during his mother's reign for purposes of military conscription, Joseph initiated the compilation of a complete land register of his dominions in 1785, and in 1789 he fixed the rate of 12-2/9 per cent as a uniform land tax, payable by lords as well as commoners.

And yet Joseph was not nearly so univocally egalitarian as his resentful aristocracy thought, or, indeed, as the dominant tendency of his measures does suggest. For it was this same Joseph who in 1777, shortly before his initiation of his own peasant reforms (in 1781) opposed a similar project of his mother's for Bohemia alone. He described it, in terms that would fit his own legislation at least as well, as an abolition of serfdom and an "arbitrary" fixing of customary peasant dues and payments that were "without the slightest consideration for the lord" and would be the nobility's ruination. The radical difference between the two stages of his policy on land reform does not seem attributable to the obvious tactical shift from the attitude of a critical coregent to that of a glory-seeking exclusive sovereign, for the attitude behind his earlier reservations on peasant reform continued to play a role in his later legislation as well, limiting its scope and its effect.

First, the reforms did not apply at all to the "dominical" peasants—that is, to peasants with terminable tenures on the lord's own demesne—or even to the poorer of the peasants with their own hereditary tenures ("rustical" peasants). Second, the reforms left intact the lord's crucial authority to exercise patrimonial jurisdiction, which gave him local police and judicial powers over the peasantry and perpetuated the public basis of his privileges. Thus Joseph's agrarian policy limited the lord's exercise of his monopolies—above all, the vexatious hunting rights across land held by peasants—but did not abrogate them in principle precisely because they stemmed from original perquisites of the aristocracy's governmental functions, and these functions were still visible in the form of its patrimonial jurisdiction.

In Prussia and Russia, the ambiguities of agrarian policy were at least as striking as in Austria, but for Frederick and Catherine the social proportions were the reverse of Joseph's: the main tendency of their measures sustained or even, as in Catherine's case, intensified the regime of aristocratic privilege and peasant bondage, while they announced liberal principles that seemed to vitiate this regime and proposed ameliorations that would put limits upon it. The rift between Frederick's principles and his practice appeared, on the surface at least, to be categorical. Not only did his law code promulgate, as a fundamental principle of the law, the equal "natural rights of the individual" to exercise his "natural freedom to seek his own good" but Frederick himself explicitly condemned the institution of serfdom for the subservience to his lord forced upon the peasant by his bondage to the soil. But the net effect of what Frederick actually did in this field was to perpetuate the existing servile relations between peasants and lords in his Prussian dominions, and the reforms that he initiated to

A Russian peasants' school in the time of Catherine the Great.

limit the exploitation of the former by the latter tended rather to make the peasants' bonds more secure than to increase their freedom in line with his liberal principles. He attempted no general emancipation of the peasants either from their attachment to the soil or from their dues to the lords. For the country as a whole he succeeded only in preventing the lords from appropriating peasants' holdings, and even in his own royal demesne he did not go beyond assuring the peasants security of tenure on the hereditary holdings to which they remained bound by law, and attempting—with only modest success—some restrictions on the most onerous of his own peasants' compulsory labor services. But even these palliatives were more than offset by Frederick's sponsorship of cooperative credit associations, trading companies, and entailed estates for the benefit of the landed aristocracy, since these institutions encouraged the kind of large-scale agriculture which in eastern Europe extended the direct exploitation of peasant labor by the estate owners.

Catherine stood at the pro-aristocratic extreme of monarchical social policy. Although the debate still rages about the effect of this policy on the Russian aristocracy's relations with the government—that is, whether Catherine's concessions were silken bonds subjecting the aristocracy more tightly to government or real privileges purchasing the voluntary cooperation of the aristocracy with government—there is no doubt about the effect of the policy in expanding the already considerable powers of the aristocracy over the Russian peasantry. This policy was, moreover, more deeply rooted in Catherine than was conceded by the old interpretation which attributed it to her later years and to her fearful experience of the nobles' opposition to her presumed liberalism in her early years. Actually,

alleviate without curing why Catherine?

Catherine's declaration of policy made her pro-aristocratic position clear from the start. Immediately after her accession, in July, 1762, a decree declared her general policy to be her "resolution to preserve inviolate the estates and possessions of the landlords and to maintain the peasants in their dutiful obedience to them." She voluntarily submitted the draft of her *Instruction* of 1767 to an informal committee of noblemen and accepted their thorough emasculation of its proposals for agrarian reform. Even this draft, moreover, did not go beyond advocating "restrictions on the abuses and dangers of serfdom"; it did not question the institution itself. Indeed, she explicitly warned that "a great many serfs should not be liberated at once by a general law" and she gave, as a prominent ground of the modest amelioration of peasant conditions that she did advocate, the merely prudential need "to remove the causes for the serfs' rebelliousness against their lords."

In view of these assertions, it is hardly surprising to find that Catherine's government enacted concrete measures strengthening the hand of the aristocracy over the peasantry from the very morrow of her accession and continued to make such enactments throughout her long reign. She converted large tracts of the public domain into the property of the nobility and thereby condemned almost a million state peasants, with their comparatively larger personal freedom and lesser obligations, to the more onerous private status of serfs—first by gift to the conspirators who enthroned her and then by a series of grants to her favorites. She bound the free peasants of Little Russia (the recently conquered region in the west and southwest) to the lord whose lands they inhabited, thereby recognizing the illegal expropriations of peasant land by the nobility and establishing the actual conditions of serfdom on it, although, characteristically and uncomfortably, she avoided calling it by that name.

For Russia as a whole, moreover, the conditions of serfdom were not only extended but intensified by governmental decrees. For the most part, such measures confirmed aristocratic privileges which had been conferred by earlier legislation, or they affirmed in law encroachments upon peasant rights which the nobility had already accomplished in practice. But these apparently formal enactments had a massive social effect, for they meant the withdrawal of state control over the aristocracy's legal exercise of its social power and the abandonment of state guardianship over the remnants of serfs' rights. Thus one set of decrees acknowledged the lord's authority to sentence serfs to exile or to military service at his own discretion, not only for felonies, as formerly, but for attempted flight from the land and for insubordination, and capped this alienation of public power over agrarian relations by prohibiting petitions by the serfs to the government against the practices of the lords.

Another set of decrees gave the force of law to the aristocratic monopolies that excluded any alternatives to the servile relations between lord and peasant. Only nobles could own land. Only nobles could own serfs. Only nobles could employ serfs in factories. Only nobles could engage in the lucrative production of alcoholic beverages. Only nobles could authorize serfs to contract a loan, a lease, or outside employment. Only nobles could elect officials to the district administrations. Still another set of decrees, finally, encouraged the nobles, with their specially advantaged position, to compete favorably in activities where they did not have a monopoly. As epitomized in the decree of 1775 on provincial and district government and in the Charter of the Nobility of 1785, such preferences for the nobles included: the right to dominant posts in both town governments and peasant courts; full personal rights, based on freedom from service to the state (save by special call of the sovereign on occasions of urgent political necessity) and the right to corporate organizations as a self-administering social class; full rights of ownership and disposition over property including the purchase, sale, and entail of land, the establishment of industries on their lands, the ownership of and disposition over all timber on their lands and of the minerals beneath them, and the ownership of and disposition over habitable and industrial property in the towns; finally, the right to engage in both wholesale and export trades. Thus the nobility was authorized to participate in the activities authorized to other classes, and its participation was legally favored in activities from which the other classes were barred and the government self-excluded.

But despite the predominantly elitist tendency of Catherine's policy—she once declared that "I am an aristocrat by profession"—it had its counterpoint. Even if the pro-peasant paragraphs of her *Instruction* of 1767 are discounted for the rhetoric designed to draw the praise of the *philosophes* and for the careful preservation of serfdom as an institution, there remains a steady undercurrent of agrarian reform in Catherine's statements of policy. Her draft of the *Instruction* asserted the general principle that every citizen has a right to the equal protection of the laws and every man to food and clothing. This statement may not have been designed for literal application to the Russian peasantry, but a set of more specific declarations in the draft was so designed. Her recommendations that lords be required to moderate their dues, that serfs be assured by law of their right to their own property, and that serfs be encouraged to buy their own freedom were based on one genuinely held practical principle. "Agriculture cannot flourish," she wrote, "where the peasant or the agricultural laborer has nothing to call his own. Every man cares more for what belongs to himself than for what belongs to somebody else, and he does not care at all for what can be taken from him."

In this same category of unrealized declarations were Catherine's two projects for state peasants that were never put into execution. In 1765 she drew up a plan providing for the freedom of those peasants who would settle on crown lands, but withdrew it when it met ministerial opposition.

She was later reported to have drafted a proposed law that would have emancipated all serfs' children born after 1785. Although this draft remains undiscovered and the report unconfirmed, the general intent is supported by her project, which was definitely drawn up but never published or effected, of a charter for the state peasantry to accompany the charters of 1785 for the nobility and for the towns. In this draft charter Catherine would have granted full personal freedom and property rights to all crown peasants, and as if to prove the authenticity of her frustrated agrarian liberalism, these conditions were actually ordered into effect during 1787 for Ekaterinoslav, the new province that Catherine named after herself.

Catherine's actual record of peasant reform lagged far behind her professions of it in principle. Still, her attention to the issue on the operational as well as the planning level is attested by her boast of having issued more than a hundred decrees "for the relief of the people." Even if historians do agree that the effect of such measures was minimal in contrast with the massive impact of her pro-aristocratic policy, enough official action was taken to lend some credence at least to her abstract claims of concern for the peasantry. Decrees of a liberal cast forbade the reenserfment of freed peasants and the public auction of serfs without land, and others cited humanitarian grounds for ordering lords to feed their peasants when harvests failed, forbidding lords to liberate old serfs (and therewith abandon the seigneurial responsibility for them), and instructing officials to watch for egregious maltreatment of serfs by lords.

But more important than any of these kinds of concern for the peasant was Catherine's admission of the peasantry, free and serf alike, into the economic rights of free individual enterprise. This admission consisted not only in the government's tacit toleration of the practice by which serfs conducted their own businesses under the cover of their lords' name, but also in the explicit governmental acknowledgment in all peasants of the right to pursue both wholesale and retail trade in the countryside and both handicraft and factory production in the countryside and the towns alike. This acknowledgment, moreover, embodied though it usually was in specific decrees on particular commodities, was capped by the decree of 1775 which included serfs in the enactment of the general principle of free industrial enterprise—that "nobody from anywhere be hindered from setting up mills of any kind and from making in them manufactures of any kind without permit or order."

The Urban Sector

The economic policies of the enlightened monarchs have an ambiguity that parallels the tensions in their social attitude toward the rural classes, and because their economic ambiguity is more readily comprehensible than their social equivocations it can be used to explain them. Each and every enlightened ruler was committed simultaneously to a regime of state economic controls and the principle of individual economic liberty. In the field of commerce, they combined prohibitive protective tariffs with domestic free trade. Joseph of Austria was especially noteworthy both for the height of his duties on foreign imports and for his removal of trading restrictions within an expanded Austro-Bohemian domestic market.

In the field of industry, the combination of policies was even more startling. On the one hand, armies of inspectors continued to regulate the production and control the quality of industrial goods, governments continued to subsidize industries and tempt foreign entrepreneurs, and rulers persisted in skimming heavy excise taxes from the returns of the industries they had encouraged—all in good old mercantilist style. On the other hand, however, the industrial policies of both Joseph and Catherine, as well as of lesser monarchical lights like Charles Frederick of Baden and Joseph's brother, Leopold of Tuscany, also showed visible traces of the Physiocratic *laissez-faire* literature they imbibed. They rejected the old mercantilist predilection for either exercising or conferring industrial monopolies; Joseph went so far as to emasculate the coercive power of the Austrian guilds on the principle that "every man should be permitted to earn his bread in the way that seems best to him." Catherine, whose problem was simplified by the virtual absence of guilds in Russia, needed only to issue the antimonopolistic decree of 1767 prescribing that "no trade and handicraft by which town inhabitants can make themselves an honest living . . . be forbidden."

This combination of interventionist and liberal economic policies was held together by two assumptions which made these policies seem consistent to the enlightened rulers and their like-minded officials. First, they believed that economic growth increased political power and that government therefore had to stimulate and regulate all economic activities. In Austrian terms, ". . . the promotion of the welfare and prosperity of the community . . . is the most important object of political office." Second, the only source of the economic growth which the government had to promote was the free activity of individuals. In Joseph's words, ". . . nothing is more necessary than liberty for commerce and industry." For the enlightened sovereigns, in short, the wealth they needed had to have its source in the free activities of individuals that lay necessarily beyond the competence of the state, but the state could and should control the conditions of production and direct the allocation of resources for the financial benefit, the civil order, and the moral unity of the collective society.

The mutual congruity of these apparently opposite policies in the minds of the enlightened monarchs found its clearest expression in their attitude toward the burghers who were engaged in trade and manufacturing. Frederick complained bitterly precisely because of their lack of entrepreneurial initiative, while Catherine went beyond the familiar employment of subsi-

dies, tax rebates, and trade treaties to promote specific economic performance. She recommended governmental controls that would enforce the
conditions of economic freedom upon a stagnant burgher class—and she
saw no incongruity in such a policy for such a purpose. In her *Instruction*
for the Legislative Commission of 1767 she proclaimed the necessity for
Russia of a large and active economic bourgeoisie, and she proceeded to
entice the Russian burghers to participate in setting the legal conditions
for their own growth by grossly overrepresenting them in the Legislative
Commission. With membership in the Commission based on elections by
estate, the Russian towns were granted three-eighths of the seats—more
than any other social group, including the aristocracy—at a time when
Russia's urban population amounted only to about one twenty-fifth of
the total. To assist their cohesion, moreover, the townsmen were not
divided into subgroups, with the result that almost 200 of their 208 deputies were merchants. The burghers, however, did not rise to the opportunity which the Empress thus provided: not only did their lethargy and obse-
quiousness permit the aristocracy to dominate the proceedings of the
Commission but their own claims were limited to the restoration of their
old narrow municipal monopolies of trade and industry and to the appropriation of such aristocratic privileges as sword bearing and serf employment.

It was at least in part because the burghers thus proved ineffective both
at counterbalancing the power of the aristocracy and at developing the
conditions for their own free enterprise that Catherine abruptly adjourned
the Commission *sine die* in 1767. For the next two decades she applied
governmental goads of a purely economic kind in the effort to galvanize
the burghers into taking the initiative, catering to their old caste monopoly
of trading within the towns but otherwise exposing them to the challenges
of free commercial and industrial enterprise by courtesy of governmental
decree and of expanded foreign markets by courtesy of governmental
treaty.

In this context of Catherine's protracted effort to provoke free initiative
by state fiat, her legislation of 1785, which included a charter for the town
burghers as well as the famous Charter of the Nobility and the abortive
charter for the state peasants, can be seen as her final attempt to develop
the traditional social privileges and duties of the separate Russian castes
into generalized economic rights and governmental functions.

Like the others, the town charter sought to organize its social object—in
this instance the burghers—into a self-administering corporation which
minimized the traditional internal rankings within the estate and
established the elective institutions designed both to guard the economic
liberties of its individual members and to represent the estate's share in
the state. Where the nobles were legally recognized as provincial corporations, the burghers were legally recognized as municipal corporations.

Where the nobles were organized into provincial and district assemblies under elected marshals who together administered the common will within the corps of nobility and represented it to the provincial and district governments, the burghers were organized under elected town councils and mayors who together were to run the towns and represent their interests to the financial and police officials of the provincial and district governments. Where the nobles' charter distinguished six different sources of noble status (Imperial appointment, military and civil service, ancient birth, and so on) but prescribed the equality of all nobles in the enjoyment of the aristocracy's freedom from service and other civil and economic rights, the town charter ranked the burghers in six classes but prescribed their equal participation in the election of the municipal authorities and the district burgher courts and in the executive board nominated by the town council. Where the distinction between the service aristocracy and the aristocracy by birth was recognized in the nobles' charter by granting political rights in the provincial noble assemblies—that is, both the right to vote in them and the right to be elected to corporate or public office by them—only to aristocrats with civil or commissioned military service, the distinction of merchants from the rest of the burghers was recognized in the town charter by the granting of civil rights—that is, freedom from compulsory state service (both civil and military), immunity from corporal punishment, and the right to substitute a business tax for the servile poll (or "soul") tax—only to the merchants.

The Meaning of Enlightened Social Policy

Catherine's charter for the urban burghers thus made explicit what was implicit in her social policy toward the nobles and the peasants: the conversion of the older social regimen of particular obligations and particular rights into a combination of political function and economic liberties. Here, indeed, is the key to the ambiguities of the enlightened absolutists' social policies in general. Their attention to both aristocratic privilege and peasants' rights, like their attention to both the official tutelage over and the entrepreneurial freedom of the economic bourgeoisie, was predicated on their reorganization of incompatible social claims into the compatible combination of political function and economic right. They used political function as a valid means of favoring one or another social class for its contribution to the state. They used economic right as a valid means of favoring one or another social class for the greater enterprise of its individual members.

The parallel of these social policies with the enlightened monarchs' policies toward the religious and intellectual institutions over which they extended political control, and toward the freedom of conscience and of thought which they deemed beyond political control, is patent. But since man's practical economic and social activities were, in the eighteenth century, still considered less sacrosanct and less essential to his individuality than his spiritual activities, the emphasis on collective political privilege over individual suprapolitical rights was correspondingly greater in the practical than in the spiritual sphere of enlightened-absolutist policy. Thus the primarily pro-aristocratic orientation of both Frederick's and Catherine's social policies was geared to their view of the aristocracy as the most important social contributor to the order of the state—in Frederick's case for its essential qualities of civil and military leadership, in Catherine's for the prudential considerations of its potential for disorder and its monopoly of authority over the vast Russian countryside. In Frederick, indeed, the political ground of his preference was explicit: in addition to "the general rights of man," which are based on the natural freedom of all individuals, he acknowledged "the hierarchy of particular rights," which are appropriate to membership in the various estates, primarily because he measured such particular rights by the differential contribution of the estates to the welfare of the state.

Even behind the apparent consistency of Joseph's policy of peasant liberation with his principles of natural-rights individualism there lay not the radical dogmatism of which he has so often been accused but the coincidence of the two different criteria. Certainly his humanitarian doctrine was more authentic than his enlightened rivals', but so was his preoccupation with politics. If, then, his peasant liberation was of a piece with his far-reaching program of publicly administered social welfare—his government built and ran hospitals, orphanages, lying-in homes, and institutions for the handicapped all over Austria—in testifying to his general feelings and principles in favor of the underprivileged and the unfortunate, both the liberation and the welfare were equally effects of his political conviction that "the working class" is "the most useful class in the nation." When sympathy for the exploited classes was detached from considerations of political utility, as Joseph had been convinced it was in his mother's concern for the Bohemian peasants, he was suspicious of it, and showed an anxiety for the viability of a noble class that was also vital to the state. In general, however, Joseph favored the peasants and restricted the lords in a way that agreed with Frederick's and Catherine's principles but diverged from their policies simply because, unlike them, he judged the interests and rights of the masses to be more needful to the state than the exemptions and privileges of the classes.

In the long run, the combination of political collectivism and economic individualism that was common to the social policy of all the enlightened monarchs proved to be more important than the differences of social preference that came out of their respective applications of this double standard. For a policy that made social status a resultant of political function and economic right had the permanent effect of weakening the autonomy of all social groups and of strengthening the power of the sovereign political authority, who now could add to his categorical monopoly of collective force over all social classes his protection of the individual rights on which his resources depended. The enlightened absolutists thus equipped the autocracies of central and eastern Europe with the capacity to survive through the liberal atmosphere and the social unrest of the nineteenth century. As a matter of fact, all these autocracies without exception—including the Habsburg empire after Joseph—first appropriated the old nobility as the political governing class par excellence. Then, when subsequent industrialization in the western powers placed a greater political premium on the rights of free economic enterprise, these states were prepared to accommodate the economic and civil rights of the rising social classes—liberal aristocrats, bourgeoisie, peasant farmers—and thus to perpetuate the authoritarian state, together with its dependent nobility, through the nineteenth into the twentieth century.

RESULTS OF ENLIGHTENED ABSOLUTISM

Like its social policies in particular, the results of enlightened absolutism in general varied from country to country in their specifics, but its joint effect upon the great powers of central and eastern Europe was massive and uniform.

Joseph's measures were, by and large, undoubtedly the shortest-lived and Catherine's undoubtedly the longest. In the latter 1780's opposition to Joseph arose both from the conservative clergy, nobles, and particularists (that is, Hungarians and Belgians) who felt violated by the liberal and centralistic features of his legislation and from the liberal intellectuals and peasants who were disappointed by the utilitarian limits as well as the centralistic oppressiveness of the reforms. Joseph responded to the resistance from 1785 on by increasing the central controls and diminishing the liberty in his reforms, and after his death in 1790 his successor, Emperor Leopold II, enlightened reformer though he had proved himself to be as Grand Duke of Tuscany, rolled some of them back entirely. Except for the retention of the peasant's right to leave his holding, a dubious right when thus isolated, Joseph's measures of peasant liberation were repealed, and some of the strongholds of aristocratic and clerical influence that he had dismantled were now restored—the administrative committees of the provincial diets, the corporate constitutions of Hungary and the Austrian Netherlands, and the Church-run seminaries and Church-controlled liturgy.

In Russia, on the other hand, the reaction against Catherine's characteristic policies after her death in 1796 was brief and ineffective. Her son and heir, Paul I (ruled 1796–1801), did indeed translate his hatred for his mother into an anti-aristocratic policy that not only attacked the preeminent position of the nobility in district and local government but abridged the personal rights and tax immunity which had been guaranteed in the

Charter of the Nobility. But even he coupled this policy with a further extension and intensification of serfdom, and after he was murdered by aristocrats in 1801 his anti-aristocratic measures were repealed while his enserfments were not. True, the corporate vitality that Catherine had hoped to stimulate as a kind of social feeder of human energies to her state did not develop in the nobility any more than in the burgher group; yet through the nineteenth century the alliance of state and aristocracy that had been cemented by Catherine continued to dominate Russian public life.

The fate of the particular policies associated with Prussia's Frederick fell between the Austrian tendency to repudiate what Joseph did and the Russian tendency to continue what Catherine did. In Prussia, Frederick's achievements were built upon. The decade of reaction which followed immediately upon his death in 1786 turned out to be, like Paul's briefer reign in Russia, evanescent and inconsequential. The lasting revision of Frederick's work was taken up, under quite different auspices, by liberal bureaucrats who reacted against the rigid mercantilist side of Frederick's policies. With the accession of the diligent Frederick William III in 1797, Frederick's fundamental policy of mobilizing Prussia's intellectual and social resources on principles taken from the advanced societies of the west was resumed. After the Prussian defeat by Napoleon at Jena in 1806, the Frederician heritage was adapted to the new conditions of power created by the revolutionary French. What was rejected was not the Frederician system as such but the persistence of its literal institutions which had become anachronisms—like the personal absolutism that had degenerated into government by irresponsible private secretaries, and the association of social castes with political authority that was now squeezing life out of the society and force out of the state. The modernization of the Prussian state was undertaken by aristocrats who had been attracted into the Prussian service by Frederick and who sought to adapt the merger of authoritarian government and liberalized society which had been initiated by Frederick on the basis of intellectual principle to the new real possibilities of free economic and social endeavor.

But the net effect of enlightened absolutism went beyond the variable destinies of its specific policies to establish a pattern of domination that would pervade vast sections of the European continent and influence the lives of future generations down to the present day. The enlightened absolutists adjusted the instruments of government—that is, bureaucracies, laws, and political values—to enforce a collective power, stability, and order over a society that required spontaneity, mobility, and freedom. Thus they pioneered a mode of politics which reconciled authoritarian government with the growing self-determination of a developing society precisely by making a necessity of the antithesis between them—by demonstrating to autonomous social groups in various stages of modernization that a viable community among them was possible only if their conflicting social claims from below were transmuted into compatible political programs by adjudication from above.

In these part-archaic, part-modern societies of central and eastern Europe (measuring modernity by the usual standards of western industrial society) authoritarian governments have imposed the advanced standards of the west upon their military, diplomatic, and economic instruments to enlarge their peoples' international capacities; and across the resulting fault of static and mobile strata in their societies they have constructed overarching policies which no group or combination of groups could construct by itself. To do this work, authoritarian governments long continued to employ the two main instruments of rule from above that their "enlightened" forebears employed as a joint principle—monarchy and philosophy. Thus they perpetuated the union of kings and philosophers in new guises.

The longevity of the Romanovs, the Habsburgs, and the Hohenzollerns, as dynasties that not only reigned but ruled until the end of the First World War, was only the physical expression of the modern function of autocracy in the fissured societies of Russia, Austria-Hungary, and Germany that under other forms persisted even deeper into our century. The merger of such autocracy with philosophy has likewise proved to be something much more fundamental in these nations than the mere historical memory of their coincidence in some eighteenth-century ancestors. For these are nations which have in fact been especially susceptible to philosophies of politics—that is, to political and social theories which call for political means to realize total social systems whose validity comes from outside the contemporary societies themselves. The legitimacy of the philosophies has been precisely like the legitimacy of the kings which it has accompanied in these countries where both have governed for so long. It consists, for both, in the derivation of their authority from a source transcending the existing society as a society and the derivation of their function from a single, supreme, collective goal—whether racial, national, or social—that must be imposed upon a fragmented society.

For better or for worse, the kings' appropriation of philosophy in the eighteenth century has developed into a fundamental mode of politics.

CHAPTER 11

The End of an Era:
The Social Movement
in the West, 1763-1789

WHEN THE LAST third of the eighteenth century is reviewed from the vantage point of its climax in the great French Revolution of 1789, the most important historical strand of the whole era is the generation-long revolutionary turmoil which gave it a European context. Starting from the obscure local circumstances of a scurrilous London newspaper article in 1763, a factional squabble in the little city-republic of Geneva in 1768, and a distant colonial struggle across the sea in 1776, diffuse social movements against established authority spread erratically across Europe during the decade of the 1780's. They erupted in Ireland and England during 1780 and zig-zagged eastward across the Continent, returning to Geneva in 1782, disrupting the Netherlands from 1783 to 1787, and infecting the Austrian Netherlands, Poland, and Sweden in 1788, before the outbreak of decisive and violent revolution in France during 1789 triggered the Hungarian rising of that year.

All these movements were social (that is, they involved groups other than those actually exercising political rights and functions accorded by the established constitution), rebellious (that is, they undertook active resistance to legal authority, whether through civil disobedience, physical violence, or irregular organizations), and liberal in their appeal (that is, they resisted in the name of the rights of man). Finally, and most concretely, these movements were all revolutionary, whether they succeeded or not, in the sense that each of them sought a transfer of political power through a sudden and decisive change in its country's constitution.

TYPES OF REVOLUTIONARY MOVEMENTS

In view of the number of movements with such qualities during the final decades of the Old Regime, and in deference to our own rising con-

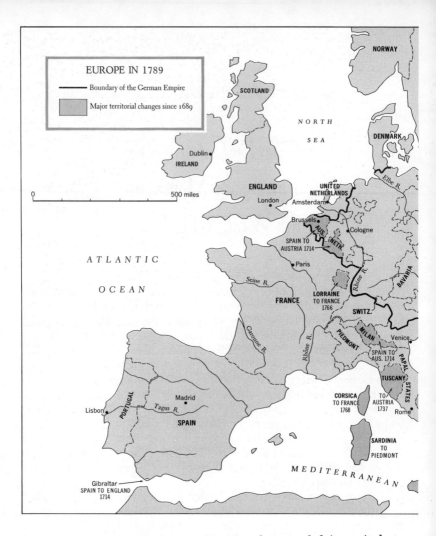

EUROPE IN 1789

——— Boundary of the German Empire

Major territorial changes since 1689

NORWAY

SCOTLAND

NORTH SEA

DENMARK

Elbe R.

Dublin

IRELAND

0 ———— 500 miles

ENGLAND

London

UNITED NETHERLANDS

Amsterdam

Brussels

AUS. NETH.

Cologne

ATLANTIC

SPAIN TO AUSTRIA 1714

Paris

Rhine R.

BAVARIA

OCEAN

Seine R.

LORRAINE TO FRANCE 1766

FRANCE

SWITZ.

Rhône R.

Garonne R.

PIEDMONT

MILAN

Venice

SPAIN TO AUS. 1714

PAPAL STATES

PORTUGAL

Madrid

Tagus R.

TUSCANY

Lisbon

SPAIN

CORSICA TO FRANCE 1768

TO AUSTRIA 1737

Rome

SARDINIA TO PIEDMONT

MEDITERRANEAN

Gibraltar
SPAIN TO ENGLAND 1714

cern with revolutionary processes, historians have tended increasingly to stress the alienation of life in these decades from the characteristic institutions of the Old Regime and its continuity rather with the cataclysmic events of 1789 and after in a general European "Age of Revolution."

From this retrospective angle of their ultimate issue in the authentic revolutions of the 1790's, the radical events of the two preceding decades can be analyzed into four different types of revolution. Each revolutionary situation contained several types of revolutionary movements, one often setting off the others, but for clarity we shall separate in interpretation what were mixed in reality.

First, there were the interventionist revolutions, where the intrusion by

foreign powers played a crucial or determining role in the transfer of political power. This kind of revolution came in two models. The intervention of France (supported by Zurich and Bern) on behalf of the patriciate in the Genevan civil strife of 1782, the Prussian intervention in 1787 on behalf of the conservative coalition of Dutch oligarchs and monarchists loyal to the prince of Orange against an independent party of the liberal middle classes, and even, on a more modest scale, the French intervention of 1778–1783 on behalf of the North American colonists against Great Britain, were cases of *imposed* revolution, where the intervening power directly affected the result of a constitutional conflict. The progressive movement of enlightened Polish magnates (that is, upper nobility) in alliance with the equally enlightened King Stanislas II (ruled 1764–1795) and what there was of an intellectual and mercantile Polish commoner class in the towns became the outstanding case of *patriotic* revolution, where the intervening power provoked a nationalistic opposition to the satellite constitution supported by the intruder. The traditional Polish constitution, whose provisions for a severely limited elective kingship and for unanimity (*liberum veto*) in the decisions of the national Diet guaranteed the sovereignty of the provincial assemblies of local serf-owning nobles whose delegates composed the Diet, received the puppet's taint from its support by Russia under cover of the joint guarantee by the partitioning powers of 1772, and the patriotic movement in rump Poland received from the shock and the continuing humiliation of foreign intrusion the cohesion which led to the enactment of administrative, educational, and censorship reforms between 1772 and 1789 as prelude to the revolutionary establishment of a liberal constitutional monarchy in 1791. The revolutionary movements in North America (1776–1783), Ireland (1780–1785), and the Austrian Netherlands (1788–1790) also shared this quality of national resistance, albeit in diluted form since the British and Habsburg powers whose intrusions seemed alien had acknowledged if ambiguous rights of sovereignty over the nations concerned. The deliberate assumption of the name "Patriot" by all these movements symbolized the provocative power of the interventionist motif in their revolutions.

Second, there were the revolutions by enlightened monarchy—that is, by enlightened kings or by kings' enlightened ministers. These revolutions also came in two models. Gustavus III's forceful imposition of a formal new constitution upon Sweden in 1789, like the Habsburg Joseph II's equally formal abrogation of his Belgian provinces' constitutional charters of self-government during the same year, climaxed *objective* revolutions by enlightened monarchy—that is, revolutions that actually shifted constitutional powers to the monarch. Neither the timid, malleable, and well-meaning Louis XVI nor the persistent, myopic, legalistic George III can be rehabilitated into an enlightened monarch by any stretch of the term, but the successive efforts of Louis' reforming ministers at tax equalization and judicial centralization in France, and attempts by the Grenvilles and the Townshends under George III to organize a rational colonial system of controls in place of the haphazard accumulation of rights and regulations for North America, were, like Joseph II's analogous centralization of local administration and his imposition of governmental controls on serfdom in Hungary, cases of *subjective* revolutions by enlightened monarchy—that is, reforms that were taken to be despotic revolutions by the privileged groups immediately affected by them.

Third, there were the conservative revolutions. In Britain's American colonies, France, the Austrian Netherlands, and Hungary, privileged groups answered the revolutionary threat of royal centralization by going beyond mere counterrevolution for the *status quo* to their own revolution for a new permanent share in the sovereign power that would preempt such threats in the future.

Finally, there were the popular revolutions, evoked by the example and appeals of the monarchical or conservative parties, temporarily joining one or another of them in its revolutionary movement, but growing essentially independent of either. The popular revolutionaries were a coalition of liberal notables (from the lower ranks of the aristocracy and from enfranchised commoners) with the insecure stake of vulnerable privileges and subordinate public functions in the old society and of commoners with no stake of either privilege or public function in the old society. They drove for the organization of a new society without privilege and with public functions based on common consent rather than distributive hierarchy. These popular revolutions came in two models. In Britain, Ireland, the Netherlands, and the Austrian Netherlands the exclusive predominance of the old society's mobile elite in the liberal coalition produced *abortive* popular revolutions. In Britain's North American colonies and in France the more balanced coalition of subordinate elite and the unprivileged produced *effective* popular revolutions.

REVOLUTIONARY MOVEMENTS AND THE OLD REGIME

This retrospective classification of the revolutionary preludes to Europe's Age of Revolution identifies the four main factors of this coming revolution, but it tells little of their connection with the European past and hence little of their real historical character. For this knowledge, we must consider the turbulent movements from 1763 to 1789 from the genetic point of view and look to their origins and growth in the Old Regime rather than to their destination beyond it. From this vantage point the radical events of the period are patterned not by the shape of the democratic revolution that was emerging but by the strands of the Old Regime that was unraveling. The political and social "revolutionaries" of the last generation before the French Revolution had, indeed, the same kind of relationship to the Old Regime in the realm of action as the "unworldly philosophers" of the same era had to the Enlightenment in the realm of thought (see pp. 208–10). Just as the thinkers were post-Enlightenment rather than anti-Enlightenment in that each of them sought to develop to a categorical extreme a single strand—such as reason, liberty, or passion—of the Enlightenment culture that had consisted in the balance of them all, so were most of the actors post-Old-Regime rather than anti-Old-Regime in that each of them sought to develop a consistent system of political authority out of one or another of the particular institutions— such as the royal bureaucracy or the aristocratic assembly—which had coexisted in time-tested, if inconsistent, equilibrium. Only the popular revolutionaries had contributed to the balanced order of the Old Regime no such particular institution that was capable of being generalized into a system of political authority, and only they, consequently, turned against the whole authoritarian and hierarchical structure of the Old Regime.

The light thrown on the four types of radical movements by their respective relations with the centrifugal tendencies of the Old Regime shows the real pattern connecting the prerevolutionary Europe of the early modern centuries to the revolutionary Europe of 1789 and after. What was decisive in this pattern was not the common social and political revolutionary effect of the four kinds of radical movements but the differences between them which made the interventionist, monarchical, and aristocratic movements crucial alternatives to the popular movement and perpetuated the regional diversities of the old Europe's political geography into the new era.

We must distinguish, therefore, between the qualified revolutionary character of the foreign intervention, the enlightened absolutism, and the social conservatism which sponsored unbalanced movements by pitting one standard institution of the Old Regime against another and the unqualified revolutionary character of the popular revolution which would transform all the standard institutions of the Old Regime. And we must note the geographical pattern of these different kinds of movements. The interventionist, monarchical, and aristocratic movements were revolutionists of Europe's political periphery. They erupted in minuscule or debilitated states like Geneva, Sweden, Poland, and the Netherlands or in the outlying dependencies of the Habsburg and British empires—in places where the combination of social hierarchy and territorial sovereignty that constituted the characteristic controls of the Old Regime was most attenuated. Of Europe's political heartland only France was struck by these revolutionary outcroppings of the Old Regime, and the exception would prove fatal. For France was also implicated in the entirely different regional pattern of popular revolution. This, the most authentic of the revolutionary movements, was spawned only by the mobile, commercialized, western societies of the Atlantic seaboard even in its abortive form of a movement by a suppressed elite, and among these societies, only in France and America in its effective form of a movement by a coalition of the subordinate elite and unenfranchised commoners.

The regional pattern created by the varying degrees of revolution from the stability of aristocratic absolutism to the popular movement against both the social and the political pillars of the traditional European order was the legacy of the Old Regime to the modern world. Just as the great powers of central and eastern Europe were the strongholds of the enlightened monarchy which equipped the balance of social hierarchy and political authoritarianism for continued viability into the twentieth century, so was the Atlantic complex of peoples the reservoir of the social movement which would again and again change elites and authorities alike in a continuing response to the growing economic and intellectual pressures for equality. These would be the two major poles of modern European history, and between them the smaller continental nations at the Old Regime's periphery would follow the pattern of partial revolution into the gradual and experimental mold of modern small-nation social politics.

Thus the political heritage of Europe's Old Regime took its final form from the absence of revolution in some nations and from the specific type of revolutionary movement, in the nations where there was revolution, during the generation preceding the epochal transformation of France in the summer of 1789. To our sketches of the stabilized regimes in Austria, Prussia, and Russia under their enlightened monarchs and to our discussion of the interventionist revolution which these domestically stabilizing rulers introduced into Europe's international relations (see chapter 9), we must now add sketches of enlightened absolutism and of aristocratic rebellion in their late posture of partial "revolutions" and a concluding discussion of the popular revolutions that initiated a new social, political, and intellectual era of European civilization.

The Revolution of Enlightened Monarchy

Of the two ways in which the later development of enlightened monarchy had revolutionary effect, the course taken in France by the enlightened ministers of Louis XVI (ruled 1774–1792) was the most important instance of the subjective model, where administrative and fiscal reforms were received as acts of constitutional revolution, and the course taken by Gustavus III in Sweden was the most prominent case of the objective model, where the enlightened ruler actually did make a forcible change in the constitution.

The French leading ministers, from Turgot in 1774 through Necker and Calonne to Loménie de Brienne in 1788, were steeped in the culture of the Enlightenment and were committed to liberal administrative change as the means of increasing the economic and social resources available to the king's government—a commitment that was actually in the best style of the reforming type of enlightened monarchy. Mortmain—the anachronism that recognized the permanently inalienable property rights of feudal corporations—was abolished on the royal domain in 1779, and the corvée—compulsory peasant labor—in 1787. Penal procedures were amended during the 1780's to prohibit the use of torture for securing confessions and to limit the use of the notorious *lettres de cachet*, which authorized imprisonment without due process. Vergennes, the foreign minister who first plotted the French intervention on behalf of the revolutionary Americans against the common British rival, subsequently initiated the negotiations with the younger William Pitt which led to the liberal—that is, low-tariff—Anglo-French commercial treaty of 1786, on the equally good royalist grounds that a larger trade for France meant a larger power for France and that a détente with England might aid the rekindled French interest in the Netherlands. Finally, the French Toleration Edict of 1787 granted civil rights to Protestants and acknowledged he validity of Protestant marriages —a reform which may be viewed as the partial restoration, on a generalized basis, of the many special Huguenot rights and liberties that had been abolished with the revocation of the Edict of Nantes a century before.

Even the two main lines of the French ministerial attempts at far-reaching reforms that could not be executed were outgrowths of older absolutist policies. Behind both was a financial crisis which was itself the culmination of the expensive old royal addiction to two-front wars and of the ruinous old royal addiction to "fiscalism"—the policy of paying for them through the creation and sale of public offices that had the effect of diverting public revenues into private fees of the office-owners and through the levying of unequal imposts that extended immunities and dried up future revenues. Hence the grave imbalance of expenditure over income which resulted from French participation in the Americans' was against Great Britain from 1778 to 1783 and which impelled the reform proposals of the 1780's climaxed both the chronic burden of royal policy on French society and the equally old paralysis of royal fiscal policy by duplicating the social conflict between privileged and commoner groups within the institutions of the state.

The first line of reform was the general land tax which Turgot devised as a solution for the chronic financial problem in 1776 and to which Calonne recurred under the immediate threat of bankruptcy in 1787. It was, for both ministers, a part of a plan for a general reorganization of the royal administration that would cut costs and increase revenue, but it also conformed to the centuries-old autocratic model of equality as the equal subjection of all citizens to the king's law. The second main line of enlightened ministerial policy—opposition to the *parlements*—also had its precedent in the French absolutist past. Even the attempt to emasculate the *parlements* in 1788 by removing their right to register royal decrees, the step that triggered uprisings against the government throughout France and led directly to the revolution of 1789, was viewed by Louis XVI as a defense of monarchy against the unlawful pretensions of an aristocracy rather than as a constitutional change (the judicial right to register was retained, and transferred to a new Plenary Court). The measure looked back, indeed, to the abolition of the *parlements* between 1771 and 1774 which had been engineered by his grandfather's imperious chancellor, René Charles de Maupeou. Louis himself had restored them upon his accession as a gesture of good will and now considered himself fully entitled to do once more what he had undone. He felt all the more authorized since he deemed the *parlements'* refusal to register his new taxes without the convo-

Anne Robert Turgot, Baron de l'Aulne. *The one French statesman who was himself a wholehearted* philosophe *and who tried to legislate Physiocratic ideas. Turgot carried down with him the hope of reforming the French monarchy from above when he fell from power in 1776.*

cation and approval of the Estates-General both unconstitutional and subversive.

Insofar as the French ministers of the decade and a half before the French Revolution thus plotted their reforms within the framework of political absolutism and limited their espousal of social change to the leveling only of those privileges directly incidental to the financial resources of the state, it would be wrong to accept the judgment of their conservative opponents and call them revolutionary. Like the Habsburg case of Joseph II, indeed, the reforms sponsored by the French autocracy had the effect of provoking conservative revolutions before the reforms could develop their own revolutionary consequences.

But one French project of the period, did indicate a possible development from reform to revolution by enlightened absolutism. Turgot's plan to associate new provincial assemblies, elected not by order or estate but by property owners as such, with the royal government for consultation on the administration of new taxes could not be implemented before he was forced from the office of Controller General in 1776 by aristocratic pressure upon the court. After Calonne adopted this project along with so many others of Turgot's some eleven years later, it was again frustrated by his enforced resignation from the same office under the same influence. When the idea was finally translated into reality under Calonne's successor, the enlightened, charming, and compliant Archbishop Loménie de Brienne, for whom the post of prime minister was resurrected, it took the old form of provincial diets which represented the three traditional estates under the chairmanship of a churchman or a noble, and in this form played a role in fomenting the conservative revolution. But in its original concept the plan for representative assemblies of the propertied citizenry in a country like France, where of the agricultural land alone some 35 per cent seems, according to the best estimates, to have been owned by peasants and some 30 per cent by burghers, does show the possible transition whereby enlightened absolutism could exchange the hierarchical for the representative principle as the final link of its administration with the body politic and thus transfer to the whole propertied citizenry the share of executive power traditionally reserved to the aristocracy. By building representative assemblies into a system of formal absolutism as the King's administrative agencies, the French plan serves to demonstrate the continuity between monarchial absolutism and monarchial revolution.

In Sweden, where the role of the aristocracy in the king's executive authority was formally guaranteed by the constitution, an enlightened monarch took the revolutionary step the French just failed to take: he forcibly changed the constitution to reduce decisively the aristocracy's share of the public power.

The Swedish monarchical revolution was consummated in two widely separated stages—the seizure of effective legislative sovereignty by the king from the mutually hostile aristocratic and commoner parties of the Swedish Diet in 1772, and the transfer of the aristocracy's dominant share of the administrative power to the commons by the king early in 1789.

A scant year after the young Gustavus III (ruled 1771–1792) had acceded to the Swedish throne, he carried through what has been called the *coup d'état* of 1772. Since it brought an immediate transfer from the estates to the king of the actual power to make laws, and anticipated the later transfer from the aristocracy to the king of the power to administer them, its implications were more revolutionary than the king's bloodless assumption of the authority of the Diet seemed to indicate. The coup itself brought Sweden a new constitution and a *de facto* absolutism to replace the "era of liberty" and its *de facto* sovereignty of aristocracy. The chief organs of aristocratic rule were the nobles' chamber of the four-chambered Swedish Diet and the civil and military services, headed by the central executive council, which the aristocrats dominated and through which they retained their social privileges over the disposition of land. Seizing the occasion of a growing social conflict between the aristocracy and the commoners, who were represented in the other three chambers of the Swedish Diet (clergy, burghers, and peasants), Gustavus enlisted the physical support of the aristocratic faction and the theoretical slogans of the popular faction against "aristocratic despotism" to take sovereign power from the Diet, where both factions had been fighting over it.

The written constitution of 1772, which he composed and imposed upon the Diet, was the ambiguous product to be expected from an

Literary conversation during the reign of Gustavus III of Sweden. *Although the king's readiness to undertake authoritarian and egalitarian* coups d'état *against the Swedish constitution indicated a revolutionary temperament not usually to be found in his fellow rulers, his intellectual tastes aligned him with the enlightened monarchs of the eighteenth century.*

ambitious royal disciple of Montesquieu and Voltaire who used the *philoso-phes'* language of constitutional monarchy to cover the distance between the absolute sovereignty he coveted and the legislative powers of the Diet he had both to acknowledge and to minimize. It granted the King full powers to govern the kingdom and the right to call the Diet at his discretion, but the Diet's concurrence was required for the imposition of new taxes, for the renewal of old taxes, and for the declaration of offensive war. Once called, moreover, it possessed the power of initiative for all legis-lation. As a matter of fact, the king convoked the Diet only for two regular sessions under this constitution—in 1778 and in 1786—and for the rest governed autocratically, bypassing the council for which provision had been made in the constitution and governing, like his uncle Frederick the Great, through his unofficial secretaries on the basis of decisions taken in his own "cabinet." But if the king thus minimized the legislative rights of both the aristocrats and the commons in the Diet for whose share in legis-lation there remained constitutional warrant, he continued to favor the aristocracy in the civil and military services that carried out his policies in the country and abroad.

The ambiguities of Gustavus' incomplete revolution came to the surface in the Diet of 1786 when he demanded approval and support for a modern army to carry out his decision to fight Russia for the control of the Baltic. When the aristocrats led the resistance in the Diet, and after his unconsti-tutional declaration of war against Russia in 1788, organized subversive leagues against him, Gustavus proceeded to complete his revolution by reducing to the bare minimum of an administrative instrument the rights of the Diet and by leveling the privileged position of the aristocracy in the administration. Convoking an extraordinary session of the Diet in February, 1789, Gustavus banished the nobles' chamber and issued a set of constitutional amendments—called the Act of Union and Security—in alliance with the three chambers of the lower estates. The new version of the constitution, which went into effect despite the formal disapproval of the nobles' chamber when it was later reconvened, provided for the consistent application of the king's "complete powers to govern" by denying the Diet's right of legislative initiative. The new constitution also provided for the equality of all classes in their access to the state services (with certain formal exceptions), and since civil inequalities had long been justified by the aristocracy's special role in these state services, these inequalities too were now minimized. The Act of Union provided for equal rights before the law and in the courts, and it extended to all classes the right to own and dispose of land.

The epilogue of Gustavus' monarchical revolution was an ironic demonstration of its separate identity vis-à-vis both conservative and modern revolutions. The last years of his reign were filled on the one hand by the continuing opposition of his aristocracy, resentful of the loss both of their legislative rights and their administrative and civil privileges, and on the other by his own fanatic desire to lead a monarchical crusade against the French revolutionaries. He was assassinated, finally, in 1792 by an ambiguous aristocratic coalition of conservative revolutionary nobles and of liberal aristocrats who sympathized with the French revolutionaries—a coalition which could agree only on its joint resistance to the revolutionary despot.

Aristocratic Revolutions

Because the most pervasive factors for change in the late eighteenth century—the extension of the market economy and the intellectual diffusion of liberal ideas—impinged upon the European aristocracy as both a tempting opportunity and a grave threat, aristocratic political radicalism for socially conservative purposes was the most widespread of all the revolutionary movements. Social elites were parties, indeed, to every kind of revolution. They were satellites or resisters of foreign intervention; they overreacted to royal limitations of privilege; and they paved the way for the popular movements which they had evoked for their own support. Thus the patriciates of Geneva and the Netherlands were the beneficiaries of the interventions by France and Prussia, respectively, into their civil strife against the plebeians of their cities for political supremacy. British Presbyterian and Congregationalist lawyers and merchants in North America, like factions of even more respectable lords and gentlemen in Great Britain itself, were first goaded into movements to change the British constitution by the alterations which they convinced themselves a despotic King George III had already made in it. Similarly in France, where the opposition to the crown would develop even more radically than elsewhere, the initial stage was dominated by an aristocratic revolt. The nobility of the robe (*i.e.* the judicial nobility), acting through the sovereign courts (*parlements*), first made constitutional opposition to the king's government honorable between 1763 and 1770 by defending as items in the fundamental rights of the people the tax immunities of their own lands and offices against Louis XV's bureaucratic reformers headed by Chancellor Maupeou. The *parlements* expanded this defense to the protection of privilege and the corporate hierarchy in principle against Turgot's enlightened program of 1776 for a uniform land tax and the suppression of the restrictive guilds. In both cases they developed the possession of a judicial right to register such royal legislation into the claim of a constitutional right to deliberate on its legality. When, in 1787, the most urgent of all French financial crises triggered the most imminent of all the royal threats of tax equalization, the nobility of the robe developed this claim into a general aristocratic campaign for a permanent share in the sovereign power on behalf of "the people"—and thereby took the fateful step of appealing to the masses and initiating the cycle of revolutions.

The purest conservative revolutions were in the Austrian Netherlands and Hungary, for in both of these outlying Habsburg possessions the aristocratic social groups who rose to undo the innovations of Joseph II not only initiated the resistance movement but retained their domination over it.

The Hungarian movement is outside our orbit, since neither the agitation of the Magyar magnates for the suspension of agrarian reform and for the restoration of the violated constitution of noble-dominated and self-governing estates nor the competing movements of peasants and radical gentry reached revolutionary proportions before the stimulus of the French events of 1789. But the Austrian Netherlands (later Belgium) does merit our attention, for there the outbreak of revolution was an autonomous development prior to the decisive news from France.

The Belgian movement revealed clearly a fundamental fact about social conservatism in the Old Regime which the overt preeminence of the nobility in eighteenth-century Europe obscured elsewhere: the recognition of privilege in many kinds of exclusive social corporations, of which the titled aristocracy was only the most favored and the most prominent. In the Austrian Netherlands, the Austrian Habsburgs, like the Spanish Habsburgs before them, governed a collection of the ten Lowland provinces whose political and social constitution had undergone surprisingly few changes since the halcyon era of local and corporate self-government in the Middle Ages. Unconnected save through the common Habsburg overlord, each of the provinces was administered by provincial estates representing the three self-administering social oligarchies of the community—the landed nobility, the Catholic hierarchy, and the municipal guildsmen.

Joseph's program—anti-aristocratic, anti-clerical, and anti-guild—had

something socially offensive to every privileged corporation, and the result
was a conservative coalition of social groups against it. But it was not until
1787, when Joseph passed from social to constitutional legislation by sup-
planting the traditional mixed judicial and administrative tribunals of the
corporate oligarchs with his centralized system of separate judicial and
administrative authorities in redrawn judicial and administrative districts,
that two of the provincial estates declared a tax strike and resistance
became active. When Joseph responded, in January, 1789, with the abrogation of the Belgian constitution—that is, of the paradigmatic Joyous Entry
of 1355, the Brabant provincial charter confirming the historic rights of
corporate self-government—his escalation of the conflict into constitutional politics brought a similar escalation of the resistance, and the whole
conservative front broke into open revolution.

The Belgian movement was distinguished not only by the comparatively
broad social base of its conservative parties but also by the collaboration of
a genuinely liberal middle class group. Called Patriots or Vonckists (after
their leader, the progressive lawyer Jean François Vonck, 1743–1792), it
joined the aristocratic Estatists to expel the Austrian authorities in November and December, 1789. The coalition drew up an Act of Union, patterned on the American Articles of Confederation and designed as the
constitution of a united Belgium. Both parties at this stage were committed to the revolutionary goal of an independent Belgium, but they clashed
violently on the political form it should assume. The Patriots pushed for a
genuinely representative constitution, based on an expanded electorate and
embodying national sovereignty. The Estatists pushed for the reinstate-
ment of the pre-Josephinian corporate constitution, returning sovereignty
to the unreformed estates of each province and limiting the revolution to
the substitution of a weak confederation of the estates for the mild Habsburg suzerainty. The Patriots—or the Democrats, as they now came to call
themselves—undoubtedly belonged to the really new political movement
which was beginning to appear in western Europe during the 1780's, but
of more immediate importance was their comparative weakness, for the
triumph of the Estatists over the Democrats in Belgium was symptomatic
of the preponderance of conservative over liberal elements in European
society until the very end of the Old Regime.

Only France proved to be an exception to this rule, and consequently it
was in France, and in France alone, that the new political movement succeeded and brought down the complex of institutions and values that composed the Old Regime. A comparison of the French and Belgian patterns
isolates the decisive difference in the balance of social forces between
France and the rest of Europe. In Belgium, as in France, the reforming
monarchy ultimately lined up with the aristocracy against the liberals: the
new Habsburg Emperor, Leopold II, took advantage of the civil strife to
reoccupy Belgium in December, 1790, and consolidated the Habsburg

The revolt in Belgium. *A crowd gathers outside the Town Hall of Brussels.*

return by reaching an agreement with the Estatists that restored the traditional corporate constitution of the Austrian Netherlands. But in Belgium,
unlike France, this alliance of monarchy and aristocracy succeeded in
ending the revolution, and it succeeded because the mass movement of
peasants and artisans in Belgium, unlike the analogous mass movement in
France, supported the corporate establishment. More attached to their
church than their French counterparts, and far less burdened by the crush-
ing taxation imposed by an expensive court and war machine, the Belgian
rural masses rose in a form not very different from that of their risings
since time immemorial. They joined their priests and their lords in the
defense of their customary faith and way of life against innovation in
church and state.

Since the conservative revolutionary movements of the 1780's partook so
much of the age-old resistance by self-administering and privileged corporations to centralizing and leveling absolutism, the questions arise: What
was new in them? What was revolutionary about them?

Two features of the movements distinguish them from the assertion of
corporate rights and exemptions against bureaucratic encroachment which
had been standard in the Old Regime.

First, the aristocrats of the revolutionary generation demanded the preservation of their social privileges no longer merely as chartered group liberties appropriate to their special status in the state but as particular
instances of universal rights which imposed general limits on the power of
the state as such. This language of natural rights, particularly in the context of the American Revolution, gave a radical flavor to the advocacy of

social privilege. Thus the *Parlement* of Paris gave such an argument for its protection of corporate privilege against Turgot's reforms in 1776 when it insisted that "a fundamental rule of natural law and civil government . . . not only upholds property rights but safeguards rights attached to the person and born of prerogatives of birth and estate."

Second, and more important, the aristocrats of the revolutionary generation sought a new constitutional basis for the recovery of the public functions that monarchs had taken from them. Unlike the social privileges which they attempted merely to retain, the corporate political rights of local self-government and of participation in the central sovereign power, which the aristocrats now sought, represented a demand for immediate constitutional change, and it was only at the stage of this demand that the conservative movement became truly revolutionary. It was revolutionary, indeed, not only because it claimed for itself a shift of political power in favor of the aristocracy but also because the aristocracy's actual dependence upon the support of other social groups for the seizure of political power from the monarchy committed it to doctrines of national sovereignty and representative government that were far more revolutionary than the rhetoric of social privilege. The Belgian Estatists, as we have seen, explicitly used a constitutional model of revolutionary America to bring about the recovery of their old corporate liberties. The Hungarian country assemblies which Joseph had destroyed would reemerge upon his death in 1790 to reinstitute the traditional Hungarian constitution, and then the serf-owning magnates who dominated these assemblies would touch off a wide-ranging revolutionary movement by basing their actual monopoly of corporate power on the constitutional claim that "the social contract which creates the state places sovereignty in the hands of the people."

The French notables went a step further than the Belgians and the Hungarians in demonstrating the revolutionary implications of the aristocratic renewal of conservative constitutions. Whereas the aristocrats of the Habsburg Empire sought to save all their social privileges by taking a share of political power, the French were willing to give up the foremost of these privileges—tax exemption—for a share of political power. The Assembly of Notables of 1787 approved the principle of a uniform land tax, and during that same year the *Parlement* of Paris surrendered a bastion of the judicial nobility's special right to verify royal legislation when it denied its own long-cherished claim to virtual "representation" of the people. But both sacrifices were for the purpose of concentrating the entire weight of the conservative party and its popular support on the convocation of the Estates-General, which would restore the medieval corporate constitution of France in modernized form. Under it the aristocracy would be assured a permanent preeminent position in the representative organ of the nation and in the sovereign authority of the monarchy to tax and to legislate. The aristocracy thus hoped to translate the letter of particular social privileges

The Assembly of Notables, 1787. *On this occasion the French monarchy called upon its aristocracy for financial assistance and was refused, to the ultimate distress of both parties.*

into the substance of a political power which would guarantee the general conditions of its social superiority.

The merger of reactionary privilege and radical politics in a movement toward conservative revolution has been a recurrent feature of European history from the Reformation to National Socialism, and in each instance the combination has seemed so anomalous as to require precise social analysis of the group that led the movement. For the aristocratic revolutions of the late eighteenth century, the characterization of the leading group as "aristocrats" is only the beginning, rather than the conclusion, of such an analysis, since the contemporary eighteenth-century use of the term—a use that we have so far followed here—referred to the *political* party fighting for hierarchical constitutions and guarantees of privilege and not to the *social* group behind it. Recent studies of the social groupings in Europe on the eve of the French Revolution have stressed their internal divisions and increasing varieties, to the effect that the social group which twentieth-century analysts identify as the aristocracy was much too variegated to be represented as a single class by the political group which eighteenth-century publicists identified as aristocracy. Aristocracy, in its modern connotation, is defined as a social status actually held by all those who possess superior privilege, power, or influence over the rest of the society and who share a distinctively coded way of life, compounded of license in private, formality in public, and elegance in company. In its application to late eighteenth-century society it includes both old and recent nobility (dividing usually at four generations of hereditary title) and both traditional and new non-noble elites (such as old gentry families in Britain and parvenu banking families in France, respectively)—an assortment of social subgroups and interests that provided social aristocratic support to the politics of enlightened monarchy and of popular liberal constitutionalism as well as to the radical conservatism of the political "aristocrats."

The social grouping with which men linked the political "aristocrats" in the 1780's was thus not the aristocracy in our comprehensive sense of the term but a particular one of its subgroups, the old nobility, defined then as now as a stipulated legal status conferring definite title, hallowed by long familial possession, and guaranteeing exclusive privileges—most importantly, in our context, political access to high deliberative, judicial, or administrative offices of state. The contemporary testimony was undoubtedly correct, for the old nobility was indeed the social grouping that led the movement for conservative political "revolution," representing, defending, and followed by their clients among the old non-noble elite of country gentry and urban oligarchs. But this social identification does not, by itself, suffice to explain the movement toward a "revolutionary" reconstitution of the state on the part of lords who had hitherto preferred to move for feudal immunities from the state. The change is explicable by two novel features in the nobles' situation. First, when enlightened monarchs or the enlightened ministers of monarchs withdrew the political guarantees of social privilege from the alliance of sovereignty and hierarchy which had composed the settled order of the Old Regime, nobles rushed to fill the void of the political authority upon which they had become dependent for their security. Second, the growth and reorientation of the larger social aristocracy whose status the old nobility actually shared but consciously rejected reached dimensions, with its absorption of contemporary economic and cultural elites, which drew from the nobles a political response as ambivalent as their social position within the aristocracy. Thus both the collective aristocratic status which eighteenth-century men did not recognize and the noble status which they exclusively recognized were factors in the politics of conservative revolution. This politics grew in good measure out of the actual relations between the inclusive aristocracy and the exclusive nobility, and for a social explanation of the politics it is to these relations that we now turn.

The most prominent common attribute of the European aristocracy throughout the eighteenth century remained what it had traditionally been for the nobility it counted within its ranks: the possession of landed estates. But this formal mark of unity covered a myriad of distinctions, old and new, which actually divided both the landowning aristocracy and its partial subset, the titled nobility, into a myriad of separate, often conflicting, interests. The aristocracy still included both noble and non-noble estate owners within its ranks. Within the nobility, by the same token, aristocrats had still to be distinguished from the non-aristocrats who commanded neither power, prestige, wealth, nor, often enough, even a landed estate. As one went from east to west in Europe the coincidence of nobility and aristocracy diminished from the full overlay in Russia to the mere peerage in Great Britain, which would have been impotent without the untitled gentry that with it made up the British aristocracy.

Again, within the European landed aristocracy the distinction persisted between the eastern serf-owning noble who wielded public administrative and judicial powers over his peasants and the western landlord who collected rents and dues from free tenants. Within the eastern serf-owning nobility, in turn, there was the further distinction between those who cultivated their own demesne with servile labor and those who let it out in servile tenures. Among the western landlords there was the distinction between those who rented their own lands to farmers through terminal leases, as in Britain, and those who possessed customary obligations upon hereditary tenures legally owned by the occupying peasants, as in France. If, finally, the old legal distinction between high and low nobility persisted with diminished force, the equally hoary social differentiations of ancient from new nobility, of the nobility of blood and sword from the nobility of administrative and judicial office, of court from country nobility, persisted with increasing force.

To these familiar divisions within the aristocracy, the growth of wealth, the attractions of the great cities, and the spread of secular culture during the eighteenth century added new distinctive criteria, bringing in additional ranks of aristocrats and redrawing some of the lines among the old. If the landed estate and the manor house remained the most uniform overt marks of aristocracy, they were now much more often than previously the signs rather than the bases of aristocratic status: men acquired them to make visible the social position they had actually attained in other ways. The possession of wealth in particular now became a widespread and accepted ground of aristocracy, bringing rich commoners into the ranks of the privileged and increasing the ratio of monied aristocrats to poor nobles. If, moreover, the magnet of commercial profits still drew comparatively few landowners, outside of England, into the class of progressive farmers who applied scientific techniques to agricultural production, it did increase the class of landlords who were oriented toward a market economy, whether indirectly, by using enclosures (as in England) or the dusty old claims of the "manorial reaction" (as in France) to increase their rents, or directly, by participating or investing in manufacturing or in wholesale and international trade. Second, the vogue of Enlightenment culture changed the standards of the way of life that was deemed both common and essential to members of the aristocracy. Intelligence, knowledgeability, the arts of communication, and good taste, now brought some of the intellectual elite—like Voltaire—into the aristocracy as a distinct group and sowed a new seed of distinction within the older aristocracy between its cultured and its unlettered sectors. Finally, the development of the cities—both capital and, to a lesser extent, provincial—into centers of social concourse, intellectual discussion, and performance of the arts developed a new kind of urbanized aristocracy with an ambition, an openness, and a mobility quite distinct from the qualities of the old rural nobility.

The superimposition of the newer upon the older criteria of aristocracy pointed in two contrary directions. On the one side, it tended to break down the old aristocratic barriers, and this attenuation included both the barriers separating the aristocratic from the nonaristocratic sectors of the society and the barriers separating one kind of aristocracy from another. The accommodation of the aristocracy to the standards set by the possession and the expenditure of monetary wealth and by the participation in and consumption of a generally accessible urban culture opened it to the elite of talent and intelligence, whatever its social provenance. Through commoners' purchase of landed estates, intermarriage into the families of needy nobles, and purchase of or skillful performance in high public office, the magic circle of aristocracy was in fact expanded, and in France and Great Britain particularly, the expectation of such upward social mobility became widespread among ambitious commoners. So permeable, indeed, did the expansion of aristocracy seem to make the barrier between noble and deserving commoner that many Frenchmen awarded themselves titles as their own just desserts and simply used them on their own authority as befitting their acquired station. Under these influences, too, such older distinctions within the aristocracy as those between the military and the judicial nobility in France or between the peerage and the gentry in Britain or between the landed and the bureaucratic nobility in Germany became quite blurred in reference to both their social prestige and their political influence.

On the other side, however, this same overlay of new upon old varieties of aristocracy led to a process of segregation through which the newly joined forces of older aristocrats sealed themselves off from the threatened inundation by new aristocrats and the pressing hordes of ambitious commoners behind them. The most striking evidence of this tendency occurred in Britain, where an economic and legal situation that made the relations between commonalty and aristocracy more fluid than anywhere else was accompanied, in the second half of the eighteenth century, by surprisingly few intermarriages between commoners and the great aristocratic families, sales of estates by nobles to commoners, or entries by commoners into the peerage. Throughout Europe, indeed, the formal creation of new nobles by the kings failed to keep pace with the pressure of the new aristocratic elite which was being increasingly populated by practitioners of the noble way of life recruited from the beneficiaries of rising incomes and from the ranks of cultivated men.

The important fact about this lag was that it was not simply a matter of institutional inertia. It was part of a more general policy on the part of the ensconced nobility, who used their growing influence in the royal governments to reinforce the definite legal criteria of nobility against the flood of claimants admitted through the actual porous standards of the new aristocracy. More and more, indeed, as the century wore on, the institutions of state became the battleground of the social conflict between the new *de facto* aristocracy and the bourgeois aspirants to that status on one side and the older nobility who would reassert their preeminence on the other. Thus, of the letters of nobility that monarchs did issue in the second half of the century far more were rewards for government service than for any other cause, and to counter this pressure the older nobility tried to anchor social caste in political privilege by making noble status of ancient lineage the necessary qualification for high governmental position. The French *parlements*' reservation of their top posts to men with four quarters (*i.e.* generations) of nobility during the 1770's and the official French stipulation, by the royal edict of 1781, of the same social requirement for army commissions were clear indications of the political lever which the conservative nobility sought to use upon the shifting social basis of the aristocratic class.

The very variety of aristocratic types and the tensions between them that historians have stressed in their social analyses of the European aristocracy during the second half of the eighteenth century give the clue to the main agents of the conservative revolutions. The conservative revolutionaries were representatives of the older nobility who took account of contemporary conditions and responded to them in two related ways. They accommodated themselves to the concentration of power in central governments, to the popular culture of the Enlightenment, and to the mobile society of a mercantile economy. But they also were in mortal fear of the leveling consequences of these contemporary conditions. Hence the members of this nobility sought to take political control of the modernizing tendencies in their society in order to direct them to the support of a stabilized aristocracy.

The connection between the ambivalent social attitude of the nobility toward the broader aristocratic culture of the age and its equally ambivalent politics of conservative "revolution" was epitomized in the leadership of the political nobles: the old Whigs in England and the judicial nobility in France were precisely those aristocrats who had long since joined the old nobility and appropriated its exclusive standards but who also retained the capacity to adapt their interests and policies to changing conditions. This connection between the social and the political positions of the old nobles was epitomized too in the terminology of their liberal opponents. The liberals gave the label of "grandees" to the great noble families which used their positions of power in the high offices of state to oppose all politics of reform by the king's government, and the overtones of the label indicated precisely the balance between their exploitation of the contemporary monetary and intellectual culture and their arrogant deprecation of the society that produced it.

The schizoid attitudes of the old high nobility toward its kings and its

contemporary society explain both the limits and the result of the conservative "revolution" it led. Driven to political opposition against the sovereigns they needed by what they considered to be the royal unbalancing of
traditional constitutions, the "grandees" and their clients in the lower old
aristocracy could not take their "revolution" beyond the conquest of only
enough political power to enforce permanent cooperation upon the monarch. But the progressive and universal character of the appeals in which
the old nobles, given their contemporaneity, could not help but dress their
claims, galvanized the newer mobile elites and underprivileged commoners
first into subordinate support of the nobiliar movement and then, in the
active societies of the Atlantic coast, into independent and authentic
popular revolution.

THE POPULAR REVOLUTIONS

Because the movements which sought to shift the ultimate political
power over the general rules of the society from the hierarchies of authority
to the people as a homogeneous body organized themselves outside the
institutions of the Old Regime and opposed both the political and the
social bases of the Old Regime, they made the only integral revolution of
the revolutionary generation that closed out the eighteenth century. In
this kind of revolutionary movement, underprivileged and unprivileged
social groups did what had never been done before. They created their own
political mass movement, and they worked out their own program, appropriate to it. Instead of sovereign kings these groups demanded royal agents
symbolic of and accountable to the sovereign will of the nation. Instead of a
many-tiered social hierarchy they demanded a single body of equal citizens, differentiated only by the simple assignment of its socially independent members to participate in government on behalf of all. And instead of
exalting philosophies for the principles of explanation that justified an ultimate order of reality, they produced ideologies to serve as principles of action that would realize the ultimate rights of all men.

The distinction between the underprivileged and the unprivileged
groups in the revolutionary movements of the period was a crucial one.
The underprivileged consisted of those who had status in the existing
society, but a status that put them in the lower reaches of the privileged
hierarchy. Ranging from country gentlemen to master artisans, they consisted mainly of the merchants, professional men (especially lawyers),
larger shopkeepers, new manufacturers, middle-income farmers, and writers—the group that was called the "middling set" in Britain and that would
speak for the Third Estate in France. The unprivileged group, called the
"inferior set" in Britain and the Fourth Estate in France, consisted largely
of the unpropertied in town and country: journeymen, small shopkeepers,
peasant sharecroppers and farm workers.

These two revolutionary groups had different positions in the society, and, consequently, different aims for it. The members of the underprivileged group enjoyed some of the exemptions from obligations, and often enough, even a measure of the political rights, that the Old Regime had to offer substantial property owners, but as beneficiaries of the commercial prosperity and as avid consumers of the Enlightenment, their ambition was to extend their influence, not as of yore, by ascending the available ladder of social privilege, but by creating a new channel to political power outside the old. Whether this new road to political power—which was usually identified with representative government based on a broad propertied electorate—would be an addition to or a replacement of the traditional avenues of aristocratic and bureaucratic influence depended upon the responsiveness of the privileged groups on the one hand and the unprivileged on the other.

For the great mass of unprivileged men and women in towns and countryside who made up the overwhelming majority of Europe's population, life during the late eighteenth century remained nearly as precarious, brutal, and miserable as it had ever been, and much of their response to the exigent conditions of their existence was correspondingly as immediate, visceral, and compulsively conservative as it had ever been. Very few of these people, indeed, were practically affected by the improvements in medical science and public sanitation that were a restricted feature of the age, and the general increase of population from mid-century on, accompanied as it was by a general price rise and the persistence of sporadic crop failures, actually swelled the numbers of landless peasants, underemployed drifters, and other consumers dependent on market supplies, whose sufferings grew with the rising cost of living. Hence the bulk of the popular disturbances in the period took the traditional forms of the food riot against the inflated price of grain, the strike for higher wages by journeymen, apprentices, and common laborers, risings against real or fancied violations of customary rights by landlord or public officials, and the mass frenzy in favor of one kind of popular faith against another kind of unpopular faith. The Gordon Riots of 1780, when anti-Catholic crowds burned, looted, and took over the streets of London for more than a week in support of Lord George Gordon's protest against the grant of civil rights to Roman Catholics by the liberal Catholic Relief Act of 1778, was only the most prominent case of the preference for good old social and religious causes on the part of those who had ever been without privilege, were now increasingly numerous and insecure as well, and hankered more than ever for the familiar certainties.

But there also were changes of degree in these conditions that helped to produce, among some men in some places, a political attitude that was new in kind. If there were more of the poor and the desperate than ever, the slight ameliorations of their lot which the late eighteenth century did witness sufficed to make the familiar blind riot for material or fanatical ends somewhat more infrequent than heretofore and thus to leave some of the unprivileged disengaged and ready for a more constructive appeal. The increase in the numbers of the unprivileged meant more actual misery, but because it also meant increased longevity, it changed their attitude toward their misery. The implications of this fall in mortality were such as to divert growing numbers of men from participation in the chronic rioting of what has been called the "preindustrial mob." The psychic implications of an increased life expectancy are indeterminable for the short-run period of a single generation, but the economic corollary of an improved system of life support was confirmed by the new crops and the better means of transportation that made famine a much rarer calamity in the later eighteenth century than it had ever been before. In some of the mobile western societies of the Atlantic seaboard, morover, the same demographic and economic growth that was dislocating the lowest orders of the society from their accustomed places and readying them for novelty was also producing a special kind of unprivileged group that coud receive and transmit the liberal political appeals diffused by the literate underprivileged groups in the name of equal rights for all. Out of the ranks of sharecroppers, artisans, and small shopkeepers, a growing layer of enterprising and prosperous peasants, traders, and manufacturers emerged to join the interests of the unprivileged with the programs of the underprivileged. They were abetted by a restive group of intellectual have-nots, dissatisfied ideologists who separated themselves from the intellectual elite and translated the social needs of the unprivileged into the political language of the underprivileged.

Popular revolutionary movements of a new type, involving either the underprivileged alone or the underprivileged and the unprivileged in combination, founding political concentrations (they were still too loose and informal to be called organizations) of their own outside the regular corporate institutions of the society, and asserting goals transcending the rearrangement of the regular corporate institutions in the state, made their appearance in the Netherlands, the Austrian Netherlands, Great Britain and its American and Irish dependencies, and finally in France.

The Free Corps movement in the Netherlands and the Vonckists in the Austrian Netherlands were liberal mcvements of the underprivileged and enlightened middle classes who fought for the end of oligarchic domination within the provinces and for national constitutions which would give representation to the bulk of property owners. But they were not joined by the unprivileged mass, which in the Netherlands tended to remain loyal to the house of Orange and in the Austrian Netherlands supported the traditional corporations against the Vonckists.

The American and Irish developments were special cases, since the separate legislative institutions in each of these dependencies—the colonial assemblies in America and the Irish Parliament at Dublin—provided rallying points for coalitions of conservatives, liberals, and sections of a mass movement. In America the coalition persisted at least until the achievement of independence. In Ireland, however, where liberal political reform rather than national independence was the main issue, the European pattern prevailed: the coalition dissolved before the essential institutions of the Old Regime were breached. In the late 1770's the example of the American Revolution, the crippling effect of British restrictions on Irish trade, and the temporary vacuum of British military force in Ireland produced the Irish volunteers, a militia organization led by such members of the liberal Anglo-Protestant Irish gentry as Henry Grattan (1746–1820) and Henry Flood (1732–1791), including both Protestant peers and the Protestant middle class in its ranks, and drawing support from a small active sector of the unenfranchised Catholic minority. As long as the Volunteers concentrated on the issues of Irish free trade and the legislative independence of the Irish Parliament, the coalition was effective. But with the rise of the issue of parliamentary reform the process of dissolution set in. The British concession of complete legislative autonomy to the unreformed Irish Parliament in 1782 bought off the more conservative sections of the Anglo-Irish establishment, while the liberals split between those who would simply remove political disabilities from the more substantial Catholics within the existing electoral system and those who would fundamentally change the whole traditional system of voting by historic counties and incorporated boroughs. By 1785 the liberal movement had run down, enervated by its own divisions, by Catholic passivity, and by the ties between the Irish and English Protestant establishments.

The defeat of these popular revolutions by coalitions of aristocracy and monarchy was a more faithful reflection of the balance of internal power even in the waning years of the Old Regime than was the impression of democratic strength given by the frequency of such revolutions. For they achieved their greatest force, as has been noted, in the politically or geographically peripheral areas of the European political system, where the continuing traditions of the city-state kept alive the possibility of direct popular participation in government, or where the combination of great distance from the political center with viable local institutions debilitated both the physical and the moral hold of the sovereign central authority so typical of the Old Regime. Certainly the turmoil in these outlying societies did reflect, in exaggerated form, strains in the states and societies of Western Europe at large, but for the proper perspective on the role of popular revolutions in the territorial societies whose growth had been most characteristic of the Old Regime we must look to the great states of England and France. We shall find such movements, to be sure, but we must attend carefully to their spatial and social limitations in the former case and their temporal limit in the latter.

England

As might be expected from the lively memories of their seventeenth-century revolutions, the first popular revolutionary movement in eighteenth-century Europe arose among the English. Anticipating the pattern that would become standard elsewhere, the mass movement that gathered in 1763 around the slogan "Wilkes and liberty" had its origins in a situation prepared by the opposition of a politically displaced aristocratic group to what it conceived to be the despotic innovations of royalty.

George III (ruled 1760–1820) is now generally conceded to have been not nearly so authoritarian, nor the Whig opposition so libertarian, as the rhetoric of the latter and of their later advocates on both sides of the Atlantic seemed to indicate. The first of the Hanoverians to have been born in England, the new king was in accord with the fundamentals of the balanced constitution as we have seen them laid down at the revolutionary settlement after 1688 and developed by Walpole and his Whig successors. Indeed, George III's policies and problems alike stemmed from the very literalness with which he took his rights within the constitution. But despite the underlying continuity between his reign and the Whig ascendancy that preceded him, his abrupt changes of ministers after 1760 and his persistent search for managers hostile to the Whig connection until he settled down with the younger William Pitt after 1783 was caused by more than the personal pique at his father's hated entourage that has been standard for the ruling houses of Europe. His politics were an attempt to develop the constitution by restoring to the substance of the royal power the management of the constitutional keys which the Whigs had actually controlled by informal conventions in the name of the royal power. Thus the King was neither a despot nor a revolutionary, but within the flexible constitution he certainly did intend a change of system that would, as the Whigs feared, sheer them of political power. The King was interested not in asserting his royal prerogative at the expense of Parliament, as his seventeenth-century forebears had been, but in asserting his constitutional prerogative to approve the actions of his own ministers—actions which lay in the no-man's-land between King and Parliament—and to use patronage, connections, influence on the politically dependent members and persuasion on the independent members to secure a majority for his government in the House of Commons, just as the great Whig families had used these means to make the mixed constitution work when they had formed the ministries under the earlier, more passive Hanoverians.

But whatever the constitutional rights of the matter, the political effect was clear enough. Powerful factions of the Whig governing class accused the King of upsetting the balance of the constitution by using the appointments and emoluments in the possession of the Crown and the government to control Parliament by pushing the election of his "placemen"—i.e., servants of the Crown—and by corrupting members otherwise selected. The group around the elder William Pitt—his brother-in-law Richard Grenville, Earl of Temple, and his successors, William Petty, Earl of Shelbourne, and his son, William Pitt the Younger—and the group around Charles Wentworth, Marquis of Rockingham—especially the radical Charles Lennox,

Great Britain's King George III,
of American ill-fame.

Duke of Richmond, and the American and Irish sympathizer, Edmund
Burke—not only opposed the King's party in Parliament but encouraged
and associated with the two main popular, extraparliamentary movements.
These two groups pioneered revolutionary modes of political action and
aimed at the radical reorganization of Parliament itself in the generation
before the French Revolution.

The first of these was the movement of 1763–1774 that focused on the
career and tribulations of John Wilkes (1727–1797). The unstable character
of the man, the sporadic violence of his following, and the recurrent sympathy with its cause by one or another group in the Whig opposition show
immediately how limited the revolutionary possibilities of the movement
were. Wilkes was a profligate, dissolute, shrewd, charming, and desperate
careerist who had married into the gentry and bought an election, in a
style not unusual for the time, to the House of Commons. He turned to
demagoguery as his only alternative for political and pecuniary salvation
when his early attachment to Pitt's and Temple's following in the House
of Commons failed to save him from prosecution by the King's government for seditious libel. He was prosecuted on the basis of an article which
was simply a more scurrilous attack than usual against the character and
credibility not of the King but of his "Minister." He was arrested on a general warrant—that is, a warrant specifying the alleged crime but not the
accused—and his court appearances in London, where the empire-oriented
Pitt party had a large following, were attended by unruly crowds who demonstrated under the banner of "Wilkes and Liberty." Wilkes immediately
responded to them in kind by declaring that his case represented not only
"the liberty of all peers and gentlemen," but "what touches me more sensi-

bly, that of all the middling and inferior set of people, who stand most in need of protection." The "liberty" that was at stake was hardly new: it involved the legality, by the standards of the traditional rights of Englishmen, of particular instruments of governmental prosecution—in this case, the general warrant—and it involved the immunities of members of Parliament. Wilkes was released in May on the ground of his parliamentary immunity, and his case also had as a permanent, albeit indirect, result, the definitive outlawing of general warrants both by the Court of King's Bench and by the House of Commons.

But the Wilkes affair was far from over, and its subsequent course centered around a far more revolutionary issue of liberty involving Parliament—the political rights of electors. Late in 1763 Wilkes's decision to reprint the earlier indirect attack upon the King and to print a pornographic *Essay on Woman* not only brought a new prosecution on joint-charges of seditious libel, obscenity, and blasphemy but transformed the nature and backing of his cause. Wilkes went into exile to escape arrest, and his aristocratic allies, now scandalized, withdrew their support. When he finally returned to England in 1768, he made his appeal directly to the constituencies, over the heads of all the parties, for election to the House of Commons. After one false start in the City of London itself, where he was roundly defeated, Wilkes ran for a county seat in Middlesex, a suburb of London. Pitching his campaign primarily at "the middling and inferior sets," who responded enthusiastically with demonstrations and occasional riots, Wilkes was elected in March, 1768, and upon successive disqualifications by the House of Commons, was reelected three times. The House brought the issue to a climax by admitting Wilkes's defeated opponent in the fourth election (April, 1769) to Wilkes's seat as member for Middlesex.

Between 1769 and 1774, before Wilkes's election as mayor of London and his qualification by the Commons for his Middlesex seat diverted him into respectability and his support into regular institutional channels, the Wilkite movement took on its most organized and its most revolutionary form. It was revolutionary in its appeal. However legal it felt its specific demands to have been, the movement summarized them under the call for a generic "liberty" which attracted all who felt, however vaguely, that their rights of whatever kind were being violated and which made freedom, for such people, the primary principle of the constitution and the primary value in politics. Again, it was revolutionary in its method. The Society of the Supporters of the Bill of Rights, which was organized to support Wilkes's right to his seat in Parliament and campaigned in 1769 for the rights of electors, the dismissal of the king's ministers, and the dissolution of Parliament, was the first of the many political pressure groups whose organization of mass movements outside the regular institutional channels of public opinion would be instrumental in the "bloodless revolutions" of

The Battle of Temple Bar. A *Wilkite mob breaks up a merchants' procession in a scene of striking modernity.*

nineteenth-century England. There was, finally, a revolutionary factor in the social identity of the people who were mobilized. Contemporaries often referred to Wilkes's supporters, particularly in the metropolitan area, as the "mob," and if, as we shall soon see, this characterization was far too indiscriminate for accuracy, the fact is that he did bring into action under the liberal political banner the kind of unprivileged, unenfranchised, and unpropertied members of the lower orders who had been traditionally subject only to stimuli of an economic or bigoted kind.

But if the development focusing on John Wilkes is thus important as the first appearance in a great state of a popular and extraconstitutional movement for liberal change, the limits of the development are equally important, for they indicate the weighty factors militating against the success of such a movement in a viable state of eighteenth-century Europe.

The development had, first, its geographic limits. Wilkes's popular support was centered in London and was for the most part limited to the contiguous counties of Middlesex and Surrey.

Again, the development had its social limits. The crucial fact was that the social group characterized as the "mob" or "inferior set" included a large proportion of county and borough voters, since traditional electoral rights in Middlesex and London extended far down the social ladder. Consequently, Wilkes's sporadic appeal to the unprivileged journeyman and laborer, precedent though it later proved to be, was actually far less important to the contemporary movement than his continuing appeal to the enfranchised traders and craftsmen of the inferior set, and in lesser degree, to the merchants and professional men of the middling set, who felt themselves an underprivileged part of the political nation.

The Wilkite development was limited, finally, by the moderate nature of its program. The main direction of the movement was, in the early terms of the Society of the Supporters of the Bill of Rights, "to defend and maintain the legal, constitutional liberty of the subject." Thus the main effort of the movement, aside from the support of Wilkes in his trials and campaigns, lay in such respectable enterprises as extending safeguards against unjust prosecution, securing the immunities of members of Parliament against the crown, securing the rights of electors against Parliament, and extending the freedom of the press to the publication of parliamentary debates. There were proposals, to be sure, that were not so compatible with the existing constitution. The Society of the Supporters of the Bill of Rights, in particular, spawned demands for constitutional change that focused on shorter terms of Parliament than the existing seven years and on radical revisions of its popular base which would involve both the extension of suffrage and the destruction of aristocratic influence, especially in the boroughs. Wilkes himself, indeed, introduced such a measure into the House of Commons in 1776. But this aspect of the movement was a product of its fragmentation. It rose in the Society as a function of its radicalization and helped to split it both internally and from the country at large. Like Wilkes' own presentation of it to the House, in short, the radical content in the Wilkite movement was a dud.

The second stage of the English development toward popular revolution—The Association movement of 1780–1785—showed a similar blend of radical tendencies and moderate limits, but with the terms reversed. This time the aims were radical but the methods moderate. The center of the revived radical movement was a very different man from John Wilkes. Christopher Wyvill (1740–1822) was a member of an old and respected Yorkshire gentry family, a possessor of a prosperous estate in that county, and a retired clergyman. In him this background combined to make a man of independent and highly moralistic mind who abominated the "corruption" of the court, of the Parliament he deemed controlled by it, and of the aristocratic factions through which he deemed the control exercised. For him, then, the reform of corruption entailed not only the exclusion of "placemen" from Parliament but the thoroughgoing expansion of the electorate to increase the independent members of Parliament. Thus he exemplified the development of the English revolutionary movement from the traditional defense against the powers of the king to the popular offensive against the combined powers of king and aristocracy.

But Wyvill tempered the radicalism of his political morality with the caution of a country gentleman. Although he recognized the theoretical validity of annual Parliaments based on universal manhood suffrage, he worked for triennial Parliaments based on independent property owners—an accommodation which in practice came down to the demand for increasing by one hundred, in proportion to population, the eighty members who represented the forty counties equally, regardless of size, in the unreformed House. Similarly, he took over, for the organization of his movement, the idea of an Association of deputies from reform-minded constituencies—an idea which had first been broached in James Burgh's *Political Disquisitions* of 1774 as a revolutionary proposal for a constituent assembly with the sovereign power to enforce reform on Parliament—but turned it into a collaboration among the gentry of the several counties to present commonly designed petitions to Parliament for its own reform.

Like Wilkes, Wyvill found allies both in the aristocratic opposition to the king's government and in the radical movement of metropolitan London. But Wyvill, who retained the initiative in what there was of the movement outside of London, opted first for an organization of county gentry over the appeal to the middling and lower freeholding electorate, and then for cooperation with the aristocratic reform movement in the Commons over the popular radical movement in the country at large. When his aristocratic support failed him Wyvill had no resource left.

Given the respectability of Wyvill's social status and the moral fastidiousness of his temperament, the revolutionary qualities of the Association movement he led stand out like beacons: like the Wilkite movement it proposed to effect change by organizing people for action outside the regular institutions of the society, and even more than the Wilkite movement it proposed to achieve changes in the constitution that would in effect shift sovereignty from the Parliament (which, it will be remembered, constitutionally included king, lords, and commons) to the House of Commons and would shift the constituent power from the corporate interests to the propertied electorate of the kingdom.

Over and above these obvious qualities, the Association movement produced a more subtle contribution to the modern syndrome of revolution. In the Society for Constitutional Information it produced an early grouping of the kind of intellectuals who would play their due role in the revolutions of all the western countries. Its leaders were intellectual activists who were distinguished not by the cogency of their theory but by the concrete application they gave to a mixture of current political ideas. John Jebb (1736–1786) adapted to Wyvill's movement James Burgh's theory of a sovereign Association which would represent "the acknowledged right of the people to new-model its constitution." John Cartwright (1740–1824) applied the old Leveller argument for equal suffrage on the basis of the right of "personality" to the same purpose. They represented, in general, the eighteenth-century "Commonweathman", who perpetuated the English seventeenth-century revolutionary tradition in simplified and modernized form. The Society thus gathered pamphleteers and journalists who were themselves neither philosophers nor theorists, but who created a new social role for philosophical and theoretical ideas.

But overshadowing these revolutionary facets of the Association movement were the two crucial antirevolutionary features that ultimately undermined it. First—in contrast to the Wilkite movement—the social groups concerned in the Association organization not only were limited entirely to those whom we have called the underprivileged rather than the unprivileged—that is, to those with political rights, albeit not with equal political rights, in the established constitution—but also to those who had their center of gravity in the upper rather than the lower set of these underprivileged—that is, in the independent country gentry rather than in the ambitious tradesmen and craftsmen of the city.

Second, the actual effect of the movement was not to foment popular revolutionary forces, since these drained away by the mid-1780's, but rather to flow into the preestablished channels of aristocracy and king, as might have been expected from a movement which increasingly depended upon the factions in the established Parliament. In the Fox-North ministry of 1783, the former Rockingham Whigs under Burke enacted the measure of "economical reform"—that is, the reduction of governmental patronage through which the king could influence Parliament—which had been their joint plank with the Associationists, but in itself, this measure served not to make Commons less subject to influence as such or more responsible to its electorate or representative of a wider electorate, but only to reduce the king's influence in comparison with the aristocracy's. And when the younger Pitt began his long tenure as prime minister on behalf of the Crown in the waning days of 1783, the country gentry and the metropolitan trading classes that had backed the Association movement for constitutional change threw their support behind his reform of the king's administrative services, since his combination of efficiency in government and collaboration with the independent members of Parliament reconciled the underprivileged groups to the material and moral efficacy of the monarchy as a counterweight to the power of the "grandees" in the Lords and Commons.

The net result of the two decades of revolutionary unrest in England was to foreshadow the pattern of popular pressure and institutional response through which the aristocratic monarchy would ultimately reform itself. But this same unrest also demonstrated the persistent strength of both aristocracy and crown that would postpone the reform for half a century.

France

In France alone did the conditions that produced the great powers of eighteenth-century Europe also develop into the conditions of a massive popular revolution against the monarchical and aristocratic institutions characteristic of those powers. Oddly enough, in view of the profound effects of the events of 1789 in France, the prehistory of those events is brief. The French Revolution of 1789 was as convulsive as it was because in France, and only in France, an elemental explosion of the unprivileged mass groups of the society converged with a political revolution by the articulate underprivileged groups for an equalized representative constitution. The conditions making for the massive unrest of peasants, artisans, shopkeepers, and unpropertied laborers in the countryside and the towns included long-range economic developments as well as a short-range crisis, and this side of the popular revolt certainly belongs to the Old Regime. But it was the political revolt of the middling classes that turned the mass unrest into a popular revolution, and this part of the story was a sudden growth that dated back only to the closing weeks of 1788 and that gave the end of the Old Regime the form of a sudden cataclysm.

The factors making for the unrest of the unprivileged masses—that is, primarily, the peasants and artisans—in eighteenth-century France were demographic and economic rather than social. The long-range social tendencies favored the easing rather than the aggravation of social tensions. In the countryside, the recognition of the peasants' personal freedom and of their property rights in the lands to which they held hereditary tenures joined with the growing markets for agricultural products and the rising price levels of the middle half century from 1730 to 1780 to produce a growing class of free and prosperous peasant proprietors. Certainly, manorial obligations on peasant land—rents, labor services, hunting and milling rights, all in favor of the lord—persisted and were even aggravated by the rediscovered dues associated with the lords' manorial reaction of the eighteenth century, but neither they nor the continuing burden of unequal taxes galvanized the French peasantry before 1789. Agrarian risings caused by deep-seated social and political grievances, such as occurred in eastern Europe, were not a feature of eighteenth-century France. In the towns, similarly, the expansion of small-scale trade and manufacturing and the deliberate governmental neglect of the restrictive guilds were reinforcing the growth of the independent class of small-scale proprietors so that they were becoming analogous to the peasant landholders in the countryside.

But against these pacifying social tendencies the effect of the dislocating changes wrought by population growth on the stagnant sectors of the economy increased, and these changes were intensified by the effects of the economic cycle. Beneath the group of prosperous peasants, artisans, and shopkeepers there grew an ever-larger group of sharecroppers, journeymen, and laborers who had only their lagging wages to balance their consumers' status and who consistently suffered under the long curve of rising prices.

The effect, against this long-term background, of a short-term recession after 1778 and an immediate crisis triggered by the catastrophic crop failure of 1788 was to depress the marginal producers, increase unemployment, worsen the position of those who were dependent on market sales, make desperate the position of those who were dependent on market purchases, and thus to spread fear throughout the unprivileged classes, prosperous and impoverished alike. It was in this situation, with the unprivi-

leged feeling themselves in the grip of forces beyond their control, that the
political revolution of the underprivileged who were legally grouped with
them in the order of the Third Estate suddenly provided the unprivileged
with the notion of king and aristocracy as the controlling powers of their
malign destiny.

Those belonging to the educated and literate group of merchants, lawyers, doctors, government officials, and writers whose influence, self-
confidence, articulateness, and expectations had risen far faster than their
legal rights and honors in eighteenth-century France were late indeed in
embarking on an independent political movement. Through almost the
entire century they had aligned themselves with the Crown or with aristocracy in the struggle between these two titans of the Old Regime, either
backing the equalizing reforms of the monarchy along with Voltaire and
Turgot, or following Montesquieu and the *parlements* and espousing the
privileges of the aristocratic corporations as the bastions of the whole
society against despotism. Even in the bitter struggle of 1787 and 1788
between the King's reforming ministers Calonne and Loménie de Brienne,
on the one side, and the aristocratic notables, led by the *parlementaires*,
on the other, over such vital issues as tax equalization and the convocation
of the Estates-General, the underprivileged bourgeois groups took no independent role but contented themselves with supporting the aristocratic
advocates of the constitutional cause.

The popular revolutionary movement thus rose only toward the end of
1788, after the *Parlement* of Paris affirmed the traditional procedure for
the Estates-General in September and a second Assembly of Notables confirmed the decision in December. This procedure, according to the precedent of the Estates' last meeting in 1614, entailed the separate voting by
the three orders and, consequently, the subordination of the commons to
the clerical and lay aristocracies. To their disaffection from royal absolutism the educated and propertied bourgeoisie now added an articulate rejection of aristocratic privilege. From this sequence of oppositions there followed not only a spate of pamphlet literature for an equality of commoner
representation in an Estates-General with real constitutional powers but
the organization of a "patriot" party, complete with committees of correspondence, already familiar from American, English, and Netherlandish
precedents of popular revolution.

But the French movement went beyond its other European counterparts
in its conjunction with the restive unprivileged masses on the land and in
the towns. In part this was accountable to the coincidence of the economic
crisis. In part it was accountable to the mechanics of the elections to the
Estates-General, for the breadth of the suffrage brought the underprivileged
and literate bourgeois together with unprivileged and illiterate peasants in
local or district assemblies of the Third Estate. In part, it was accountable to
the social geography of France, with its myriad towns spotted through the

countryside and their propertied citizens and officials in continuing contact with the small-town artisans and the surrounding peasantry. In part, finally, it was accountable to the fateful decision of the King to support the constitutional position of the aristocracy. For the merger of authorities removed the last possibility for the underprivileged or the unprivileged to rest their cases with one of the pillars of the Old Regime.

Thus was the first of the popular fronts created in France. Its program was formulated by a new kind of intellectual, a man who started from the particular practical grievances announced by the various unprivileged and underprivileged groups and used principles as the means of connecting them so that these groups might act in concert. The most notable of these ideologues was Abbé Emmanuel Joseph Sieyès, who replied to the titled question of his pamphlet, *What Is the Third Estate?* with the answer that essentially it was "everything" because he would reduce philosophy's absolute principles of universal human rights to a general appeal on behalf of the practical claims of the Third Estate.

And so, along with the age of kings, the age of the philosophers passed into history.

SUGGESTIONS
FOR FURTHER READING

(Books marked * are available in paperback.)

Single-volume surveys of the approximate period covered in this book tend to begin from the Peace of Utrecht in 1713 or the death of Louis XIV in 1715. Of these, the most valuable by recent standards is *M. S. Anderson, *Eighteenth Century Europe, 1713–1789* (New York, 1966) (Oxford Galaxy) because of its attention to economic, social, and political institutions and despite its comparative neglect of intellectual history. For political narrative, see *David Ogg, *Europe of the Ancien Régime, 1715–1783* (New York, 1966) (Harper Torchbook). For analytical chapters, see *R. J. White, *Europe in the Eighteenth Century* (New York, 1965) (St. Martin's). For light essays on eighteenth-century "states of mind," see Sir Harold Nicolson, *The Age of Reason* (Garden City, N.Y., 1961). For a good brief survey, see *Frank Manuel, *The Age of Reason* (Ithaca, N.Y., 1957) (Cornell). For the last generation of Europe in the Old Regime, R. R. Palmer, *The Age of the Democratic Revolution: A Political History of Europe and America, 1760–1800*, 2 vols. (Princeton, N.J., 1959–1964) is now required reading.

The more familiar and more minutely subdivided series on European history have entries for our whole period. It is covered for the *Rise of Modern Europe series (Harper & Row) by John B. Wolf, *The Emergence of the Great Powers, 1685–1715* (New York, 1951); Penfield Roberts, *The Quest for Security, 1715–1740* (New York, 1947); Walter L. Dorn, *Competition for Empire, 1740–1763* (New York, 1940); and Leo Gershoy, *From Despotism to Revolution, 1763–1789* (New York, 1944). The latter two volumes are particularly useful for their analysis of the relationships between politics and administration and between politics and society, respectively. From the *New Cambridge Modern History* we have Vol. VII, *The Old Regime, 1713–1763*, ed. by J. O. Lindsay (Cambridge, Eng., 1957) and Vol. VIII, *The American and French Revolutions, 1763–1793*, ed. by Albert Goodwin (Cambridge, Eng., 1965). What can be said for these series as a whole holds for their volumes covering our period in particular: their strength lies rather in their intensive descriptions or their particular essays than in their historical continuity or their development of themes over a considerable time span. The same disjointed and uneven excellence holds for the collection of essays in the sumptuously illustrated volume, *The Eighteenth Century: Europe in the Age of the Enlightenment*, ed. by Alfred Cobban (London, 1969).

There are satisfactory general national histories for the major countries of western and central Europe in the period. British developments are covered by one volume in Dorothy Marshall, *Eighteenth Century England* (New York, 1962) and by three volumes in the Oxford History of England series: George

Clark, *The Later Stuarts, 1660–1714* (Oxford, 1955); Basil Williams, *The Whig Supremacy, 1714–1760* (Oxford, 1939); and J. Steven Watson, *The Reign of George III, 1760–1815* (Oxford, 1960). See also *J. H. Plumb, *England in the Eighteenth Century* (Harmondsworth, 1950) (Pelican) and *R. J. White, *The Age of George III* (New York, 1969) (Doubleday Anchor). Among the recent general works on eighteenth-century France, both *Alfred Cobban, *A History of Modern France*, Vol. I, *1715–1799* (New York, 1965) (Penguin) and Gordon Wright, *France in Modern Times: 1760 to the Present* (Chicago, 1960) are recommended for the coverage indicated in their titles, and among the classics *Alexis de Tocqueville, *The Old Regime and the French Revolution* (New York, 1955) (Doubleday Anchor) remains important. For central Europe Hajo Holborn's *A History of Modern Germany: 1648–1840* (New York, 1964) covers both Germany and Austria in a work that remains alone in its field.

POLITICAL HISTORY

On Europe as a whole, the most recent work is E. N. Williams, *The Ancien Régime in Europe: Government and Society in the Major States, 1648–1789* (New York, 1970), a state-by-state survey in social context. For the rest, the history of eighteenth-century politics has been devoted either to absolutism or to diplomacy. *Max Beloff, *The Age of Absolutism, 1660–1815* (New York, 1966) (Harper Torchbook) is a political survey which includes the entire period, while Ronald W. Harris, *Absolutism and Enlightenment, 1660–1789* (London, 1964) deals far more with absolutism than with Enlightenment. *John G. Gagliardo, *Enlightened Despotism* (New York, 1967) (T. Y. Crowell) is a recent essay on the same aspect of the age which was covered earlier in *Geoffrey Brunn, *Enlightened Despots*, second ed. (New York, 1967) (Holt, Rinehart and Winston). On the diplomatic history of the age, *Ludwig Dehio, *The Precarious Balance* (New York, 1962) (Vintage) shows the long-range effects of the duel between Louis XIV and William III; *Albert Sorel, *Europe under the Old Regime* (Harper Torchbook), the first section of *L'Europe et la Révolution française*, 9 vols. (Paris, 1895–1911), is the classical cynical view of eighteenth-century diplomacy; Harold Temperley, *Frederick the Great and Kaiser Joseph*, second ed. (New York, 1968) is an intriguing account of the European policies and relations of the two monarchs; and Herbert Kaplan, *The First Partition of Poland* (New York, 1962) is a detailed case study of eighteenth-century diplomacy in its most notorious case.

What is available in English of national political history for the eighteenth century tends to revolve around political biography. For Great Britain, see especially two books by J. H. Plumb: *Sir Robert Walpole*, 2 vols. (Boston, 1956–1960) and *The First Four Georges* (New York, 1956); Sir Lewis B. Namier's two pioneering works in collective biography, *The Structure of Politics at the Accession of George III*, second ed. (New York, 1957) (St. Martin's Papermac) and *England in the Age of the American Revolution*, second ed. (New York, 1961) (St. Martin's Papermac); his classic essay on George III in *Personalities and Powers* (New York, 1955); and the development of his methods by Robert Walcott, *English Politics in the Early Eighteenth Century* (Cambridge, Mass., 1956); John B. Owen, *The Rise of the Pelhams* (London, 1957); John Brooke, *The Chatham Administration* (New York, 1956) and **The House of Commons, 1754–1790* (New York, 1968) (Oxford). On the side of conflict rather than consensus, Richard Pares, *King George and the Politicians* (Oxford, 1953) Herbert Butterfield, *King George, Lord North and the People* (London, 1949); **George Rudé, Wilkes and Liberty* (New York, 1962) (Oxford); and I. R. Christie, *Wilkes, Wyville and Reform* (New York, 1963), all relate political personalities to the upheavals of George III's reign. For France, see **John B. Wolf, Louis XIV* (New York, 1968) (Norton); George P. Gooch, *Louis XV: Monarchy in Decline* (London, 1956); Bernard Fay, *Louis XVI: The End of a World* (Chicago, 1968); Arthur M. Wilson, *French Foreign Policy during the Administration of Cardinal Fleury* (Cambridge, Mass., 1936); John M. S. Allison, *Lamoignon de Malesherbes* (New Haven, 1938); and Douglas Dakin, *Turgot and the Ancien Régime in France* (London, 1939). On Germany, see Pierre Gaxotte, *Frederick the Great* (London, 1941); George P. Gooch, *Frederick the Great* (London, 1947). On Austria, see Nicholas Henderson, *Prince Eugen of Savoy* (London, 1964); Edward Crankshaw, *Maria Theresa* (New York, 1970); Robert Pick, *Empress Maria Theresa: The Early Years* (New York, 1966); and, for Joseph II, Saul Padover, *The Revolutionary Emperor*, revised ed. (Hamden, Conn., 1967). On Russia's chief autocrats, N. Kliuchevski, *Peter the Great* (London, 1958) is a selection from a larger classic, and **G. S. Thomson, Catherine the Great and the Expansion of Russia* (New York, 1962) (Collier-Macmillan) is a useful survey.

Among the impersonal studies of national political events and institutions which are of more than monographic interest the following may be singled out for special attention. For Great Britain, **E. N. Williams, Eighteenth Century Constitution* (New York, 1960) (Cambridge U.); **D. L. Keir, Constitutional History of Modern Britain since 1485* (New York, 1967) (Norton); Betty Kemp, *Kings and Commons, 1660–1832* (New York, 1957); J. H. Plumb, *The Origins of Political Stability in England, 1675–1725* (Boston, 1967); and Vol. X of William Holdsworth's *History of English Law*, third ed., 16 vols. (London, 1922–1932) give standard accounts of the eighteenth-century constitution and its consolidation, while G. S. Veitch, *Genesis of Parliamentary Reform* (Hamden, Conn., 1967) and the first two volumes of Simon Maccoby, *English Radicalism*, 4 vols. (London, 1935–1961) give standard accounts of the rise of opposition to it. For France, aside from older narrative histories like J. B. Perkins, *France under the Regency* (Boston, 1892) and *France under Louis XV*, two vols. (Boston, 1897), English-language works on prerevolutionary politics have tended to focus on the limits of absolutism, as in Lionel Rothkrug, *Opposition to Louis XIV* (Princeton, N.J., 1965); Vivian R. Gruder, *The Royal Provincial Intendants: A Governing Elite in Eighteenth Century France* (Ithaca, N.Y., 1968); James D. Hardy, *Judicial Politics in the Old Regime: The Parliament of Paris under the Regency* (Baton Rouge, La., 1967); and *The Brittany Affair and the Crisis of the Ancien Régime*, ed. by John Rothney (New York, 1969). For Germany, as one might expect, the structure of Prussian government has attracted special scholarly concern, as in

*Hans Rosenberg, *Bureaucracy, Aristocracy, and Autocracy* (Boston, 1966) (Beacon); *Sidney B. Fay, *The Rise of Brandenburg-Prussia*, second ed. (New York, 1964) (Holt, Rinehart and Winston); and R. A. Dorwart, *Administrative Reform under Frederick William I* (Cambridge, Mass., 1953). But the reader's particular attention should be called to F. L. Carsten, *Princes and Parliaments* (New York, 1959) and Helen P. Liebel, *Enlightened Bureaucracy versus Enlightened Absolutism in Baden, 1750–1792* (Philadelphia, 1965), rare analyses of political relations in German states apart from both Prussia and Austria, and to Klaus Epstein, *The Genesis of German Conservatism* (Princeton, N.J., 1966), an analysis of the social and intellectual basis of conservative politics in all of eighteenth-century Germany. For the Habsburg dominions, see P. Frischauer, *The Imperial Crown* (London, 1939); H. J. Kerner, *Bohemia in the Eighteenth Century* (New York, 1932); H. Marczali, *Hungary in the Eighteenth Century* (New York, 1910); and Bela Kiraly, *Hungary in the late Eighteenth Century: The Decline of Enlightened Despotism* (New York, 1969). For Russia, Vol. IV and V of N. Kliuchevski, *History of Russia*, 5 vols. (New York, 1911–1931) remain brilliant and profound, albeit hobbled by a poor translation.

ECONOMIC AND SOCIAL HISTORY

Although students of modern history are accustomed to the close connection between economic development and social structure which has characterized industrial society and has been reflected in the historical writing about Europe in the nineteenth and twentieth centuries, such a connection does not hold for the historical writing about Europe in the eighteenth century. Economic history, especially in the English language, tends to be sparse, but social history is rich.

For economic history proper, the available literature—aside from isolated chapters in works of general history (see above)—is focused primarily on the origins of the agricultural and industrial revolutions, starting in the latter part of the eighteenth century. Thus the standard economic-history texts are too unspecific about the eighteenth century to be very useful to historians of the period, and the two outstanding economic histories cover, at the date of this writing, only aspects of the second half of the century. *The Cambridge Economic History of Europe* still lacks Vol. V, the eighteenth-century volume. Vol. VI (in two parts), *The Industrial Revolutions and After*, ed. by M. M. Postan and H. J. Habakkuk (Cambridge, Eng., 1965), reaches back into the eighteenth century for the beginnings of the Industrial Revolution, most valuably in David S. Landes, "Technological Change and Development in Western Europe, 1750-1914," a chapter which has been expanded in the same author's *Unbound Prometheus* (London, 1969). The other, much briefer and much older general work which historians have found especially appropriate to their own work—Witt Bowden, Michael Karpovich, and A. P. Usher, *Economic History of Europe since 1750* (New York, 1937)—also begins, as the title indicates, in the middle of our period. So do *W. W. Rostow's schematic *Stages of Economic Growth* (New York, 1960) (Cambridge U.) and W. O. Henderson's comparative *Britain and Industrial Europe, 1750–1870*, second ed.

(New York, 1965). In a more specialized vein, Vols. III and IV of Charles Singer, *et al.*, *History of Technology*, 5 vols. (Oxford, 1954–1958) is most informative on the details of technical innovation. Eli Heckscher, *Mercantilism*, second ed., 2 vols. (New York, 1955) is another larger work on a special economic function—in this case, governmental economic policy—which includes the eighteenth century in its purview.

Most of what is available on the national economic history of the period deals with Great Britain, both because of linguistic accessibility and because of the indisputable focus of primary economic growth there. Two books by Thomas S. Ashton—*An Economic History of England: The Eighteenth Century* (London, 1955) and **The Industrial Revolution, 1760–1830* (London and New York, 1948) (Oxford Galaxy)—and J. D. Chambers and G. E. Mingay, *The Agrarian Revolution, 1750–1880* (New York, 1966) are recent and substantial works along the future looking line. Only sporadic special studies are available to English-language readers on French economic history of the period: Warren C. Scoville, *The Persecution of the Huguenots and French Economic Development, 1680–1720* (Berkeley, Calif., 1960) and Shelby McCloy, *French Inventions of the Eighteenth Century* (Lexington, Ky., 1952). For central Europe the economic literature is similarly scattered. W. O. Henderson has two overlapping books on Prussian policy and economic growth—*The State and the Industrial Revolution in Prussia, 1740–1870* (New York, 1958) and *Studies in the Economic Policy of Frederick the Great* (New York, 1963). For Austrian and German economic thinking Albion Small, *The Cameralists* (Chicago, 1909) should still be consulted. For Russia, the eighteenth-century chapters of **Jerome Blum's* important *Lord and Peasant in Russia* (Princeton, N.J., 1961) (Atheneum) should be read for the economic basis of Russian agrarian relations.

Social history has traditionally been an amorphous field which has tended to shade off either into irrelevant details of daily existence or into politics and economics. But the historiography of eighteenth-century Europe has been benefited by the recent emphasis upon the independence of social history as the study of the kind of ordinary relations within and between groups of men and women which are prior to politics, connected with economics but not derivative from it, and definitive of the real life lived by most human beings in the past. On the European level, relevant documents and commentary for many groups are collected in **European Society in the Eighteenth Century*, ed. by Robert Forster and Elborg Forster (New York, 1969) (Harper Torchbook). For particular groups, we have **The European Nobility in the Eighteenth Century*, ed. by Albert Goodwin (New York, 1967) (Harper Torchbook); **Charles Morazé, Triumph of the Middle Classes* (New York, 1968) (Doubleday Anchor), which, however, as the title implies, emphasizes the nineteenth century; and for France and England, **George Rudé, The Crowd in History, 1730–1884* (New York, 1964) (Wiley).

Of the rich historical literature on social groups within the major European countries—in addition to the above-mentioned works by Namier on the politics of the British aristocracy, by Rudé on popular upheaval in Wilkite England, by Rosenberg on the interaction of Prussian aristocracy with Prussian monarchy, by Landes on the social impact of early industrialization, and by Blum on the social impact of agricultural change—the following are especially illuminating for the conditions of social life as such. For Great Britain, Dorothy Marshall, *English People in the Eighteenth Century* (New York, 1956); *Dorothy George, *England in Transition* (London, 1951) (Pelican); A. R. Humphreys, *The Augustan World* (London, 1954); and *Man versus Society in Eighteenth Century Britain*, ed. by James L. Clifford (Cambridge, Eng., 1968) have superseded, in substance if not in style, Vol. III of George M. Trevelyan, *Illustrated Social History*, 4 vols. (New York, 1949–1952). On particular aspects of British social life, see G. E. Mingay, *English Landed Society in the Eighteenth Century* (Toronto, 1963) for the stabilizing factor; the opening chapter of *Asa Briggs, *The Making of Modern England, 1783–1867: The Age of Improvement* (New York, 1965) (Harper Torchbook) sketches the social basis of change late in the century.

For France, *Franklin L. Ford, *Robe and Sword* (New York, 1953) (Harper Torchbook) and Robert Forster, *The Nobility of Toulouse in the Eighteenth Century* (Baltimore, 1960) are important studies of the French aristocracy; *Elinor G. Barber, *Bourgeoisie in Eighteenth Century France* (Princeton, N.J., 1955) (Princeton) is an equally important study of the urban commoners; George Rudé, *The Crowd in the French Revolution* (New York, 1959) gives background on the French masses in the *ancien régime*; *C. B. Behrens, *The Ancien Régime* (New York, 1967) (Voyager) and *Georges Lefebvre, *The Coming of the French Revolution*, trans. by R. R. Palmer (New York, 1957) (Vintage) give the social background of all classes. Shelby McCloy, in *The Humanitarian Movement in Eighteenth Century France* (Lexington, Ky., 1957) and *Government Assistance in Eighteenth Century France* (Durham, N.C., 1946), deals with national movements for social welfare. On the local level, *Franklin L. Ford, *Strasbourg in Transition, 1648–1789* (New York, 1966) (Norton) is a microcosm of social development; John McManners, *French Ecclesiastical Society under the Ancien Régime* (New York, 1961) is a microcosm of social stability.

For German society, the standard works in English are two books by W. H. Bruford: *Germany in the Eighteenth Century* (Cambridge, Eng., 1935) (Cambridge U.) and *Culture and Society in Classical Weimar, 1775–1806* (Cambridge, Eng., 1962). See too the recent study on the German peasantry by John Gagliardo, *From Pariah to Patriot* (Lexington, Ky., 1969). On the Austrian peasantry, see Edith M. Link. *The Emancipation of the Austrian Peasant, 1740–1798* (New York, 1949).

For Russian society in the eighteenth century, the outstanding recent work is *Marc Raeff, *Origins of the Russian Intelligentsia: The Eighteenth Century Nobility* (New York, 1966) (Harbinger), but P. Dukes, *Catherine the Great and the Russian Nobility* (Cambridge, Eng., 1968) and the relevant sections of *G. T. Robinson *Rural Russia under the Old Regime* (Berkeley, Calif., 1967) (U. of California) can also be consulted with profit. Valentine Bill, *The Forgotten Class: The Russian Bourgeoisie from the Earliest Beginnings to 1900* (New York, 1959) is disappointingly thin on a promising subject.

INTELLECTUAL HISTORY

The main theme in the recent literature on the intellectual history of
the eighteenth century is the refutation, both for the culture as a whole
and for its individual representatives, of its homogeneous characterization
as an age of secularized reason, the characterization often inferred from
such formerly standard works as *Carl Becker, *The Heavenly City of the
Eighteenth Century Philosophers* (New Haven, 1932) (Yale) and *Basil
Willey, *The Eighteenth Century Background* (New York, 1941)
(Beacon). These refutations insist both that the particular intellectual
movement called "the Enlightenment" was far from being co-extensive
with the entire variegated culture of eighteenth-century Europe and that
the Enlightenment was itself far too variegated a movement to admit of
simple definition, or indeed, for some historians, of any definition at all.
Such recent refutations are exemplified by the cultural diversity shown in
the essays of *The Age of Enlightenment*, ed. by W. H. Barber, *et al.*
(Edinburgh, 1967) and *Aspects of the Eighteenth Century*, ed. by Earl R.
Wasserman (Baltimore, 1965); by the plurality of Enlightenment motifs
shown in Alfred Cobban, *In Search of Humanity* (New York, 1960); by
the existentialist variety of eighteenth-century attitudes in Lester G.
Crocker, *An Age of Crisis: Man and World in Eighteenth Century French
Thought* (Baltimore, 1959); and by the unexpected views of some eighteenth-century intellectuals on religion in *Frank Manuel, *The Eighteenth
Century Confronts the Gods* (New York, 1967) (Atheneum), and on
social science in Louis I. Bredvold, *The Brave New World of the Enlightenment* (Ann Arbor, Mich., 1961). The great modern synthesis, which
accounts for all such critiques and reconstructs the Enlightenment in the
light of them as a coherent movement, is Peter Gay, *The Enlightenment:
An Interpretation*, 2 vols. (New York, 1966–1969). Vol. I has appeared in
paperback as *The Enlightenment: The Rise of Modern Paganism* (Vintage). This work is a mobile intellectual portrait, in contrast to *Ernst
Cassirer, *The Philosophy of the Enlightenment* (Boston, 1955) (Beacon),
which also argues for the integrity of the Enlightenment, but helped to provoke the challenges to it by imposing a rigid dialectical logic upon eighteenth-
century culture. Similar to Gay in their flexible reconstructions of eighteenth-
century thought are two volumes by Paul Hazard—*The European Mind
(New York, 1963) (Meridian), on the 1680–1715 generation, and *European
Thought in the Eighteenth Century* (New York, 1963) (Meridian) for the
succeeding period—and the recent convenient survey by Norman Hampson,
The Enlightenment (Baltimore, 1968) (Penguin).

For the various special branches of Enlightenment thought, the following readings may be recommended:

On religion and the churches in general, see *Gerald R. Cragg, *The
Church and the Age of Reason, 1648–1789* (London, 1962) (Pelican) and
the relevant chapters of J. H. Nichols, *A History of Christianity,
1650–1950* (New York, 1956). For Catholicism in general, Vol.
XXX–XL of Ludwig von Pastor, *History of the Popes* (London,
1938–   ) and the introduction of F. Nielson, *The History of the*

Papacy in the Nineteenth Century (New York, 1906) are still instructive, while *R. R. Palmer, *Catholics and Unbelievers in Eighteenth Century France* (Princeton, N.J., 1939) and *Richard Herr, *The Eighteenth Century Revolution in Spain* (Princeton, N.J., 1969) (Princeton) consider the responses of Catholic churchmen to the secular attack in those countries. On the sundry denominations and locales of Protestants, there are B. C. Poland, *French Protestantism and the French Revolution, 1685–1815* (Princeton, N.J., 1957); A. L. Drummond, *German Protestantism since Luther* (London, 1951); Koppel S. Pinson, *Pietism as a Factor in the Rise of German Nationalism* (New York, 1934); Norman Sykes, *Church and State in England in the Eighteenth Century* (London, 1934); Roland N. Stromberg, *Religious Liberalism in Eighteenth Century England* (New York, 1954), and on English Wesleyanism, *Methodism and the Common People of the Eighteenth Century* (London, 1945); and *Elie Halévy, *England in 1815* (Barnes & Noble), the first volume of his *History of the English People in the Nineteenth Century*, second revised ed., 6 vols. (London, 1949–1952).

On natural science in the eighteenth century—in addition to the above-cited general works on the Enlightenment—see the appropriate chapters in *Charles Gillispie, *The Edge of Objectivity* (Princeton, N.J., 1960) (Princeton); *Natural Philosophy through the Eighteenth Century*, ed. by Allan Ferguson (London, 1948); *Alexander Koyre, *From the Closed World to the Infinite Universe* (Baltimore, 1968) (Johns Hopkins), and *Alfred R. Hall, *The Scientific Revolution, 1500–1800*, revised ed. (Boston, 1966) (Beacon). The detailed A. Wolf, *A History of Science, Technology, and Philosophy in the Eighteenth Century*, revised ed., 2 vols., (London, 1952) is the one extensive book on the general subject for the period, but Aram Vartanian, *Diderot and Descartes* (Princeton, N.J., 1953) and Philip C. Ritterbush, *Overtures to Biology* (New Haven, 1964) are interesting treatments of particular eighteenth-century scientific subjects.

For special inquiries into eighteenth-century views of human nature (*i.e.* psychology and morals), in addition to Lester G. Crocker's *Age of Crisis* (cited above), reference should be made to the same author's *Nature and Culture: Ethical Thought in the French Enlightenment* (Baltimore, 1963) and to *Elie Halévy, *The Growth of Philosophic Radicalism* (Boston, 1955) (Beacon), the standard work on the origins and early history of utilitarianism.

Much of the available literature on the political and social ideas of the eighteenth century focuses on individual thinkers (see below). For what there is of more general treatments, see especially *Kingsley Martin, *French Liberal Thought in the Eighteenth Century* (New York, 1963) (Harper Torchbook); *J. L. Talmon, *The Origins of Totalitarian Democracy* (New York, 1960) (Norton); Elizabeth V. Souleyman, *The Vision of World Peace in Seventeenth and Eighteenth Century France* (New York, 1941); *Caroline Robbins, *Eighteenth-century Commonwealthman* (New York, 1959) (Atheneum); Harold J. Laski, *Political Thought in England: Locke to Bentham* (London, 1919); Gladys Bryson, *Man and Society*:

The Scottish Inquiry of the Eighteenth Century (Princeton, N.J., 1945); and Leonard Krieger, *The German Idea of Freedom* (Boston, 1957). On economic ideas, see William Letwin, *The Origin of Scientific Economics* (Garden City, N.Y., 1963) and *The Economics of Physiocracy*, ed. by Ronald L. Meek (Cambridge, Mass., 1962). On the main line of Enlightenment ideas of history, see J. B. Black, *The Art of History* (New York, 1926). On the related ideas of historical progress and regress, see *Frank Manuel, *The Prophets of Paris* (New York, 1962) (Harper Torchbook); Charles Frankel, *The Faith of Reason* (New York, 1969); Charles Vereker, *Eighteenth-Century Optimism* (Liverpool, 1967); and Henry Vyverberg, *Historical Pessimism in the French Enlightenment* (Cambridge, Mass., 1958).

The bulk of the available general literature on the Enlightenment is, like the Enlightenment itself, oriented toward France, and until recently there has been little on the shape of the movement in other national contexts. But now for England *Leslie Stephen's old but still informative *History of English Thought in the Eighteenth Century*, new ed., 2 vols. (New York, 1962) (Harbinger) can be supplemented with Gerald R. Cragg, *Reason and Authority in the Eighteenth Century* (Cambridge, Eng., 1964) and Ronald W. Harris, *Reason and Nature in the Eighteenth Century, 1714–1780* (London, 1968). For the Spanish Enlightenment, Richard Herr (cited above) is excellent. For Germany, two of the essays in *Introduction to Modernity: A Symposium on Eighteenth-Century Thought*, ed. by Robert Mollenauer (Austin, Tex., 1965) are relevant, and so is, for Austria, the middle section of Robert A. Kann, *A Study in Austrian Intellectual History: From Late Baroque to Romanticism* (New York, 1960). Of particular interest for the distinctive intellectual development of France are Ira O. Wade, *The Clandestine Organization and Diffusion of Philosophic Ideas in France from 1700 to 1750* (New York, 1967), for the early spread of Enlightenment in France, and Robert Darnton, *Mesmerism and the End of the Enlightenment in France* (Cambridge, Mass., 1968) for the radical temper in the generation before the revolution which grew out of it.

We may conclude this bibliographical essay with a list of particularly noteworthy recent works on individual intellectuals. On main-line representatives of the Enlightenment: Ronald Grimsley, *Jean D'Alembert, 1717–1783* (New York, 1963); Isabel Knight, *The Geometric Spirit: The Abbé de Condillac and the French Enlightenment* (New Haven, 1968); Arthur Wilson, *Diderot: The Testing Years, 1713–1759* (New York, 1957); Lester G. Crocker, *Diderot: The Embattled Philosopher* (New York, 1966); David Kettler, *The Social and Political Thought of Adam Ferguson* (Columbus, Ohio, 1965); John B. Stewart, *The Moral and Political Philosophy of David Hume* (New York, 1963); David W. Smith, *Helvétius* (New York, 1965); Henry S. Allison, *Lessing and the Enlightenment* (Ann Arbor, Mich., 1966); Robert Shackleton, *Montesquieu* (New York, 1961); Ira O. Wade, *The Intellectual Development of Voltaire* (Princeton, N.J., 1969); and *Peter Gay, *Voltaire's Politics* (New York, 1965) (Vintage). On figures who developed away from the main line: Mary P. Mack, *Jeremy Bentham: An*

Odyssey of Ideas (London, 1962); F. M. Barnard, *Herder's Social and National Thought* (New York, 1965); Karl Vietor, *Goethe the Thinker* (Cambridge, Mass., 1950); *Ernst Cassirer, *The Question of Jean-Jacques Rousseau* (Bloomington, Ind., 1963) (Midland), Judith Shklar, *Men and Citizens: A Study of Rousseau's Social Theory* (New York, 1969); Alfred Cobban, *Edmund Burke and the Revolt Against the Eighteenth Century*, second ed. (New York, 1960); and *Peter Stanlis, *Edmund Burke and the Natural Law* (Ann Arbor, Mich., 1958) (Ann Arbor).

Index

364 / Index

Orry, Philibert, 78, 80
Ottoman Empire, 45, 56, 266
 decline of (late 17th, early 18th centuries), 2, 57–58
 German wars, 28, 34
  from 1683 to 1699, 14, 15, 30, 31–32
  from 1714 to 1718, 53
  from 1736 to 1739, 58, 62, 63
  Holy League alliance against, 30
  links with War of the League of Augsburg, 30–32
  Peace of Karlowitz (1699), 30, 31–32
  Peace of Passarowitz, 53
 involvement in Great Northern War, 52–53
 Russian wars, 46, 48
  from 1736 to 1739, 55
  from 1768 to 1774, 58, 258, 272–73
  truce at Constantinople (1700), 31
"Ostend Company," 77

Paine, Thomas, 181, 189
Paley, William, 208
Pamela, 151, 152, 223
Panin, Nikita, 270
Pantheism, 143
Papacy, 287
 Holy League alliance, 30
 Louis XIV and, 21
 see also Roman Catholic Church
Paris, Peace of (1736), 269
Parliament, English, *see* Great Britain
Parliament, Irish, 332–33
Parma, 62
Party, political, modern concept of, 234–35
Pascal, Blaise, 141, 143, 144, 147
Passarowitz, Peace of (1718), 2, 53, 62
Pastoral Letters, 73
Patino, José, 61
Paul I (of *Russia*), 306–7
Peasantry: Austrian, after Joseph II's death, 306
 and Joseph II's agrarian reforms, 295–97
 Prussian, Frederick II and, 295, 297–98
 Russian, 86, 87, 129, 130
  Catherine II and, 295, 297, 298–301
  Paul I and, 307
  Pugachev rebellion (1773), 130, 131
Pelham, Henry, 111
Pelham, Thomas, 111
Persia, 51
Persian Letters (Montesquieu), 163
Peter I (of *Russia*), 1, 2, 9, 85, 86, 87, 88, 90, 94, 106, 146, 291
 alliance with France (1717), 54
 biographical, 46–47, 51-52
 compared to Charles XII, 46
 domestic reforms and policies, 48–51
 enlightened absolutism and, 243, 244
 Great Northern War, 33, 42–43, 44–45, 47, 48–49, 51, 52–54
Peter II (of *Russia*), 85, 86

Peter III (of *Russia*), 85, 130, 247–48, 252, 268, 269
Peter the Great, *see* Peter I (of *Russia*)
Peterwardein, Battle of (1716), 53
Petty, William, Earl of Shelbourne, 334
Philip II (of *Spain*), 249–50
Philip V (of *Spain*), 9, 24, 32, 36, 41, 76
 governmental reforms under, 60–61
Philosopher king, *see* Absolutisms, enlightened
Philosophical and Political History of European Settlements and Trade in the East and West Indies, 214
Philosophical Dictionary, 185
Philosophical Inquiry into the Origin of Our Ideas of the Sublime and Beautiful, 230
Philosophical Letters (Voltaire), 158, 163
Philosophy, see Enlightenment
Physics, 141
Physiocracy, 134, 135, 196, 197–198, 199, 200, 201, 202, 203, 302
 see also Laissez-faire
Piacenza, 62
Piedmont-Savoy, *see* Savoy
Pietism, 148–51, 157, 229
Pitt, William (the Younger), 111, 132, 133, 245, 315, 334, 335, 336, 340
Plan for a Royal Tithe, 72
Plato, 197
Podolia, 31
Poland, 3, 53, 56, 266, 268, 270, 309, 314
 Augustus the Strong deposed, 44
 Confederation of the Bar, 270
 constitutional monarchy of 1791, events leading to establishment of, 311–12
 decline of in early 1700's, oligarchic tradition continues, 57
 and Habsburg-Turkish wars, 31
 Holy League alliance, 30
 Louis XV and, 81,
 partition of (1772), 257, 258, 260, 262,
  events leading to, 269–74
  results of, 275–79
  terms of, 274–75
 Treaty of Karlowitz and, 31
 see also Europe
Polish Succession, War of the (1733–1735), 55, 57, 62, 63, 68
Political Disquisitions, 339
Political Justice, 225
Political Testament, 253
Poltava, Battle of (1709), 45, 48
Pomerania, 17, 53, 89, 90
Pompadour, Madame de, 80, 83
Poniatowski, Stanislas, 270
Pope, Alexander, 157, 180
Population explosion, 8, 118–19, 331
Popular sovereignty, concept of, 190, 191
Portugal, 41, 289
Power(s), balance of, 39, 41
 separation of, 190–191, 254
Pragmatic Sanction (1720), 9, 65–66